Given the controversies and difficulties which preceded the coming into force of the Lisbon Treaty, it is easy to forget that the Treaty is a complex legal document in need of detailed analysis for its impact to be fully understood. Jean-Claude Piris, the Director-General of the Legal Service of the Council of the European Union (EU), provides such an analysis, looking at the historical and political contexts of the Treaty, its impact on the democratic framework of the EU and its provisions in relation to substantive law. Impartial legal analysis of the EU's functions, its powers and the treaties which govern it make this the seminal text on the most significant recent development in EU law.

SINCE 1988, JEAN-CLAUDE PIRIS has served as the Legal Counsel of the Council of the EU and Director-General of its Legal Service. He is an Honorary Counsellor of State of France, a former diplomat at the UN and the former Director of Legal Affairs of the OECD. He was the Legal Advisor of the successive Intergovernmental Conferences which negotiated and adopted the treaties of Maastricht in 1992, Amsterdam in 1997 and Nice in 2001, the Constitutional Treaty signed in Rome in 2004 and, finally, the Lisbon Treaty in 2007.

REFERENCE

CAMBRIDGE STUDIES IN EUROPEAN LAW AND POLICY

This series aims to produce original works which contain a critical analysis of the state of the law in particular areas of European law and set out different perspectives and suggestions for its future development. It also aims to encourage a range of work on law, legal institutions and legal phenomena in Europe, including 'law in context' approaches. The titles in the series will be of interest to academics; policymakers; policy formers who are interested in European legal, commercial and political affairs; practising lawyers including the judiciary; and advanced law students and researchers.

THE LISBON TREATY

A Legal and Political Analysis

JEAN-CLAUDE PIRIS

CAMBRIDGE
UNIVERSITY PRESS

CAMBRIDGE UNIVERSITY PRESS
Cambridge, New York, Melbourne, Madrid, Cape Town, Singapore,
São Paulo, Delhi, Dubai, Tokyo

Cambridge University Press
The Edinburgh Building, Cambridge CB2 8RU, UK

Published in the United States of America by Cambridge University Press, New York

www.cambridge.org
Information on this title: www.cambridge.org/9780521197922

First published 2010

Printed in the United Kingdom at the University Press, Cambridge

A catalogue record for this publication is available from the British Library

Library of Congress Cataloguing in Publication data
Piris, Jean-Claude.
The Lisbon Treaty : a legal and political analysis / Jean-Claude Piris.
p.   cm. – (Cambridge studies in European law and policy)
Includes bibliographical references and index.
ISBN 978-0-521-19792-2 (hardback)
1. Treaty on European Union (1992). Protocols, etc., 2007 Dec. 13.   2. Constitutional
law – European Union countries.   I. Title.   II. Series.
KJE4443.32007.P57   2010
341.242′2 – dc22   2010011465

ISBN 978-0-521-19792-2 Hardback
ISBN 978-0-521-14234-2 Paperback

DISCLAIMER
All opinions expressed in this book are purely personal. They do not
represent the views of the Council of the European Union.

To Margrét Thoroddsdottir-Piris and Anne-Sophie Sunna Piris, my wife and daughter, for their constant support and patience during the time of writing this book.

I do absolutely believe in the European project.
I think it is the most noble political ideal
in European history in a thousand years.*

* Peter Sutherland, chairman of British Petroleum, chairman of Goldman Sachs International, chairman of London School of Economics, former EU Commissioner and former Director-General of the World Trade Organization. Interview by Harry Eyres, *Financial Times*, 3–4 January 2009.

CONTENTS

ix

BOXES

FOREWORD

Mit dem Vertrag von Lissabon wurde ein neues Kapitel der europäischen Geschichte aufgeschlagen. Einen entscheidenden Impuls für diesen neuen Vertrag gaben die Feierlichkeiten zum 50. Jahrestag der Unterzeichnung der Römischen Verträge am 25. März 2007. Denn hier bekannten sich die europäischen Staats- und Regierungschefs in der "Berliner Erklärung" zu den gemeinsamen Werten, Aufgaben und Strukturen der Europäischen Union – und dazu, die Europäische Union auf eine erneuerte gemeinsame Grundlage zu stellen.

Diesen Willen in ein Mandat für eine Regierungskonferenz umzusetzen, war sicherlich nicht einfach. Dass dieses Ziel schließlich noch während der deutschen Ratspräsidentschaft auf dem Europäischen Rat vom 21. bis 23. Juni 2007 erreicht wurde, ist auch ein Verdienst von Jean-Claude Piris als Generaldirektor des Juristischen Dienstes des Rates. Die Mühen haben sich gelohnt. Denn der Vertrag von Lissabon macht die Europäische Union nach außen stärker und selbständiger und nach innen demokratischer. Die Union ist damit für die neuen Herausforderungen der zunehmend globalisierten Welt besser gerüstet.

Mit Inkrafttreten des Vertrags von Lissabon am 1. Dezember 2009 wurde ein vielschichtiger Reformzyklus erfolgreich abgeschlossen, der bereits mit den Verhandlungen zum Vertrag von Maastricht begann. Das vorliegende Buch zeichnet die historischen Linien nach. Dadurch werden die Wurzeln und Bezüge der zentralen Regelungen klar herausgearbeitet. Daneben stellt das Werk auch die wichtigsten Urteile zum Vertrag von Lissabon dar – beispielsweise das Urteil des deutschen Bundesverfassungsgerichts. Das Buch leistet somit eine umfassende Einordnung des geltenden Primärrechts der Europäischen Union aus einer berufenen Hand.

Angela Merkel
Bundeskanzlerin
Bundesrepublik Deutschland

The Lisbon Treaty opened a new chapter in European history. The celebrations on 25 March 2007 to mark the fiftieth anniversary of the signing of the Treaties of Rome were a significant driver of this new Treaty, for it was on this occasion that the European heads of state or government, in signing the Berlin Declaration, committed themselves not only to a set of shared values, tasks and structures within the European Union but also to placing the European Union on a renewed common basis.

Converting this commitment into a mandate for an Intergovernmental Conference was by no means easy. The fact that this goal was indeed accomplished at the European Council meeting held on 21–23 June 2007 – and still within the period of the German EU Council Presidency – was thanks in no small part to Jean-Claude Piris in his role as Director-General of the Council Legal Service. It was worth the effort. For the Lisbon Treaty makes the European Union stronger and more independent in foreign policy but internally more democratic, which means it is better equipped to face the new challenges of an increasingly globalised world.

With the entry into force of the Lisbon Treaty on 1 December 2009, a complex cycle of reform that had in fact begun with the negotiations for the Maastricht Treaty was successfully completed. This book traces the outline of the historical process and in so doing clearly elucidates the roots of the core provisions and also the relationships between them. At the same time the work illuminates the most significant judgments relating to the Lisbon Treaty – for instance the judgment by the German Federal Constitutional Court. The book achieves in effect a comprehensive assessment of existing primary law in the European Union, written by an authoritative hand.

Angela Merkel
Chancellor
Federal Republic of Germany
(Berlin, November 2009)

ACKNOWLEDGEMENTS

The author thanks Thérèse Blanchet for her invaluable assistance in the writing of this book.

He also thanks Patricia Hancq for her constant help, as well as Vendula Kuncová.

He thanks all his friends and colleagues, in particular Michael Bishop, who agreed to read the manuscript, for the many improvements they brought to it. Any mistakes are those of the author.

TABLE OF CASES

Other international courts

European Court of Human Rights (ECHR) and European Human Rights Commission

International Court of Justice

National Constitutional Courts
Czech Republic

France

Germany, Federal Republic of

ABBREVIATIONS

CAP	common agricultural policy
CFSP	Common Foreign and Security Policy
Coreper	Committee of Permanent Representatives[1]
COSAC	Conference of European Affairs Committee of national parliaments[2]
COSI	Standing Committee on operational co-operation on internal security[3]
CSDP	Common Security and Defence Policy
Cst	Treaty establishing a Constitution for Europe
EAEC	European Atomic Energy Community (Euratom)
EC	European Community/Communities
ECB	European Central Bank
ECHR	European Court of Human Rights
ECJ	European Court of Justice
ECSC	European Coal and Steel Community
EEAS	European External Action Service
EEC	European Economic Community ('EC' after the 1992 Maastricht Treaty)
EIB	European Investment Bank
EMU	Economic and Monetary Union
EP	European Parliament
ESDP	European Security and Defence Policy
EU	European Union
Euratom	European Atomic Energy Community (EAEC)
Eurojust	European Union's Judicial Co-operation Unit
Europol	European Police Office
FP	Financial Perspectives
FSJ	Freedom, Security and Justice
FYROM	Former Yugoslav Republic of Macedonia
GNI	Gross National Income

1 French acronym for 'Comité des Représentants Permanents'.
2 French acronym for 'Conférence des Organes Spécialisés dans les Affaires Communautaires et européennes des parlements de l'Union européenne'.
3 French acronym for 'Comité permanent de coopération opérationnelle en matière de Sécurité Intérieure'.

HR	High Representative (of the Union for Foreign Affairs and Security Policy) (after the Lisbon Treaty)
HSG	heads of state or government
IGC	Intergovernmental Conference
IIA	Interinstitutional Agreement
JHA	Justice and Home Affairs
MEP	member of the European Parliament
MFF	Multiannual Financial Framework
NATO	North Atlantic Treaty Organization
OECD	Organisation for Economic Co-operation and Development
OJ	*Official Journal of the European Union* (before 1 January 2003: *Official Journal of the European Communities*)
OLAF	European Anti-Fraud Office[4]
QMV	qualified majority voting
SG/HR	Secretary General/High Representative for CFSP (before the Lisbon Treaty)
SIS	Schengen Information System
TEC	Treaty establishing the European Community
TEU	Treaty on European Union ('former TEU': refers to the Treaty on European Union in force before 1 December 2009)
TFEU	Treaty on the Functioning of the European Union
VIS	Visa Information System
WEU	Western European Union

---

4 French acronym for '*Office européen de Lutte Anti-Fraude*'.

~

Introduction

May and June 2005: the peoples of two of the six founding members of the European Union, France and the Netherlands, consulted by referendum, refuse to ratify the Constitutional Treaty for Europe.[1]

June 2008: the people of Ireland, one of the countries which has benefited most from the European Union, rejects the ratification of the Lisbon Treaty .

What is happening?

Does this mean that the dreams of a reconciled and more united Europe are dying? What exactly are those dreams? And, to begin with, which countries and peoples are concerned?

It is not easy to give a definition of Europe, whether geographically, historically or culturally.

Geographically, Europe is not a precise concept. It is not a continent, but rather a peninsula at the western edge of the Eurasian continent. Its eastern borders are far from being precise. It presents a vast variety of landscapes and climates, from the driest places of its Mediterranean coasts to the polar regions of Lapland.

It has always been populated by many diverse peoples, mainly but not only Christians, using dozens of languages and even different alphabets.

Historically, these peoples have organised themselves into national entities, according to their religions, languages or geographical situation. Over the centuries, Europeans have developed and strengthened the concept of the nation state. The European nation states have nurtured their differences, thus favouring nationalism, something which often led to wars with their neighbours. Nationalism explains why European nations have been fighting each other over the centuries.

---

1 See J.-C. Piris, *The Constitution for Europe: A Legal Analysis* (Cambridge University Press, 2006).

1

Despite that, for centuries they have, competing and fighting, dominated the world, economically, culturally and militarily. At the beginning
of the twentieth century, Europeans could clearly have a feeling of supe-
riority: they were indeed the masters of the world.

However, barely half a century later, in 1945, the situation had completely changed. After two world wars Europe was left destroyed, poor,
weak and divided, and de facto, or even de jure, under the control of
the two new superpowers – the United States and the Soviet Union.
Nationalism, which had been the strength and fortune of all the great
European nations, had been exalted to a point which had led them to
self-destruction.

One may hope, however, that this time the lesson was learned.

Immediately after the end of the Second World War, with the financial
and military help of the United States, western Europe quickly began to
reorganise itself in order to restore its destroyed economy and protect
its security, perceived as endangered by the USSR. The Organisation for
European Economic Co-operation (OEEC, which in 1961 became the
Organisation for Economic Co-operation and Development, OECD) was
established in 1948. It was designed to make better use of the financial
help of the United States and to restore and organise liberal economies
in Europe. On the defence side, the Western European Union (WEU)
was also created in 1948, followed by NATO, under the leadership of the
United States, in 1949. The Council of Europe was established in 1949.

At the same time, following the famous speech of Robert Schuman, the
French Foreign Minister, on 9 May 1950, efforts began to build a smaller
and more integrated Europe around France and Germany. Right from
the beginning the purpose was obviously political – that is, to avoid the
resurgence of another war between them. The issue was to find the ways
and means to achieve this goal. The choice was made to begin with economic links, to build powerful supranational institutions, and to use the
so-called 'Jean Monnet method', which consisted in progressively building up 'through practical achievements which will first of all create real
solidarity, and through the establishment of common bases for economic
development'.[2]

The European Coal and Steel Community (ECSC), established by six
founding States, entered into force in 1952. Then followed, with the same
Member States, the European Economic Community (EEC) in 1958,

2 Quoted from the third paragraph of the Preamble to the Coal and Steel Treaty, 1950.

together with the European Atomic Energy Community (EAEC, better known as Euratom). That was the start of the historic adventure which led to the establishment of the European Union.

Over the first half-century of its existence, the EU developed and changed very fast. Its membership increased from six in 1952 to twenty-seven in 2007 (Box 1), and will probably increase in the future. Even its name has been changed twice: first from 'European Economic Community' (EEC) to 'European Community' (EC), and then to 'European Union' (EU).

BOX 1. THE SUCCESSIVE ENLARGEMENTS OF THE EU

1952	Belgium, France, Germany, Italy, Luxembourg, Netherlands
1973	Denmark, Ireland, United Kingdom
1981	Greece
1986	Portugal, Spain
1995	Austria, Finland, Sweden
2004	Cyprus, Czech Republic, Estonia, Hungary, Latvia, Lithuania, Malta, Poland, Slovakia, Slovenia
2007	Bulgaria, Romania

Its scope of action has been considerably enlarged over the years, from the establishment of a customs union to an internal market flanked by common policies for agriculture, competition and external trade, and economic cohesion between its various regions. Later, these policies were extended to cover the protection of the environment, foreign policy, justice and home affairs, and a monetary policy.

Since 2007 the EU has consisted of twenty-seven Member States. It is a single market of half a billion people. The internal market is an area without internal frontiers in which the free movement of persons, goods, services and capital is ensured. The EU manages a single currency (the euro) and a monetary union for sixteen of its Member States. It speaks more and more with a single voice and acts as a single protagonist on the international scene, whatever the subject matter.

For the first few decades of its existence, the decision-making process in the EU was, at least de facto, similar to that of a classic international organisation, through negotiations and unanimous decisions of the representatives of the governments of its Member States meeting as a Council of Ministers. Nowadays, the EU can no longer be considered an 'ordinary' international organisation.

Very early, the legal Acts adopted by the EC institutions within the fields of EC competences were recognised as having primacy over the law of the Member States and as being able to have direct effects on their citizens. However, in its early years the scope of action of the EC was not very large. Over the years, the Member States decided to delegate to the EC institutions some of their powers to adopt legislation and to negotiate international agreements in a number of new fields. They decided that, in a number of those fields, the EC legislature (the European Parliament and the Council deciding in codecision or the Council alone) may adopt legal Acts even when there is no unanimity among the Member States (abolition of the right of veto); these Acts are legally binding upon them and they are obliged to implement them fully and correctly. The Commission ensures that this is the case, and may take a Member State to the EC Court of Justice if it fails to fulfil its obligations correctly. Such a Member State may then be faced with having to pay a lump sum and/or penalty payment, as well as paying compensation to those who have been adversely affected.

The institutions of the EU are no longer fully in the hands of the governments of the Member States. The members of the European Parliament (MEPs), which, with each treaty modifying the founding treaties, has gained more legislative and budgetary powers, have been, since 1979, directly elected by the EU citizens. The members of the Commission, which has the power to initiate EU legislation and to control its implementation, are not freely appointed by the governments, the European Parliament having the power to approve or to disapprove their choice. The independent European Court of Justice plays the role of a supreme court, ruling on disputes between the institutions and the Member States about the extent of their respective powers as well as on complaints by individuals on the legality of EU Acts.

It was against this background that the transformation of the EU into a federal entity was seen by some as a possibility in the short or medium term. At the same time, others underlined important factors indicating that this would be difficult to conceive. If a union composed of between six and fifteen Member States that were relatively homogeneous in their economic development had not been able to become a federal State, then a greater number of Member States, with a lesser degree of homogeneity, would make it impossible. These observers also stressed that, while some of the larger Member States (notably the United Kingdom, France and Poland) have never been keen on a federal EU, many of the smaller Member States, which may in the past have been more inclined towards it, have today changed their mind. Many of them are now strongly in favour of establishing an equality between States in all areas, be it their 'representation' in the Commission, the Court of Justice or the Court of Auditors, their 'right of veto' in the European Council, an 'equal right for all' to preside over the different configurations of the Council and their preparatory bodies, and so on. These States, which constitute by far the majority of the EU members, have the feeling that they need to protect themselves better against what they perceive to be the excessive weight and powers that, they believe, larger Member States would tend to have within a federal entity. They have thus become the strongest force of resistance against moves aimed at rebalancing the distribution of powers within the EU in accordance with the democratic principle, under which every citizen should have the same weight in the political decision-making process. This is one of the reasons why the basic treaties establishing the EU are complex. The other major reason is that the Member States want to remain 'the masters of the treaties' and wish to limit in a detailed and precise way the powers they decide to confer on the EU institutions, according to the subject matter concerned.

However, as soon as 1972, the idea emerged of transforming the EEC into a 'European Union'. The establishment of such a single entity, while not being a move towards a federal State, would have merged all aspects of European integration and co-operation. During the 1972 summit of the heads of state or government (HSG) in Paris, the HSG 'declared their intention of converting their entire relationship into a European Union before the end of this decade'.[3] The idea was then lost for the rest of the decade, due to the turmoil of the economic crisis of the 1970s and to the lack of political will among the governments of the Member States, which were divided on the issue.

In June 1983, in Stuttgart, the HSG relaunched the idea in their 'Solemn Declaration on European Union', by reaffirming their 'will to transform the whole complex of relations between their States into a European Union'.[4] Meanwhile, in 1981, the European Parliament had mandated one of its members, Altiero Spinelli, to propose amendments to the existing treaties. This work resulted in a 'draft Treaty instituting the European Union', accepted by the European Parliament by a vote of 237 to 31 in February 1984, but this document, which purported to be a 'constitution', was ignored by the Member States.

---

3 Communiqué of the Conference of the Heads of State or Government, Paris, 19–21 October 1972 (Bulletin EC 10–1972), 16.
4 Denmark did not agree on this point.

It was finally in 1993 that the Maastricht Treaty established the European Union, not, however, as a single entity, but alongside and in parallel with the existing European Communities. Four entities then existed side by side, three of them recognised as separate legal entities with their own legal personality: the EC, the ECSC and Euratom. The EU was the odd one out, containing the second and third pillars (i.e. the area of Common Foreign and Security Policy and the area of Justice and Home Affairs), which were to be managed quite differently from the three communities, and which was not formally given legal personality.

It was only ten years later, in 2003, that the proposal was again made to merge the EU and one of the two remaining communities – the EC – into a single entity.[5] This was approved in the Constitutional Treaty, solemnly signed in Rome in October 2004. However, that Treaty failed to be ratified by all Member States. The Lisbon Treaty, signed in December 2007 and which entered into force on 1 December 2009, was built with many elements taken from the Constitutional Treaty, but it has a different structure and is based on different political characteristics, making it a very different political turning point in the history of the European Union.

The purpose of this book is to present the main elements of the Lisbon Treaty and to explain their legal and political meaning and effects, putting them in their historical and political context.

5 The ECSC had lapsed in 2002 and Euratom would remain a separate Community.

I

The origins and birth of the Lisbon Treaty

Section 1 The process that led to the establishment of the European Union

The point of departure was the 1951 Paris Treaty, by which the six found-ing Member States established the European Coal and Steel Community (ECSC). They then adopted the Rome Treaty establishing the European Economic Community (EEC) and the Treaty establishing the European Atomic Energy Community (EAEC or Euratom), in 1957.

That was the beginning of the process which led to the establishment of the European Union (EU). Since then, and before the Lisbon Treaty, the original Rome Treaty has been modified by a number of successive amending treaties: the most important ones[1] came into effect in 1987 (the Single European Act), in 1993 (the Maastricht Treaty), in 1999 (the Amsterdam Treaty) and in 2003 (the Nice Treaty).

The **1957 Rome Treaty** (signed on 25 March 1957), which entered into force on 1 January 1958, established the EEC. The aim was to cre-ate a customs union, flanked by a common agricultural policy and by co-operation in other areas, in order to try and build a 'common mar-ket'. The Council, composed of ministers representing the government of each Member State, took all the important decisions on the basis of pro-posals from the Commission, mostly on the basis of unanimity, sometimes consulting a Parliamentary Assembly composed of members delegated by the national parliaments of the Member States. It was decided later on (in 1976) that the members of this assembly would be elected by direct universal suffrage.[2] This reform aimed at achieving a more democratic basis for the decisions of the EC institutions, but at the same time had the effect that national parliaments were no longer directly involved. The

---

1 It has also been amended by a few other treaties which aimed at limited reforms on institutional and budgetary matters.
2 See the Act concerning the election of representatives of the European Parliament by direct universal suffrage, annexed to Council Decision 76/787/ECSC, EEC, Euratom (OJ

first elections took place in 1979. The name of the Assembly was officially changed to the European Parliament by the Single European Act of
1986.

Taking into account past experience, the **1986 Single European Act**
(signed on 17 and 28 February 1986), which entered into force on 1
July 1987, gave a decisive impulse for the completion of the internal
market, with a deadline (1992) and the means to achieve it, through
the use of 'qualified majority voting'[3] in the Council for the adoption of the many pieces of legislation required. It also introduced a
new decision-making procedure, the 'co-operation procedure', which
gave a stronger role to the European Parliament than the consultation
procedure.

It was the fall of the Berlin Wall in 1989, the end of the Cold War and the
reshaping of the geopolitical landscape in Europe which, in 1992, triggered
the establishment of the European Union and the renaming of the EEC
as the EC. This was done by the Treaty on European Union, known as
the **1992 Maastricht Treaty** (signed on 7 February 1992), which entered
into force on 1 November 1993. The Treaty enlarged the scope of action
of the EC (the first pillar), in particular assigning it the task of creating
a single currency. It also added two further pillars: the second pillar –
the Common Foreign and Security Policy (CFSP) – and the third pillar –
Justice and Home Affairs (JHA). The Treaty retained most characteristics
of intergovernmentalism for the second and third pillars: decisions were to
be taken unanimously by the Council, while the European Parliament, the
Court of Justice and the Commission were given no role, or rather a very
limited one. However, the European Parliament was given an increased
say on the EU budget, as well as on legislation in the first pillar, through the
introduction of the so-called 'codecision procedure' with the Council. The
entry into force of the Maastricht Treaty was difficult: a first referendum
in Denmark (26 June 1992) was negative (50.7 per cent voting 'no');
after the adoption in the Edinburgh European Council (December 1992)
of different texts concerning Denmark but not modifying the Treaty, a
second referendum (18 May 1993) was positive (56.7 per cent voting
'yes').

No. L278, 8 October 1976, 5, last amended in 2002, which can be found in a consolidated form at http://eur-lex.europa.eu/LexUriServ/LexUriServ.do?uri=CONSLEG:
1976X1008:20020923:EN:PDF).

3 'Qualified' because each member of the Council has a different number of votes according
to the size of the Member State which he or she represents.

The **1997 Amsterdam Treaty** (signed on 2 October 1997), entered into force on 1 May 1999. It 'communitarised' – that is, submitted to ordinary Community rules – some parts of the third pillar (visas, asylum, immigration and civil judicial co-operation). It incorporated into the EC Treaty the so-called 'Schengen *acquis*' on the removal of checks on persons at internal borders, which had been developed outside the Treaties by certain Member States. It also created the office of High Representative for the CFSP, in order to give an impetus to the development of this area of action of the EU (the second pillar). Again, the European Parliament gained more powers in the legislative field, the 'codecision' procedure being modified to put the European Parliament on an almost equal footing as the Council to adopt legislation in some areas.

The main purpose of the **2001 Nice Treaty** (signed on 26 February 2001), which entered into force on 1 February 2003, was to adapt the institutions to accommodate the future enlargement of the EU to twelve new Member States, in particular by adapting the weighting of votes of the representatives of the governments of the Member States in the Council and by limiting the size of the Commission. It also gave more powers to the European Parliament, notably through extending to new areas its right of codeciding legislative Acts with the Council, and by making this right a real codecision by conferring the same deciding power on the European Parliament as that of the Council. Again, the ratification of the Nice Treaty was difficult, as a first referendum in Ireland gave a negative result on 7 June 2001 (54 per cent voting 'no'); after the adoption of declarations recalling that the Irish policy of neutrality would remain untouched, a second referendum was positive on 19 October 2002 (62.85 per cent voting 'yes').

When the Nice Treaty came into force – that is, in 2003 – the EU was composed of fifteen Member States. In less than four years this number nearly doubled, increasing its membership first to twenty-five, on 1 May 2004, and then to twenty-seven, on 1 January 2007.

This massive enlargement of the membership of the EU, which would undoubtedly have a significant impact on its institutions and on its decision-making, was already in planning at the time when the Amsterdam Treaty and the Nice Treaty were being negotiated – that is, between 1996 and 2000.[4] As early as June 1993, the European Council,

---

4 On these consequences with regard to the functioning of the Council, see also the so-called 'Trumpf–Piris Report', 1999, available at www.ena.lu/rapport_trumpf-piris_fonctionnement_conseil_perspective_union_elargie_mars_1999–010007265.html.

meeting in Copenhagen, had 'agreed that the associated countries in Central and Eastern Europe that so desire shall become members of the European Union'.[5] In June 1995, it added Malta and Cyprus to the list.[6] In December 1997 it decided that accession negotiations with six of those States would start in spring 1998, and in December 1998 it decided that negotiations with the six other States would start in February 2000. That meant that twelve new States could be invited to join the fifteen existing ones.

In spite of the pressure resulting from this ambitious enlargement calendar, the Amsterdam Intergovernmental Conference (IGC), which took place from March 1996 to June 1997, was not able to resolve the most difficult institutional issues. That is the reason why, at the end of the IGC, a number of Member States were not satisfied with its results. They ensured that the IGC agreed on a protocol (nicknamed 'The Amsterdam Leftovers', Box 2).

BOX 2. PROTOCOL ON THE INSTITUTIONS WITH THE PROSPECT OF ENLARGEMENT OF THE EUROPEAN UNION (AMSTERDAM 1997)

Article 1

At the date of entry into force of the first enlargement of the Union . . . , the Commission shall comprise one national of each of the Member States, provided that, by that date, the weighting of the votes in the Council has been modified, whether by reweighting of the votes or by dual majority, in a manner acceptable to all Member States, taking into account all relevant elements, notably compensating those Member States which give up the possibility of nominating a second member of the Commission.

Article 2

At least one year before the membership of the European Union exceeds twenty, [an IGC] shall be convened in order to carry out a comprehensive review of the provisions of the Treaties on the composition and functioning of the institutions.

---

5 Presidency Conclusions, Copenhagen, 21 and 22 June 1993, 13. These conclusions set out the 'Copenhagen criteria' which should be respected by the future enlargements of the EU. All Presidency Conclusions since 1993 may be found on the Internet site of the Council at consilium.europa.eu, under 'European Council', 'European Council meetings' and 'Presidency Conclusions'.
6 Presidency Conclusions, Cannes, 26 and 27 June 1995.

One of the main reasons for this disagreement in Amsterdam was the issue which also proved to be one of the most difficult nuts to crack in the IGCs which would follow (the Nice IGC, the Constitutional Treaty IGC and the Lisbon IGC) – that is, the issue of the composition of the Commission.

It was on the basis of the Amsterdam Leftovers Protocol that the IGC which was to approve the Nice Treaty was convened. The five topics to be discussed were the size of the Commission, the weighting of votes in the Council, the possible extension of qualified majority voting in the Council, the organisation of the Court of Justice and the issue of facilitating 'enhanced co-operation' among some Member States.

The Nice IGC did its best to give at least minimal answers to these five issues. However, its mediocre results, as well as the horse-trading with which it finished its work, after several days and nights of tough bargaining, left a bad atmosphere. Once again, a number of Member States were unhappy with the results, and they convinced the IGC to adopt, in December 2000, the 'Nice Declaration'. In this Declaration, the IGC called 'for a deeper and wider debate about the future of the EU' which should address, *inter alia*, four questions (Box 3).

BOX 3. THE FOUR QUESTIONS PUT BY THE DECLARATION ON THE
FUTURE OF THE UNION (NICE 2000)

(1) How to establish and monitor a more precise delimitation of competences between the European Union and its Member States, reflecting the principle of subsidiarity;
(2) the status to be given to the Charter of Fundamental Rights of the Union;
(3) a simplification of the Treaties with a view to making them clearer and better understood without changing their meaning; and
(4) the role of national parliaments in the European architecture.

During the second semester of 2001, the Belgian Presidency of the Council decided to work intensively in order to propose a procedure which could help to find agreed answers to these four questions. In order to prepare these answers, the Belgian Prime Minister, Guy Verhofstadt, pushed for establishing a 'Convention on the Future of Europe'.

In **December 2001**, the European Council, on the proposal of Verhof-stadt, adopted the **Laeken Declaration**.[7] According to that Declaration, 'the Union needs to become more democratic, more transparent and more efficient'; it should resolve 'three basic challenges' which are 'how to bring citizens . . . closer to the European design', 'how to organise . . . the European political area in an enlarged Union and how to develop the Union into a stabilising factor and model in the new, multipolar world'. The Declaration put several questions, among which were how to simplify and reorganise the existing treaties and whether this 'might not lead in the long run to the adoption of a constitutional text in the Union' (Box 4).

BOX 4. DECLARATION ON THE FUTURE OF THE EUROPEAN UNION
(LAEKEN, DECEMBER 2001)

I. Europe at a crossroads

For centuries, peoples and states have taken up arms and waged war to win control of the European continent. The debilitating effects of two bloody wars and the weakening of Europe's position in the world brought a growing realisation that only peace and concerted action could make the dream of a strong, unified Europe come true. In order to banish once and for all the demons of the past, a start was made with a coal and steel community. Other economic activities, such as agriculture, were subsequently added in. A genuine single market was eventually established for goods, persons, services and capital, and a single currency was added in 1999. On 1 January 2002 the euro is to become a day-to-day reality for 300 million European citizens . . .

The European Union is a success story. For over half a century now, Europe has been at peace. Along with North America and Japan, the Union forms one of the three most prosperous parts of the world. As a result of mutual solidarity and fair distribution of the benefits of economic development, moreover, the standard of living in the Union's weaker regions has increased enormously and they have made good much of the disadvantage they were at.

Fifty years on, however, the Union stands at a crossroads, a defining moment in its existence. The unification of Europe is near. The Union is about to expand to bring in more than ten new Member States, predominantly Central and Eastern European, thereby finally closing one of the darkest chapters in European history: the Second World War and the ensuing artificial division of Europe. At long last, Europe is on its way to becoming one big family, without bloodshed, a real transformation clearly

---

7 Presidency Conclusions, Laeken, 14 and 15 December 2001, Annex 1 (SN 300/1/01 REV1).

calling for a different approach from fifty years ago, when six countries first took the lead.

II. Challenges and reforms in a renewed Union

The Union needs to become more democratic, more transparent and more efficient. It also has to resolve three basic challenges: how to bring citizens, and primarily the young, closer to the European design and the European institutions, how to organise politics and the European political area in an enlarged Union and how to develop the Union into a stabilising factor and a model in the new, multi-polar world. In order to address them a number of specific questions need to be put.

- A better division and definition of competence in the European Union...
- Simplification of the Union's instruments...
- More democracy, transparency and efficiency in the European Union...
- Towards a Constitution for European citizens...
- ...

III. Convening of a convention on the future of Europe

In order to pave the way for the next Intergovernmental Conference as broadly and openly as possible, the European Council has decided to convene a Convention composed of the main parties involved in the debate on the future of the Union. In the light of the foregoing, it will be the task of that Convention to consider the key issues arising for the Union's future development and try to identify the various possible responses.

...

Some of the elements of the 2001 Laeken Declaration reflected the concern that for several years had already been worrying national political leaders as well as European institutions: European integration was being seen with less and less enthusiasm by European citizens. There had been two successive negative referend on the approval of EU treaties, in 1992 in Denmark and in 2001 in Ireland. Moreover, the turn-out trends for the European elections have also shown a worrying decline, from 63 per cent in 1979 (date of the first direct elections) to 49.8 per cent in 1999 (Box 5).[8]

8 Source: Internet site of the European Parliament, www.elections2009-results.eu/fr/turnout_fr.html#.

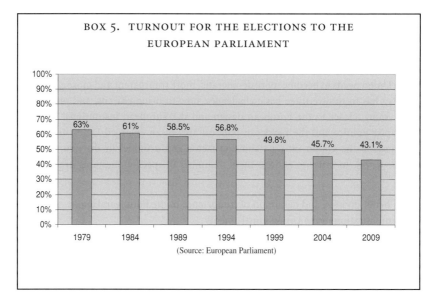

BOX 5. TURNOUT FOR THE ELECTIONS TO THE
EUROPEAN PARLIAMENT

(Source: European Parliament)

In addition, the usual method of negotiating amendments to the Treaties – in diplomatic conferences (IGCs) between representatives of the governments of the Member States – was denounced in some quarters (notably in the European Parliament) as being too secretive and elitist. However, the form of an IGC was unavoidable, as it is legally required by the Treaty.

Therefore in December 2001 the European Council decided that the next IGC would be prepared by a convention. This kind of body had been established in 1999–2000 for the drafting of the EU Charter of Fundamental Rights, a text which was then approved and proclaimed by the European Parliament, the Council and the Commission in Nice on 7 December 2000. The new convention would also involve democratically elected representatives of Member States and would debate in public. According to its proponents and supporters, the method of the convention would have the advantage of avoiding the usual horse-trading between diplomats arguing behind tightly closed doors. The idea was that it would allow public opinion in the Member States to have the opportunity of following and influencing the debates and the content of the future treaty in the direction the people would wish.

Section 2 The 2002–2003 European Convention and the 2004 Constitutional Treaty and its failed ratification

The 2002–2003 European Convention proposing the draft Constitutional Treaty

It was on this premise that the European Council decided that the Convention on the Future of Europe[9] would be composed not only of representatives of the heads of state or government of the Member States and of the Commission, but also, and mainly, of representatives of national parliaments and of the European Parliament. It would be chaired by the former French president, Valéry Giscard d'Estaing, and vice-chaired by former heads of Italian and Belgian governments, respectively Giuliano Amato and Jean-Luc Dehaene. The ten acceding States and the three candidate States would also be represented and involved in the proceedings. All in all, including the alternates and the observers from different committees and social partners, the Convention numbered 220 persons, of whom about two-thirds were elected parliamentarians (51 per cent from national parliaments and 14 per cent from the European Parliament) and only 25 per cent were appointed by governments. This is to be compared with IGCs, where all members are government representatives (with the participation of Commission representatives and, more recently, with representatives of the European Parliament as observers).

The mandate of the Convention in the 2001 Laeken Declaration was rather vague. It was 'to consider the key issues arising for the Union's future development and try to identify the various possible responses' and to 'draw up a final document which may comprise either different options . . . or recommendations if consensus is achieved'. This final document was to 'provide a starting point for discussions in the Inter-governmental Conference, which [would] take the ultimate decisions'.

---

9 The work of the Convention has been the subject of a large number of books and articles, and it will not be developed here. See, among others, P. Magnette and K. Nicolaïdis, 'The European Convention: Bargaining in the Shadow of Rhetoric' (2004) 27 *West European Politics* 381; G. Milton and J. Keller-Noëllet, *The European Constitution: Its Origins, Negotiation and Meaning* (London: John Harper Publishing, 2005); J. Jarlebring, 'Taking Stock of the European Convention: What Added Value Does the Convention Bring to the Process of Treaty Revision?' (2003) 4 *German Law Journal* 785; P. Norman, *The Accidental Constitution: The Making of Europe's Constitutional Treaty* (Brussels: EuroComment, 2005).

The Convention started in February 2002, completing its work a year and a half later, in July 2003, with a 'draft Treaty establishing a Constitution for Europe'. It created eleven working groups and three 'discussion circles'.[10]

Interestingly enough, no working group was established on institutional questions, which were obviously the most important and difficult ones, thus reflecting the will of the præsidium or of its president to keep these delicate questions under their control. All the meetings of the Convention itself and of its bodies were public, as well as its documents.[11] The work was prepared by a steering board, the Præsidium, which was composed of twelve members plus one invitee for all the acceding states. This body had a crucial role in preparing the documents and draft legal texts that would be submitted to the plenary sessions of the Convention. As opposed to the Convention itself, the præsidium did not work in public and was in fact very secretive.

The Convention and its Præsidium were both chaired by Giscard d'Estaing and were supported by a Secretariat of about twenty people, whose secretary-general was Sir John Kerr (now Lord Kerr of Kinlochard), a former UK permanent representative at the EU. There was neither a legal advisor nor a drafting or legal committee. Towards the end of the Convention's work, a small group of legal experts of the Legal Services of the European Parliament, the Council and the Commission helped, at the request of the præsidium of the Convention, in quickly reviewing the adaptations to be made to the provisions of Part III on EU competences, which had mostly been recopied from the existing provisions of the Treaty.

Following an initial so-called 'listening phase' which lasted quite a long time (six to seven months), the Convention was in October 2002 presented by its president with a draft table of contents of what Giscard d'Estaing proposed calling a 'Constitutional Treaty'. This treaty would merge the EC and EU Treaties into a single text, resulting in a new 'European Union' with a single legal personality. The first set of draft provisions prepared

---

10 The eleven working groups were on Subsidiarity (WG I), the Charter of Fundamental Rights (WG II), the Legal Personality of the EU (WG III), National Parliaments (WG IV), Complementary Competences (WG V), Economic Governance (WG VI), External Action (WG VII), Defence (WG VIII), Simplification (WG IX), Freedom, Security and Justice (WG X), and Social Europe (WG XI). The three discussion circles were on the Court of Justice, on the budgetary procedure and on the own resources.

11 The address of the Internet site of the Convention is http://european-convention. europa.eu.

by the præsidium was presented in February 2003. From then on, the process accelerated. Hundreds of amendments were tabled by Convention members. They were then discussed in the præsidium and, accompanied by the præsidium's suggestions, submitted to the next plenary session. Further sets of provisions were progressively suggested and approved. Finally, a first 'complete' draft 'Treaty establishing a Constitution for Europe' (which did not contain Part III, the largest one) was submitted to the Convention at the end of May 2003. This partial text was presented by the Convention's president to the heads of state or government on 20 June 2003 in Thessaloniki (Greece). The draft was then quickly completed by its long Part III and was approved by a vast majority (which its president determined to be 'a consensus') of the Convention at its fnal plenary session on 10 July 2003. It was officially transmitted to the president of the European Council on 18 July 2003.[12]

This draft prepared by the Convention served as the basis for the work of the IGC which, pursuant to Article 48 of the EU Treaty, was convened by the Italian Presidency of the Council by a letter of 30 September 2003.

The 2003–4 Intergovernmental Conference which approved the Constitutional Treaty

The IGC held it first meeting on 4 October 2003 in Rome. It was composed of the representatives of the governments of the fifteen Member States and of the ten acceding states at the level of foreign minister. Two representatives from the Commission and two from the European Parliament were also invited to participate, as well as observers from the candidate countries Bulgaria, Romania and Turkey. As had been the case in previous IGCs, the Secretariat of the IGC was provided by the General Secretariat of the Council.

At the outset, it was decided that the IGC would meet only at the level of prime ministers or heads of state (who held five meetings), with a preparation at the level of ministers for foreign affairs (who held nine meetings). No meeting was scheduled at the level of civil servants. Two informal meetings of diplomats in fact took place in Rome, during the

---

12 See doc. CONV 850/03 of 18 July 2003, on the Internet site of the Convention. A minority of the Convention ('Euro-sceptics') expressed its disagreement. The representatives of the Spanish and Polish governments also expressed reservations, in particular on the Qualified Majority Voting (QMV) system.

Italian Presidency, and one in Dublin, during the Irish Presidency, but they did not negotiate texts.

The IGC did not hold its meetings in public. However, all its documents, as well as the contributions by the presidency, the delegations and the IGC Secretariat, were made public on its Internet site.[13]

The IGC immediately established a Working Party of Legal Experts to review the legal drafting of the text of the Constitution as proposed by the Convention. The text of the Constitutional Treaty as drafted by the Convention was not well drafted from a legal point of view; it contained a number of inconsistent provisions, serious lacunae, and incorrect legal drafting or ambiguities. The Italian Presidency therefore proposed to the IGC in September 2003[14] that a Working Party of Legal Experts should be established to carry out a 'legal verification' of the draft Treaty. This working party was to be the only group of civil servants officially set up by the IGC. In order to stress the purely legal-technical character of its mandate, the working party would be chaired not by the usual six-monthly rotating presidency, but by the Legal Counsel to the IGC (Director-General of the Council Legal Service). The working party was composed of representatives from the twenty-five participating states (including the ten which would join the European Union on 1 May 2004) and the three candidate states (Bulgaria, Romania and Turkey), as well as from the Commission and from the European Parliament (Directors-General of their Legal Services).

The Group started its work in the week following the launch of the IGC, at the beginning of October 2003, and held a total of twenty-three meetings ending in April 2004. It worked on the basis of a wholly revised text of the Treaty (in French) which had been drafted, with a great number of added suggestions, by members of the Council's Legal Service working for the IGC Secretariat (with the help from the Commission's Services as regards the existing Protocols and Acts of Accession).

Among the hundreds of suggestions approved unanimously by the Group, all of which were adopted later by the IGC, it is worth mentioning the following:

---

13 The 2003–4 IGC documents are accessible on the Internet site of the Council, under 'Lisbon Treaty' and 'Previous IGCs'.

14 Letter of 29 September 2003 from Franco Frattini, the Italian Foreign Minister, to his colleagues and to the European Parliament and the Commission (see Internet site of the Council, under 'Lisbon Treaty' and 'Previous IGCs').

- in the preamble, the addition of a reference to succession between Treaties and to legal continuity of the *acquis communautaire,* and the deletion of a sentence written in Greek (a quotation from Thucydides);
- the combining, in a single Protocol, of the various transitional provisions which had been scattered throughout the draft Constitutional Treaty;
- the addition of transitional provisions which had not been drawn up by the Convention;
- a complete redrafting of the Protocol amending the Euratom Treaty (which would remain in force as a separate treaty);
- drafting adaptations to the thirty-six Protocols and Annexes I and II which were annexed to the Treaties and which had not been examined by the Convention (nine of these Protocols were repealed);
- the establishment of three new protocols: the Protocol on the Acts and Treaties which have supplemented or amended the EC and EU Treaties, and two Protocols taking over the substantive contents still in force of the previous four Accession Treaties (1972, 1979, 1985 and 1994)[15] and the latest Accession Treaty (2003) respectively. It was necessary to preserve explicitly those elements of these Acts and Treaties which had to remain in force, because the Acts and Treaties themselves were repealed pursuant to Part IV of the draft Constitutional Treaty, and also to make the necessary technical adjustments to bring them into line with the draft Constitutional Treaty, without altering their legal effect;
- the decision to use continuous Arabic numbering for the entire text of the Constitutional Treaty.

The IGC, at the level of ministers of foreign affairs and of heads of state or government, did not fundamentally modify the essential features of the draft issued from the Convention. The IGC concentrated on those institutional issues which had not obtained a consensus in the Convention and resolved them – that is, the definition of qualified majority voting (QMV) in the Council, the composition of the Commission and the new organisation of the Presidency of the Council. It also modified the texts on defence policy and the scope of QMV in certain fields, notably justice and home affairs. It also revised the budgetary procedure. The text was approved in June 2004, including all the suggestions made by the Legal Experts. The Treaty was solemnly signed in Rome on 29 October 2004.

15 In approving that Protocol, the Working Party agreed to retain certain provisions as historical references, in spite of the fact that its Chairman noted that, since the expiry of the deadlines specified therein, those provisions no longer had any legal effect.

The main features of the 2004 Constitutional Treaty

The Constitutional Treaty repealed all existing Treaties, and replaced them by a single text. It streamlined legal instruments and procedures and codified long-standing principles and rules.

Up until 2004, the original 1957 Treaties had been amended and complemented fifteen times. As a result, there were about 2,800 pages of primary law contained in seventeen Treaties or Acts, three legal personalities,[16] the three pillars, fifteen types of different legal instruments and several types of decision-making procedures. Restructuring and simplifying this complicated system and trying to make it more readable and understandable was one of the objectives of the Constitutional Treaty.[17]

The restructuring was the most visible and, in a way, the most 'revolutionary' work achieved by the Convention and the IGC, despite the fact that it was a mere codification of existing texts. The choice was made to repeal all existing Treaties[18] and to replace them by a single text. The problem was that this choice would entail the re-ratification by Member States of all existing provisions which had been copied without any substantial change from the preceding Treaties. This re-ratification would open the way for Euro-sceptics to criticise the new Constitutional

16 Without taking into account the Agencies of the EC or of the EU, which are often given separate legal personalities for functional purposes.

17 See the article written by the author of this book in 1995, before the Amsterdam IGC, under the pseudonym 'Justus Lipsius', 'The 1996 Intergovernmental Conference' (1995) 20 *European Law Review* 235: 'The ideal would be to replace the present Treaties (EU, EC, ECSC, EAEC, Merger Treaty, Single European Act, plus the Treaties amending budgetary and financial provisions) by a single Treaty Charter. This is technically feasible but entails political choices which will sometimes be difficult . . . It is legally and politically feasible . . . to agree on the merger into one entity of the three existing Communities and of the Union, the new entity being a European Union which should be given legal personality and treaty-making power. This will in no way prevent the IGC from deciding that the decision-making process will be completely different in one or other of the areas pertaining to Union competence, in, for instance, CFSP or co-operation in justice and home affairs, and that the Court of Justice will have a different role or no role at all regarding these last areas, etc. These are separate questions, which can be solved technically while avoiding a legal architecture which is of such complexity that nobody can understand. That being said . . . the single Treaty would still remain too long and too complex if the exercise was limited to merging all the provisions of the present Treaties into a single consolidated text. Therefore, the best solution would be to draft, on the one hand, a "Treaty-Charter", as short and readable as possible, dealing with principles, competence and institutional matters, and, on the other hand, a number of protocols annexed to it, dealing in detail with specific matters.'

18 Apart from the Euratom Treaty.

Treaty, pretending that it conferred new powers on the Union, even though the provisions in question had already been in force for a long time.

The Constitutional Treaty aimed at 'One Treaty, One Legal Personality and One Pillar'. It repealed the two main existing Treaties – that is, the EC and EU Treaties, as well as all the previous Treaties and Protocols.[19] The substance of all these Treaties was to be merged into a single 'Constitutional Treaty'. Only the Euratom Treaty would remain separate. The number of pages of primary law would diminish from 2,800 pages to 560 pages (including the Euratom Treaty), the Constitutional Treaty as such being only 200 pages (400 pages including its thirty-six protocols).

The Constitutional Treaty was structured in four parts:

- Part I laid down, in about thirty pages (sixty Articles), the main elements of the EU: its values and objectives, citizens' rights, the Union's competences, its institutions, its legal instruments, its finances and its membership.
- Part II, with fifty-four Articles, in about ten pages, reproduced (with only a few minor changes) the EU Charter of Fundamental Rights as it had been adopted in Nice in December 2000 by the European Parliament, the Council and the Commission.
- Part III, with 322 Articles, in about 130 pages, contained the details of internal and external 'policies', or rather of the competences conferred on the Union.[20] Most of it was a mere reproduction, with no change of substance, of the provisions of the EC and EU Treaties.
- Part IV, with twelve Articles, in six pages, contained the general and final provisions.

With the Protocols, the Constitutional Treaty ran to 400 pages, which is still very long. However, one has to realise that a short treaty will always be impossible, given the will of the Member States, its authors, to have it detailed. Actually, they want to control exactly how many competences

---

19 See Art. IV-437 and the Protocol on the Acts and Treaties which have supplemented or amended the EC Treaty and the EU Treaty. Ten existing protocols were repealed (i.e. Protocols no. 9, 10, 12, 13, 19, 23, 24, 30, 33 and 35 from the list of Protocols in the consolidated version of the Treaties in OJ No. C325, 24 December 2002, 37–8) but ten new protocols were added (i.e. Protocols no. 1, 2, 8, 9, 12, 23, 32, 33, 34 and 36 from the list of Protocols, OJ No. C310, 16 December 2004).

20 The Constitutional Treaty, as all other EU Treaties, did not determine in itself what kind of policies would be decided by the competent legislative authorities, but enabled them to act and set out the limits within which they would be authorised to adopt the policies they would determine. The term 'policies' was therefore not well chosen and gave rise to misunderstandings.

they confer on the EU and to limit in a precise manner, according to the subject matter concerned, how much power they confer on the EU institutions to exercise these competences.[21]

Therefore, one could say that the Constitutional Treaty, in particular with its user-friendly Part I, would have achieved, in terms of readability, the objective of simplifying the Treaties 'with a view to making them clearer and better understood without changing them' (see the four questions of the 2000 Nice Declaration, Box 3). To a non-specialist, reading the first sixty Articles in Part I of the Constitutional Treaty (i.e. only thirty pages) gave a reasonably clear idea of what the Union is, of what it does, and how it does it. In addition, a more interested reader would have been able to find almost everything in a single document, instead of having to go through seventeen Treaties and Acts.

Legally, and despite its name, the 'Treaty establishing a Constitution for Europe' remained a treaty agreed between sovereign states. It could only enter into force (and then be amended) by the agreement of all Member States. Calling it a 'Constitution' did not change anything about that. The EU would not have become 'sovereign' – that is, it would not have obtained 'Kompetenz-Kompetenz', it would not have acquired the right to define the extent of its own powers. This competence would have continued to belong to the 'Masters of the Treaties' – that is, the Member States. The relationship between the EU and its Member States would not have been changed. The EU would not have become a state.

It is true that, despite indifference and ambiguity,[22] the European Union had progressively developed as a constitutional order of its own, with what the Court of Justice had already called in 1964 a 'new legal order',[23] established by a 'basic constitutional charter, the Treaty'[24] and 'for the benefit of which the States have limited their sovereign rights, in ever wider fields, and the subjects of which comprise not only Member States

---

21 See J. Straw, UK Foreign Secretary at the time: 'Were it a superstate, writing its constitution would be easy, and the result short. You would declare that power resided in its parliament, government and supreme court, and leave those institutions to make and enforce the law. It is precisely because the EU is not a superstate that it needs a more complicated rule-book spelling out, policy by policy, the areas of its competence. This is what gives the document its length.' *The Economist*, 10 July 2004, 30.

22 On this ambiguity, see Y. Mény, 'Europe, la grande hésitation', *Le Monde*, 12 June 2004. See also the article by the author of this book, 'Does the European Union Have a Constitution? Does It Need One?' (1999) 6 *European Law Review* 557.

23 Judgment of 13 November 1964, Cases 90/63 and 91/63 of *Commission v. Luxembourg and Belgium*, [1964] ECR 625, and Case 6/64, *Costa v. ENEL*, 593.

24 See Case 294/83, *Les Verts v. Parliament*, para. 23. See also Opinion 1/91 of 14 December 1991, *EEA Agreement*, [1991] ECR 6102, para. 21.

but also their nationals'. The essential characteristics of this legal order have been in particular 'its primacy over the law of the Member States and the direct effect of a whole series of provisions which are applicable to their nationals and to the Member States themselves'.[25]

This legal reality – that is, the existence of a constitutional charter in a material sense – would have been made more explicit and visible by the so-called 'Constitution'.

Therefore, although legally the Constitutional Treaty would not have been a revolution, as it would have changed neither the nature of the Union, nor the nature of the Union's relations with the Member States, and although it would have been shorter and clearer than the current treaties, by the same token it appeared to be a great novelty and was presented as such, both by its supporters and by its opponents. The indisputable result, finally, was that it was presented and appeared to the public as being a major political innovation – that is, as a completely new symbolic and political step in the history of the EU. The use of words such as 'laws', 'minister', 'flag' or 'anthem' and, above all, of the word 'constitution' indeed had a powerful political effect. Using these words provoked a psychological shock which proved to be politically much larger than the legal nature and substantive content of the Constitutional Treaty.[26]

The failed ratification of the 2004 Constitutional Treaty

Article IV-447 of the Constitutional Treaty required, for it to enter into force, the ratification of all Member States. This was in accordance with Article 48 of the Treaty on European Union (TEU), which was obviously applicable.

Among the twenty-five governments signatories of the Treaty, fifteen requested the authorisation of their parliament to ratify. As at September

---

25 See para. 21 of Opinion 1/91, *EEA Agreement.*
26 As the author of this book wrote in 2003, at the same time as the Convention was deliberating about the use of those words, 'such symbolic gestures should be used with great care. They could create hopes on the part of the "utopians", who will be disappointed that the EU is not delivering on its promises or that the actual content of the draft Constitutional Treaty does not correspond to the grandeur of the symbols. They could create added fears on the part of the "realists", who will become even more nervous about the whole thing. These disappointments and fears could, added to each other, result in more people rejecting the EU than welcoming it. Forcing reality may backlash heavily, especially when ratification is submitted to popular referendums (as would be the case in a number of Member States for the ratification of the Constitutional Treaty).' J.-C. Piris, 'The European Union: Towards a New Form of Federalism?', in J. Fedtke and B. Markesinis (eds.), *Patterns of Regionalism and Federalism*, The Clifford Chance Lectures, Vol. 8 (Oxford: Hart Publishing, 2006), 69, at 85.

2006, fourteen had obtained that authorisation (in chronological order: Lithuania, Hungary, Slovenia, Italy, Greece, Slovakia, Austria, Germany, Latvia, Cyprus, Malta, Belgium, Estonia and Finland). Sweden decided to delay its parliamentary procedure, and the Czech Republic delayed its choice between a referendum or a parliamentary procedure. The other nine governments decided to organise a referendum on the ratification, two for constitutional reasons (Denmark and Ireland) and seven for political reasons (Luxembourg, France, the Netherlands, Spain, Poland, Portugal and the United Kingdom). During 2005, four of these States organised a referendum, two of them being positive (Spain and Luxembourg) and two negative: France (29 May 2005) and the Netherlands (1 June 2005).

The results of the referendums in France and in the Netherlands, two founding Member States, both having always been at the centre of European integration, were perceived as a political earthquake. The question of what to do with the ongoing ratification process of the Constitutional Treaty was discussed during the European Council in June 2005, when the twenty-five HSG unanimously adopted a Declaration[27] (Box 6).

BOX 6. DECLARATION ON THE RATIFICATION OF THE TREATY ESTABLISHING A CONSTITUTION FOR EUROPE, EUROPEAN COUNCIL, 15–16 JUNE 2005

. . .

The recent developments do not call into question the validity of continuing with the ratification processes. We are agreed that the timetable for the ratification in different Member States will be altered if necessary in response to these developments and according to the circumstances in these Member States.

We have agreed to come back to this matter in the first half of 2006 to make an overall assessment of the national debates and agree on how to proceed.

. . .

Nothing much happened during the following year.

In June 2006, the European Council again discussed what to do, but again extended the period of reflection, while giving specific tasks to the Council Presidency in the first semester of 2007 (i.e. the future German Presidency) (see Conclusions, Box 7).

---

27 See Declaration by the Heads of State or Government on the ratification of the Treaty establishing a Constitution for Europe (SN 117/05) on the Internet site of the Council, together with the Presidency Conclusions.

BOX 7. EUROPEAN COUNCIL, 15–16 JUNE 2006, PRESIDENCY
CONCLUSIONS

47. [T]he Presidency will present a report to the European Council during the first semester of 2007, based on extensive consultations with the Member States. This report should contain an assessment of the state of discussion with regard to the Constitutional Treaty and explore possible future developments.

48. The report will subsequently be examined by the European Council. The outcome of this examination will serve as the basis for further decisions on how to continue the reform process, it being understood that the necessary steps to that effect will have been taken during the second semester of 2008 at the latest. Each Presidency in office since the start of the reflection period has a particular responsibility to ensure the continuity of this process.

49. The European Council calls for the adoption, on 25 March 2007 in Berlin, of a political declaration by EU leaders, setting out Europe's values and ambitions and confirming their shared commitment to deliver them, commemorating fifty years of the Treaties of Rome.

By 1 January 2007, the date on which Bulgaria and Romania became members of the EU, eighteen Member States had ratified the Constitutional Treaty,[28] seven had suspended their ratification process (the Czech Republic, Denmark, Ireland, Poland, Portugal, Sweden and the United Kingdom) and two had failed in their ratification (France and the Netherlands).

Section 3 From the Constitutional Treaty to the Lisbon Treaty

Discussions between the heads of state or government which followed the two negative referendums in France and the Netherlands concluded that it was politically impossible to hope for the ratification of an unchanged Constitutional Treaty by all the Member States. However, most of the heads of state or government were convinced that it was politically necessary to strengthen the EU and to democratise further its decision-making process, and, in order to do that, to negotiate and adopt a new treaty as soon as possible. Otherwise, the climate of distrust and the feeling that the European Union was in crisis would continue and even deepen. On this

---

28 Austria, Belgium, Cyprus, Estonia, Finland, Germany, Greece, Hungary, Italy, Latvia, Lithuania, Luxembourg, Malta, Slovakia, Slovenia and Spain, as well as Bulgaria and Romania through the ratification of their Accession Treaty.

basis, the two major questions about a new possible treaty were when? and with what content?

The possible timing for a new European treaty

The two most important sentences of the June 2006 European Council Conclusions were contained in paragraphs 49 and 48:

- in paragraph 49: 'The European Council calls for the adoption, on 25 March 2007 in Berlin, of a political declaration by EU leaders, setting out Europe's values and ambitions and confirming their shared commitment to deliver them, commemorating 50 years of the Treaties of Rome';
- in paragraph 48: 'The report [i.e. the report requested of the German Presidency for the first semester of 2007], will subsequently be examined by the European Council. The outcome of this examination will serve as the basis for further decisions on how to continue the reform process, it being understood that the necessary steps to that effect will have been taken during the second semester of 2008 at the latest. Each Presidency in office since the start of the reflection period has a particular responsibility to ensure the continuity of this process.'

The German Presidency was thus given two mandates:

- a first mandate for March 2007, when it should convince the 'EU leaders' (i.e. the heads of state or government and the presidents of the European Parliament and of the European Commission) to adopt a declaration 'setting out Europe's values and ambitions and confirming their shared commitment to deliver them, commemorating 50 years of the Treaties of Rome';
- a second mandate for June 2007, when, after 'extensive consultations with the Member States' it should convince the European Council to adopt a report which should 'contain an assessment of the state of discussion with regard to the Constitutional Treaty and explore possible future developments'.

These conclusions showed that the heads of state or government had not yet made up their mind about the date when a new treaty could be negotiated, as they mentioned that 'The report will subsequently be examined by the European Council. The outcome of this examination will serve *as the basis for further decisions on how to continue the reform process, it being understood that the necessary steps to that effect will have been taken during the second semester of 2008 at the latest'* (emphasis added).

These terms were quite ambiguous, allowing for two possible interpretations.

According to a first possible interpretation, the reference to the second semester of 2008 – that is, the semester during which France would preside over the EU Council (after Germany, Portugal and Slovenia) – meant that the aim would be to try and reach political decisions under the leadership of France. That could refer either to a political agreement on the essential content of a possible future treaty, or a complete agreement on a full text of the treaty already approved in legal terms. In both cases, the ratification of the treaty would take place during 2009–10 or later. This first interpretation was shared by most, because it appeared to be the most realistic one.

According to a second possible interpretation, however, the reference to the second semester of 2008 and the 'necessary steps' could be to the end of the ratification process of the future treaty, in order to allow it actually to enter into force at the beginning of 2009. This was a bold interpretation, not shared by many, because it implied a very tight and optimistic calendar. However, this interpretation was also based on the political fact that a decision to wait until 2010 would have some disadvantages, taking into account the three following events, which were due to happen before then.

The European elections in June 2009

Most MEPs insisted that the revision of the Treaties should enter into force *before* the elections of June 2009. They feared that, without a relaunching of the European project before that date, the rate of abstention, which had reached 55 per cent in 2004, could be disastrous. The European Parliament adopted a Resolution on 14 June 2006[29] to put forward that political wish. One had also to take into account the fact that the future treaty would probably provide for a new composition of the European Parliament, by modifying the total number of MEPs and enabling a modification of the numbers of MEPs attributed to each Member State. Therefore, in order to be able to organise the European elections, the Member States would

---

29 See Resolution on the next steps for the period of reflection and analysis on the Future of Europe (No. P6_TA(2006)0263), available on the Internet site of the European Parliament, www.europarl.europa.eu.

need to know how many seats they would have and modify their electoral legislation accordingly, in order to be ready in time before the June 2009 elections.

The new composition of the Commission
in November 2009

In case no new treaty had entered into force before or on 1 November 2009, the provisions of the treaty in force on that date would naturally apply to the appointment of the new Commission. According to Article 4(2) of the Protocol on the enlargement of the EU annexed to the Treaties by the Nice Treaty, 'as from the date on which the first Commission following the date of accession of the 27th Member State of the Union takes up its duties [i.e. on 1 November 2009[30]] . . . the number of Members of the Commission shall be less than the number of Member States'. They would have to be chosen 'according to a rotation system based on the principle of equality, the implementation arrangement for which shall be adopted by the Council acting unanimously', and 'the number of Members of the Commission shall be set by the Council, acting unanimously'.

Therefore, without a new treaty on 1 November 2009, the Council would have to adopt, before the beginning of the procedure leading to the appointment of the Commission due to take office on 1 November 2009, the necessary decisions[31] setting out the number of Commissioners and the implementing arrangements for the rotation system, which would be extremely difficult decisions to reach in an isolated manner.

The 'mid-term' review (2008–9) of the EU
Financial Perspectives

The mid-term review of the Financial Perspectives is foreseen in the December 2005 agreement on the Financial Perspectives for 2007–13,[32] which provided that 'The European Council . . . invites the Commission to

30 Although this could theoretically happen before that date, in case either of the resignation of the Commission, or of a vote of a motion of censure by the European Parliament.

31 According to Art. 4(3) of the Protocol on enlargement, such decisions were supposed to have been adopted straight after the signature 'of the treaty of accession of the 27th Member State to the Union' – that is, after the signature on 25 April 2005 of the Accession Act of Bulgaria and Romania.

32 See doc. 15915/05, in particular paras. 79 and 80, available on the Council Internet site in the public register of Council documents at http://register.consilium.europa.eu/pdf/en/05/st15/st15915.en05.pdf.

undertake a full, wide-ranging review covering all aspects of EU spending, including the CAP, and of resources, including the UK rebate, to report in 2008/9.'

This review will raise political difficulties in a number of, if not all, Member States. It would be even more difficult to resolve if discussed at the same time as the revision of the Treaties.

*

Therefore, these events appearing unavoidable, it was desirable that the issue of the new treaty should be resolved in time, in order for the new treaty to enter into force on or around 1 January 2009. Taking into account a delay of at least twelve months for ratification, that meant that the new treaty should be signed at the end of 2007 or, at the latest, at the very beginning of 2008.

Calculating backwards, that meant that the report required from the German Presidency for June 2007 could not be limited to a presentation of different options, or even to a political description of what a possible revision of the treaties could be, but should already present a clear and precise mandate to the IGC, describing the future legal solutions to be adopted by the IGC, which would have to be convened immediately after the European Council and work very quickly.

On this point, the Berlin Declaration, adopted on the occasion of the fiftieth Anniversary of the Rome Treaty, was very important and was actually a decisive turning point. It is in this short but powerful text that all heads of state or government took the political commitment to place the European Union 'on a renewed common basis before the European Parliament elections in 2009'. This could not be interpreted otherwise than that the new Treaty should be in place before that date (i.e. before June 2009) (see Box 8).

BOX 8. BERLIN DECLARATION, 25 MARCH 2007

. . .

With European unification, a dream of earlier generations has become a reality. Our history reminds us that we must protect this for the good of future generations. For that reason, we must always renew the political shape of Europe in keeping with the times. That is why today, 50 years after the signing of the Treaties of Rome, we are united in our aim of placing the European Union on a renewed common basis before the European Parliament elections in 2009.

For we know, Europe is our common future.

The possible content of a new treaty

During the first three months of the German Presidency, until the adoption of the Berlin Declaration at the end of March 2007, the time was used essentially to advance the climate change file, which enabled all forces to be concentrated later on finding a solution to the 'institutional issues', as this matter was called. The consultations with delegations in view of the Berlin Declaration also enabled links and trust to be created for the work to follow and the concept of the possible solution to be developed. The German Chancellor, Angela Merkel, as well as her government, showed a cautious approach. They did not want to create too-ambitious expectations that they would not be able to meet.

It was actually difficult to imagine what to do in concrete terms while the French presidential election had not yet taken place. It was a fact that one of the two main contenders in that election, Nicolas Sarkozy, had taken a position in favour of a 'simplified treaty', which he said would be ratified through a parliamentary procedure, thus excluding a new referendum. However, the structure and the content of the so-called 'simplified treaty' as described by Sarkozy, whilst not precise, appeared insufficiently ambitious to be accepted by the eighteen Member States which, in the meantime, had ratified the Constitutional Treaty. Moreover, the other main contender, Ségolène Royal, promised that, whatever the new treaty looked like and whatever its content, she would put its ratification to a referendum. The German Presidency kept informal and confidential contacts with the entourages of both Sarkozy and Royal, as well as with the advisors of the third main candidate, François Bayrou.

Within the German Presidency, things were directly in the hands of Chancellor Merkel. She decided to give her close advisors leadership on this issue within the German administration. Therefore her closest advisor, Uwe Corsepius, was the one in charge, helped by his deputy, Nikolaus Meyer-Landrut. They worked in co-operation with the Ministry of Foreign Affairs, notably with the Secretary of State Rainer Sielberberg.

With the legal and technical help of the General Secretariat of the Council, in particular of the Legal Service of the Council, Corsepius and his colleagues tried to imagine what the structure and content of a possible new treaty could be. This treaty would have to be acceptable, on the one side, to the eighteen states which had ratified the Constitutional Treaty and, on the other side, not only to France and the Netherlands, whose people had rejected the Constitutional Treaty, but also to the seven states which had put their ratification process on hold. This was particularly the case for the United Kingdom, Poland and the Czech Republic, where either public opinion or the government was not keen on approving a new European Treaty. In the United Kingdom, for example, a referendum on the Constitutional Treaty had been promised, whereas most observers thought that the results of a referendum on any kind of European Treaty, whatever its shape and content, would probably be negative. At first glance, solving that political conundrum looked like trying to square the circle.

However, thinking more about it gave shape to some concrete ideas.

The starting point was to analyse the factors which had determined the negative results of the referendums in both France and the Netherlands. In both countries there is no doubt that the 'no' votes were due both to domestic and to European factors. Nothing could be done, of course, with regard to domestic factors, except for hoping that national elections would change the general mood of the electors. With regard to some of the 'European' factors, such as worries about the enlargement of the EU or the links made between European integration and globalisation, nothing could be done either, except for explanations and information.

However, one of the main 'European driven' motivations for a number of voters in both countries was that, due to the symbolic vocabulary used, there had been a misunderstanding over what the 'Constitution for Europe' was. The use of expressions such as 'Constitution', 'laws', 'minister', 'flag', 'anthem' and so on, as well as some declarations made, for instance by Valéry Giscard d'Estaing, who compared the work of the Convention to the work done in Philadelphia, at the end of the eighteenth century, by the Convention which established the United States of America, were responsible for this misunderstanding. The reality was that, in itself, the legal content of the Constitutional Treaty would have far from revolutionised either the specific character of the EU or the nature of its relationship with the Member States. Nor would it have significantly increased the powers conferred on the EU by the Member States.

Therefore the first outline of a possible deal between the eighteen states which had ratified the Constitutional Treaty and the nine other states slowly began to appear. For the first group of countries, any future treaty would have to keep as many as possible of the concrete legal reforms foreseen in the failed Constitutional Treaty. For the second group, particularly France and the Netherlands, but also the United Kingdom, the Czech Republic, Poland and Denmark, any future treaty would have to present itself as a different political text from the Constitutional Treaty.

In particular, it should distinguish itself from a 'Constitution for Europe', in concept as well as in name. This was particularly stressed by Nicolas Sarkozy after his election as President of the French Republic on 6 May 2007. This was equally vital for Jan Peter Balkenende, Prime Minister of the Netherlands, where the decision whether or not to launch a referendum was in the hands of the parliament, on the basis of a legal analysis to be made by the independent Raad van State (Council of State). It was also vital for Tony Blair, Prime Minister of the United Kingdom, if he was going to decide to abandon the idea of a referendum. It was equally the case for Anders Fogh Rasmussen, Prime Minister of Denmark, where the decision to call a referendum or not, based on Article 20 of the Danish Constitution, would largely be in the hands of lawyers of the Ministry of Justice, who would have to report on the issue of whether the new treaty would (or would not) entail the transfer of new competences from the Member States to the EU. In its analysis of the Constitutional Treaty in November 2004, the Danish Ministry of Justice had concluded that eleven provisions would have entailed such a transfer of new competences. That Treaty would therefore have required a ratification according to Article 20 of the Danish Constitution – that is, through the approval either of five-sixths of the members of the Folketing (Danish parliament), an option which appeared politically out of reach, or via a referendum, which was the only practicable option.

The possible outline for a new treaty

On this basis it was possible to imagine a possible outline for a draft treaty. The first requirement for France, the Netherlands and the United Kingdom was that the treaty would not repeal the existing treaties in order to replace them by a single one. Therefore, it should be a classic amending treaty, as had been the case with all previous treaties (Single European Act, Maastricht, Amsterdam and Nice), which amended existing treaties without replacing them. That was a must, because it meant renouncing the concept of 'constitutionalisation'. The second requirement was the disappearance of the words 'constitution' and 'constitutional'. The third was the deletion of the words 'minister', 'law', 'flag', 'anthem' and any other wording which would evoke the possible transformation of the EU into a state or which would be ambiguous on this point.

These three requirements were the necessary points of departure for France, the Netherlands and the United Kingdom, before even accepting the principle of entering into negotiations. Several other points were then raised. All these three countries wanted a new treaty that appeared to modify the existing treaties as little as possible and kept as much as possible of their structure. Each of these three countries had various other requirements, and kept the German Presidency very busy. On its side, Denmark had its own requirements, in the light of the report of its Ministry of Justice on the Constitutional Treaty. If one wanted to avoid a referendum in Denmark, each and all of the eleven provisions involving a transfer of powers would have to be amended in the new treaty.

The Presidency organised bilateral meetings (with the participation of the Council's Secretariat) in Berlin with each of the other Member States. These bilateral meetings took place at least twice with each Member State's representatives, more often with the most 'difficult' ones – that is, France, the Netherlands, the United Kingdom and Denmark, whose problems were legally very delicate. There were also two plenary meetings of the twenty-seven in Berlin, at the level of senior civil servants or secretary of state (the so-called 'focal points') and in a confidential manner.

During that period the advisors of Angela Merkel continued to work with the Council's Legal Service in order to get a full and precise picture of a 'would-be treaty' in a legal presentation.

The next step was to try and describe this 'would-be treaty' in a document which should be as short but as precise as possible, in order to be adopted by the 2007 June European Council as being the mandate for the IGC to be convened immediately afterwards. In view of the tight calendar described above, this mandate would, ideally, be 100 per cent 'exhaustive' – that is, it should describe the legal solutions to be given to all issues – in order to facilitate as much as possible the work of the future IGC, which should be very short.

The detailed IGC mandate adopted in June 2007

Having followed a well-planned preparatory process, Angela Merkel was able to present her proposal for the IGC mandate to the European Council which met on 21 and 22 June 2007 in Brussels. The negotiations and adoption of the mandate were not easy and finished in the early hours of 23 June. It may be estimated that the result was a 95 per cent 'exhaustive' mandate – that is, covering 95 per cent of the substantive issues.[33]

---

33 The text of the mandate is annexed to the Presidency Conclusions, Brussels, 21 and 22 June 2007, doc. 111777/1/07 REV 1, 15–30, available on the Internet site of the Council.

However, two issues remained unresolved, due to lack of time: both issues related to the tough position taken by the United Kingdom, the first one on Schengen and the second one on the provisions on JHA.[34] These two issues were left to the IGC.

It was the first time that such a detailed mandate was adopted for an IGC. This was due to the fact that the elements of the possible deal were already widely known, since they had been under negotiation for many years, first as 'left-overs' from the Amsterdam and Nice IGCs and then in the Convention and in the following IGC. The method was to list, in a precise manner, what would be different from the known deal and to provide legal texts already drafted in a number of cases, mostly in footnotes and in annexes to the mandate.

The strict character of the mandate was clear from its first sentence, which stated that it '[provides] the exclusive basis and framework for the work of the IGC that will be convened'.

The mandate then set out the purpose of the IGC:

- 'to draw up a Treaty . . . amending the existing Treaties' (see paragraph 1);
- to abandon 'the constitutional concept, which consisted in repealing all existing Treaties and replacing them by a single text called "Constitution"' (see paragraph 1). 'The *TEU* and the *Treaty on the Functioning of the Union* will not have a constitutional character. The terminology used throughout the Treaties will reflect this change: the term "Constitution" will not be used, the "Union Minister for Foreign Affairs" will be called High Representative of the Union for Foreign Affairs and Security Policy and the denominations "law" and "framework law" will be abandoned, the existing denominations "regulations", "directives" and "decisions" being retained. Likewise, there will be no article mentioning the symbols of the EU such as the flag, the anthem or the motto' (see paragraph 3).

For a detailed account of the work done by the German Presidency and of the IGC which ensued (in particular the work of the Group of Legal Experts), see C. Herma, 'Intergovernmental Conference on the Lisbon Treaty', in *Treaty of Lisbon: Provisions, Evaluation, Implications* (UKIE Analytical Paper Series, Office of the Committee for European Integration, Department of Analyses and Strategies (available at www.ukie.gov.pl).

34 In particular, Art. 10 of the Protocol on the transitional provisions and Art. 5 of the Protocol on the application to the United Kingdom and Ireland of the Protocol on Schengen.

The content and the structure of the future treaty were then outlined:

- the new treaty 'will introduce into the existing Treaties, which remain in force, the innovations resulting from the 2004 IGC' (see paragraph 1). The wording 'innovations resulting from the 2004 IGC' in fact referred to the substantive modifications which the Constitutional Treaty would have made to the existing Treaties, but which could not be easily identified because they were diffused throughout the text of the Constitutional Treaty, which, to a very large extent, 'codified' the existing Treaties;
- the new treaty 'will contain two substantive clauses amending respectively the *Treaty on the European Union (TEU)* and the *Treaty establishing the European Community (TEC)*. The *TEU* will keep its present name and the *TEC* will be called *Treaty on the Functioning of the Union*, the Union having a single legal personality. The word "Community" will throughout be replaced by the word "Union"; it will be stated that the two Treaties constitute the Treaties on which the Union is founded and that the Union replaces and succeeds the Community' (see paragraph 2).

Part II and Annex 1 of the mandate set out the amendments to be made to the EU Treaty. The method chosen was to list, in the mandate, the amendments which would be made to the EU Treaty, stating that 'in the absence of indications to the contrary in [the] mandate, the text of the existing Treaty remains unchanged'.

Part III and Annex 2(A) of the mandate set out the amendments to be made to the EC Treaty (renamed the Treaty on the Functioning of the European Union, TFEU). Because it would have been too complicated, given the length of the EC Treaty and the number of amendments required, the method followed for the TFEU was the reverse of that followed for the EU Treaty. It consisted in '[inserting] into the [EC] Treaty by way of specific modifications in the usual manner' all 'the innovations as agreed in the 2004 IGC', the mandate listing only the 'modifications . . . introduced compared to the results of the 2004 IGC' (see paragraphs 18 and 19).

Finally, Annex 2(B) identified the place of a number of provisions (identified mostly through a reference to their numbering in the Constitutional Treaty) in the TEU or in the TFEU. In particular, it was decided that the great majority of enabling clauses formerly contained in Part I of the Constitutional Treaty would be put into the TFEU, in order to avoid burdening the TEU with technical provisions.

In addition to abandoning the 'constitutional' concept and all the related vocabulary, the main modifications agreed in the June 2007 mandate as compared with 'the results of the 2004 IGC' (i.e. to the text of the Constitutional Treaty) were the following:

- on the structure of the treaties (i.e. two Treaties – the TEU and TFEU), the insertion of new provisions explaining the relation between the two Treaties and the purpose of the TFEU[35] (see paragraphs 2 and 19(a) of the mandate);
- on the Union's objectives (Article 3 TEU[36]), a limited redrafting by distinguishing more clearly between the provisions on the internal market and those on the area of freedom, security and justice,[37] by adding a new paragraph on economic and monetary union and the euro[38] and by inserting in the paragraph on external relations a reference to the protection of its citizens by the Union[39] (see point 3 of Annex 1 to the mandate);
- on the primacy of EU law, the removal of the provision[40] which 'codified' into the Treaty the principle of primacy which had been laid down by the Court of Justice in the 1960s (see paragraph 3);[41]
- on the relations between the Union and its Member States (Article 4 TEU[42]), the addition as a new paragraph 1 of the last sentence from Article 5(2) TEU[43] according to which 'competences not conferred upon the Union in the Treaties remain with the Member States', and the addition at the end of paragraph 2 of a sentence stating that 'national

35 See the new 3rd subparagraph in Art. 1 TEU, which states that 'the Union shall be founded on the [EU Treaty and TFEU]. Those two Treaties shall have the same legal value.' See also Art. 1 TFEU, whose paragraph 1 states that the TFEU 'organises the functioning of the Union and determines the areas of, delimitation of, and arrangements for exercising its competences'.
36 Compare with Art. I-2 of the Constitutional Treaty.
37 The wording of the 4th indent of Art. 2 of the former TEU was reproduced in Art. 3(2) TEU, and a first sentence on the internal market was inserted at the beginning of paragraph 3, first indent, of that Article. In this operation, the wording 'where competition is free and undistorted' from Art. I-3(2) was removed, which created some reaction and was the reason why Protocol no. 27 on the internal market and competition was added.
38 See Art. 3(4) TEU.   39 See the end of the first sentence of Art. 3(5) TEU.
40 Art. I-6 of the Constitutional Treaty.
41 The last sentence of this paragraph provided that 'concerning the primacy of EU law, the IGC will adopt a Declaration recalling the existing case law of the EU Court of Justice' (see Declaration no. 17).
42 Compare with Art. I-5 of the Constitutional Treaty.
43 Art. I-11(2) of the Constitutional Treaty.

security remains the sole responsibility of each Member State' (see point 4 of Annex 1);

- with regard to the Charter of Fundamental Rights, the non-inclusion in the Treaty, but the insertion in Article 6(1) TEU of a cross-reference to the Charter specifying that 'it shall have the same legal value as the Treaties', and the addition of two subparagraphs recalling that the Charter does not extend the competences of the Union and that it 'shall be interpreted in accordance with the general provisions in [its] Title VII . . . and with due regard to the explanations' (see paragraph 9 and point 5 of Annex 1);
- on national parliaments, the insertion of a new provision highlighting their particular role in the EU (Article 12 TEU), an extension from six to eight weeks of the period for them to give a reasoned opinion on subsidiarity,[44] and the addition of a new possibility (i.e. enhanced 'yellow card') for national parliaments, with regard to proposed acts in the codecision procedure, to oblige the Commission to re-examine the draft and for the EU legislature to consider specifically the issue of subsidiarity[45] (see paragraph 11 and point 7 of Annex 1);
- on the new 'double majority' voting system in the Council, the postponement of its entry into force from 1 November 2009 to 1 November 2014,[46] until which date the previous QMV system (i.e. as introduced by the Nice Treaty) will continue to apply, and the possibility of continuing to use this system, upon request by a Council member in a given case, until 31 March 2017 (see paragraph 13);
- on the so-called 'Ioannina Decision',[47] the parallel postponement to 1 November 2014 of its application, and the addition of a possibility of applying it as from 1 April 2017 upon request from Council members representing at least 55 per cent of the population or 55 per cent of the number of Member States necessary to constitute a blocking minority under the new 'double majority' system (see paragraph 13);
- on enhanced co-operation (Article 20(2) TEU[48]), the setting at nine Member States, instead of one-third of the number of Member States,

---

44 See Art. 6 of Protocol no. 2 on the application of the principles of subsidiarity and proportionality.
45 See Art. 7(3) of Protocol no. 2 on the application of the principles of subsidiarity and proportionality.
46 See Art. 16(4) and (5) TEU and Art. 3 of Protocol no. 36 on transitional provisions.
47 Which is contained in Declaration no. 7.
48 Compare with Art. I-44(2) of the Constitutional Treaty.

as the minimum number required for launching such co-operation (see paragraph 14);

- on CFSP (and ESDP), the retention of the title devoted to this area in the EU Treaty, instead of placing it in the TFEU together with the other provisions on the Union's external,[49] the insertion of a new paragraph setting out the specificities of CFSP,[50] the addition of a specific legal basis on personal data protection in this area,[51] and a specification that the flexibility clause cannot be used in the area of CFSP[52] (see paragraphs 7, 15, 19(r) and 19(w) and point 8 of Annex 1);
- on revision procedures for the treaties (Article 48 TEU[53]), the addition of a new second sentence in the first paragraph of the ordinary revision procedure specifying that proposals for amending the treaties may serve to increase or to reduce the competences conferred on the Union (see paragraph 16);
- on the accession procedure (Article 49 TEU[54]), the addition of a new last sentence on taking into account 'the conditions of eligibility agreed upon by the European Council', which actually refers in particular to the famous 'Copenhagen criteria' for enlargement agreed by the European Council in June 1993[55] (see paragraph 16 and point 9 of Annex 1);
- on shared competences (Article 2(2) TFEU[56]), the addition of a new last sentence specifying that Member States can exercise their competence again to the extent that the Union has decided to cease exercising its competence (see paragraph 19(b));
- on supporting competences (Article 6 TFEU[57]), the addition in the introductory sentence of a reference to the fact that the EU's competence

---

49 See Chapters 1 and 2 of Title V of the TEU, to be compared with Chapter II of Title V of the Constitutional Treaty. However, both the CFSP and the other external action chapters are placed under a common 'umbrella' provision stating that 'the Union's action on the international scene shall be guided by the principles, shall pursue the objectives of, and be conducted in accordance with the general provisions laid down [in Arts. 21 and 22 TEU]' (see Art. 23 TEU and Art. 205 TFEU).

50 See Art. 24(1), 2nd subparagraph, TEU.

51 See Art. 39 TEU. This provision is limited, however, to the processing of personal data by the Member States when carrying out activities falling within CFSP. It does not concern data processed by EU institutions, which remain subject to the general data protection legal basis (Art. 16 TFEU).

52 See Art. 352(4) TFEU.

53 Compare with Arts. IV-443–445 of the Constitutional Treaty.

54 Compare with Art. I-58 of the Constitutional Treaty.

55 See Presidency Conclusions, European Council, 21 and 22 June 1993 (SN 180/1/93 REV 3).

56 Compare with Art. I-12(2) of the Constitutional Treaty.

57 Compare with Art. I-17 of the Constitutional Treaty.

is to support, co-ordinate or supplement 'the actions of the Member States' (see paragraph 19(c));

- on co-ordination of social security systems (Article 48 TFEU[58]), the addition of a new possibility of preventing the adoption of a legislative act, by providing that if the European Council takes no action when seized under the 'emergency brake' system, the act proposed will be deemed not to have been adopted (see paragraph 19(g));

- on services of general interest, the addition of a new protocol (see paragraph 19(i));

- in the area of freedom, security and justice (FSJ), the addition of a new provision on co-ordination in the field of national security (Article 73 TFEU), the addition of a no-objection procedure for national parliaments in the *passerelle* on family law (Article 81(3) TFEU),[59] the simplification of the 'brake–accelerator' procedures in judicial co-operation in criminal matters (Articles 82(3) and 83(3) TFEU[60]), the addition of a new 'accelerator' procedure in the provision on the Public Prosecutor's Office and in operational police co-operation (Articles 86(1) and 87(3) TFEU[61]) and the extension of the scope of the opt-out Protocol for the United Kingdom to cover the whole FSJ area (see paragraph 19(j)–(l) and point 2 of Annex 2(A));

- in the area of energy (Articles 122 and 194 TFEU[62]), the addition of a reference to the spirit of solidarity between Member States and to the interconnection of energy networks (see paragraph 19(m) and (q) and points 3 and 5 of Annex 2(A));

- on the environment (Article 191 TFEU[63]), the addition of 'combating climate change' in the list of objectives (see paragraph 19(p) and point 4 of Annex 2(A));

- on the classification and adoption of EU legal acts (Articles 288–293 TFEU), a definition of what is a 'legislative act'[64] and a description of codecision (called 'ordinary legislative procedure') and other legislative procedures ('special legislative procedure') (see paragraph 19(u) and (v)).

---

58 Compare with Art. III-136(2)(b) of the Constitutional Treaty.
59 Compare with Art. III-269(3), 2nd subparagraph, of the Constitutional Treaty.
60 Compare with Arts. III-270(3) and (4) and III-271(3) and (4) of the Constitutional Treaty.
61 Compare with Arts. III-274(1) and III-275(3) of the Constitutional Treaty.
62 Compare, respectively, with Arts. III-180(1) and III-256(1) of the Constitutional Treaty.
63 Compare with Art. III-233(1), 4th indent, of the Constitutional Treaty.
64 Classification as a legislative act has a number of consequences in terms of openness for proceedings and documents, the role of national parliaments, etc.

On this basis, in its conclusions approved by consensus, the European Council '[agreed] to convene an Intergovernmental Conference and [invited] the Presidency without delay to take the necessary steps in accordance with Article 48 of the TEU, with the objective of opening the IGC before the end of July as soon as the legal requirements have been met'.

It also '[invited] the incoming Presidency to draw up a draft Treaty text in line with the terms of the mandate and to submit this to the IGC as soon as it opens. The IGC will complete its work as quickly as possible, and in any case before the end of 2007, so as to allow for sufficient time to ratify the resulting Treaty before the European elections in June 2009.'[65]

Following that, the German Presidency, through a letter from its permanent representative Wilhelm Schönfelder, submitted to the Council, in accordance with Article 48 of the EU Treaty, 'a proposal for the amendment of the Treaties on which the Union is founded'.[66] This proposal contained paragraphs 8 to 14 of the Presidency Conclusions of the June European Council, as well as the IGC mandate.

The IGC which adopted the Lisbon Treaty

In accordance with what had been agreed by the European Council and following the favourable opinion delivered by the Council on 16 July 2007,[67] the Portuguese Presidency, which succeeded the German one, decided immediately to convene the IGC.[68] As early as 23 July 2007, the IGC officially opened at the level of foreign minister, and the Presidency, on the basis of the work done by the Council's Legal Service, transmitted the text of the draft treaty to the twenty-six other Member States.[69] The IGC could meet at three levels: heads of state or government, ministers of foreign affairs, and personal representatives of the heads of state or

---

65 See Presidency Conclusions, Brussels, 21 and 22 June 2007, paragraphs 10 and 11.

66 See doc. 11222/07, available on the Internet site of the Council at http://register. consilium.europa.eu/pdf/en/07/st11/st11222.en07.pdf.

67 See doc. 11597/07, available on the Internet site of the Council at http:// register.consilium.europa.eu/pdf/en/07/st11/st11597.en07.pdf. Before that, the European Parliament (on 11 July), the Commission (on 10 July) and the European Central Bank (on 5 July) had also delivered a favourable opinion (see, respectively, Council docs. 11626/07, 11625/07 and 11624/07).

68 See letter of Luis Amado, Minister of Foreign Affairs of Portugal, of 17 July 2007 (doc. 12004/07, available on the Internet site of the Council at http://register. consilium.europa.eu/ pdf/en/07/st12/st12004.en07.pdf).

69 Documents CIG 1/07 (draft Treaty amending the EU and EC Treaties), 2/07 (draft Protocols), 3/07 (draft Declarations), and 4/07 (draft Preamble of the amending Treaty).

government or so-called 'focal points'. The Portuguese Presidency also decided on 17 July to convene a Group of Legal Experts of the twenty-seven Member States (including representatives from the European Parliament and the Commission). Taking into account its largely legal mandate, this Group, the only group of civil servants officially set up by the IGC, would be chaired by the Legal Counsel to the IGC, as had been the case for the Group of Legal Experts of the 2003–4 IGC. This Group began to work immediately after the official opening of the IGC and finished its work on 3 October 2007, after having held twenty-four meetings.

The Group worked on the basis of the four documents which had been transmitted by the Presidency on the day the IGC was opened. These drafts were transmitted in one legally edited language version (French), and the other twenty-two language versions were made available in the following weeks. In its paper on the organisation of the work of the IGC, the Presidency specified that if issues were not resolved at the meetings of legal experts, personal representatives could be consulted. This proved not to be necessary.

The line taken from the beginning of the work of the Group of Legal Experts was to abide strictly by the detailed IGC mandate which had been agreed by the heads of state or government. Any amendment to the texts transmitted by the Presidency would have to respect the IGC mandate and be agreed by common agreement of the legal experts.

The Group began its work on 24 and 25 July 2007 by going through the draft Preamble to the Lisbon Treaty and most of the amendments to the EU Treaty. It resumed its work on 29 August and held meetings at a rate of three or four days per week until mid-September. The Group completed a first reading of all the texts before the informal meeting of ministers of foreign affairs (the so-called 'Gymnich meeting') on 8 September 2007, at which the chairman of the Group informed the ministers on the state of play. A second reading of the texts was carried out by mid-September.

As from 12 September, and until its final meeting on 3 October 2007, the work of the Group of Legal Experts concentrated almost exclusively on the difficult negotiation and drafting of the only two issues which had been left open in the IGC mandate of June. These issues were the opt-out provisions for the United Kingdom and Ireland regarding the measures building on the Schengen *acquis* and the third-pillar *acquis*, as well as the transitional period for the powers of the Commission and the Court of Justice regarding the third-pillar *acquis*. Most of that negotiating work took place in informal small gatherings, in between the plenary meetings of the Group taking stock of the situation, until final agreement was reached on 3 October. Thus, out of the five weeks of intensive work of the Group, half of the time was dedicated to these two issues.

During its work the Group agreed on about 350 adaptations or improvements, ranging from minor corrections to substantial provisions. In addition to the above-mentioned provisions related to Schengen and the third pillar, the Group agreed *inter alia* on the following:

- a simple and straightforward Preamble for the Lisbon Treaty (the Treaty is 'to complete the process started by the Amsterdam Treaty and by the Nice Treaty with a view of enhancing the efficiency and democratic legitimacy of the Union and . . . improving the coherence of its action');
- a procedure and timetable for the proclamation and the publication of the Charter of Fundamental Rights (proclamation before the signature of the Treaty and publication in the *Official Journal*, together with the explanations, immediately after);[70]
- the deletion of subtitles attached to Articles of the EU Treaty (because it was too difficult to agree on subtitles for the CFSP Articles in the EU Treaty);
- the addition in Article 9 of the EU Treaty of the definition, taken from Article 20(1) TFEU, of citizenship of the Union, which is additional to national citizenship and does not replace it;
- the addition in Article 13 of the EU Treaty of a paragraph (4) recalling the advisory role of the Economic and Social Committee and the Committee of the Regions;
- a specification in Article 15(3) of the EU Treaty that the European Council will meet 'twice every six months' instead of 'quarterly' as originally proposed;
- the addition in Article 17(5), 2nd subparagraph, of the EU Treaty, concerning the composition of the Commission, of the word 'strictly' in relation to the equal rotation between Member States, as stated in Article 244(a) of the TFEU, and of a phrase on 'the demographic and

---

70 The revised version of the Charter was proclaimed by the European Parliament, the Council and the Commission in Strasbourg on 12 December 2007, on the eve of the signature of the Treaty on 13 December in Lisbon, and it was published, with the explanations, in the *Official Journal of the European Union* (OJ) on 14 December 2007 (OJ No. C303, 14 December 2007, 1 and 17). In the draft texts transmitted by the Presidency on 23 July, the Charter and the explanations thereto had been put into two Declarations (nos. 11 and 12).

geographical range of all the Member States', also taken from Article 244(b) TFEU;

- the addition in Article 24(1), 2nd subparagraph, of the EU Treaty of the word 'rules', so that the first sentence reads 'The [CFSP] is subject to specific rules and procedures';
- the addition in Article 26(2), 2nd subparagraph, of the High Representative as also being entrusted, with the Council, 'to ensure the unity, consistency and effectiveness of the action of the Union' in CFSP;
- the insertion in Article 48(2) of the EU Treaty of the words '*inter alia*' in the second sentence so that it reads 'These proposals [for amendments to the Treaties] may, *inter alia*, serve either to increase or to reduce the competences conferred on the Union in the Treaties';
- keeping unchanged the three final provisions of both Treaties (TEU and TFEU) (i.e. on the unlimited duration of the Treaties, on the procedure for their ratification and entry into force, and on their original language versions), with the addition of a paragraph on their possible translation into other languages as determined by the Member States among languages which have official status on their territory;
- the insertion, in Article 1(1) of the TFEU on the purposes of the Treaty, of the word 'delimitation', so that the sentence reads 'this Treaty organises the functioning of the Union and determines the areas of, delimitation of, and arrangements for exercising its competences';
- a specification, in certain legal bases within the TFEU, that the EU legislature should act by means of regulations;[71]
- the placing of Articles 15 (openness) and 16 (personal data protection) within Title II on provisions having general application of the TFEU;

---

71 In Art. 14(2), last sentence, on services of general economic interest; in Art. 15(3), on openness; in Art. 24, on the procedures required for a citizens' initiative; in Art. 75, on the freezing of assets in terrorism cases; in Art. 121(6), on multilateral surveillance; in Art. 127(6), on prudential supervision; in Art. 164, on the European Social Fund; in Art. 161, on the Structural Funds; in Art. 178, on the European Regional Development Fund; in Art. 197(2), on administrative co-operation; in Art. 207(2), on the common commercial policy; in Art. 214(5), on the European Voluntary Humanitarian Aid Corps; in Art. 223(2), on the general conditions governing the duties of MEPs; in Art. 224, on political parties at European level; in Art. 226, on temporary committees of inquiry of the European Parliament; in Art. 228(4) on the European Ombudsman; in Art. 257, on specialised courts; in Art. 291(3), on the mechanisms for controlling the Commission's exercise of implementing powers; in Art. 298(2), on the European administration; in Art. 311, on the Union's own resources; in Art. 312(2), on the multiannual financial framework; in Art. 322, on the financial rules; in Art. 336, on staff rules; and in Art. 342, on language rules.

- the addition of the words '*inter alia*' in the introductory sentence of Article 20(2) of the TFEU, which lists the rights and duties of the Union's citizens;
- the redrafting of the sentence, in Article 275, 1st subparagraph, of the TFEU, concerning the absence of jurisdiction of the Court of Justice 'with respect to the provisions relating to the [CFSP] [or] with respect to acts adopted on the basis of those provisions';
- the partial redrafting of Article 289 of the TFEU on legislative procedures and acts, including the addition of paragraph (4) concerning cases where the author of the proposal for a legislative act is not the Commission;
- a clarification in Articles 203, 349 and 352 of the TFEU (respectively on overseas countries and territories and on the flexibility clause) that the Council may use either a legislative or a non-legislative procedure, and that if it uses a legislative procedure, it will be a special legislative procedure;
- the insertion in Article 314(1) of the TFEU, concerning the budgetary procedure, of an exception for the European Central Bank to the obligation for each institution to draw up estimates of its expenditure, since it has a separate budget, in accordance with Article 26 of its Statute (Protocol no. 4);
- the addition of a subparagraph in Article 1 of Protocol no. 36 on transitional provisions to make clear that until the end of the 2004–9 parliamentary term, 'the composition and the number of [MEPs] shall remain the same as on the date of entry into force of the Treaty of Lisbon' (which was foreseen on 1 January 2009).

All these modifications agreed by the Group were incorporated in a revised version of the draft texts issued on 5 October 2007, in view of the IGC meeting at the level of ministers of foreign affairs in Luxembourg on 15 October. No other changes to the texts were made at that meeting.

The texts were then transmitted to the IGC at the level of heads of state or government which met at Lisbon on 18 October 2007, and which agreed on the last substantive amendments and additions to the texts and gave their final political agreement to what would become the Lisbon Treaty. Six political issues were solved directly by the heads of state or government:

- the composition of the European Parliament: taking into account the position of Italy, the number of MEPs was increased from 750 to 751 in order to give one additional MEP to Italy; this was done by inserting the words 'plus the President' in Article 14(2) of the EU Treaty and by adding two declarations specifying that this additional seat will be attributed to Italy and stating that the European Council will give its political agreement to a draft Decision on the composition of the Parliament, revised accordingly (Declarations nos. 4 and 5);

- QMV in the Council: taking into account the position of Poland, the so-called 'Ioannina Decision', contained in Declaration no. 7, was modified (change in the date of adoption of the decision by providing that it would be adopted on the date of signature of the Treaty,[72] removal of a preambular clause on the duration of the Decision, removal of the provision of 1 November 2014 as the date on which the Decision would take effect) and addition of a Protocol no. 9 laying down an obligation that the European Council holds a 'preliminary deliberation . . . acting by consensus' on any draft aiming at amending or abrogating the 'Ioannina Decision';
- the spelling of 'euro' in the Cyrillic alphabet: taking into account the position of Bulgaria, agreement on the spelling of 'euro' as 'евро' in Cyrillic;
- the conferral of competences: taking into account the position of the Czech Republic, the addition of a declaration on the delimitation of competences (notably the possibility for the Council to request the Commission for a proposal to repeal a legislative act, and for an IGC to amend the Treaties in order to reduce the competences conferred on the Union) (Declaration no. 18);
- the Court of Justice: taking into account the position of Poland, the addition of a declaration concerning the increase, from eight to eleven, of the number of advocates-general and stating that, should the Court of Justice request such an increase, Poland would get a 'permanent' advocate-general, like the other large Member States (Germany, France, Italy, Spain and the United Kingdom) (Declaration no. 38);
- the appointment of the High Representative: the addition of a declaration on 'appropriate contacts' to be made with the European Parliament in advance of the appointment of the High Representative for Foreign Affairs and Security Policy (Declaration no. 12).

Having solved these problems, the heads of state or government agreed on the whole text of the Treaty as suggested by the Group of Legal Experts.

72 The Decision was indeed adopted by written procedure on the day the Lisbon Treaty was signed – that is, on 13 December 2007 (see doc. 16013/07). It entered into force on the same day as the Lisbon Treaty.

Following this final political agreement of the IGC, the texts were, as usual, transmitted to the jurist-linguists of the Council[73] for a final review of their concordance in the twenty-three EU official languages. The suggested corrections by the jurist-linguists were sent to the Member States' delegations on 30 October 2007, and jurist-linguist meetings together with the twenty-seven delegations and representatives from the European Parliament and the Commission took place from 12 to 16 November. The verified versions were sent to delegations on 3 December and put on the Internet site of the Council on 4 December 2007.[74]

The Treaty was then solemnly signed in Lisbon on 13 December 2007. It was published in the *Official Journal of the European Union* (OJ) on 17 December.[75] A consolidated version of the TEU and TFEU, incorporating the amendments made by the Lisbon Treaty, was published in the OJ on 9 May 2008.[76]

*

It follows from the above that both teams (the 'Euro-enthusiasts' and the 'Euro-sceptics') may claim to have scored goals with the content of the Lisbon Treaty.

We would suggest that these two teams are not called the 'federalists' and the 'sovereignists', because this no longer corresponds to the reality of today. They should rather be called the 'integrationists' and the 'co-operationists'.[77] Why this change of terminology?

Because, in fact, none of the most 'Euro-enthusiast' among today's political leaders of the twenty-seven Member States wants to establish a 'United States of Europe'. However, they do favour greater integration of policies in some fields, in order to help their countries and their citizens to face today's challenges. They also favour a European Union which would be an active and effective power on the international scene.

On the opposite side, none of the most Euro-sceptic European leaders opposes the existence of the European Union. Most of them would even accept some reasonable progress in European co-operation. However, they want the EU to remain an international organisation (albeit of a special character), in which the Member States do co-operate, sometimes

---

73 This department of the Council Legal Service is called the Directorate on 'Quality of Legislation'.

74 The Treaty is reproduced in document CIG 14/07 and the Final Act in document CIG 15/07. This text has been the subject of technical legal corrections in the different language versions which have to be agreed upon by all Parties.

75 OJ No. C306, 17 December 2007, 1.   76 OJ No. C115, 9 May 2008, 1.

77 On this point, see M. Cini, *European Union Politics*, 2nd edn (Oxford University Press, 2007).

very closely, but while preserving their characteristics as sovereign and independent nation states.

Any negotiation, in order to reach a result, has to finish in a compromise. Normally, the compromise between the 'integrationists' and the 'co-operationists' over a given issue where the former want 'white' and the latter 'black', should lead to the adoption of a colour in a nuanced shade of 'grey'. However, in the EU the compromise is sometimes found by putting two distinct issues together in a package deal, and by agreeing that one half of it will be white and the other half black! Apparently, both sides win, and thus both teams have the feeling that they have scored goals. Of course, each side thinks that it has had the better share. But this is not the issue. The issue is whether the result of the negotiation is a viable one, good enough to allow the EU to work effectively in real life. If the result is not workable, both sides lose, and the question may be asked whether this situation is durable.

Let us see which of the two teams won the match with the adoption of the Lisbon Treaty.

The **co-operationists** scored an impressive number of goals, more political than legal, as none of them reduces the existing powers of the EU:

- the idea of a 'constitution', which had been the big success of the 'integrationists', must be forgotten, probably for a long time, along with the use of the vocabulary normally used for a state (minister for foreign affairs, anthem, flag, laws, etc.);
- for the first time, the Treaty legally guarantees that the essential functions of the Member States are to be respected by the Union;
- for the first time, the Treaty allows a Member State, if and when it wishes, to withdraw from the EU;
- all major areas close to the core attributes of sovereign states remain, either reserved for the exclusive competence of the Member States or subject to the right of veto of any one of them: revision of the Treaties, foreign policy, defence and security, taxation, financial resources for the EU budget, economic policy, the most delicate or sensitive parts of environmental protection and energy, social policy, family law, health, culture, education and so on; moreover, in foreign policy (and defence), the EU 'federal' institutions (European Parliament, Court of Justice, Commission) are not given the powers they have in other EU areas of action, the Union therefore actually remaining organised in two separate pillars;
- for the first time, the possibility of controlling respect for subsidiarity is given to entities which are external to the EU institutions – that is, to

the national parliaments, with the possibility of going to the EU Court of Justice.

The goals scored by the **integrationists** might be less numerous, but they concern important and concrete substantive reforms:

- in about forty additional cases, the decision-making in the Council will be done by QMV: however, apart from most of the former third pillar, the right of veto of each of the twenty-seven Member States is preserved for the most sensitive and important decisions;
- an increased role is given to the 'federal' institutions (European Parliament, Court of Justice and Commission) especially significant for the former third pillar;
- an important potential role is given to the two new 'Brussels-based jobs', the President of the European Council and the High Representative for Foreign Affairs and Security Policy: of course, nobody can predict today whether these two figures will be able to play an important political role, as their legal powers, as laid down in the Treaties, are, at least for the European Council President, rather limited;
- a greater possibility is opened up for closer co-operation among some Member States, especially in the area of CFSP/ESDP and the former third pillar.

Therefore, on the whole, the Lisbon Treaty:

- on the one hand, gives to the EU a new legal framework which offers better potential to progress. Most, if not all, of the substantive reforms envisaged in the Constitutional Treaty have been preserved. The Treaty brings forward structures, procedures and mechanisms which will potentially allow the Union to develop further in the future. Therefore, without giving significant new competences to the EU, it strengthens the possibility, if there is a political will for it, of more integration of the policies of the Member States and of greater visibility of the EU in the world;
- on the other hand, the Lisbon Treaty is a political backlash for the integrationists. For the first time, they have been obliged to retreat and to accept that their retreat is visible. They have been obliged to accept the disappearance of any word or symbol which aimed at stressing that the Union could be compared to an entity having more and more elements in common with a state. This is an important political event, and the ideal of a federal European entity has been seriously damaged.

If this assessment is accurate, one might call the match a draw.

Section 4 The difficult ratification of the Lisbon Treaty

Hungary was the first Member State to ratify the Lisbon Treaty, on 17 December 2007 – only a few days after its signature. All the Member States, except Ireland, decided to go through a parliamentary procedure.

In Denmark, this had to be preceded by a legal study by the Ministry of Justice. As mentioned above, such a study had been carried out in November 2004 for the Constitutional Treaty. It had concluded that, on eleven points, the Constitutional Treaty would have transferred new powers from the Member States to the EU. For this reason its ratification required, as provided for in Article 20 of the Danish Constitution, either five-sixths of the votes in the Folketing or a referendum. These eleven points having been modified, the legal study of 4 December 2007 made by the Danish Ministry of Justice on the Lisbon Treaty concluded that the new Treaty did not entail any new transfer of sovereignty to the EU. Therefore the government decided on 11 December that the ratification of the Lisbon Treaty could take place according to the normal procedure provided by the Constitution for the conclusion of international treaties. On the same day, the Danish parliament agreed with that procedure. It ratified the Treaty on 24 April 2008.

In France, the Conseil constitutionnel (Constitutional Council) was seized, and decided on 20 December 2007, as it had done previously for the Constitutional Treaty, that the Lisbon Treaty was incompatible with the French Constitution on several points.[78] The government therefore decided on a revision of the French Constitution, which was done by means of a vote on 4 February 2008 of both chambers of the Parlement, which ratified the Treaty on 7 and 8 February 2008.

In the Netherlands, the Raad van State (State Council) issued an opinion on 12 September 2007 in which it determined, on the basis of the IGC mandate, that the proposed new Treaty 'is substantially different from the [Constitutional Treaty]'. The government then decided, on 21 September 2007, that it was not necessary to proceed through a referendum. The States-General (parliament) reached the same conclusion about two weeks later and the Treaty was ratified by the States-General on 5 June and 8 July 2008.

---

78 Decision no. 2007–560 DC, 20 December 2007. See comment by J. Roux, 'Le Conseil constitutionnel et le contrôle de constitutionnalité du Traité de Lisbonne: bis repetita', (2008) 49(1) *Revue Trimestrielle de Droit européen*, which refers to Decision no. 2004–505 DC, 19 November 2004, by which the Conseil constitutionnel decided that the ratification of the Constitutional Treaty required a modification of the French Constitution. For an analysis of this decision see my book, *Le Traité constitutionnel pour l'Europe: une analyse juridique* (Brussels: Bruylant, 2006), Annex 2, 299–308.

In the United Kingdom, the opponents of the Lisbon Treaty argued that the Prime Minister, at the time Tony Blair, had promised a referendum to authorise the ratification of the Constitutional Treaty. Since, according to them, the Lisbon Treaty was more or less a reproduction of the Constitutional Treaty, a referendum should therefore take place in the United Kingdom before ratifying the Lisbon Treaty. This gave rise to long debates in both the House of Commons and the House of Lords. Finally, both Houses gave their approval (the House of Commons on 11 March and the House of Lords on 18 June 2008) and the Royal Assent was given on 19 June 2008. The referendum issue was also submitted to the High Court of Justice, which, in its judgment of 25 June 2008, dismissed the case.[79] The main reasons were, notably, that the Lisbon Treaty was substantially different from the Constitutional Treaty and that a promise of holding a referendum '[did not] give rise to legitimate expectations enforceable in public law . . . The subject matter, nature and context of a promise of this kind place it in the realm of politics, not of the courts.'

In Germany, both chambers of the legislature quickly gave their authorisation to ratify (on 24 April and 23 May 2008). However, the German President, Horst Köhler, suspended his signature of the instrument of ratification in order to wait until the Federal Constitutional Court, which had been seized by a number of individuals, ruled on the compatibility of the Treaty with the German Constitution (the Basic Law). The German Constitutional Court did so on 30 June 2009 in a very thorough judgment which ruled that the Lisbon Treaty was compatible with the German Basic Law, but that, before the ratification instrument could be deposited by Germany, the powers of the German parliament (the Bundestag and the Bundesrat) should be substantially increased in a number of instances.[80] New legislation on this was passed on 8 September in the Bundestag and on 18 September 2009 in the Bundesrat (by a unanimous vote). It was published in the German *Official Journal* on 24 September and on 25 September 2009 the President signed the instrument of ratification, which, on the same day, was deposited in Rome.

79 See *Wheeler v. Prime Minister and Secretary of State*, Case No. CO/1915/2008, of 25 June 2008.
80 See Joint Cases 2 BvE 2/08, 2 BvE 5/08, 2 BvR 1010/08, 2 BvR 1022/08, 2 BvR 1259/08 and 2 BvR 182/09. A press release by the Constitutional Court itself (no. 72/2009) summarises the judgment and is available at www.bundesverfassungsgericht.de/pressemitteilungen/ bvg09–072en.html. The Court also made an English translation of its judgment available on its Internet site (see preliminary version at www.bundesverfassungsgericht.de/ entscheidungen/es20090630_2bve000208en.html). For an analysis of this important judgment see Appendix 1. See also below, Section 17.

In Poland, both chambers of the parliament also soon gave their autho-risation to ratify (on 1 and 2 April 2008), but the Polish President, Lech Kaczynski, decided to suspend his signature of the instrument of ratifi-cation, following the negative referendum in Ireland of 12 June 2008. He later declared that he would wait for the solution to be found regarding the Irish situation and that if the second referendum in Ireland was positive, he would sign the instrument of ratification. He did so on 10 October 2009 and the Polish instrument of ratification was deposited in Rome on 12 October 2009.

The guarantees given to Ireland and the second referendum

Ireland was the only Member State where the ratification had to be autho-rised, not by its national parliament, but by referendum, according to the interpretation given by the Irish government to the judgment of 9 April 1987 by the Supreme Court in the *Crotty* case.[81] The referendum was held

81 See *Crotty v. Taoiseach*, Judgment of 9 April 1987, 1986 No. 12036P. The *Crotty* case concerned the ratification of the Single European Act (SEA). Mr Crotty had claimed that any amendment to the Treaties made after Ireland joined the EC in 1973 would require a further amendment to the Irish Constitution. The Court stated that the authorisation given to the State in Art. 29.4.3 of the Constitution to become a member of the EC 'must be construed as an authorisation given to the State not only to join the Communities as they stood in 1973, but also to join in amendments of the Treaties so long as such amendments do not *alter the essential scope or objectives of the Communities*' (emphasis added). The Court went on to examine the amendments brought to the Treaties by the SEA to check whether they required an amendment to the Irish Constitution, and therefore a referendum, because the Irish Constitution can only be amended though a referendum. The Court concluded that neither the changes from unanimity to qualified majority, nor the addition of new legal bases which were within the original aims and objectives of the EC, nor the addition of a Court of First Instance, nor the introduction of provisions on the approximation of laws would alter the essential character of the Communities or create a threat to fundamental constitutional rights. The Court therefore unanimously rejected this part of the appeal. With regard to the second part of the appeal on Art. 30 SEA on European Political Cooperation (EPC), according to which the High Contracting Parties 'shall endeavour jointly to formulate and implement a European foreign policy', the judges were divided. A majority of three out of five judges decided in favour of the appeal. The main reason was that the ultimate purpose of EPC was to create a European Union and that this would go beyond the authorisation given in Art. 29.4.3 of the Irish Constitution and the necessities of EC membership and therefore require an amendment to the Constitution. As a consequence, a referendum was held in Ireland for ratifying the SEA. After that, the government decided to hold referendums for each subsequent Treaty (Maastricht, Amsterdam and Nice), with the exception of the accession Treaties. On the necessity or not for holding referendums on such cases in Ireland, see R. Barrington, 'Was Holding a Referendum on Lisbon Treaty Really Necessary?', Opinion, *Irish Times*, 11 July 2008; L. Pech, '*Le référendum en Irlande pour ratifier les traités européens: obligatoire ou coutumier?*', Questions d'Europe no. 115, Fondation Robert Schuman, 28 October

on 12 June 2008. The turn-out was 53.13 per cent – 1.6 million voters – of whom 53.4 per cent – 862,415 voters – voted 'no'.

On 18 and 19 June 2008, at its first meeting following the negative referendum in Ireland, the European Council adopted the conclusions[82] given in Box 9.

BOX 9. EUROPEAN COUNCIL, 19–20 JUNE 2008, PRESIDENCY
CONCLUSIONS

LISBON TREATY

1. The European Council took note of the preparatory work carried out in line with its December 2007 conclusions.
2. The European Council noted the outcome of the referendum in Ireland on the Lisbon Treaty and took stock of the situation on the basis of an initial assessment provided by the Taoiseach Brian Cowen.
3. The European Council agreed that more time was needed to analyse the situation. It noted that the Irish government will actively consult, both internally and with the other Member States, in order to suggest a common way forward.
4. Recalling that the purpose of the Lisbon Treaty is to help an enlarged Union to act more effectively and more democratically, the European Council noted that the parliaments in 19 Member States have ratified the Treaty and that the ratification process continues in other countries.[1]
5. The European Council agreed to Ireland's suggestion to come back to this issue at its meeting of 15 October 2008 in order to consider the way forward. It underlined the importance in the meantime of continuing to deliver concrete results in the various policy areas of concern to the citizens.

   . . .

---

[1] The European Council noted that the Czech Republic cannot complete its ratification process until the Constitutional Court delivers its positive opinion on the accordance of the Lisbon Treaty with the Czech constitutional order.

Opinion polls[83] conducted after the referendum on the reasons for the 'no' vote showed that the main reason for voting 'no' had been a lack

2008. See also G. Barrett, 'Building a Swiss Chalet in an Irish Landscape? Referendums on European Union Treaties in Ireland and the Impact of Supreme Court Jurisprudence' (2009) 5 *European Constitutional Law Review* 32.

82 See doc. 11018/1/08 REV 1.

83 The two main opinion polls which were commissioned were the 'Post-Referendum Survey in Ireland', conducted between 13 and 15 June 2008 at the request of the Commission (see Flash Eurobarometer 245) and the 'Post-Lisbon Referendum', conducted between 24 and 31 July at the request of the Irish Department for Foreign Affairs (see Research Findings issued in September 2008 by Millward Brown MS). For an analysis of the referendum results see M. Pilecka, 'Homework for the Irish, Reasons for the Rejection of the Lisbon

of information about the Lisbon Treaty (42 per cent according to the Millward Brown poll and 22 per cent according to the Eurobarometer poll), followed by a perceived loss of power or independence and the desire to protect Irish identity (16 per cent Millward Brown, 12 per cent Eurobarometer). The next most mentioned reasons were the protection of Irish neutrality (6 per cent Eurobarometer, 5 per cent Millward Brown), the protection of the corporation tax system (6 per cent Eurobarometer), the loss of an Irish Commissioner (6 per cent Eurobarometer, 4 per cent Millward Brown) and ethical issues (gay marriage, abortion, euthanasia) (2 per cent Eurobarometer).

In a speech to the Dáil (parliament) on 18 June 2008, Brian Cowen, the Prime Minister (Taoiseach), gave his initial reaction to, and assessment of, the referendum. Among the reasons he put forward, he mentioned in the first place the loss of an Irish Commissioner, followed by a perceived threat to Ireland's right to maintain its tax system and tax rates, the need for assurances about the right of Ireland to maintain its traditional policy of neutrality and, finally, worries about abortion, public services, workers' rights and the protection of farmers in the World Trade Organization (WTO) negotiations.

At the next meeting of the European Council, on 15 and 16 October 2008, the Irish Prime Minister explained that a parliamentary committee had been established to examine in particular concerns highlighted by opinion polls and that this committee would give its report by the end of November.[84] The Prime Minister also declared that, according to his own assessment, the issues of most concern during the referendum campaign included the future composition of the Commission, issues related to defence and neutrality, social or ethical matters, and taxation. He announced that in the coming months there would be a comprehensive exploration of ways in which these concerns could be adequately addressed.

The European Council stated in its October 2008 Conclusions that

> [R]ecalling its conclusions of June 2008, [the European Council] took note of the analysis of the results of the referendum on the Lisbon Treaty

---

Treaty as Seen through Opinion Polls', in *Lisbon Treaty: Provisions, Evaluation, Implications* (UKIE Analytical Paper Series, Office of the Committee for European Integration, Department of Analyses and Strategies (www.ukie.gov.pl)), 38.

84 This report was published on 27 November 2008; see 'Ireland's Future in the European Union: Challenges, Issues and Options', House of the Oireachtas, Sub-Committee on Ireland's Future in the European Union. The Committee identified six issues of importance: taxation, workers' rights, public services, ethical questions, neutrality and an Irish Commissioner.

presented by the Irish Taoiseach, Brian Cowen. The Irish government will continue its consultations with a view to contributing to finding a way to resolve the situation. On that basis, the European Council agreed to return to this matter at its meeting in December 2008 with a view to defining the elements of a solution and a common path to be followed.

On 11 and 12 December 2008, the European Council adopted among others the Conclusions given in Box 10.[85]

BOX 10. EUROPEAN COUNCIL, 11–12 DECEMBER 2008, PRESIDENCY
CONCLUSIONS

The Treaty of Lisbon

1. The European Council re-affirms that the Treaty of Lisbon is considered necessary in order to help the enlarged Union to function more efficiently, more democratically and more effectively including in international affairs. With a view to enabling the Treaty to enter into force by the end of 2009, the European Council, while respecting the aims and objectives of the Treaties, has defined the following path.

2. On the composition of the Commission, the European Council recalls that the Treaties currently in force require that the number of Commissioners be reduced in 2009. The European Council agrees that provided the Treaty of Lisbon enters into force, a decision will be taken, in accordance with the necessary legal procedures, to the effect that the Commission shall continue to include one national of each Member State.

3. The European Council has carefully noted the other concerns of the Irish people presented by the Taoiseach as set out in Annex 1 relating to taxation policy, family, social and ethical issues, and Common Security and Defence Policy (CSDP) with regard to Ireland's traditional policy of neutrality. The European Council agrees that, provided Ireland makes the commitment in paragraph 4, all of the concerns set out in the said statement shall be addressed to the mutual satisfaction of Ireland and the other Member States.

   The necessary legal guarantees will be given on the following three points:
   - nothing in the Treaty of Lisbon makes any change of any kind, for any Member State, to the extent or operation of the Union's competences in relation to taxation;
   - the Treaty of Lisbon does not prejudice the security and defence policy of Member States, including Ireland's traditional policy of neutrality, and the obligations of most other Member States;
   - a guarantee that the provisions of the Irish Constitution in relation to the right to life, education and the family are not in any way affected by the fact that

---

85 See doc. 17271/1/08 REV 1.

the Treaty of Lisbon attributes legal status to the EU Charter of Fundamental Rights or by the justice and home affairs provisions of the said Treaty.

In addition, the high importance attached to the issues, including workers' rights, set out in paragraph (d) of Annex 1 will be confirmed.

4. In the light of the above commitments by the European Council, and conditional on the satisfactory completion of the detailed follow-on work by mid-2009 and on presumption of their satisfactory implementation, the Irish Government is committed to seeking ratification of the Treaty of Lisbon by the end of the term of the current Commission.

. . .

Moreover, Brian Cowen made a statement, which was annexed to the Presidency Conclusions at the European Council of 11 and 12 December 2008 (Box 11).

BOX 11. STATEMENT OF THE CONCERNS OF THE IRISH PEOPLE ON THE LISBON TREATY AS SET OUT BY THE TAOISEACH, 11–12 DECEMBER 2008

a) Ensuring that Ireland's requirements regarding maintenance of its traditional policy of neutrality are met;

b) Ensuring that the terms of the Treaty of Lisbon will not affect the continued application of the provisions of the Irish Constitution in relation to the right to life, education and the family;

c) Ensuring that in the area of taxation the Treaty of Lisbon makes no change of any kind to the extent or operation of the Union's competences;

d) Confirming that the Union attaches high importance to:
   • social progress and the protection of workers' rights;
   • public services, as an indispensable instrument of social and regional cohesion;
   • the responsibility of Member States for the delivery of education and health services;
   • the essential role and wide discretion of national, regional and local Governments in providing, commissioning and organising non-economic services of general interest which is not affected by any provision of the Treaty of Lisbon, including those relating to the common commercial policy.

The package offered to the Irish government at the European Council of 18 and 19 June 2009 with a view to obtaining the assent of the Irish people consisted of four elements:[86]

---

86 The Presidency Conclusions which contain the package may be found in doc. 11225/1/09 REV 1. The package had been carefully prepared by the Czech Presidency, in close

- five paragraphs in the European Council Conclusions (Box 12);
- Annex 1 to the Conclusions which contained a 'Decision of the Heads of State or Government of the twenty-seven Member States of the EU, meeting within the European Council, on the concerns of the Irish people on the Treaty of Lisbon' (Box 13);
- Annex 2 which contained a 'Solemn Declaration on workers' rights, social policy and other issues'; and
- Annex 3 which contained a 'National Declaration by Ireland'.

The shape of the solution found for Ireland is to a large extent similar to that which was adopted in Edinburgh in December 1992 after the negative referendum in Denmark on the Maastricht Treaty. In that case, a Decision was also adopted by the heads of state or government which was fully compatible with the Treaty and therefore did not require the other Member States to re-ratify the Maastricht Treaty or to ratify the Decision itself. Declarations were also adopted in 1992.[87]

The first element of the package (paragraphs 1 to 5 of the Conclusions) recalls the December 2008 Conclusions, confirms the agreement already reached in December 2008 about the composition of the Commission (one national of each Member State) and states that the Decision of the heads of state or government is 'legally binding' and that it 'is fully compatible with the Treaty of Lisbon and will not necessitate any re-ratification'. The Decision makes certain 'clarifications' about the Lisbon Treaty but it does not change the Treaty. This was the condition for the other Member States to accept it.

The Conclusions also explain what will happen in the future with the Decision. Its content will be given 'full Treaty status' through its transfer into a Protocol to be decided 'at the time of the conclusion of the next accession Treaty'. The Protocol will be attached to the TEU and the TFEU. It is stated that this Protocol 'will clarify but not change either the content or the application of the Treaty of Lisbon' and that it 'will in no way alter the relationship between the EU and its Member States'.

co-operation with the Irish government, in particular with its Attorney General, Paul Gallagher, and with the assistance of the Legal Counsel of the EU Council.

87 The 'package' of solutions for Denmark was published in the *Official Journal* (OJ No. C348, 31 December 1992, 1). See O. Vigant Ryborg, *Det utoenkelige: NEJ...!* (Denmark: Informations Forlag, 1998).

BOX 12. EUROPEAN COUNCIL, 18–19 JUNE 2009, PRESIDENCY
CONCLUSIONS

Ireland and the Treaty of Lisbon

1. The European Council recalls that the entry into force of the Treaty of Lisbon requires ratification by each of the twenty-seven Member States in accordance with their respective constitutional requirements. It reaffirms its wish to see the Treaty enter into force by the end of 2009.

2. Having carefully noted the concerns of the Irish people as set out by the Taoiseach, the European Council, at its meeting of 11–12 December 2008, agreed that, provided the Treaty of Lisbon enters into force, a decision would be taken, in accordance with the necessary legal procedures, to the effect that the Commission shall continue to include one national of each Member State.

3. The European Council also agreed that other concerns of the Irish people, as presented by the Taoiseach, relating to taxation policy, the right to life, education and the family, and Ireland's traditional policy of military neutrality, would be addressed to the mutual satisfaction of Ireland and the other Member States, by way of the necessary legal guarantees. It was also agreed that the high importance attached to a number of social issues, including workers' rights, would be confirmed.

4. Against this background, the European Council has agreed on the following set of arrangements, which are fully compatible with the Treaty, in order to provide reassurance and to respond to the concerns of the Irish people:

   (a) Decision of the Heads of State or Government of the 27 Member States of the European Union, meeting within the European Council, on the concerns of the Irish people on the Treaty of Lisbon (Annex 1);

   (b) Solemn Declaration on Workers' Rights, Social Policy and other issues (Annex 2).

   The European Council has also taken cognisance of the unilateral declaration of Ireland (Annex 3), which will be associated with the Irish instrument of ratification of the Treaty of Lisbon.

5. Regarding the Decision in Annex 1, the Heads of State or Government have declared that:

   (i) this Decision gives legal guarantee that certain matters of concern to the Irish people will be unaffected by the entry into force of the Treaty of Lisbon;

   (ii) its content is fully compatible with the Treaty of Lisbon and will not necessitate any re-ratification of that Treaty;

   (iii) the Decision is legally binding and will take effect on the date of entry into force of the Treaty of Lisbon;

   (iv) they will, at the time of the conclusion of the next accession Treaty, set out the provisions of the annexed Decision in a Protocol to be attached, in

> accordance with their respective constitutional requirements, to the Treaty on European Union and the Treaty on the Functioning of the European Union;
>
> (v) the Protocol will in no way alter the relationship between the EU and its Member States. The sole purpose of the Protocol will be to give full Treaty status to the clarifications set out in the Decision to meet the concerns of the Irish people. Its status will be no different from similar clarifications in Protocols obtained by other Member States. The Protocol will clarify but not change either the content or the application of the Treaty of Lisbon.
>
> . . .

The second element of the package – that is, the Decision by the heads of state or government, has the same format as the 1992 Edinburgh Decision. It is divided into sections and its final provision states that it 'shall take effect on the same date as the Treaty of Lisbon'. As stated in its Preamble, the Decision is 'in conformity with [the Lisbon] Treaty' (see Box 13). As indicated in the Conclusions, its purpose is to *clarify* the Lisbon Treaty in order to meet the concerns of the Irish people. It addresses the three points on which, as agreed in December 2008, legal guarantees would be given: the right to life/family/education, taxation and security/defence.

BOX 13. DECISION OF THE HEADS OF STATE OR GOVERNMENT OF THE 27 MEMBER STATES OF THE EU, MEETING WITHIN THE EUROPEAN COUNCIL, ON THE CONCERNS OF THE IRISH PEOPLE ON THE TREATY OF LISBON, 18–19 JUNE 2009

The Heads of State or Government of the 27 Member States of the European Union, whose Governments are signatories of the Treaty of Lisbon,

Taking note of the outcome of the Irish referendum of 12 June 2008 on the Treaty of Lisbon and of the concerns of the Irish people identified by the Taoiseach,

Desiring to address those concerns in conformity with that Treaty,

Having regard to the Conclusions of the European Council of 11–12 December 2008,

Have agreed on the following Decision:

Section A
Right to life, family and education

Nothing in the Treaty of Lisbon attributing legal status to the Charter of Fundamental Rights of the European Union, or in the provisions of that Treaty in the area of Freedom, Security and Justice affects in any way the scope and applicability of the protection of the right to life in Article 40.3.1, 40.3.2 and 40.3.3, the protection of the family in Article 41 and the protection of the rights in respect of education in Articles 42 and 44.2.4 and 44.2.5 provided by the Constitution of Ireland.

Section B
Taxation

Nothing in the Treaty of Lisbon makes any change of any kind, for any Member State, to the extent or operation of the competence of the European Union in relation to taxation.

Section C
Security and defence

The Union's action on the international scene is guided by the principles of democracy, the rule of law, the universality and indivisibility of human rights and fundamental freedoms, respect for human dignity, the principles of equality and solidarity, and respect for the principles of the United Nations Charter and international law.

The Union's common security and defence policy is an integral part of the common foreign and security policy and provides the Union with an operational capacity to undertake missions outside the Union for peace-keeping, conflict prevention and strengthening international security in accordance with the principles of the United Nations Charter.

It does not prejudice the security and defence policy of each Member State, including Ireland, or the obligations of any Member State.

The Treaty of Lisbon does not affect or prejudice Ireland's traditional policy of military neutrality.

It will be for Member States – including Ireland, acting in a spirit of solidarity and without prejudice to its traditional policy of military neutrality – to determine the nature of aid or assistance to be provided to a Member State which is the object of a terrorist attack or the victim of armed aggression on its territory.

Any decision to move to a common defence will require a unanimous decision of the European Council. It would be a matter for the Member States, including Ireland, to decide, in accordance with the provisions of the Treaty of Lisbon and with their respective constitutional requirements, whether or not to adopt a common defence.

Nothing in this Section affects or prejudices the position or policy of any other Member State on security and defence.

It is also a matter for each Member State to decide, in accordance with the provisions of the Treaty of Lisbon and any domestic legal requirements, whether to participate in permanent structured cooperation or the European Defence Agency.

The Treaty of Lisbon does not provide for the creation of a European army or for conscription to any military formation.

It does not affect the right of Ireland or any other Member State to determine the nature and volume of its defence and security expenditure and the nature of its defence capabilities.

It will be a matter for Ireland or any other Member State, to decide, in accordance with any domestic legal requirements, whether or not to participate in any military operation.

Section D
Final provisions

This decision shall take effect on the same date as the Treaty of Lisbon.

The third element of the package is a Declaration on workers' rights and other social issues, as was also mentioned in December 2008 (in the last subparagraph in point 3 of the Conclusions). The Declaration starts with language mostly taken from the statement of the Taoiseach in December 2008 and continues with text taken from provisions introduced by the Lisbon Treaty (such as certain objectives of the EU, the general social clause or certain provisions from Protocol no. 26 of services of general interest).

The fourth element of the package is a National Declaration by Ireland on issues of neutrality and defence, similar to the National Declaration made in Seville in June 2002 before the second referendum on the Nice Treaty.[88]

The second Irish referendum took place on 2 October 2009 and resulted in a clear and strong 67.13 per cent 'yes' vote (32.87 per cent 'no'), with a 59 per cent turnout. A few days later, on 16 October, the Irish President, Mary McAleese, signed the Twenty-Eighth Amendment of the Irish Constitution (Treaty of Lisbon) Bill 2009, and the instruments of ratification of the Lisbon Treaty were deposited in Rome on 23 October 2009.

The last problems raised in the Czech Republic

In the Czech Republic the ratification process in the parliament was suspended, due to the fact that the Senate had asked the Constitutional Court

---

88 See Annex IV to the Presidency Conclusions, European Council, 21–22 June 2002 (doc. 13463/02).

On the second Irish referendum, see P. J. Kuijper, 'The Second Second Irish Referendum: Finally a Fair Choice', (2009) 36(2) *Legal Issues of Economic Integration* 101.

to provide an opinion on the compatibility of the Charter of Fundamental Rights and of certain provisions of the Lisbon Treaty with the Czech constitutional order.[89] The Constitutional Court gave its (unanimous) judgment on 26 November 2008, in which it stated that the provisions in question of the Treaty, as well as the Charter, were not contrary to the Czech constitutional order.[90] Thereafter, both chambers of the Czech parliament authorised the ratification of the Treaty (the Chamber of Deputies on 18 February and the Senate on 6 May 2009). However, the President of the Czech Republic, Vaclav Klaus, decided not to sign the act of ratification immediately.

A few months later, on 29 September 2009, three days before the second referendum in Ireland on 2 October, seventeen Czech senators filed a second request at the Constitutional Court on the compatibility of the remaining provisions of the Lisbon Treaty with the Czech Constitution. The Constitutional Court convened a first hearing on 27 October and a second hearing on 3 November 2009. On that date, it gave its judgment according to which the Lisbon Treaty is in conformity with the Czech constitutional order and that there was nothing to prevent its ratification.[91]

In parallel to this procedure President Klaus made a public statement on 9 October 2009, according to which he 'conditioned the completion of the ratification process of the Lisbon Treaty upon the granting of a guarantee that an opt-out, similar to that which Poland and the United Kingdom have been granted, will be negotiated for the Czech Republic'.[92] This referred to Protocol no. 30 on the application of the Charter of Fundamental Rights of the EU to Poland and the United Kingdom.[93]

---

89 257th Resolution of the Committee for EU Affairs of the Parliament of the Czech Republic, 6th session, 3rd meeting, 9 April 2008 (Senate Bulletin no. 181).

90 For an analysis of this judgment see Appendix 2.

91 Judgment of 3 November 2009, *Treaty of Lisbon (II)*, Pl. US 29/09. See the Czech Constitutional Court press release, 3 November 2009, at www.usoud.cz/clanek/2144. The Court rejected the objections raised by the petitioners on the 'Irish guarantees'. With regard to the use of the right to contest the constitutionality of an international treaty before the Constitutional Court, it said that this right cannot be used to contest, over and over again, judgments already given by the Court on the international treaty's conformity with the constitutional order. This right should be used without unnecessary delay. This cannot be in the order of several months after the parliament consented to ratification, but only weeks.

92 See Statement by the Government of the Czech Republic on the ratification process of the Lisbon Treaty made on 12 October 2009.

93 Mr Klaus argued that the Beneš decrees adopted in the 1940s (which confiscated property and removed Czechoslovak nationality from Sudeten Germans and people of Hungarian origin who had been considered disloyal to Czechoslovakia) would be at risk

An answer was given to this request in the form of conclusions adopted at the European Council of 29 and 30 October 2009 together with a draft Protocol to be attached to the TEU and TFEU 'at the time of the conclusion of the next Accession Treaty' (see Box 14). Attentive readers will note the text of paragraph 2 of the Conclusions, in particular its third subparagraph. The wording was the result of difficult negotiations involving all Member States in the region.

BOX 14. EUROPEAN COUNCIL, 29–30 OCTOBER 2009, PRESIDENCY CONCLUSIONS

. . .

2. The European Council recalls that the entry into force of the Treaty of Lisbon requires ratification by each of the 27 Member States in accordance with their respective constitutional requirements. It reaffirms its determination to see the Treaty enter into force by the end of 2009, thus allowing it to develop its effects in the future.

   On this basis, and taking into account the position taken by the Czech Republic, the Heads of State or Government have agreed that they shall, at the time of the conclusion of the next Accession Treaty and in accordance with their respective constitutional requirements, attach the Protocol (in Annex I) to the Treaty on European Union and the Treaty on the Functioning of the European Union.

   In this context, and with regard to legal application of the Treaty of Lisbon and its relation to legal systems of Member States, the European Council confirms that:

a) The Treaty of Lisbon provides that 'competences not conferred upon the Union in the Treaties remain with the Member States' (Art. 5(2) TEU);
b) The Charter is 'addressed to the institutions, bodies, offices and agencies of the Union with due regard for the principle of subsidiarity and to the Member States only when they are implementing Union law' (Art. 51(1) Charter).

   . . .

---

because of the EU Charter of Fundamental Rights acquiring primary law status under the Lisbon Treaty. This argument was legally unfounded. On this question see S. Peers, 'The Beneš Decrees and the EU Charter of Fundamental Rights', Statewatch, 12 October 2009, at www.statewatch.org/news/2009/oct/lisbon-benes-decree.pdf. See also legal opinions which were given during the accession negotiation of the Czech Republic to the EU: J. A. Frowein, U. Bernitz and Lord Kingsland, 'Legal Opinion on the Beneš-Decrees and the accession of the Czech Republic to the European Union' (October 2002), Working Paper, Directorate-General for Research, European Parliament (available on the Internet).

Annex I
Protocol on the application of the Charter of Fundamental Rights of the European Union to the Czech Republic

The Heads of State or Government of the 27 Member States of the European Union, taking note of the wish expressed by the Czech Republic,

Having regard to the Conclusions of the European Council,

Have agreed on the following Protocol:

Article 1

Protocol No. 30 on the application of the Charter of Fundamental Rights of the European Union to Poland and to the United Kingdom shall apply to the Czech Republic.

Article 2

The Title, Preamble and operative part of Protocol No. 30 shall be modified in order to refer to the Czech Republic in the same terms as they refer to Poland and to the United Kingdom.

Article 3

This Protocol shall be annexed to the Treaty on European Union and to the Treaty on the Functioning of the European Union.

. . .

Following the green light given by the Czech Constitutional Court on 3 November 2009 and the solution found to the last-minute request from President Klaus, he finally signed the instrument of ratification on the same day, 3 November 2009, after which the instrument was deposited in Rome on 13 November 2009.

This twenty-seventh ratification enabled the Lisbon Treaty to enter into force on 1 December 2009.

Section 5 The structure of the Lisbon Treaty

A complex Treaty

The main characteristic of the Lisbon Treaty is that, contrary to the failed 2004 Constitutional Treaty, it follows a similar pattern to all the other preceding European treaties. It does not repeal and replace them, but only amends them. It contains only seven articles, the two most important making numerous amendments to the existing Treaties. Article 1 of the Lisbon Treaty amends the Treaty on European Union (former TEU), while Article 2 amends the Treaty establishing the European Community (TEC). The TEC is renamed 'Treaty on the Functioning of the European Union' (TFEU), because the European Community is replaced by the European Union, which legally succeeds it.

Article 1 contains 61 amendments to the former TEU and Article 2 contains 295 amendments to the TEC. In order to help the reader a little, subtitles in capital letters indicate the subject matter concerned. As a way of reducing the number of technical amendments, a new technique of 'horizontal amendments' is used, by which certain words are automatically replaced throughout the Treaty, such as the word 'Community', which is replaced throughout by 'Union', or the word 'ecu', which is replaced throughout by 'euro' (see Article 2(A) of the Lisbon Treaty).

Article 3 states that the Treaty 'is concluded for an unlimited period' and Article 4 refers to the Protocols which are annexed to the Lisbon Treaty. Article 5, together with the Annex which contains a table of equivalences, organises the renumbering of the Articles of both the TEU and the TFEU and the adaptation of the cross-references to renumbered Articles, sections, chapters, titles and parts of the Treaties. It is similar to Article 12 of the Amsterdam Treaty which did the same. Articles 6 and 7 contain the usual provisions, respectively, on the conditions for entry into force and on the twenty-three official languages in which the Treaty is authentic. In accordance with Article 48 of the former TEU, Article 6 requires the unanimous ratification by all Member States. The date originally stated for entry into force (1 January 2009) was, of course, not met. The Treaty entered into force on the first day of the month following the twenty-seventh (Czech) ratification – that is, on 1 December 2009.

The Lisbon Treaty also contains eleven new Protocols which are annexed to the existing Treaties. Two Protocols, attached to the Lisbon Treaty itself, respectively amend the pre-existing Protocols which were, and remain, annexed to the two main treaties (TEU and TFEU) and adapt the Euratom Treaty to the new institutional provisions introduced by the Lisbon Treaty.

As was the case for most other amending Treaties which did not contain self-standing provisions,[94] the Lisbon Treaty does not remain as a new treaty in itself. On the date of its entry into force, the amendments that it made to the former TEU and the TEC produced their legal effect.

---

94 Except for the Single European Act and the Treaty of Maastricht.

Therefore, in the so-called 'consolidated texts',[95] the Lisbon Treaty does not appear as such. It was the vector for introducing amendments to the two main treaties governing the EU and it had then 'lived its life'. The same legal method was used for previous treaties.

The IGC which approved the Lisbon Treaty also agreed on a number of Declarations, which it attached to the Final Act. These Declarations do not have legally binding value, but most of them, since they were approved by all the twenty-seven States parties to the IGC, may shed some light on the interpretation given to the Treaty by the parties or on their political intentions.

The result is a very complex structure. One of the advantages of the failed Constitutional Treaty would have been the consolidation of most EU 'primary law' (texts having the legal value of a treaty), which was spread over seventeen treaties and Acts, into one single document. However, the Lisbon Treaty, instead of simplifying the structure and the readability of the treaties, adds one more layer of complexity. One has to admit that, on its own, this Treaty is simply unreadable.

However, after having been consolidated into the existing treaties, the Lisbon Treaty does bring more simplicity to a few issues.

A single legal personality for the EU

Until the Lisbon Treaty, there were two separate legal personalities: the EC (Article 281 TEC) and the EU (through its treaty-making power under Article 24 former TEU); Euratom also had a separate legal personality (Article 184 Euratom Treaty). The Lisbon Treaty merges the two legal personalities of the EC and of the EU into a new single EU legal personality (see Section 9); although the Euratom legal personality will remain separate (it is a sectoral treaty).

The pillar structure

In 1993, the Maastricht Treaty added two pillars to the existing Community first pillar – that is, the second pillar on CFSP and the third pillar on JHA – preserving the main characteristics of intergovernmentalism for those areas. This structure in three pillars was placed under the common

---

95 Published in OJ No. C115, 9 May 2008, 1. These 'consolidated treaties' are not an official codification of the Treaties which would replace and repeal previous Treaties. These 'consolidated treaties' have not been formally adopted; they were published only 'for information purposes'. The Lisbon Treaty will therefore itself remain in force.

umbrella of the Union, the EC being supplemented by these two new areas of co-operation.

The EC was the most integrated pillar, where all the institutions played a full role. The Commission had an almost exclusive role of initiative for the adoption of legal acts. The European Parliament was often closely associated with the Council for the adoption of legislative acts. The Court of Justice had full jurisdiction to interpret and review the legality of legal acts.

In the second pillar, the CFSP, which included the European Security and Defence Policy (ESDP), was served by the same institutions, but their respective powers were not the same as in the EC. The Council was the most powerful institution, adopting, generally by unanimity, all acts in this area. The Commission did not have an exclusive right of initiative. The European Parliament was consulted only 'on the main aspects and the basic choices' of the CFSP, and the Court of Justice had no jurisdiction in this field. Although some people claim that the Lisbon Treaty makes the three pillars disappear, one has to recognise that the institutional specificities which characterised the second pillar are mostly preserved by that Treaty. While the procedures and rules governing all other fields of action of the EU are described in the TFEU, those governing the CFSP are contained in the new TEU, thus underlining the fact that CFSP will remain different from the other areas.

The third pillar covered Police and Judicial Co-operation in criminal affairs, commonly known as JHA (Justice and Home Affairs). Here again, the respective powers of the institutions were not the same as in the EC. However, in 1999, the Amsterdam Treaty had already given to the European Parliament, the Commission and the Court of Justice a greater role than they had under the Maastricht Treaty. The Commission was given a right of initiative, but not an exclusive one, as the Member States also had such a right. The European Parliament gained a consultative role. The Court of Justice saw the scope of its judicial review enlarged, even if it remained more limited than in the EC. This is substantially modified by the Lisbon Treaty. The European Parliament gains codecision powers in almost all cases. The Court's jurisdiction is extended to cover the whole area of the JHA (which is now called 'FSJ': Freedom, Security and Justice) sector. Therefore the introduction of preliminary ruling procedures, infringement procedures and actions brought by individuals have become possible. The only limitation is that, with regard to judicial co-operation in criminal matters and police co-operation, the Court will still be prevented from reviewing 'the validity or proportionality of operations carried out by the police or other law-enforcement services of a Member State or the exercise of the responsibilities incumbent upon Member States with regard to the maintenance of law and order and the safeguarding of internal security' (Article 276 TFEU).

Another limitation is that the new rules on the competence of the Court of Justice will not apply immediately for the JHA acts which were adopted in the past on the basis of the former EU Treaty. There will be a transitional period of five years before the Court obtains these new powers for such acts adopted in the past, unless the acts are meanwhile amended under the new rules.[96]

The legal effects of the removal of the pillar structure

The Lisbon Treaty removes the pillar structure and therefore does not preserve the second pillar, but in reality it does preserve its main characteristics. These specific characteristics are expressly listed in a paragraph which was added by the IGC mandate agreed in June 2007. Hence the second subparagraph of Article 24(1) TEU[97] states that

> [T]he common foreign and security policy is subject to specific rules and procedures. It shall be defined and implemented by the European Council and the Council acting unanimously, except where the Treaties provide otherwise. The adoption of legislative acts shall be excluded. The [CFSP] shall be put into effect by the High Representative of the Union for Foreign Affairs and Security Policy and by Member States, in accordance with the Treaties. The specific role of the European Parliament and of the Commission in this area is defined by the Treaties. The Court of Justice of the European Union shall not have jurisdiction with respect to these provisions, with the exception of its jurisdiction to monitor compliance with Article 40 of [the TEU] and to review the legality of certain decisions as provided for by the second paragraph of Article 275 of the [TFEU].

However, it has to be recalled that, according to Article 40 TEU (to be compared with the Article 47 of the former TEU),

> [T]he implementation of the [CFSP] shall not affect the application of the procedures and the extent of the powers of the institutions laid down by the Treaties for the exercise of the Union competences referred to in Articles 3 to 6 of the [TFEU]. Similarly, the implementation of the policies listed in those Articles shall not affect the application of the procedures

96 See Art. 10(1) to (3) of Protocol no. 36 on transitional provisions.
97 Compare with Art. III-16(1) of the Constitutional Treaty.

and the extent of the powers of the institutions laid down by the Treaties
for the exercise of the Union competences under [the CFSP].

One does not know what the effect will be of the addition of this second
subparagraph, which did not exist in Article 47 of the former TEU. The
case law of the Court has, up to now, been extremely protective of (or
even generous to) the first pillar, notably in the *ECOWAS* case,[98] which is
ambiguous on the question of whether the first pillar is really limited by
the competences conferred on the EC by the Member States. Would such
an audacious judgment still be possible with the second subparagraph of
Article 40 TEU?

As regards the third pillar, it does disappear. Therefore acts adopted in
this area are now regulations, directives and decisions. They are generally
adopted in codecision (ordinary legislative procedure) by the European
Parliament and the Council, on a proposal from the Commission. The
jurisdiction of the Court of Justice covers the whole area.

The removal of the pillar structure has certain consequences. Thus the
basic principle relating to the relationship between EU law and national
law (primacy), the delimitation of EU competences (conferral, Article
5(1) and (2) TEU) and of the institutions' powers (conferred powers,
Article 13(2) TEU), the principles governing the use of such competences
(subsidiarity and proportionality, Article 5(3) and (4) TEU), the principle of loyalty between the EU and the Member States and between the
institutions (sincere co-operation, Articles 4(3) and 13(2) TEU), as well
as the principle of 'indirect administration', whereby the responsibility
for implementing and applying EU law belongs primarily to the Member
States (Article 4(3), 2nd subparagraph, TEU, and Article 291(1) TFEU),
apply to all areas of EU activity. Until the Lisbon Treaty some of these
principles applied only to the EC and not, at least expressly, to the EU
outside the first pillar.

Likewise, the so-called 'flexibility clause' contained in Article 352 TFEU
(ex-Article 308 TEC) also applies to the former third pillar (judicial and
police co-operation in criminal matters). However, paragraph 4 of Article
352 excludes the CFSP from its scope.[99]

---

98 See judgment of 20 May 2008, Case C-91/05, *Commission v. Council (small arms)* [2008]
    ECR I-3651.
99 Paragraph 4 reads, 'This Article cannot serve as a basis for attaining objectives pertaining
    to the [CFSP] and any acts adopted pursuant to this Article shall respect the limits set
    out in Article 40, second paragraph, of the [TEU] .'

The protection of personal data extends to all EU sectors (Article 16 TFEU), the sole exception being 'the processing of personal data by the Member States when carrying out activities which fall within the scope of [the CFSP Chapter], and the rules relating to the free movement of such data' which fall under a specific legal basis within the CFSP Chapter (Article 39 TEU). However, the processing of personal data 'by Union institutions, bodies, offices and agencies' in CFSP matters falls under the general legal basis (Article 16 TFEU).

The powers of the European Ombudsman (Article 228 TFEU) and of the temporary Committees of Inquiry set up by the European Parliament (Article 226 TFEU) extend to all EU sectors, including FSJ and CFSP.[100]

The territorial scope of the EU Treaty also covers all EU sectors (Article 52 TEU and Article 355 TFEU), whereas before the entry into force of the Lisbon Treaty only the EC Treaty had a provision on territorial scope (Article 299 TEC).

The Protocol on privileges and immunities (Protocol no. 7) also covers all EU sectors, whereas before the entry into force of the Lisbon Treaty it was annexed to the EC Treaty alone and therefore covered only EC and not EU agencies. This obliged the Member States to conclude specific privileges and immunities agreements to cover agencies set up under the EU Treaty in CFSP matters.[101] The extended scope of the Protocol will allow lengthy ratification procedures when establishing new agencies on these matters to be dispensed with.

*

Finally, after the Lisbon Treaty, as before, the EU is governed by two main Treaties which have equal legal value. However, one can say that the division of substance between the two new Treaties, the TEU and the TFEU, brings more clarity than the division which existed before between the former TEU and the TEC.

---

100 Before the Lisbon Treaty, the powers of the European Ombudsman were limited to the first and third pillars (EC and JHA) and the powers of temporary committees of inquiry were limited to the EC pillar alone.

101 There are three agencies of this kind:

- the EU Institute for Security Studies (Council Joint Action 2001/554/CFSP of 20 July 2001, OJ No. L200, 25 July 2001, 1);
- the EU Satellite Centre (Council Joint Action 2001/555/CFSP of 20 July 2001, OJ No. L200, 25 July 2001, 5);
- the European Defence Agency (Council Joint Action 2004/551/CFSP of 12 July 2004, OJ No. L245, 17 July 2004, 17).

The TEU contains the general provisions applying to the EU, its values and objectives, its basic principles, the delimitation of its powers, the way the Treaty may be revised and the main characteristics of its institutions and of their powers.

The TFEU contains the legal bases which enable the EU and its institutions to act, while setting limits to their powers. It is true that the result of the Lisbon IGC is difficult to grasp and to read and that there are inconsistencies (the main one being the location of the provisions on CFSP in the TEU and not in the TFEU). However, on the whole, it does represent progress. Thus a reading of the 'consolidated' TEU on its own might be enough for the man in the street to understand what the EU is about and how it functions, and all that in a reasonably short text (fifty-five Articles in thirty pages).

II

General provisions

Section 6 Values and objectives

One striking characteristic of the Lisbon Treaty is that it is deeply rooted in human rights, as was the case of the failed Constitutional Treaty. As mentioned by an American author, 'much of the Constitution is given over to the issue of fundamental human rights. It might be said that human rights are the very heart and soul of the document.'[1]

The Lisbon Treaty puts to the forefront the values on which the EU is based (see Box 15). It also takes the highly symbolic steps both of giving the Charter of Fundamental Rights the same legal value as the treaties (Article 6(1) TEU) and of providing for an obligation for the EU to accede to the European Convention for the Protection of Human Rights and Fundamental Freedoms (Article 6(2) TEU).

BOX 15. THE UNION'S VALUES (ARTICLE 2 TEU)

The Union is founded on the values of respect for human dignity, freedom, democracy, equality, the rule of law and respect for human rights, including the rights of persons belonging to minorities. These values are common to the Member States in a society in which pluralism, non-discrimination, tolerance, justice, solidarity and equality between women and men prevail.

Article 2 TEU on the Union's values is not only a political and symbolic statement. It has concrete legal effects.

First, it is a condition which a European State has to respect in order to be allowed to apply for membership: 'Any European State which respects the values referred to in Article 2 and is committed to promoting them may apply to become a member of the Union' (Article 49 TEU).

Second, serious breaches of these values by a Member State may lead to a suspension of some of its rights resulting from Union membership:

---

1 J. Rifkin, *The European Dream* (New York: Jeremy P. Tarcher/Penguin, 2004), 212.

'the European Council . . . may determine the existence of a serious and persistent breach by a Member State of the values referred in Article 2' (Article 7(2) TEU).[2]

Moreover, the promotion of its values is one of the first objectives of the EU, as mentioned in Article 3(1) TEU. The Union's values are therefore part and parcel of the very essence of the EU.

In addition, Article 3 enumerates the objectives of the EU (see Box 16). This Article tries to give answers to two basic questions: why has the EU been established? what is the EU aiming at? Clear and ambitious, it merges objectives previously contained in Article 2 of the former TEU and in Article 2 TEC and adds new objectives or rephrases them.

BOX 16. THE OBJECTIVES OF THE EU (ARTICLE 3 TEU)

1. The Union's aim is to promote peace, its values and the well-being of its peoples.
2. The Union shall offer its citizens an area of freedom, security and justice without internal frontiers, in which the free movement of persons is ensured in conjunction with appropriate measures with respect to external border controls, asylum, immigration and the prevention and combating of crime.
3. The Union shall establish an internal market. It shall work for the sustainable development of Europe based on balanced economic growth and price stability, a highly competitive social market economy, aiming at full employment and social progress, and a high level of protection and improvement of the quality of the environment. It shall promote scientific and technological advance.

   It shall combat social exclusion and discrimination, and shall promote social justice and protection, equality between women and men, solidarity between generations and protection of the rights of the child.

   It shall promote economic, social and territorial cohesion, and solidarity among Member States.

   It shall respect its rich cultural and linguistic diversity, and shall ensure that Europe's cultural heritage is safeguarded and enhanced.
4. The Union shall establish an economic and monetary union whose currency is the euro.

---

2 The list of values in Art. 2 TEU whose breach may result in suspension is longer than the previous list in Art. 6(1) of the former EU Treaty (referred to in Art. 7(2) on the suspension of rights), which reads, 'The Union is founded on the principles of liberty, democracy, respect for human rights and fundamental freedoms, and the rule of law, principles which are common to the Member States.'

5. In its relations with the wider world, the Union shall uphold and promote its values and interests and contribute to the protection of its citizens. It shall contribute to peace, security, the sustainable development of the Earth, solidarity and mutual respect among peoples, free and fair trade, eradication of poverty and the protection of human rights, in particular the rights of the child, as well as to the strict observance and the development of international law, including respect for the principles of the United Nations Charter.

6. The Union shall pursue its objectives by appropriate means commensurate with the competences which are conferred upon it in the Treaties.

Compared with the objectives set out in previous Treaties, an important addition is the aim to work for 'a highly competitive social market economy',[3] which may be considered as bringing in an important nuance as compared with the objective of an 'open market economy' set out in Article 119 TFEU (previously Article 4 TEC) in the Title on economic and monetary union.

While a majority of the objectives are similar to previous ones, such as 'a high level of protection and improvement of the quality of the environment',[4] the '[combating of] social exclusion and discrimination',[5] social protection,[6] social progress,[7] equality between men and women[8] or solidarity among Member States,[9] some wording is new compared with previous Treaties. One could mention, for instance, 'full employment' instead of 'high level of employment' which was in both Article 2 of the former TEU and Article 2 TEC, as well as 'social justice', 'solidarity between generations' or 'rights of the child', which were not mentioned in previous Treaties. The same goes for the objectives of 'respect[ing] [the Union's] rich cultural and linguistic diversity' and 'ensur[ing] that Europe's cultural heritage is safeguarded and enhanced'. All these additions, when compared with the past Treaties, go in the direction of respecting human values and caring for the well-being of the people.

3 The system of 'social market economy' was developed in Germany by Ludwig Erhard, the first minister of economy in the post-war Federal Republic. Being a balance between the market and social policy, it is quite representative of the so-called 'European Social Model' in its various nuances. On the one hand, it enables the free play of forces on the market, with the State creating the framework for competition to work and, on the other hand, it provides for a complete system of social protection.

4 Compare with Art. 2 TEC.   5 Compare with Art. 137(1)(j) TEC.
6 Compare with Art. 2 TEC.   7 Compare with Art. 2, 1st indent, former TEU.
8 Compare with Art. 2 TEC.   9 Compare with Art. 2 TEC.

As to the list of EC activities which was set out in Article 3 TEC, it has in effect been replaced by the provisions listing the EU competences in Articles 3 to 6 TFEU.[10] An element in this list referring to 'a system ensuring that competition in the internal market is not distorted' (Article 3(1)(g) TEC) had been reproduced in Article I-3(2) of the Constitutional Treaty on the Union's objectives, using the words 'an internal market where competition is free and undistorted'.[11] These words were not retained in the IGC mandate adopted in June 2007 and are therefore not in Article 3 TEU. However, this deletion does not entail any modification of substance (see Section 39).

Section 7 Delimitation and clarification of the EU competences

The Lisbon Treaty codifies categories of EU competences which had already been identified by the Court of Justice or had been mentioned in the previous Treaties. It puts them into a more coherent order.

Classifying EU competences into three categories

In order to divide more clearly the respective powers of the Member States and of the EU, the Treaty lists and defines three categories of EU competences (Article 2 TFEU):[12]

- **exclusive competences**, where only the EU may legislate and adopt legally binding acts; the Member States are allowed to do so only if they are specifically empowered by the EU,[13] or, of course, when they need to legislate for ensuring a proper implementation of EU acts;
- **shared competences**, where both the EU and Member States may legislate and adopt legally binding acts, but, when the EU has legislated,

---

10 An indication in that sense is given in the table of equivalences between the old and new numbering of Articles (see footnote 26 of that table, OJ No. C115, 9 May 2008, 367).

11 This wording had caused a lot of debate in France during the referendum campaign.

12 These categories had already either been identified by the Court in its case law (see e.g. as regards exclusive competences, Opinion 2/91 of 19 March 1993, *ILO*, ECR I-1061, para. 19) or mentioned in the Treaties (e.g. in Art. 43(d) of the former TEU, in Art. 5 TEC or in Art. 133(6), 2nd subpara., TEC).

13 See judgment of 15 December 1976, Case 41/76, *Donckerwolcke*, [1976] ECR 1921 (para. 32). The fact that the EU has not exercised its competence may not be used by a Member State for claiming that it has freedom to act, without having been first authorised to do so. In such a situation, 'Member States may henceforth act only as trustee of the common interest' (see judgment of 5 May 1981, Case 804/79, *Commission v. UK*, [1981] ECR 1045 (paras. 18, 20, 27, 28, 30 and 31).

the Member States may exercise their competences only to the extent that the EU has not exercised its competence, or to the extent that the EU has decided to cease exercising its competence;
- **supporting competences**, where the EU may support, co-ordinate or supplement the actions of the Member States, but without being allowed to adopt legislative harmonisation rules.

The Treaty lists the policy areas in which the EU has exclusive, shared and supporting competences (respectively Articles 3, 4 and 6 TFEU; see Box 17). As can be seen from these lists, and contrary to what is sometimes thought, the number of areas of exclusive competences is very limited (only five), while the list of shared and supporting competences is much longer.

BOX 17. THE DIVISION OF COMPETENCES BETWEEN THE EU AND
ITS MEMBER STATES

Exclusive competences	Shared competences	Supporting competences
1. Customs union	1. Internal market	1. Protection and improvement of human health
2. Establishment of the competition rules necessary for the functioning of the internal market	2. Social policy, for the aspects defined in the TFEU	2. Industry
	3. Economic, social and territorial cohesion	3. Culture
	4. Agriculture and fisheries (except conservation of marine biological resources)	4. Tourism
3. Monetary policy for the Member States whose currency is the euro	5. Environment	5. Education, vocational training, youth and sport
4. Conservation of marine biological resources (fisheries policy)	6. Consumer protection	6. Civil protection
	7. Transport	7. Administrative co-operation
	8. Trans-European networks	
5. Common commercial policy	9. Energy	
	10. Area of freedom, security and justice	
	11. Common safety concerns in public health matters, for the aspects defined in the TFEU	

Specific cases
1. Co-ordination of economic and employment policies.

2. Common foreign and security policy (CFSP and ESDP).
3. Research, technological development and space.
4. Development co-operation and humanitarian aid.

Although the classification of these areas into the three categories of competences defined by the Treaty did not in all cases follow a purely Cartesian logic, the new Articles on competences have the merit of codifying and clarifying the existing delimitation of competences between the Union and the Member States. They do not change the balance, and preserve a margin of flexibility. They also establish a mechanism which allows for a more effective control of respect for the subsidiarity principle by the EU institutions.

The debate on the issue of division of competences and the solutions chosen

The issue of the division of competences was one of the four items listed in the 2000 Nice Declaration on the future of the Union: 'how to establish and monitor a more precise delimitation of powers between the European Union and the Member States, reflecting the principle of subsidiarity'. It was included at the request of the government of Germany, whose Länder had criticised a lack of clarity in the delimitation of these competences. It was argued that this lack of clarity made it difficult for the citizen to understand 'who does what in Europe' and risked permitting a 'creeping' increase in the powers of the EU's institutions.

In the Convention, the idea of establishing a precise and rigid catalogue of competences was discussed but quickly abandoned: it was found to be too difficult to establish and, in any case, inappropriate, given the characteristics of the EU. Afterwards, discussions focused on:

- defining the different categories of competences;
- devising a new mechanism in order to better ensure a strict respect for the principles of subsidiarity and proportionality by the institutions.

Reaching a consensus on the definition of the different categories of EU competences and on the listing of the areas belonging to each category was not an easy task. The wish to preserve some flexibility in the system, the fact that the EU competences evolve and that in most areas these competences are shared with the Member States, made it difficult to establish closed lists of areas of competences. While the lists of areas of exclusive and supporting competences are exhaustive (Articles 3 and 6 TFEU), the list of areas of shared competences is not (Article 4 TFEU). It starts with the sentence, '[t]he Union shall share competence with the Member States where the Treaties confer on it a competence which does not relate to the areas referred to in Article 3 and 6.' It implies, therefore, that the list of areas of shared competences is not exhaustive and that Article 5 TFEU on co-ordination of economic and employment policies and Article 2(4) TFEU on CFSP belong to the category of shared competences.

That was also the means of resolving the difficulty caused by the fact that the classification made in the Lisbon Treaty (which, on this issue, follows the Constitutional Treaty) did not fit exactly with the variety of competences of the EC and the EU. Areas such as research and development, development co-operation and humanitarian aid, found themselves between shared and supporting competences (Article 4(3) and (4) TFEU), with legal bases showing that the EU has neither a shared, nor a supporting competence, but a complementary competence of its own, in addition to the Member States' competence.

With regard to economic and employment policies (Article 5 TFEU), the EU has only a competence of co-ordination, while the Member States retain the competence on substance. This area should thus have been classified as a 'complementary' competence and not as a 'shared' one. Nevertheless, it was decided politically within the Convention that the importance of the co-ordination done by the EU in this area made it difficult to make it appear as a mere 'complementary' competence. Neither the 2003–4 IGC nor the Lisbon IGC corrected the work of the Convention on this point.

With regard to CFSP, the provisions on which, contrary to what was provided for in the Constitutional Treaty, are located in the TEU and are thus separated from the other legal bases on EU competences in the TFEU, it was considered that the specificity of the EU competence in this area, where both the EU and the Member States have a competence, made it politically difficult to include this area in one of the three general categories of competences.

The classification of the internal market was also subject to discussion, because, in this area, the Union has a functional competence of harmonisation (which, logically, can only be done by the Union and, therefore, should be regarded as an exclusive competence) but, as long as the Union has not exercised its competence, Member States keep their power to legislate and to adopt legally binding acts.

In any case, the inclusion of an area in one or other category cannot modify the substance of the competences as they are defined precisely in other parts of the Treaties, given that, according to Article 2(6) TFEU, 'the scope of and arrangements for exercising the Union's competences shall be determined by the provisions of the Treaties relating to each area'. Actually, the definition of the shared competences in Article 2(2) TFEU, which might appear as too vague, is much more precise when set out in detail by each relevant legal basis in the TFEU.

In addition, and as requested by the 2007 IGC mandate, a Protocol no. 25 on the exercise of shared competence was annexed to the Treaties by the Lisbon Treaty. Its sole Article states that 'With reference to Article 2 [TFEU] on shared competence, when the Union has taken action in a certain area, the scope of this exercise of competence only covers those elements governed by the Union act in question and therefore does not cover the whole area.' One does recognise in this drafting the results of negotiation involving the negotiating efforts made on behalf of Member States having difficulties in accepting the concept of 'shared competences'. The aim of the Protocol is to reproduce what is the current legal situation, while trying to avoid any flexible interpretation in the future, which could lead to an unwanted 'creeping' extension of the EU powers.

To be interpreted in the same way is the last sentence of Article 2(2) TFEU, which was also added in accordance with the 2007 IGC mandate: 'The Member States shall again exercise their competence to the extent that the Union has decided to cease exercising its competence.' The wish here was to state that the exercise by the EU of shared competences will not necessarily always go in the direction of an enlargement of the EU competences and of a parallel reduction of the Member States' competences. It is expressly provided that the Union may decide to cease exercising its competence in a given area and that, in that case, the Member States will of course be free to exercise again their competence to that extent. This sentence, which has been criticised by some as being contrary to the concept of an 'ever closer Union' (see the penultimate paragraph in the Preamble of the TEU and Article 1, 2nd subparagraph, TEU), reflects, however, something which had always been a legal possibility.

Section 8 Basic principles

The Lisbon Treaty codifies and clarifies long-standing legal principles which either were already defined in the text of the Treaties, or had already been developed by the Court of Justice.

The principle of primacy of EU law is confirmed but not formally enshrined in the Lisbon Treaty

The authors of Article I-6 of the Constitutional Treaty intended to reflect expressly the principle that EC law has supremacy over national law: 'The Constitution and law adopted by the institutions of the Union in exercising competences conferred on it shall have primacy over the law of the Member States.'

Declaration no. 1 to the Final Act of the 2003–4 IGC noted that 'Article I-6 reflects existing case-law of the Court of Justice'. This principle had indeed already been affirmed as early as 1964 by the EC Court of Justice in its landmark judgment *Costa* v. *ENEL*:[14] 'The executive force of Community law cannot vary from one State to another in deference to subsequent domestic laws, without jeopardising the attainment of the objectives of the Treaty set out in Article 5(2) and giving rise to the discrimination prohibited by Article 7.'[15]

---

14 See Case 6/64, *Costa v. ENEL*. See also Case 106/77, *Simmenthal*, in which the Court stated that 'in accordance with the principle of the precedence of Community law, the relationship between provisions of the Treaty and directly applicable measures of the institutions on the one hand and the national law of the Member States on the other is such that those provisions and measures not only by their entry into force render automatically inapplicable any conflicting provision of current national law but – in so far as they are an integral part of, and take precedence in, the legal order applicable in the territory of each of the Member States – also preclude the valid adoption of new national legislative measures to the extent to which they would be incompatible with Community provisions' (para. 17), and 'every national Court must, in a case within its jurisdiction, apply Community law in its entirety and protect rights which the latter confers on individuals and must accordingly set aside any provision of national law which may conflict with it, whether prior or subsequent to the Community rule' (para. 21).

See also judgment of 17 December 1970, Case 11/70, *International Handelsgesellschaft*, [1970] ECR 1125, in which the Court stated that 'In fact, the law stemming from the Treaty, an independent source of law, cannot because of its very nature be overridden by rules of national law, however framed, without being deprived of its character as Community law and without the legal basis of the Community itself being called in question. Therefore the validity of a Community measure or its effect within a Member State cannot be affected by allegations that it runs counter to either fundamental rights as formulated by the Constitution of that State or the principles of a national constitutional structure' (para. 3).

15 The primacy of EU law has been recognised, after some difficulty, by most national supreme courts as regards the infra-constitutional law. However, a number of supreme courts do not accept its primacy over their national constitutional law (in particular in Germany, France, Spain and Italy). This is essentially a problem of principle, a legal and political issue, of great importance, but which has had no practical impact up to now (for an overview of the situation in Member States see J.-P. Jacqué, *Droit institutionnel de l'Union européenne*, 5th edn (Paris: Dalloz, 2009), 573–87.

This case law had already been codified, in primary law, although not so clearly for non-specialists. This was in paragraph 2 of the Protocol on the application of the principles of subsidiarity and proportionality, annexed to the EC Treaty by the Amsterdam Treaty. According to this paragraph, 'the application of the principles of subsidiarity and proportionality . . . shall not affect the principles developed by the Court of Justice regarding the relationship between national and Community law'.

The primacy rule is a classic principle in multi-layered legal orders such as federal States.[16] As far as the EU is concerned, it is also a consequence of the international law principle 'pacta sunt servanda' (Article 27 of the 1969 Vienna Convention on the Law of Treaties). The primacy of EU law over national law is essential to the Union's ability to function. Without it, legislation validly adopted by the EU institutions could be ignored by a Member State whenever it was considered by that State to be contrary to its economic or political interests. In the absence of primacy, 'the legal basis of the Community itself [would be] called in question' (as the Court stated in *Simmenthal*), and the internal market and all the basic policies of the EU could not function.[17]

The objective pursued by the drafters of the Constitutional Treaty, both in the Convention and in the 2003–4 IGC, was to codify this basic principle explicitly and using simple words. In theory, the legal effect of this would have been that the primacy rule would have covered CFSP–ESDP law, as well as the rest of Union law. It would have remained the case, however, that the EU Court of Justice has no jurisdiction in CFSP or ESDP matters. Moreover, Article I-5(1) of the Constitutional Treaty recognised that the EU is bound to respect 'national identities' of Member States, 'inherent in their fundamental structures, political and constitutional, inclusive of regional and local self-government', and that 'it shall respect their essential State functions, including ensuring the territorial integrity of

---

16 See Cl. 2 of Art. VI of the US Constitution: 'This Constitution, and the Laws of the United States which shall be made in Pursuance thereof; and all Treaties made, or which shall be made, under the Authority of the United States, shall be the supreme Law of the Land; and the Judges in every State shall be bound thereby, any Thing in the Constitution or Laws of any State to the Contrary notwithstanding.'
    See also Art. 31 of the German Constitution: 'Federal law shall have primacy over Land law.'
    See also Art. 49 of the Swiss Constitution: 'Federal law shall have primacy over contrary cantonal law.'

17 However, according to the judgment of 30 June 2009 of the German Constitutional Court, 'the Federal Republic of Germany does not recognise an absolute primacy of application of Union law' (para. 331).

the State, maintaining law and order and safeguarding national security' (reproduced in the present Article 4(2) TEU). Therefore, in practice, Article I-6 of the Constitutional Treaty would not, at first sight, have had new legal effects. However, its political and symbolic importance was great.

Two constitutional courts (the French Conseil constitutionnel and the Spanish Tribunal Constitucional[18]) had carefully examined this provision of the Constitutional Treaty. They both found that it reflected a principle which already existed and that its formalisation in the Constitutional Treaty did not require a modification of their national Constitution.

However, after the two negative referendums of 2005 in France and in the Netherlands, a number of Member States were insisting, in advance of the Lisbon IGC, that this provision of the Constitutional Treaty should not be kept in the future Treaty. This request was accepted only after long and difficult discussions, including at the level of heads of state or government in June 2007, and after an agreement on the adoption of a specific Declaration no. 17 to which was annexed an opinion of the Council Legal Service which had been requested by the heads of state or government (see Box 18).

BOX 18. DECLARATION NO. 17 CONCERNING PRIMACY

The Conference recalls that, in accordance with well settled case law of the Court of Justice of the European Union, the Treaties and the law adopted by the Union on the basis of the Treaties have primacy over the law of Member States, under the conditions laid down by the said case law.

The Conference has also decided to attach as an Annex to this Final Act the Opinion of the Council Legal Service on the primacy of EC law as set out in 11197/07 (JUR 260):

Opinion of the Council Legal Service of 22 June 2007

---

18 In France, see Decision of the Conseil constitutionnel no. 2004–505 DC of 19 November 2004. In its decision, the Conseil constitutionnel, however, puts the French Constitution itself outside the EU legal order and, therefore, not bound by EU law, at www.conseil-constitutionnel.fr/decision/2004/2004505/2004505 dc.pdf. In Spain, see Decision of the Tribunal Constitucional, no. DTC 1/2004 of 13 December 2004, at www.tribunalconstitucional.es/Stc2004/DTC2004–001.htm.

For an analysis of both decisions see Annex 2 of my book, *Le traité constitutionnel pour l'Europe*, as well as J.-E. Schoettl, 'La ratification du "Traité établissant une Constitution pour l'Europe" appelle-t-elle une révision de la Constitution française?' (2004) 393(238) *Les Petites Affiches* 3.

However, the fact that these legal possibilities are now expressly included in EU texts has a political significance not to be underestimated. This was probably the purpose aimed at. These possibilities will be difficult to exploit in practice, as they would need a proposal from the Commission and the necessary majority in the European Parliament and in the Council, in accordance with the applicable legal base (or common accord in the case of Article 48(2) TEU).

The principle of subsidiarity

Article 5(3) TEU provides that 'in areas which do not fall within its exclusive competence, the Union shall act only if and in so far as the objectives of the proposed action cannot be sufficiently achieved by the Member States, either at central level or at regional and local level, but can rather, by reason of the scale or effects of the proposed action, be better achieved at Union level'.

This principle, which was mentioned for the first time in the Maastricht Treaty, was already set out in Article 5, 2nd subparagraph, TEC and referred to in Article 2, 2nd subparagraph, of the former TEU. The Lisbon Treaty refers for the first time to regional and local levels. The principle and the modalities for the control of the respect of this principle are being developed in Protocol no. 2 on the application of the principles of subsidiarity and proportionality, which has been substantially revised, as compared with the Constitutional Treaty, in order to give a more important role to the national parliaments of the Member States to exercise a control on the respect of the subsidiarity principle by the EU institutions (see Section 15).

The principle of proportionality

Article 5(4) TEU provides that 'the content and form of Union action shall not exceed what is necessary to achieve the objectives of the Treaties'.

This principle was already set out in Article 5, 3rd subparagraph, TEC. This principle and the modalities for the control of its respect are developed in Protocol no. 2.

The principle of sincere co-operation

Article 4(3), 1st and 3rd subparagraphs, TEU provides that 'the Union and the Member States shall, in full mutual respect, assist each other in carrying out tasks which flow from the Treaties ... The Member States shall facilitate the achievement of the Union's tasks and refrain from any measure which could jeopardise the attainment of the Union's objectives.' Article 13(2) TEU provides that 'the institutions shall practise mutual sincere co-operation'.

This principle was already set out in Article 10 TEC, which provided that '[Member States] shall facilitate the achievement of the Community's tasks. They shall abstain from any measure which could jeopardise the attainment of the objectives of this Treaty.' It had been interpreted by the Court of Justice as also applying to the relations between EU institutions.[21]

The principle of indirect administration

Article 4(3), 2nd subparagraph, TEU provides that 'the Member States shall take any appropriate measure, general or particular, to ensure fulfilment of the obligations arising out of the Treaties or resulting from the acts of the institutions of the Union'. Article 291(1) TFEU provides that 'Member States shall adopt all measures of national law necessary to implement legally binding Union acts'.

The Lisbon Treaty also introduced a new legal basis enabling the Union to 'support the efforts of Member States to improve their administrative capacity to implement Union law' (Article 197(2) TFEU).

This principle was already set out in Article 10, 1st subparagraph, TEC, under which 'Member States shall take all appropriate measures, whether general or particular, to ensure fulfilment of the obligations arising out of [the] Treaty or resulting from action taken by the institutions', but the Lisbon Treaty sets it out in more explicit terms.[22]

The principle of equality of Member States before the Treaties

During the 2003–4 IGC, some delegations (Portugal in particular) desired that the Treaty should establish a 'principle of equality between Member States of the Union'. This appeared to be unacceptable for a number of delegations. They rightly stressed that such a principle did not exist within the Union legal order. The Treaties themselves differentiate between

---

21 See judgment of 30 March 1995, Case 65/93, *European Parliament v. Council*, [1995] ECR I-643, para. 23.

22 On the system of 'indirect administration' see Section 11.

Member States according to certain objective criteria.[23] The Union is
not a classic international organisation between states; it is a union both
of states and of citizens. The final compromise was to refer to the 'equality
of Member States before the Treaties' (Article 4(2) TEU), which is a formulation already used by the Court of Justice in its case law and which,
therefore, did not give rise to any legal concern.[24]

Section 9 The legal personality of the EU

Article 47 TEU states that 'the Union shall have legal personality'. Article
335 TFEU states that 'in each of the Member States, the Union shall enjoy
the most extensive legal capacity accorded to legal persons under their
laws; it may, in particular, acquire or dispose of movable and immovable
property and may be a party to legal proceedings'.

The question arises of why it was necessary or opportune to give an
express legal personality to the EU. As for the former first pillar, it had
always benefited from the legal personality conferred on the Community
by Article 281 TEC. As for the former third pillar, part of it had been
integrated into the EC and the remainder (criminal matters) was under
the same regime as the second pillar. As for the former second pillar, the
EU as such had already concluded many international agreements,[25] thus

---

23 However, in its judgment of 30 June 2009, the German Constitutional Court is of the
    opinion that the principle of equality of States continues to rule the political organisation
    of the EU too much (see, among others, para. 292).
24 The Court has referred to 'the principle of equality of Member States before Community
    law' in a case concerning the elimination of quantitative restrictions on agricultural
    products, in connection with the United Kingdom's accession in 1973 (see judgment, 29
    March 1979, Case 231/78, *Commission v. UK* (potatoes), [1979] ECR 1447, para. 17). See
    also judgments of 7 February 1979, Case 128/78, *Commission v. UK* (tachographs), [1979]
    ECR I-419, para. 12; and of 7 February 1973, Case 39/72, *Commission v. Italy* (premiums
    for slaughtering cows), [1973] ECR 101, para. 24).
25 By the date of entry into force of the Lisbon Treaty, the EU had concluded about one
    hundred international agreements on the basis of Art. 24 of the former TEU. Eight of
    them may be considered particularly significant in substance:

    • two agreements concluded with the United States in the area of Justice and Home
      Affairs (one on extradition and one on mutual legal assistance);
    • two agreements with the United States on the transfer of Passenger Name Record
      (PNR);
    • a similar PNR agreement concluded with Australia;
    • one agreement with Switzerland on its association to the Schengen area;
    • two agreements with Iceland and Norway on surrender procedures and on mutual
      assistance in criminal matters.

demonstrating that it had already an implied legal personality.[26] However, the exact scope of this legal personality was still disputed among scholars and within government circles. Was the EU able to sue or to be sued in the context of a case exclusively concerning the CFSP field? Was it possible for the EU to become a member of an international organisation? Moreover, it was strange to see the two legal personalities, of the EU and of the EC, coexisting. In addition, long delays were caused by the fact that, as the conclusion of international agreements concerning either the second or the third pillars remained covered by Article 24(5) of the former TEU, national procedures were needed in most Member States for the most significant agreements. Finally, the visibility of the EU in the world was not at its best as long as the EU was not expressly conferred with a full legal personality. The Lisbon Treaty greatly improves the situation. Third countries will understand better that they are negotiating with one entity, the EU, and not with two separate entities, the EU and the EC, depending on the subject matter under negotiation.

It should also be noted that, in Declaration no. 24 concerning the EU legal personality, the IGC 'confirms that the fact that the [EU] has a legal personality will not in any way authorise the Union to legislate or to act beyond the competences conferred upon it by the Member States in the Treaties', which is legally quite obvious.

The creation of a single legal personality allowed the introduction of a single procedure to negotiate and conclude international agreements. This procedure is described in Article 218 TFEU. It replaces the two procedures which existed before, namely Article 300 TEC and Article 24 former TEU.

The other agreements are of a technical nature – that is, about sixty on the participation of third States in EU-led operations, about twenty SOFAs (status of forces agreements on the status of personnel operating abroad in an EU-led operation) and more than ten on exchange of classified information.

26 The EU fulfils all the criteria set out by the International Court of Justice, in its Advisory Opinion of 11 April 1949 on the legal personality of the United Nations (see *Reparation for injuries suffered in the service of the United Nations*, better known as the '*Bernadotte* case', at www.icj-cij.org). On the issue of the legal personality of the Union, see S. Marquardt, 'The Conclusion of International Agreements under Art. 24 of the Treaty on European Union', in V. Kronenberger (ed.), *The European Union and the International Legal Order: Discord or Harmony?* (The Hague: T.M.C. Asser Instituut, 2001), 333; updated as 'La capacité de l'Union européenne de conclure des accords internationaux dans le domaine de la coopération policière et judiciaire en matière pénale', in G. de Kerchove and A. Weyembergh (eds.), *Sécurité et justice: enjeu de la politique extérieure de l'Union européenne* (Brussels: Institut d'Etudes Européennes, Université de Bruxelles, 2003), 179.

However, some variations apply in this procedure, depending on the subject matter of the international agreement to be concluded:

- Article 218(3) TFEU gives the Council the choice of the negotiator, most probably either the Commission or the High Representative, depending on the subject matter of the agreement envisaged;
- Article 218 (6) TFEU increases the powers of the European Parliament as compared with Article 300(3) TEC, in that it provides for the consent of the European Parliament for many international agreements, in particular with regard to all agreements covering fields where codecision applies internally;
- agreements are to be concluded by the Council using qualified majority voting (QMV), save for cases where the agreement covers a field for which unanimity is required for the adoption of an EU act (Article 218(8) TFEU);
- agreements concluded under the Treaties shall be 'binding on the institutions of the Union and on its Member States' (Article 216(2) TFEU), as was the case with those concluded on the basis of the EC Treaty. The Lisbon Treaty does thus remove the former particularity in CFSP where, pursuant to Article 24(5) of the former TEU, 'no agreement shall be binding on a Member State whose representative in the Council states that it has to comply with the requirements of its own constitutional procedure'. However, all the CFSP decisions to be taken by the Council in such a process (from the authorisation to open negotiations to the decision to conclude agreements) will still be taken by unanimity (Article 218(8) TFEU and Article 31(1) TEU). This preserves the already existing system of the so-called 'constructive abstention', under which 'when abstaining in a vote, any member of the Council may qualify its abstention', in which case 'it shall not be obliged to apply the decision, but shall accept that the latter commits the Union'. At the time of writing, this mechanism had never been applied.
- Article 207 TFEU, which replaces Article 133 TEC, contains specific provisions concerning the common commercial policy under which the Commission is the sole negotiator and QMV is the general rule, save for certain matters where unanimity in the Council is required.[27]

---

27 See Section 36. Unanimity is required for the following agreements (Art. 207(4), 2nd and 3rd subparas., TFEU):

- trade in services, commercial aspects of intellectual property and foreign direct investments if unanimity is required for the adoption of internal rules;

Section 10 Variable geometry

The procedure for 'enhanced co-operation' is modified

Enhanced co-operation, which was designed to allow some Member States, using the EU framework and institutions, to co-operate further between themselves in cases where the others do not wish to do so, has existed on paper since 1997 (Amsterdam Treaty).[28] However, perhaps due to the strict conditions attached to launching it, but actually more probably due to political reasons (avoiding a 'two-speed Europe'), the procedure has never yet been used, despite the fact that the Nice Treaty made it easier to launch by providing for QMV instead of unanimity.

The Lisbon Treaty regroups the four sets of rules on enhanced co-operation of the past Treaties (due to the pillar structure)[29] into two sets of rules set out in the TEU for the generalities (Article 20) and in the TFEU for the details (Articles 326 to 334). It makes slight modifications to the procedure:

- it widens the scope of possible enhanced co-operation to cover the whole CFSP field, including defence, whereas it had previously only covered the implementation of a CSFP action which had already been decided upon;
- it removes the so-called 'emergency brake' procedure, which allowed a Council member to request that the question of an authorisation for enhanced co-operation be referred to the European Council;
- it provides for a new *passerelle* that will allow participants in an enhanced co-operation to decide in the Council to switch from unanimity to QMV (except in defence) and from a special legislative procedure to the ordinary legislative procedure (codecision).

However, the effect of these slight improvements will be somewhat reduced by:

- trade in cultural and audiovisual services, where they risk prejudicing the EU's cultural and linguistic diversity;
- trade in social, education and health services if they risk seriously disturbing the national organisation of such services and prejudicing the responsibility of Member States to deliver them.

28 Originally the idea was launched by a joint letter from Chancellor Schröder and President Chirac at the end of 1995.

29 Theses rules were in Arts. 27A to 27E former TEU (CFSP), 40 and 40A former TEU (JHA), 43 to 45 former TEU (general rules), and 11 and 11A TEC (first pillar).

- the increase in the minimum number of participants from eight to nine Member States (the Constitutional Treaty provided for one-third of the Member States, i.e. nine with twenty-seven Member States, but ten with twenty-eight);
- the requirement of unanimity in the Council for authorising any kind of enhanced co-operation in CFSP, without any exception for an enhanced co-operation that would aim at implementing CFSP decisions which have already been adopted (whereas until the Lisbon Treaty there had been QMV in such a case);
- the requirement of the consent of the European Parliament (where MEPs from all Member States have a right to vote) for launching an enhanced co-operation, even for cases where the codecision procedure does not apply (whereas, until the Lisbon Treaty, in cases where codecision did not apply, the European Parliament was only to be consulted);
- the requirement of a Commission proposal (which will have to be decided, as in all cases, by a simple majority of Commissioners from all Member States) for triggering an enhanced co-operation in matters other than CFSP.

Besides that, the existing preconditions for the launching of an enhanced co-operation remain mostly the same as they were under Article 43 of the former TEU: no undermining of the internal market, no barrier to or discrimination in trade between Member States, no distortion of competition and no enhanced co-operation in areas of exclusive EU competence.

Existing cases of 'inbuilt closer co-operation'

In the former TEU and TEC there were already cases of what could be called 'inbuilt closer co-operation', which resulted either from specific conditions on the participation of Member States in certain EU policies and/or from the fact that some Member States had requested and obtained an opt-out from certain EU policies. These particular situations also constitute tools for flexibility which the Lisbon Treaty takes over, and to which it adds 'permanent structured co-operation' in the field of defence.

The two existing cases of 'inbuilt closer co-operation', not modified by the Lisbon Treaty, are the euro zone and the Schengen area, in which, at the time of writing, sixteen and twenty-two Member States respectively participate. Participation in these areas is subject to strict criteria which have to be fulfilled by the Member States concerned.

Participation in the euro zone is subject to fulfilling, among other conditions, the 'convergence criteria' relating to a high degree of price stability, a low budgetary deficit and the durability of limited fluctuation margins within the exchange-rate mechanism (see four indents in Article 140(1) TFEU and Protocol no. 13 on the convergence criteria). The EMU and the euro zone are examined in Section 38.

Participation in the Schengen area (i.e. the removal of checks on persons at internal borders and access to the Schengen Information System (SIS)),[30] is subject to the State concerned having successfully undergone an evaluation procedure. This procedure concerns in particular the quality and level of controls at external borders; it requires a Council decision by unanimity of the representatives of the Schengen Member States.[31] The Schengen area and the specific position of the United Kingdom and Ireland are examined in Section 24.

The defence policy could also be considered, even now, as a case of 'inbuilt closer co-operation' among twenty-six Member States, since Denmark 'does not participate in the elaboration and the implementation of decisions and actions of the Union which have defence implications' (Article 5, 1st subparagraph, of Protocol no. 22 on the position of Denmark).

The new case added by the Lisbon Treaty: the 'permanent structured co-operation' in the field of defence

The Lisbon Treaty adds to the above cases a new case of 'inbuilt closer co-operation': the 'permanent structured co-operation' in the field of defence (Articles 42(6) and 46 TEU). This co-operation is open to Member States 'whose military capabilities fulfil higher criteria and which have made more binding commitments to one another in this area with a view to the most demanding missions'. The criteria concerning military capabilities to be fulfilled are set out in Protocol no. 10 on permanent structured co-operation established by Article 42 TEU. The decision-making procedure is described in Article 46 TEU. The Council will decide on the establishment of such co-operation by QMV, which is quite remarkable, as it will

---

30 The SIS is a computerised database and exchange of information system between the competent authorities of Member States.

31 See Protocol no. 19 on the Schengen *acquis* integrated in the framework of the EU.

make the launching of such a co-operation easier than the launching of a classical 'enhanced co-operation' in the field of CFSP, where unanimity is required (on the permanent structured co-operation see Section 35).

Section 11 Legislative and non-legislative procedures and Acts

The Lisbon Treaty streamlines instruments and decision-making procedures which the EU institutions have to use to exercise their powers. The Treaty reduces significantly the number of different types of legal instrument. It introduces a distinction between legislative and non-legislative procedures and a hierarchy of legislative and non-legislative acts. Drawing a logical conclusion from this distinction, it provides for full openness of Council meetings when acting in a legislative capacity. The Treaty also streamlines the different decision-making procedures.

Streamlining the legal instruments adopted by the EU institutions

The Treaty reduces from fifteen to five the different types of legal instrument.

The fifteen types of legal instruments before the Lisbon Treaty

The former TEU and TEC provided for fifteen different types of legal instruments having different legal effects, the differences in some instances being very minor:[32]

- the regulation (which is binding and directly applicable);
- the directive (which is binding as to the results to be achieved but leaves to national authorities the choice of form and methods);
- four types of decisions (EC, CFSP, JHA and *sui generis*, which all have a legally binding force);
- the recommendation and the opinion (which have no binding force);
- the framework decision (JHA, similar to a directive, although it cannot entail direct effect);[33]
- the convention between Member States (EC and JHA, i.e. the classic international agreement, existing under international law, but seldom used);

---

32 See Arts. 249 and 293 TEC, as well as Arts. 12 to 15, Art. 34 and Art. 37 of the former TEU.

33 On the consequences of this see judgment of 16 June 2005, Case C-105/03, *Pupino*, [2005] ECR I-5285.

- principles and general guidelines (listed among CFSP instruments, although not a legal act);
- the common strategy (CFSP);
- two types of common positions (CFSP and JHA, which both have binding force); and
- the joint action (CFSP, which also has binding force).[34]

While the original Rome Treaty of 1957 provided for only five legal instruments, the addition of the second and third pillars (CFSP and JHA) in the nineties and the political will to differentiate these new sectors resulted in a proliferation of legal instruments, which sometimes had similar names but different legal effects or, conversely, different names but similar legal effects. This phenomenon did not contribute to enhancing the readability and understanding of the Treaties.

The five types of legal instruments after the Lisbon Treaty

The Constitutional Treaty had aimed at reducing the number of legal instruments to six, called 'European law' (similar to a regulation), 'European framework law' (similar to a directive), 'European regulation' (a non-legislative act whose legal effects were a mixture of a regulation and a directive), 'European decision' (also a non-legislative act) and the two usual non-binding acts (recommendation and opinion). The differentiation between legislative and non-legislative acts was done through the denomination of the legal instruments. Those with the word 'law' were legislative and those without were non-legislative. This had the advantage of establishing a clear distinction of legislative and non-legislative acts. The names 'law' and 'framework law' had been chosen by the Convention for their symbolism. For the same reason, they disappeared from the Lisbon Treaty.

In the June 2007 IGC mandate, the heads of state or government decided to revert to the usual denominations for legal instruments – that is, regulation, directive and decision (see point 3 of the mandate). Therefore the Lisbon Treaty reduces the number of legal instruments to the five traditional Community instruments (i.e. three binding and two

---

34 For an analysis and suggestions made at the time of the Convention, see the contribution of the author of this book on 17 October 2002 to the Working Group IX 'Simplification' set up by the Convention, in Working document 06 (WG IX–WD 06), of 6 November 2002 (available on the Internet site of the Convention).

non-binding ones), the only difference being a slightly modified definition of the decision[35] (Article 288 TFEU):

- the regulation, which 'shall have general application. It shall be binding in its entirety and directly applicable in all Member States'(no change);
- the directive, which 'shall be binding, as to the result to be achieved, upon each Member State to which it is addressed, but shall leave to the national authorities the choice of form and methods' (no change);
- the decision, which 'shall be binding in its entirety. A decision which specifies those to whom it is addressed shall be binding only on them' (slight change);[36]
- the recommendation, and
- the opinion, both of which shall have no binding force (no change).

It was nevertheless decided to keep the differentiation between legislative and non-legislative acts, but to make it through the type of adoption procedure and not through the denomination of the act. Hence, when the legal basis provides that an act is to be adopted 'in accordance with the ordinary legislative procedure' (i.e. codecision) or 'in accordance with a special legislative procedure', the act in question belongs to the category of legislative acts (see Article 289(3) TFEU). If the legal basis does not provide for a legislative procedure, then the act does not belong to the category of legislative acts.

Delegated and implementing acts adopted under Articles 290 and 291 TFEU are non-legislative acts. In order to enable the readers to identify easily the hierarchy of legislative acts and delegated or implementing acts, the Treaty provides that the word 'delegated' or 'implementing' will each time be inserted in the title of these acts (see Articles 290(3) and 291(4) TFEU).

---

35 Under Art. 249, 4th subpara., TEC, a decision always required an addressee, even when it had a normative character (i.e. addressed to all Member States). The Lisbon Treaty has introduced a more straightforward definition which makes the decision a normative act ('binding in its entirety') and mentions the addressee only as a possibility. This ends the difference which existed in certain languages (notably German) between *Entscheidung* and *Beschluss*, as only the latter remains.

36 Decisions are the only type of act which the Council may adopt while acting in CFSP, but those decisions will not have the character of a legislative act (see Title V of TEU, in particular Art. 31(1): 'decisions under this Chapter shall be taken by the European Council and the Council acting unanimously, except where this Chapter provides otherwise. The adoption of legislative acts shall be excluded.'

Streamlining the procedures to be followed by the EU institutions

Trying to transpose to the EU a ready-made state model would not suit the political and institutional uniqueness of the EU. Thus introducing a strict, Montesquieu-like division of powers between the legislature and the executive would not make sense in the EU. However, streamlining the decision-making procedures and introducing some logic and clarity into the famous 'comitology' procedures set up to monitor the implementing powers conferred on the Commission by the legislature was needed. This has been done in Articles 290 and 291 TFEU.

New rules by default in legislative matters and other streamlining of procedures

The Lisbon Treaty streamlines the decision-making procedures in various ways.

The number of procedures is reduced by removing the 'co-operation procedure' (Article 252 TEC) which was the predecessor of the codecision procedure, and which had survived only in the monetary policy sector.

Codecision becomes the 'ordinary legislative procedure' (Articles 289(1) and 294 TFEU) whereby legal acts are adopted by the European Parliament and the Council, acting by QMV, on a proposal from the Commission.[37]

The other legislative procedure under which legal acts may be adopted is called the 'special legislative procedure'. It covers cases where legal acts are adopted either by the Council with the participation of the European Parliament (through consultation or consent) or by the European Parliament with the consent of the Council.[38] Other institutions, such as the Commission or the European Central Bank, may also have to be consulted.

---

37 As indicated in Art. 289(4) TFEU, there are some cases where the ordinary legislative procedure is not triggered by a Commission proposal but by an initiative of a group of Member States (at least a quarter of the Member States) in the FSJ area (see Art. 76 TFEU) or of the European Parliament (see Art. 223(2) TFEU) by a recommendation from the European Central Bank (see for instance Art. 129(3) and (4) TFEU) or at the request of the Court of Justice (see Art. 281 TFEU).

38 The European Parliament may adopt legislative acts in three instances: Art. 223(2) TFEU on the Statute of MEPs, with the consent of the Council; Art. 226 TFEU on Committees of Inquiry, with the consent of the Council and the Commission; and Art. 228(4) TFEU on the European Ombudsman, with the consent of the Council.

The prevailing situation, in which most legislative acts were adopted on a proposal from the Commission, is codified in Article 17(2) TEU[39] and becomes the rule by default. Acts adopted under a legislative procedure (whether ordinary or special) are therefore, in the great majority of cases, adopted on the basis of a proposal from the Commission. In some cases, the triggering of the procedure may be an initiative by a group of Member States (in the FSJ areas, with a minimum of a quarter of the number of Member States), on a recommendation from the ECB or at the request of the Court of Justice.

Likewise, the pre-existing situation under which the Council acted by QMV in most policy areas is codified in Article 16(3) TEU and also becomes the rule by default.[40]

Another general rule introduced by the Lisbon Treaty is that 'the Council shall meet in public when it deliberates and votes on a draft legislative act' (Article 16(8) TEU). This also means that, in principle, all documents regarding a legislative item on the Council agenda will also be public.

Apart from legislative procedures, there are procedures for adopting non-legislative acts – that is, in all cases where the legal basis in the Treaties does not refer to a 'legislative' procedure (ordinary or special). Article 15(1) TEU expressly specifies that the European Council is not allowed to 'exercise legislative functions'. Likewise, in the CSFP field, it is expressly specified that 'the adoption of legislative acts shall be excluded' (Articles 24(1), 2nd subparagraph, and 31(1) TEU). In this field only decisions can be adopted, and the European Council or the Council may act on either an initiative from a Member State or a proposal from the High Representative, or a proposal from the High Representative with the Commission's support (see Chapter 2 of Title V of the TEU).

Where the type of legal act is not specified in the legal basis concerned, the European Parliament, the Council, the Commission[41] and the European Central Bank may adopt any of the legal acts listed in Article 288 TFEU, in accordance with the decision-making procedure which is provided for in the legal basis.

---

39 Art. 17(2) TEU reads, 'Union legislative acts may be adopted only on the basis of a Commission proposal, except where the Treaties provide otherwise. Other acts shall be adopted on the basis of a Commission proposal where the Treaties so provide.'

40 Art. 16(3) TEU reads, 'The Council shall act by a qualified majority except where the Treaties provide otherwise.' This is in lieu of the past rule by default which was a simple majority, and which was, in reality, the least common of the voting procedures, save for procedural decisions (Art. 205(1) TEC).

41 The Commission always act by a simple majority (Art. 250 TFEU).

In three instances the legal bases do not specify whether the procedure to be followed is a special legislative procedure or a non-legislative procedure, the choice being therefore left to the Commission, in its proposal, and later on to the Council when it examines the proposal, of making it a legislative or a non-legislative procedure (and act).[42]

General principles on implementing EU law

The Community was founded on the fundamental principle of 'indirect administration', which is itself based on the political philosophy of subsidiarity. This means that the power to implement Community law lies primarily with the Member States, under the supervision of the Commission, of the national courts and of the Court of Justice. The Union does not apply the system which is in force in some federal states, such as the United States, where a power conferred at federal level comprises not only the legislative power but also the power of implementation of laws through executive measures.

The principle of indirect administration was set out in Article 10 TEC, which stated that Member States must take 'all appropriate measures, whether general or particular, to ensure fulfilment of the obligations arising out of this Treaty or resulting from action taken by the institutions of the Community'.

With the Lisbon Treaty, this principle is restated in the second subparagraph of Article 4(3) TEU, under which 'the Member States shall take any appropriate measure, general or particular, to ensure fulfilment of the obligations arising out of the Treaties or resulting from the acts of the institutions of the Union', and in Article 291(1) TFEU, under which 'Member States shall adopt all measures of national law necessary to implement legally binding Union acts'. As far as CFSP is concerned, the language used by the Treaty is different: 'The Member States shall support the Union's external and security policy actively and unreservedly in a spirit of loyalty and mutual solidarity and shall comply with the Union's action in this area' (Article 24(3) TEU, to be compared with Article 11(2) of the former TEU).

Only national administrations (tax, customs, veterinary authorities, etc.) have the necessary infrastructure and resources in terms of manpower and financial and technical means to apply and implement EU

---

42 These three instances are Art. 203 TFEU on the association of overseas countries and territories, Art. 349 TFEU on specific measures regarding certain French, Portuguese and Spanish overseas regions, and the flexibility clause (Art. 352).

law. If all EU legislation had to be implemented at EU level, the EU would have to set up a vast administrative infrastructure, which the Member States do not want. They intend the Union's central administrative bodies, including the Commission, to remain small (approximately 30,000 officials, i.e. less than the administration of a large town) and the implementation of EU law to remain the preserve of national administrations.

There are exceptions to the principle of indirect administration. In some cases the Commission has been given directly by the Treaty the task of implementing a given policy, particularly where centralisation has been judged necessary. This is the case, in particular, for measures in the field of competition law (Articles 105 and 106 TFEU) and for the control of aids granted by Member States (Article 108 TFEU).

In other, more numerous, cases, the EU legislator may entrust the Commission with the direct management and application of certain provisions, such as, for instance, programmes providing support or incentives, a management power which is then a corollary of the general power of the Commission to implement the budget of the EU (Article 317 TFEU).

The EU legislator may also find it necessary to entrust the Commission with the adoption of certain implementing rules in respect of an EU legislative act, to ensure that it is applied in a uniform and consistent manner, for example in order to avoid distorting competition or discriminating between economic operators. It is the case with regard to the centralised issuing of authorisations for placing certain products on the market (e.g. medicines) or of EU intellectual property rights by EU agencies acting under Commission supervision (e.g. trademarks).

When entrusting the Commission, the EU legislator will provide for a system of control over the exercise of such implementing powers by the Commission. This is what has become known as 'comitology'.

Comitology

The rules in force before the Lisbon Treaty

Before the Lisbon Treaty, Article 202 TEC provided that the Council may 'confer on the Commission, in the acts which the Council adopts, powers for the implementation of the rules which the Council lays down'. Article 202 also provided that the Council 'may also reserve the right, in specific cases, to exercise directly implementing powers itself'. In practice, this generic expression 'implementing powers' has covered two types of powers which are different in nature:

- not only the power to apply or to implement all or part of a legislative act at Community level, in those cases where, departing from the principle of indirect administration by the Member States, the EC legislature entrusted implementation to the Commission, at least in part;
- but also the power to update certain provisions of a basic instrument – that is, when the Commission was given the power to amend or adapt non-essential elements of the legislative act itself, for example in an annex.[43]

Although these two types of 'implementing' powers which could be conferred on the Commission were different in nature, the rules for their exercise have remained the same for a long time. The Commission had to go through a procedure involving a committee composed of representatives of the Member States before being able to adopt the measure (hence the neologism 'comitology'). The committee procedure is a logical consequence of the principle of indirect administration. It is an exception to the basic principle of 'indirect administration', whereby the responsibility for implementing and applying EU law belongs normally to the Member States, under the control of the Commission, of the national courts and of the Court of Justice. Given that implementation is normally a matter for the Member States, when the EC legislature decides to entrust it, in part, to the Commission, participation in that implementation is entrusted to committees made up of representatives of Member States' governments. These, therefore, have a say on the implementing measures to be adopted by the Commission and which they will subsequently have to apply in practice. This 'say' varies according to the type of committee laid down in a Decision on committee procedure,[44] based on Article 202 TEC, which stated that 'the Council may impose certain requirements in respect of

---

43 For example, where the Commission was authorised by the EC legislator to adapt a legislative act to technical progress or to international standards, to amend a date or a figure, to lay down in an annex additional and more detailed rules for application by the Member States of the legislative act, etc. Sometimes the mere fact of amending or setting a figure (e.g. a percentage) may have very significant implications affecting the very essence of the legislative act (e.g. the definition of chocolate according to the percentage of a particular type of fat).

44 See Council Decision 1999/468/EC of 28 June 1999, laying down the procedures for the exercise of implementing powers conferred on the Commission (OJ No. L184, 17 July 1999, 23), last amended by Council Decision of 17 July 2006 (OJ No. L200, 22 July 2006, 11).

the exercise of these powers' (i.e. the implementing powers conferred on the Commission). The committees may have only a consultative role or they may have more influence. They are distinct from the Council (as a legislative authority). They are convened and chaired by the Commission. In certain cases, if a committee has reached deadlock, the issue may be referred to the Council (which then acts as an executive body, not as a legislative authority).

However, it was not logical to apply the committee procedure, without distinction, both to the adoption of implementing measures and to the adoption of measures, described as 'quasi-legislative', which actually modified the basic legislative act itself. This practice met with criticism from the European Parliament. When it was a matter of exercising implementing powers in the strict sense – that is, cases where the legislature entrusts the Commission with partial implementation of a legislative instrument – it was logical to provide for Member States to have a role in the Commission's exercise of the powers conferred on it. However, this did not hold for scrutiny of cases where the legislature authorised the Commission to amend a legislative act. The power to amend a legislative act lies with the legislature itself, not with the Member States. Scrutiny of this delegation of powers should therefore have been entrusted to the legislature, not to the Member States.

Logically, it is the entity 'deprived' of a power normally due to it which should receive, in return, a right of participation or scrutiny: the Member States, when they are partially 'deprived' of implementation, and the legislature, when it is 'deprived' of its power of amendment. This is why, just as Member States should not be able to scrutinise the exercise of delegated legislative powers, the legislature should not be able to take part in the exercise of implementing powers.

At the same time as the Convention was working on the draft Constitutional Treaty,[45] the Commission had proposed to amend the 1999 Decision on 'comitology' and, on this basis, the Council adopted an important amendment in July 2006 (on the 'comitology system' see Box 19). This amendment introduced a new procedure, called 'regulatory procedure with scrutiny', also known in the Brussels jargon as 'PRAC', after its French acronym from *procédure de réglementation avec contrôle*. The PRAC allows the European Parliament or the Council to prevent the

---

45 See suggestions made to the Convention on 17 October 2002 on the possibility of making this distinction (pp. 20–3 of the contribution of the author of this book to the Working Group IX 'Simplification', Document WGIX–WD06 of 6 November 2002).

BOX 19. THE 'COMITOLOGY' SYSTEM BEFORE THE
LISBON TREATY*

The 'comitology' system – that is, the system by which committees composed of Member States' representatives, meeting outside the Council structure, control the exercise by the Commission of implementing powers conferred on it by the EU legislature pursuant to Article 202 TEC – was set out for the first time in a Council Decision of July 1987 (the Comitology Decision), which was substantially amended in June 1999 and again in July 2006. It provides for four types of committee, all composed of Member States' representatives and chaired by a Commission representative, which differs according to the effects of the opinion they deliver:

- *advisory committee*, which delivers a purely consultative opinion on the draft measures submitted to it by the Commission, the Commission having to 'take the utmost account of the opinion' in the measures it will adopt;
- *management committee*, which also delivers an opinion. If the measures adopted by the Commission are not in accordance with the Committee's opinion, these measures are communicated by the Commission to the Council, in which case the Commission can defer the application of the measures for a maximum period of three months, during which the Council, by QMV, can take a different decision;
- *regulatory committee*, which also delivers an opinion. However, if the draft measures are not in accordance with the Committee's opinion or if no opinion is delivered, the Commission has to submit to the Council a proposal relating to the measures and inform the European Parliament. The Council has to act by QMV within a maximum of three months, in view of the position taken by the European Parliament when the basic act is an act adopted in codecision. If the Council opposes the proposal, the Commission has to re-examine it. If the Council does not oppose or has not adopted the proposed act, the Commission automatically adopts the implementing act.
- *regulatory procedure with scrutiny committee (PRAC)*, which also delivers an opinion. In case of positive opinion, the Commission has to submit the draft measures for scrutiny by the European Parliament and the Council. Either of them can, within a period of three months, oppose the adoption of the draft measures if they 'exceed the implementing powers provided for in the basic instrument' or if the draft 'is not compatible with the aim or the content of the basic instrument or does not respect the principles of subsidiarity or proportionality'. If so, the Commission can submit to the Committee an amended draft of the measures or present a legislative proposal to the legislator. Otherwise, it can adopt the measures. In case of negative opinion by the Committee, the Council can, within two months and by QMV, oppose the adoption of the measures. If the Council envisages adopting the measures, the European Parliament is to be seized within a maximum of two months for scrutiny of the draft measures and can oppose

them for the same reasons as above. In case of opposition from the Council or from the Parliament, the measures cannot be adopted and the Commission can either submit an amended proposal of measures or a legislative proposal. In case of non-opposition to the measures or if the deadlines have elapsed without action on the part of the Council or of the European Parliament, the measures can be adopted by the Commission. This procedure applies only for measures of a general scope which seek to amend non-essential elements of a basic act adopted under the codecision procedure, *inter alia*, by deleting some of those elements or by supplementing the act by the addition of new non-essential elements.

The choice of the type of committee was left to the legislator, which was guided by certain non-binding criteria** set out in Article 2(1) of the Comitology Decision. However, the criterion for the PRAC was compulsory (see Article 2(2)).

---

  * It should be noted that, save for the 'PRAC', which is not compatible with Art. 290 TFEU, this 'comitology' system is compatible with Art. 291 TFEU and therefore remains applicable as long as it is not replaced by a regulation adopted in codecision by the European Parliament and the Council on the basis of Art. 291 TFEU.

 ** See, however, judgment of 21 January 2003, Case C-378/00, *Commission v. Council* (LIFE), [2003] ECR I-937, in which the Court stated that '51.... even though an act adopted by a Community institution does not lay down a rule of law which that institution is bound to observe, but merely lays down a rule of conduct indicating the practice to be followed, that institution may not depart from it without giving the reasons which have led it to do so ... 55. ... when the Community legislature departs, in the choice of committee procedure, from the criteria which are laid down in Art. 2 of the second comitology decision, it must state the reasons for that choice' (paras. 51 and 55).

Commission from adopting measures designed to amend a basic act which has been adopted under the codecision procedure, even if the committee is in favour of these measures. Conversely, if the committee's opinion on the draft measures is unfavourable, the measures are submitted to the Council, which can accept, amend or reject them. If the Council accepts the measures, the European Parliament can still oppose them. The PRAC thus remedied the institutional anomaly described above.

The system laid down in the Lisbon Treaty

At the same time as confirming the basic principle of indirect administration, the Lisbon Treaty has improved the situation, by finally introducing a distinction between two types of control mechanisms in case powers are entrusted to the Commission by the EU legislator, thus resolving the unsatisfactory situation of the 'comitology system':

- *control of 'delegated powers' as provided for in Article 290 TFEU*: it provides that a legislative act adopted under codecision by the European

Parliament and the Council may delegate to the Commission the power to adopt 'delegated' acts which will supplement or amend certain non-essential elements of the basic act. Since this will involve amending the text of the legislative act itself, scrutiny of the exercise of this power is entrusted to the EU legislature (the European Parliament and the Council), not to the Member States. Each legislative act will explicitly lay down the conditions to which the delegation is subject. These may either be a right of either branch of the legislature to revoke the delegation of power, or a right to object, within a certain time limit, to the entry into force of the delegated act. The adjective 'delegated' will be inserted in the titles of delegated acts. There will thus no longer be any official committee procedure for this type of Commission power;[46]

- *control of 'implementing powers' as provided for in Article 291 TFEU:* after having established, in its paragraph 1, the basic principle that implementing Union law normally belongs to the Member States, Article 291 provides that, 'where uniform conditions for implementing legally binding acts are needed', those acts shall confer implementing powers on the Commission (or on the Council, in certain cases[47]). The word 'implementing' will be inserted in the titles of these acts. Since by virtue of the principle of indirect administration, such powers normally would have been exercised by the Member States, they will continue to be associated with the control of implementing powers conferred on the Commission, in accordance with detailed rules to be determined in a Regulation to be adopted under codecision.

Pending the adoption of such a new Regulation, the current Comitology Decision, which is compatible with the Lisbon Treaty, remains applicable, except with regard to the PRAC, which is no longer needed as Article 290 TFEU provides for the procedure to be followed in such cases.[48]

---

46 However, it is very likely that the Commission, when drafting delegated acts, will consult groups composed of experts from Member States in order to ensure that the delegated acts will be properly applied later on by the Member States' authorities. This consultation was already provided for in the financial services sector (the so-called 'Lamfallussy' committees) in Declaration no. 39.

47 Such cases should be 'duly justified', which is a similar condition to that in Art. 1, 1st subpara., of the 'Comitology Decision' of 1999 ('in specific and substantiated cases'). In addition, Art. 291(2) TFEU specifies that in CFSP and ESDP cases, implementing powers will always be entrusted to the Council, not to the Commission.

48 All legislative acts adopted in the past and which contain PRAC procedures will remain applicable until they are modified.

One can only hope that this will end a long saga, at least as regards the broad thrust of a new system which is based on both legal logic and political balance between institutions.

Section 12   Procedures for the revision of the Treaties

Article 48 of the former TEU provided for the 'normal' procedure for revising the Treaties, including an IGC and the ratification by all Member States in conformity with their constitutional requirements. The 'ordinary revision procedure' provided for in this Article has been amended. It has been completed by several so-called *passerelles* (a French word for 'footbridge' which has become the Brussels jargon for naming these 'bridging clauses') and by a 'simplified revision procedure' applicable to Part III of the TFEU. Some other provisions of the Treaties also provide for simplified procedures in specific cases.

The ordinary revision procedure

The ordinary revision procedure is described in Article 48(2) to (5) TEU. The initiative for a revision may come, not only from a Member State or the Commission, as was the case until the Lisbon Treaty, but also from the European Parliament. It is expressly mentioned that the proposal may aim *inter alia* either at increasing or at reducing the competences conferred on the EU; therefore such proposal might obviously also aim at changes in the Treaties which have no effect on the competences of the EU, such as a reform of the institutions.

Another new feature in the procedure is that, if the European Council, after consulting the European Parliament and the Commission, adopts by a simple majority a decision in favour of examining the proposed amendments, a procedure which corresponds de facto to what was done up to now, it should then, instead of immediately convening the IGC, convene a convention composed of representatives of the national parliaments, of the European Parliament, of the heads of state or government, and of the Commission. The convention shall adopt by consensus a recommendation on the proposal and transmit it to the IGC. However, the European Council may decide, by a simple majority (but with the prior consent of the European Parliament) not to convene a convention and go directly to the IGC, if it is felt that the extent of the proposed amendments does not justify the convening of a convention.

After this stage, the procedure follows the pattern which has always been applicable: common accord in the IGC on the amendments to be made to the Treaties, and ratification by all the Member States in accordance with their constitutional requirements.

A specific provision (Article 48(5) TEU) states, that 'if, two years after the signature of a treaty amending the Treaties, four fifths of the Member States have ratified it and one or more Member States have encountered difficulties in proceeding with ratification, the matter shall be referred to the European Council'.

One may remark that the so-called 'ordinary' procedure looks so heavy that it might actually be quite 'extraordinary' in the future, or even that it might no longer be used because Member States are not enthusiastic about going for another complete revision of the Treaties in the foreseeable future. This is the reason why the other revision procedures, which aim at specific and partial revisions, are important.[49] A brief review of them will show that, obviously, even for specific and partial revisions, Member States will remain, in all cases, 'the Masters of the Treaties'.

The simplified revision procedure to amend Part Three of the TFEU on internal competences

Part Three of the TFEU contains the details of all EU internal competences. The simplified procedure to amend this Part is set out in Article 48(6) TFEU. Any such revision may, however, 'not increase the competences conferred on the Union in the Treaty'. As compared with the ordinary revision procedure, the simplification consists in dispensing with both the convening of a convention and of an IGC, allowing the amendments to be agreed by a decision of the European Council, acting after consulting the European Parliament and the Commission.[50] This decision will come into force once it has been approved by both a unanimous decision of the European Council and then a normal ratification procedure by all Member States, in accordance with their respective constitutional requirements.

Simplified revision procedures in specific cases

A few provisions allow the Council, acting by unanimity, to amend the scope of a specific legal basis or the provisions of a protocol:

---

49 For an overview of all *passerelles* and provisions on a simplified revision procedure, see Appendix 3. See also Appendix 1 for an indication of the cases in which the German parliament will have a role as a consequence of the judgment of the German Constitutional Court of 30 June 2009.

50 And the European Central Bank in case of institutional changes in the monetary area.

- Article 25 TEU enables the Council, by unanimity with the consent of the European Parliament and after approval by the Member States in accordance with their respective constitutional requirements, to 'strengthen or to add to the rights' of the EU citizens as laid down in Article 20(2) TEU. This Article contains the list of citizens' rights, such as the right to move freely within the Union, the right to vote and to stand as candidates in European and municipal elections, and so on. This possibility of adding to the list of citizens' rights already existed (Article 22, 2nd subparagraph, TEC);
- in three cases, in the FSJ field, the Council, by unanimity and with the consent of the European Parliament, but without the need for a ratification procedure in the Member States, is allowed to extend the scope of a provision. It can extend the list of specific aspects of criminal procedure (Article 82(2)(d) TFEU), the list of areas of crime where minimum rules concerning the definition of criminal offences and sanctions may be established (Article 83(1), 3rd subparagraph, TFEU), and it can extend the powers of the European Public Prosecutor's Office (Article 86(4) TFEU);
- two provisions allow the Council to amend, totally or in part, the provisions of certain protocols. Article 126(14) TFEU allows the Council, by unanimity and after consulting the European Parliament and the European Central Bank, to replace Protocol no. 12 on the excessive deficit procedure.[51] The same goes for amending provisions of Protocol no. 5 on the Statute of the European Investment Bank.[52]

Five provisions allow for the amendment of primary law provisions using QMV in the Council. These are the only cases in which the Treaty can be amended by QMV and not by unanimous agreement of the Council members or of the governments of the Member States:

- 'the nature of the composition' of the Economic and Social Committee and of the Committee of the Regions may be reviewed by the Council acting by QMV on a proposal from the Commission (Article 300(5) TFEU);
- the Council and the European Parliament may, in codecision, amend parts of the Statute of the ECB (Article 129(3) TFEU),[53] as well as the

---

51 This possibility already existed under the TEC in Art. 104(14).
52 See Art. 308, 3rd subpara., TFEU. This possibility already existed under the TEC in Art. 266, 3rd subpara.
53 The Council may also, by QMV, after consulting the European Parliament and ECB, amend some other provisions of the ECB Statute (see Art. 129(4) TFEU). This possibility

Statute of the Court of Justice, with the exception of its Title I and Article 64 (Article 281, 2nd subparagraph, TFEU);[54]

- the Council may, five years after the entry into force of the Lisbon Treaty (i.e. as from 1 December 2014), repeal, by QMV, specific rules allowing compensation measures for certain areas affected by the former division of Germany (Articles 98 and 107(2)(c) TFEU).[55]

The *passerelles*

As a result of the debate on whether to switch several provisions to QMV and/or codecision, or whether to allow for a simplified procedure for amending certain provisions or parts of the Treaties, a number of *passerelles* were agreed. These *passerelles* allow either the European Council or the Council to decide by unanimity to switch a particular legal basis from unanimity to QMV or from a special legislative procedure to the ordinary legislative procedure (codecision), without having to follow the full ordinary procedure for revising the Treaties.[56]

The existing *passerelles* in the EU and EC Treaties as in force before the Lisbon Treaty

Some *passerelles* had already been inserted in the Treaties. They have rarely been used. They provided for a less heavy procedure (no IGC, and sometimes consent required from neither the European Parliament nor the national parliaments).[57] They were the following:

- Article 42 of the former TEU, which allowed the Council, by unanimity, to 'communitarise' the whole or parts of the JHA pillar. Such a decision would then have to be ratified by all Member States in accordance with their respective constitutional requirements;
- Article 67(2), 2nd indent, TEC, which allowed the Council, by unanimity and without a ratification procedure in the Member States, to switch

---

of amending the ECB Statute was already in existence for the Council, by QMV, under Art. 107(5) and (6) TEC.

54 The possibility of amending the EU Court of Justice Statute was already in existence for the Council (by unanimity) under Art. 245, 2nd subpara., TEC.

55 See also Declarations nos. 28 and 29 of the IGC on these two provisions.

56 For an overview of all *passerelles* and provisions on a simplified revision procedure, see Appendix 3.

57 Of course, nothing prevents Member States wishing to do so from requesting a consultation or binding resolution from their parliament. Some of them have decided to do so. In Germany this was required by the Constitutional Court in its judgment of 30 June 2009.

the whole or parts of Title IV of Part III of the TEC (on visas, asylum, immigration and other policies, including judicial co-operation in civil matters) to codecision,[58] and to adapt the provisions on the Court's jurisdiction in the same Title;

- Article 137(2), 2nd subparagraph, TEC, which allowed the Council, by unanimity and without a ratification procedure in the Member States, to switch to QMV and codecision for adopting certain measures in the social field (protection of workers in case of termination of their employment contract, the representation and collective defence of workers and conditions of employment of third-country nationals);
- Article 175(2), 2nd subparagraph, TEC, which allowed the Council, by unanimity and without a ratification procedure in the Member States, to switch to QMV for those environment matters which were still subject to unanimity (provisions primarily of a fiscal nature, measures affecting town and country planning, management of water resources and land use).

The *passerelles* after the Lisbon Treaty

The Lisbon Treaty provides both for a general *passerelle* and for sectoral ones.

Article 48(7) TEU provides now for a **general *passerelle*** under which the European Council may decide by unanimity, with the consent of the European Parliament and if no national parliament opposes it within six months, to switch a legal basis from unanimity to QMV or from a special legislative procedure to the ordinary legislative procedure (codecision). It is to be stressed that both governments and national parliaments keep their right of veto in such a case. This general *passerelle* is applicable only to the TFEU and to Title V of the TEU (CFSP), but neither to decisions having military implications or in the area of defence, nor to Titles I to IV and VI of the TEU.

In addition, the Lisbon Treaty keeps or introduces **six sectoral *passerelles*** which are *lex specialis* to the general one:

---

58 This is the only *passerelle* which has been used before the entry into force of the Lisbon Treaty. Within the framework of the pluri-annual JHA programme ('The Hague Programme'), the European Council requested in November 2004 that the Council adopt a decision, based on Art. 67(2), 2nd indent, TEC, to switch to QMV and the codecision procedure the provisions on border crossing, visas, asylum and immigration policy, except those on legal migration. The Decision was adopted on 22 December 2004 and made codecision applicable to these areas as from 1 January 2005 (OJ No. L396, 31 December 2004, 45).

- the Lisbon Treaty retains two of the existing *passerelles* in the social policy and environment fields (Articles 153(2), last subparagraph, TFEU, and 192(2), last subparagraph, TFEU). In both cases the Council, acting unanimously on a proposal from the Commission, after consulting the European Parliament, may decide to make the ordinary legislative procedure applicable in specified cases;
- the Lisbon Treaty adds four new sectoral *passerelles*: one enabling a switch to QMV in CFSP, except for decisions having military or defence implications (Article 31(3) and (4) TEU), one enabling a switch to QMV for the adoption of the multi-annual financial framework (Article 312(2), 2nd subparagraph, TFEU), one enabling a switch to codecision in family law with cross-border implications (Article 81(3) TFEU)[59] and one enabling a switch to QMV or codecision for adopting acts within an enhanced co-operation (with the exception of military or defence matters) (Article 333 TFEU).

Two political observations may derive from what is described in this section:

- the probability of a full-scale 'horizontal' Treaty reform – similar to the Treaties of Maastricht, Amsterdam, Nice and Lisbon – appears to be very weak; this is why the Member States, authors of the Treaties, have provided for specific methods with a view to partial modifications of the Treaties;
- any Treaty revision which might take place according to these specific methods of modification will always remain subject to unanimity or common accord of all Member States, except in minor and very precise cases.

Section 13 Withdrawal of a Member State from the EU

In an enlarged EU, which has committed itself to further enlargements, and could end up with thirty-five Member States and more,[60] thus

---

59 Contrary to the situation under the TEC (Art. 67(2), 2nd indent, TEC), where the *passerelle* did not require the consent from the national parliaments, the *passerelle* under Art. 81(3) TFEU introduces the right for any national parliament to oppose the use of the *passerelle* within a period of six months from the notification of the draft decision on the use of the *passerelle*.

60 The accession negotiations with Croatia started on 17 March 2005 and those with Turkey on 3 October 2005. In addition, paras. 40 to 43 of the Presidency Conclusions at the Thessaloniki European Council of June 2003 reaffirmed 'the European perspective of the Western Balkan countries, which will become an integral part of the EU, once they

increasing the diversity and sometimes the divergence of views and inter-
ests among them, the new provision on voluntary withdrawal from the
EU would be the ultimate way to deal with a serious problem with a
Member State.

Article 50 TEU states that 'Any Member State may decide to withdraw
from the Union in accordance with its own constitutional requirements.'
Then follows a 'divorce' procedure under which, after notification by the
Member State concerned, the Union concludes an agreement with that
State, setting out the arrangements for its withdrawal. The agreement is to
be concluded by the Council, acting by QMV, after obtaining the consent
of the European Parliament, and the Treaties will cease to apply to the
State concerned from the date of entry into force of the agreement or,
failing that, two years after the request for withdrawal, unless that deadline is prolonged by common accord of the European Council (deciding
unanimously) and the State concerned.[61]

Whether such a provision only enshrines a right which previously
existed under international law, and whether it constitutes progress or
a setback, may be assessed differently. It might be observed that, even
in the past, in the case where a Member State would have wanted to
withdraw from the EU, it would have been impossible, in practice, for
the other Member States to oppose this political will. In some of the
Member States such a withdrawal would, in any case, require a revision of
their constitution. In such a case, it would obviously have been necessary
to negotiate an agreement between the EU and the Member State in
question, in order to organise economic and other relations in such a way
as to cause as little disturbance as possible.

---

meet the established criteria' (doc. 11368/03). This 'European perspective' has since been
reiterated several times by the European Council (see, for example, the Conclusions of
19–20 June 2008). These six countries are: the Former Yugoslavian Republic of Macedonia
(FYROM), which the European Council has already recognised as a 'candidate country',
Montenegro, which presented its candidacy at the end of 2008, Albania, which presented
its candidacy in April 2009, Bosnia and Herzegovina, Kosovo (not recognised by all
EU Member States), and Serbia, which presented its candidacy in December 2009. A
'European perspective' has also been requested by other countries, such as Georgia and
the Republic of Moldova. Iceland presented its candidacy in July 2009.

61 For an analysis of withdrawal rights, see R. J. Fried, 'Providing a Constitutional Framework
for Withdrawal from the EU: Article 59 of the Draft European Constitution' (2004) 53
International and Comparative Law Quarterly 407. See also by the same author 'Secession
from the European Union; Checking Out of the Proverbial "Cockroach Motel"' (2004) 27
Fordham Law Journal 590. See also J.-V. Louis, 'Le droit de retrait de l'Union européenne'
(2006) 3–4 *Cahiers de droit européen* 297.

One may note that such a right of withdrawal normally exists in con-federations of states, but not in federal states.

Therefore this provision on withdrawal is politically very significant, as it does clarify a basic issue – that is, that the Union is actually a voluntary association between states which remain sovereign as to the question of whether or not they remain in that association.[62]

---

62 The German Constitutional Court, in its judgment of 30 June 2009, underlined the link between this political significance and the nature of the EU. The Court states that the German Constitution 'prohibits the transfer [to the EU] of competence to decide on its own competence (*Kompetens-Kompetenz*)... steps of [EU] integration... must, in principle, be revocable. For this reason, withdrawal from the European union of integration (*Integrationsverband*) may, regardless of a commitment for an unlimited period under an agreement, not be prevented by other Member States or the autonomous authority of the Union. This is not a secession from a state union (*Staatsverband*)... but merely the withdrawal from a *Staatenverbund* [association of sovereign national States] which is founded on the principle of the reversible self-commitment' (para. 233; see also paras. 329 and 330).

III

Democracy

One of the major aims of the Lisbon Treaty, as set out explicitly in its very short Preamble, is to enhance the 'democratic legitimacy of the Union'.[1] This has been a leitmotiv since the 1993 Maastricht IGC Declaration no. 13,[2] the 1997 Amsterdam Protocol no. 9 on the role of national parliaments in the EU, the 2000 Nice Declaration (see Box 3), which stressed the importance of giving a role to national parliaments, and the 2001 Declaration of Laeken, which insisted on 'the democratic challenge facing Europe' (Box 20).

For the first time, the Lisbon Treaty incorporates in the basic Treaties, right at the beginning of the TEU, a section entitled 'Provisions on

---

1 On this issue, see G. Majone, 'Europe's Democratic Deficit' (1998) 4 *European Law Journal* 5, and *Dilemmas of European Integration. The Ambiguities and Pitfalls of Integration by Stealth* (Oxford University Press, 2005); A. Moravcsik, 'In Defence of the "Democratic Deficit": Reassessing Legitimacy in the European Union' (2002) 40 *Journal of Common Market Studies* 603, and 'What Can We Learn from the Collapse of the European Constitutional Project?' (2006) 47(2) *Politische Vierteljahresschrift* 219; A. Follesdal and S. Hix, 'Why There Is a Democratic Deficit in the EU: A Response to Majone and Moravcsik' (2006) 44 *Journal of Common Market Studies* 537; V. A. Schmidt, *Democracy in Europe: The EU and National Polities* (Oxford University Press, 2006); S. C. Sieberson, 'The Treaty of Lisbon and its Impact on the EU's Democratic Deficit' (2008) 14 *Columbia Journal of European Law* 445; J. H. H. Weiler, 'Does Europe Need a Constitution? Demos, Telos on the German Maastricht Decision' (1995) 1 *European Law Journal* 219, *The Constitution of Europe* (Cambridge, MA: Harvard University Press, 1999), and, with U. R. Haltern and F. C. Mayer, 'European Democracy and its Critique' (1995) 18(3) *West European Policies* 4. See also the judgment of the German Constitutional Court of 30 June 2009 on the Lisbon Treaty, which analyses in detail how and whether the requirement of democracy is, according to that Court, not satisfied at EU level (see Section 17 and Appendix 1).

2 See 'Declaration on the Role of National Parliaments in the European Union', in which the IGC encouraged greater involvement of national parliaments in EU activities, notably through increasing the exchange of information and regular contacts between them and the European Parliament and the early communication, by the governments of the Member States, of legislative proposals tabled by the Commission.

BOX 20. THE DECLARATION ON THE FUTURE OF THE EUROPEAN UNION (LAEKEN, DECEMBER 2001)

...

The European Union derives its legitimacy from the democratic values it projects, the aims it pursues and the powers and instruments it possesses. However, the European project also derives its legitimacy from democratic, transparent and efficient institutions. The national parliaments also contribute towards the legitimacy of the European project. The declaration on the future of the Union, annexed to the Treaty of Nice, stressed the need to examine their role in European integration. More generally, the question arises as to what initiatives we can take to develop a European public area.

The first question is thus how we can increase the democratic legitimacy and transparency of the present institutions, a question which is valid for the three institutions.

... Should the role of the European Parliament be strengthened? Should we extend the right of codecision or not? Should the way in which we elect the members of the European Parliament be reviewed? Should a European electoral constituency be created, or should constituencies continue to be determined nationally? Can the two systems be combined? Should the role of the Council be strengthened? Should the Council act in the same manner in its legislative and its executive capacities? With a view to greater transparency, should the meetings of the Council, at least in its legislative capacity, be public? Should citizens have more access to Council documents? How, finally, should the balance and reciprocal control between the institutions be ensured?

A second question, which also relates to democratic legitimacy, involves the role of national parliaments. Should they be represented in a new institution, alongside the Council and the European Parliament? Should they have a role in areas of European action in which the European Parliament has no competence? Should they focus on the division of competence between Union and Member States, for example through preliminary checking of compliance with the principle of subsidiarity?

...

---

democratic principles' (Articles 9 to 12), in which Article 10 is particularly relevant (Box 21).

Moreover, and more concretely, the Lisbon Treaty brings a whole set of new provisions aiming at enhancing the democratic legitimacy of the Union, among which the more important aim at strengthening the role of

---

BOX 21. ARTICLE 10 TEU

1. The functioning of the Union shall be founded on representative democracy.
2. Citizens are directly represented at Union level in the European Parliament.
3. Member States are represented in the European Council by their Heads of State or Government and in the Council by their governments, themselves democratically accountable either to their national Parliaments, or to their citizens.
4. Every citizen shall have the right to participate in the democratic life of the Union. Decisions shall be taken as openly and as closely as possible to the citizen.
5. Political parties at European level contribute to forming European political awareness and to expressing the will of citizens of the Union.

---

the European Parliament, giving a concrete role to national parliaments and providing for citizen's initiatives.[3]

Section 14 The European Parliament

The European Parliament is the only institution of the European Union whose members are elected by direct universal suffrage of all citizens of the EU. Logically, if one tried to 'democratise' the way the EU functions, one would think about increasing the European Parliament's powers. Thus, in

---

3 In its above-mentioned judgment of 30 June 2009, the German Constitutional Court notes that the German Constitution (the Basic Law) 'permits derogations from the organisational principles of democracy applying on the national level which are due to the requirements of a European Union that is based on the principle of equality of States and has been negotiated under the law of international agreements' (para. 227). It states that 'the shape of the [EU] must comply with democratic principles . . . European integration may neither result in the system of democratic rule in Germany being undermined, nor may the supranational public authority as such fail to fulfil fundamental democratic requirements' (para. 244). On the issue of 'equality between States', see in Section 8 the discussions which were held during the 2003–4 IGC.

For its part, the Czech Constitutional Court, in its second judgment on 3 November 2009, replied to the objection of a democratic deficit in the EU with regard to Art. 10(1) TEU on representative democracy, that this Article is directed at processes both at the European and domestic level, and not only at the European Parliament. According to the Court, the European Parliament is not an exclusive source of democratic legitimacy for decisions adopted on the EU level. That legitimacy derives from a combination of structures existing both on the domestic and European levels, and it is not possible to require absolute equality among voters in individual Member States. That would be possible only if decisions in the EU were adopted while at the same time ruling out legitimating connections to governments, and above all to legislative assemblies in the individual Member States (Czech Constitutional Court, press release, 3 November 2009).

treaty after treaty, the European Parliament's powers have been progressively and regularly increased. Named as the 'Assembly' by the original Treaties, it gave itself the name 'European Parliament' as soon as 1962, a name which was officially recognised only in 1986, in the Single European Act. In 1976 it was decided that its members would be directly elected by the citizens, and the first direct elections took place in 1979.[4] Since then, its powers have steadily increased. From a mere consultative role, it now has a role of codecision for most legislative acts, and a similar role in the adoption of the budget of the EU. The appointment of the Commission requires its consent. Moreover, the Commission is responsible to the European Parliament, which may vote on a motion of censure entailing the resignation of the Commission as a body. The European Parliament has also, among other powers, the ability to establish temporary committees of inquiry, to receive petitions from citizens, to elect the European Ombudsman, to put oral or written questions to the Commission and to the Council, and so on.

The composition of the European Parliament

According to Article 14(2) TEU, 'the European Parliament shall be composed of representatives of the Union's citizens . . . elected for a term of five years by direct universal suffrage in a free and secret ballot'. This wording is different from Article 190(1) TEC, according to which MEPs were 'representatives of the peoples of the States brought together in the Community'.[5]

This new wording follows that used in Article 10(1) and (2) TEU, according to which the functioning of the EU is founded on 'representative

---

4 See the Act concerning the election of representatives of the European Parliament by direct universal suffrage, annexed to Council Decision 76/787/ECSC, EEC, Euratom (OL No. L278, 8 October 1976, 5, last amended in 2002). The election of the European Parliament by direct universal suffrage was one of the conditions set out by the German Constitutional Court in its *Solange I* case of 29 May 1974 for accepting the primacy of EU law over German law (see BVerfGE 37, 271, which may be found translated into English at www.ucl.ac.uk).

5 For the German Constitutional Court, this change of wording has no consequence because in its view 'even after the new formulation [of] Art. 14.2 TEU Lisbon . . . the [EP] is not a body of representation of a sovereign European people. This is reflected in the fact that it, as the representation of the peoples in their respectively assigned national contingents of Members, is not laid out as a body of representation of the citizens of the Union as an undistinguished unity according to the principle of electoral equality' (para. 280; see also para. 284). For an overview of the different rules applied in each of the twenty-seven Member States for the 2009 European elections, see *Agence Europe*, No. 2514, 13 March 2009.

democracy' and 'citizens are directly represented at Union level in the [EP]'.

The number of MEPs 'shall not exceed seven hundred and fifty in number, plus the President' (i.e. 751). 'Representation of citizens shall be degressively proportional, with a minimum threshold of six members per Member State. No Member State shall be allocated more than ninety-six seats' (Article 14(2) TEU). This increases the number of MEPs from 736, as provided for by Article 190(1) TEC, as amended by the 2005 Accession Act,[6] to 751.

The minimum number of seats per Member State was hotly debated until the end of the 2003–4 IGC. The more populated states wanted a minimum number of four, the less populated ones a minimum of six. The final result, which provides for a minimum of six seats, is therefore favourable to the smaller Member States. It was part of an interlinked package which included the reduction in the number of Commissioners and the reform of the method of calculation of the votes in the Council, both reforms which had been very difficult for the smaller Member States to accept.[7]

The criteria retained for the European Parliament's composition ('degressively proportional', with an upper limit of ninety-six seats for a given Member State and a lower limit of six) are not sufficient to give automatically a single ready-made determination of the number of seats for each of the Member States.[8] Therefore Article 14(2) TEU provides that the European Council has to adopt by unanimity, on the initiative of the European Parliament and with its consent, a decision establishing the future composition of the European Parliament in accordance with these criteria. If the Lisbon Treaty had entered into force on 1 January 2009 as originally foreseen (see Article 6(2) of the Lisbon Treaty), this

---

6 Art. 9(2) of the Accession Act of Bulgaria and Romania provided for a total number of MEPs of 736. The European elections of June 2009 took place in accordance with these provisions.

7 Since then, the package has been reopened with the political decision of the European Council in December 2008 to abandon the idea of a 'reduced' Commission (see para. 2 of the Presidency Conclusions, doc. 17271/1/08 REV 1, repeated in the June 2009 Presidency Conclusions, as part of the package of solutions for enabling a second referendum in Ireland). This still had to be formalised in the appropriate legal form at the time of writing.

8 In its judgment of 30 June 2009, the German Constitutional Court is very critical of these upper and lower limits on the number of MEPs: 'the result of this is that the weight of the vote of a citizen from a Member State with a low number of inhabitants may be about twelve times the weight of the vote of a citizen from a Member State with a high number of inhabitants' (para. 284; see also para. 285).

decision should have been adopted in due time before the elections of June 2009.[9] During the IGC period, the European Parliament approved a draft decision[10] in order for the European Council to give its political agreement on the draft, in advance of the entry into force of the Lisbon Treaty, so that the decision could be adopted formally immediately upon entry into force of the Treaty. However, an unexpected obstacle was raised by Italy. In view of its population (59,131,300 on 1 January 2007), Italy would have obtained, according to the calculations made and the proposal put forward by the European Parliament, seventy-one seats, while the United Kingdom (60,833,800) would have obtained seventy-two seats and France (63,392,100) would have obtained seventy-four seats. The Italian political class bluntly refused this proposal. It was only at the very end of the Lisbon IGC, at the level of heads of state or government in Lisbon on 18 October 2007, that a solution was found, according to which the European Parliament would not have 750 seats, but '750 plus the President', which obviously makes 751, as the President is also a member of the European Parliament! Declaration no. 4 of the IGC on the composition of the European Parliament states that 'the additional seat in the European Parliament will be attributed to Italy'. The European Parliament did not object.

However, due notably to the negative Irish referendum in June 2008, the Lisbon Treaty could not enter into force before the European elections took place on 4–7 June 2009. As all the institutional changes incorporated into the new Treaty are carefully balanced and inextricably linked to each other, something had to be done in order to re-establish a balance. This is the reason why, at the December 2008 European Council, the following Declaration was adopted:[11]

> In the event that the Treaty of Lisbon enters into force after the European elections of June 2009, transitional measures will be adopted as soon as possible, in accordance with the necessary legal procedures, in order to increase, until the end of the 2009–2014 legislative period, in conformity with the numbers provided for in the framework of the IGC which approved the Treaty of Lisbon, the number of MEPs of the twelve Member

---

9 See Art. 2, 1st subpara., of Protocol no. 36 on transitional provisions which provided for the European Council to adopt this Decision 'in good time before the 2009 European Parliament elections'.

10 See draft Decision annexed to the European Parliament's Resolution dated 11 October 2007 and Declaration no. 5 of the Lisbon IGC.

11 See Presidency Conclusions, European Council, 11–12 December 2008 (Annex 1 to doc. 17271/1/08 REV 1).

States for which the number of MEPs was set to increase. Therefore, the total number of MEPs will rise from 736 to 754 until the end of the 2009–2014 legislative period. The objective is that this modification should enter into force, if possible, during the year 2010.

This Declaration was confirmed at the June 2009 European Council and Annex 4 to the Presidency Conclusions set out the detailed numbers of additional MEPs for each of the twelve Member States which will share the eighteen supplementary MEPs.[12] The Annex also indicates the procedure by which these additional MEPs will be designated. This still had to be formalised in the appropriate legal form at the time of writing (through an amendment of Article 2 of Protocol no. 36 on transitional provisions).

The additional powers of the European Parliament

The European Parliament's powers have been very much increased by the Lisbon Treaty, first through an extension of the scope of the codecision procedure, but also in a number of other ways.

Extension in the scope of codecision

Codecision has become the 'ordinary legislative procedure'. According to Article 289 TFEU, 'the ordinary legislative procedure shall consist in the joint adoption by the European Parliament and the Council of a regulation, directive or decision on a proposal from the Commission'. The scope of codecision has been extended to about thirty more cases of variable importance and provided for in fourteen new legal bases.[13] The most significant sectors of extension are the area of freedom, security and justice (FSJ area), co-ordination of social security for migrant workers, culture, measures necessary for the use of the euro, the structural and cohesion funds, the establishment at EU level of intellectual property

---

12 See Presidency Conclusions, European Council, 18–19 June 2009 (doc. 11225/1/09 REV 1). The additional seats will be distributed as follows: Bulgaria (1), Spain (4), France (2), Italy (1), Latvia (1), Malta (1), Netherlands (1), Austria (2), Poland (1), Slovenia (1), Sweden (2) and United Kingdom (1). Germany will keep its 99 MEPs until the 2014 elections (i.e. above the 96 maximum limit) as they were elected for five years in 2009.

13 See in Appendix 4 the list of about thirty existing cases which are switched to codecision. To this should be added the fourteen new legal bases which provide for the codecision procedure. See in Appendix 5 the list of the new legal bases; there are thirty-one cases where QMV in the Council applies and, for fourteen of those, where codecision also applies.

rights and other centralised regimes, common organisation of the markets and general objectives in agriculture, definition of the framework for implementing the common commercial policy, amendments to the Statute of the Court of Justice and rules on 'comitology'.

This extension will mean that both the European Parliament and the Council, in order to be efficient, will have to agree to adopt more acts during the first reading. This working method has been developed in order to reduce delays in the legislative procedure, by avoiding the time-consuming second (and possibly even third) readings and meetings of the Conciliation Committee (see Article 294 TFEU). This working method consists in organising informal meetings (called 'trilogues') between the Council Presidency (accompanied by the Council Secretariat and Legal Service), the Commission's representatives and the European Parliament's Rapporteur. These meetings aim at informally approving texts which can then be approved officially both by the European Parliament and by the Council in the same terms, allowing the legislative procedure to be finished with only a 'first reading'. This has proved to be very effective.[14]

Other cases of an increase in the European Parliament's powers

In addition to the extension of the scope of codecision, the European Parliament has also gained the following new powers:

- on the **appointment of the Commission**, the European Parliament has the right to 'elect'[15] the President of the Commission proposed by the European Council, whose proposal, adopted by QMV, has to take into account the results of the European elections (Article 17(7) TEU). If the European Parliament refuses to elect its nominee, the European Council has to present another candidate.[16] The European Parliament

---

14 See J.-P. Jacqué, 'Une vision réaliste de la procédure de codécision', in *Mélanges en hommage à Georges Vandersanden – Promenades au sein du droit européen* (Brussels: Bruylant, 2008), 183.

15 To be compared with Art. 214(2), 1st subpara. TEC which provided that the European Parliament 'shall approve' the nomination decided by the Council, meeting in the composition of heads of state or government.

16 As events in autumn 2004 relating to the nomination of the Commission headed by Mr Barroso showed, when the European Parliament successfully opposed the inclusion of a person in the list of Commissioners, the European Parliament is quite ready to make full use of the powers it is granted by the Treaty to approve the Commission President and the college of Commissioners. It has even, for some time and going beyond what is laid down in the Treaty, developed a practice of hearing each Commissioner-designate individually before taking its decision to approve the whole Commission. It was during this procedure

also has the right to approve the High Representative, as a member of the Commission (Article 17(7), 3rd subparagraph, TEU);

- on the **budget**, the new procedure increases the European Parliament's powers (although the 2003–4 IGC modified the Convention's draft in order to give more powers to the Council) because there is no longer so-called 'compulsory expenditure' (on which the Council had the last word), as opposed to 'non-compulsory expenditure' (on which the European Parliament had the last word). Under the TFEU, the European Parliament now 'co-decides' with the Council on all expenditure (Article 314 TFEU). An important point remains to be decided – that is, how the procedure of transfers will be organised, a procedure which will have to be agreed upon by the European Parliament and the Council as part of the Financial Regulation (see Section 37);
- on the conclusion of **international agreements** by the EU, the scope of the procedures requiring the consent of the European Parliament in some cases, or its mandatory consultation in other cases, have both been enlarged (Article 218(6) TFEU). Moreover, the European Parliament 'shall be immediately and fully informed at all steps of the procedure' of negotiations of international agreements on behalf of the EU (Article 218(10) TFEU); this might need appropriate procedures in order to preserve the confidentiality of the negotiations;
- on the **European External Action Service** (EEAS), the European Parliament has to be consulted on the Council Decision on the organisation and functioning of the EEAS (Article 27(3) TEU);
- on **delegated and implementing acts**, the European Parliament has been given a role in the control of delegated powers (Article 290 TFEU) and a codecision power for the adoption of the next 'Comitology' Decision which, before the Lisbon Treaty, was adopted by the Council, after consulting the European Parliament (Article 291 TFEU, on this issue, see Section 11);
- on the **FSJ area**, the European Parliament has been given a role for scrutinising or evaluating Europol and Eurojust (Articles 85(1), 3rd subparagraph, and 88(2), 2nd subparagraph, TEU) as well as a right

---

of hearings in September 2004 that some of the Parliamentary Committees responsible for such hearings expressed concerns, in particular about one of the Commissioner-designates. The risk of a negative vote by the European Parliament on 27 October 2004 led President Barroso to withdraw his team from the approval vote and reshuffle it before submitting it to a successful vote of approval on 18 November 2004. A similar situation occurred again in 2009/2010.

to be informed of the content and results of the 'mutual evaluation' system under Article 70 TEU;

- on the **'flexibility clause'**, the consent of the European Parliament is now required to any legal act adopted by the Council on the basis of this clause – that is, Article 352 TFEU (ex-Article 308 TEC). This Article allows for EU action when it is necessary to attain one of the objectives of the Treaties but the Treaties have not provided the specific necessary powers. The Council had, before the Lisbon Treaty, to act unanimously after consulting the European Parliament. It now has the obligation to obtain the consent of the European Parliament;[17]
- on the **revision of the Treaties**, the European Parliament is now allowed to propose a revision of the Treaties, either in the ordinary proce- dure for revision or in the simplified procedures (Article 48 TEU). This was a long-standing request by the European Parliament which, up to the Lisbon Treaty, had been regularly rejected by the Member States;
- on the possible **withdrawal of a Member State from the Union**, the consent of the European Parliament is now required to the agreement setting out the arrangement for such a withdrawal (Article 50(2) TEU).

*

On the whole, the Lisbon Treaty considerably strengthens the European Parliament's powers. This is certainly due to two factors:

---

17 In its judgment of 30 June 2009, the German Constitutional Court criticised the amended version of Art. 352 TFEU as compared with its previous version in Art. 308 TEC, which had existed ever since the 1957 Rome Treaty. The Court stated that this new version 'must lead to a new assessment of the provision. Article 352 TFEU is no longer restricted to the attainment of objectives in the context of the common market but makes reference to the 'policies defined in the Treaties' (para. 327). For the Court, 'the newly worded provision makes it possible to substantially amend Treaty foundations of the European Union without the mandatory participation of legislative bodies beyond the Member States' executive powers' (para. 328). For that reason, the Court stated that, prior to its approval of the use of Art. 352 TFEU, the German government must obtain a formal authorisation from the German parliament, as in the case of an amendment to the Treaties. The Constitutional Court might in fact have reached the same conclusion before: it is well known that the Court of Justice has, for years, interpreted Art. 308 TEC as if the reference to the common market was not there. On top of that, Art. 352 TFEU has a much narrower scope than had Art. 308 TEC, and its use is subject to the consent of the European Parliament and to the information of all national parliaments. The only logical explanation is that the Constitutional Court wished to stress that, in its opinion, the Court of Justice has taken too many liberties with its interpretation of the Treaties.

- the fact that the Convention which prepared the draft Constitutional Treaty, and whose suggestions on this matter were not greatly modified, was dominated by very active and clever MEPs;
- the fact that all Member States agreed that something had to be done in order to convince the EU citizens that the EU is a democratic entity and that its decision-making process is effectively in the hands of elected politicians.

Without any doubt, this increase in powers will have an impact on the balance of powers between the institutions (see Section 30). It remains to be seen whether the EU citizens will take this increase of the European Parliament's powers into account when deciding whether to participate in the next European elections, in 2014 (see, above, Box 5 on the trend in the turnout in European elections). So far, this factor has had no impact on the turnout in the European elections, which has continued its steady decline. It could be argued that at the June 2009 elections it was not clear that the Lisbon Treaty, and the increase in the European Parliament's powers for which it provided, would enter into force. However, one obvious difficulty is that the European election campaigns are run on national issues rather than on European ones. The European elections are often used as a 'mock' election indicating the popularity of the government before the 'real' elections – which, in the minds of most electors, are and remain the national legislative and/or presidential ones.[18]

Section 15 The national parliaments

The 'role of national Parliaments in the European architecture' was one of the four questions put by the 'Declaration on the future of the Union' adopted at the end of the Nice IGC in 2000. Until 1979, the members of the European Parliament were members of national parliaments designated by the latter. The breaking of this link had serious effects. National parliaments had the feeling that a part of their legislative power had been transferred to their governments. Some of them organised themselves in order to better control the European policy of their governments; most of them did not.

---

18 In its judgment of 30 June 2009, the German Constitutional Court noted that 'the public perception of factual issues and of political leaders remains connected to a considerable extent to patterns of identification which are related to the nation-State, language, history and culture' (para. 251). This is indeed the case.

The long journey of the national parliaments: from being victims of European integration to becoming actors in the EU decision-making process[19]

Ever since its beginning, European integration has been based on the fact that Member States have accepted exercising their powers in common in certain fields. Therefore some powers were transferred from the national institutions to the EU institutions in certain fields. The transfers of power were increased with successive Treaties. This deprived national parliaments of direct powers on the adoption of legislative acts in those fields. Because the Council is the most important EU decision-making institution, the decision-making process of the EU is very much influenced by national governments. Therefore a solution has to be that national parliaments, having lost their direct powers at national level, should control the way their respective governments act in the EU, notwithstanding the role of the European Parliament.

In some EU Member States, the reaction has been quick in order to adapt to this new situation. National parliaments have changed their rules of procedure, they have negotiated new practical procedures with their governments, and amendments have been made to national constitutions, in order to give national parliaments more control over the decisions made by the representatives of their governments in the EU Council.

Reforms of this kind have been quicker and more substantial in the Member States where, traditionally, national parliaments have a strong political position, such as in Denmark,[20] the United Kingdom and, latterly, in other Nordic countries.

However, European Affairs Committees have now been established in the parliaments of all EU Member States, and they have progressively strengthened their position vis-à-vis their government. Some national constitutions have been modified in order to establish some binding rules for governments to consult and wait for the opinion of their parliament. In practice, representatives of the governments of the Member States in the Council now frequently refer to 'parliamentary scrutiny reserves', which prevent them from voting in favour of an act or decision because they have not yet obtained the opinion (or approval) of their national parliament.

---

19 This formulation is borrowed from the interesting book, J. O'Brennan and T. Raunio (eds.) *National Parliaments within the Enlarged European Union: From 'Victims' of Integration to Competitive Actors* (New York: Routledge, 2007).

20 The system of scrutiny established by the Folketing (Danish parliament) was the earliest.

National parliaments of the Member States also began to organise co-operation between themselves, by establishing in 1989 the Conference of Community and European Affairs Committees of Parliaments of the EU (known as 'COSAC').[21] They have been requesting for years, notably through their meetings in the COSAC, that the EU institutions, in particular when drafting and adopting legislative acts, should take their opinions into account.

The EU Treaties did formally recognise the role of national parliaments, first through a Declaration on the role of national parliaments in the EU (annexed to the Final Act of the Maastricht IGC),[22] then in Protocols (annexed to the Treaties by the Amsterdam and Nice Treaties). The 1997 Protocol on the role of national parliaments in the EU did not go very far. Its paragraph 3 provided that 'a six-week period shall elapse between a legislative proposal or a proposal for a measure to be adopted under Title VI of the Treaty on European Union [i.e. in the JHA area] being made available in all languages to the European Parliament and the Council by the Commission and the date when it is placed on a Council agenda for decision either for the adoption of an act or for adoption of a common position'. This period of six weeks was supposed to allow the governments of the Member States to inform their national parliaments.

The Lisbon Treaty has given a significant response to the demands of the national parliaments, by conferring a number of rights on them, including, in particular, the right to receive information directly from the EU institutions (i.e. not through their own government) and a direct role

---

21 'COSAC' is an acronym from the full name of this Conference in French: 'Conférence des Organes Spécialisés dans les Affaires Communautaires et européennes des parlements de l'Union européenne'. The Protocol on the role of national parliaments in the European Union, as it was in force before the Lisbon Treaty, provided in Part II (paras. 4 to 7) that the Conference of European Affairs Committees of national parliaments 'may make any contribution it deems appropriate for the attention of the institutions of the European Union'. Under the Lisbon Treaty, the role of COSAC, whose official name is now the Conference of Parliamentary Committees for Union Affairs, is provided for in Art. 10 of Protocol no. 1. Among the publications of COSAC, see in particular the 12th Bi-Annual Report, 'Developments in EU Procedures and Practices Relevant to Parliamentary Scrutiny', presented by the COSAC Secretariat to the XLII COSAC in Stockholm on 5–6 October 2009 (available at www.cosac.eu).

22 In this Declaration the IGC underlined the importance of encouraging 'greater involvement of national parliaments in the activities of the [EU]'. To this end, 'the exchange of information between national parliaments and the [EP] should be stepped up' through 'the granting of appropriate reciprocal facilities and regular meetings'. Governments were encouraged to 'ensure . . . that national parliaments receive Commission proposals for legislation in good time for information and possible examination'.

in checking that the EU institutions respect the principle of subsidiarity (Article 5 TEU and Protocol no. 2). They are also given a role in different evaluation and monitoring mechanisms in the FSJ area (Articles 70, 85 and 88 TFEU). A significant increase in the powers of the national parliaments has been obtained as compared with the failed Constitutional Treaty, in particular under the impetus of the government of the Netherlands.

The fact that the European Parliament did not fully succeed in clearly and incontrovertibly establishing itself as providing *the* solution for the democratic legitimacy which the EU needs, was one of the reasons why the Lisbon Treaty gave a role to national parliaments in the EU legislative process. However, the latter role will not be easy to fulfil. First, the Lisbon Treaty's provisions will be effective if and when national parliaments reinforce their co-operation, through the COSAC or otherwise (e.g. through the establishment of a secretariat in Brussels). Second, in order to have an influence national parliaments should be able to intervene early in the process, since many draft EU legislative acts, before their adoption by the Council as so-called 'A-items' (i.e. without discussion at the Council), have already been approved at the level of the Council's working groups or Coreper (even though they are only drafts and their approval at the level of Council preparatory bodies is also given upon instructions from the governments). One has to remember that the deadline of eight weeks[23] given to national parliaments to intervene in the process is very short.

This is why the mechanism established by the Lisbon Treaty is still seen as insufficient by some Member States, which are looking for additional specific national mechanisms. This is more necessary in some countries than in others, since the extent of each parliament's control over the positions taken by the representative of its government in the EU Council and in the European Council is, for the time being, very different according to the Member State concerned.[24] In this regard, the Danish model still appears to be one of the most effective systems in practice. The German parliament has now obtained important new powers as well, following the Constitutional Court judgment of 30 June 2009. In other Member States,

---

23 See Art. 4 of Protocol no. 1 on the role of national parliaments in the EU and Art. 6 of Protocol no. 2 on the application of the principle of subsidiarity and proportionality.

24 The Danish Folketing, the Finnish Eduskunta and the Swedish Riksdag are more proactive and engaged in EU decision-making than other national parliaments (see H. Hegeland, 'The European Union in National Parliaments: Domestic or Foreign Policy? A Study of Nordic Parliamentary Systems', in O'Brennan and Raunio, *National Parliaments within the Enlarged European Union*, 95).

the ratification process of the Lisbon Treaty also provided the opportunity to negotiate and obtain more powers for the national parliament. This was the case in some countries (in France and in Portugal for instance) where the constitution has been amended to give an enhanced role to the parliament.

There are two reasons to be optimistic.

First, national parliaments now exercise deeper and tighter control than ever before over their government's positions on EU issues.

Second, it is to be hoped that the provisions of the Lisbon Treaty will be a point of departure for all national parliaments to invest more time and resources on EU issues. The direct and swift flow of information on EU issues allows them to be informed and to play a role, if they so wish.

However, the fact remains that the actual balance of powers between government and parliament is different from one EU Member State to another, according to their respective constitutional texts, practices and political cultures. The effectiveness of any mechanism will depend in the first place on the national political culture. Therefore, *if there is a need to provide further democratic legitimacy in the EU, the answer is mainly to be found at the national level.*

*

Article 12 TEU highlights all the powers attributed to national parliaments by the Lisbon Treaty (see Box 22). Two Protocols develop some of these powers, Protocol no. 1 on the role of national parliaments in the EU (which replaced the 1997 Protocol) and Protocol no. 2 on the application of the principles of subsidiarity and proportionality.

BOX 22. ARTICLE 12 TEU

National Parliaments contribute actively to the good functioning of the Union:

(a) through being informed by the institutions of the Union and having draft legislative acts of the Union forwarded to them in accordance with the Protocol on the role of national Parliaments in the European Union;

(b) by seeing to it that the principle of subsidiarity is respected in accordance with the procedures provided for in the Protocol on the application of the principles of subsidiarity and proportionality;

(c) by taking part, within the framework of the area of freedom, security and justice, in the evaluation mechanisms for the implementation of the Union policies in that area, in accordance with Article 70 [TFEU], and through being involved in

> the political monitoring of Europol and the evaluation of Eurojust's activities in accordance with Articles 88 and 85 of that Treaty;
> (d) by taking part in the revision procedures of the Treaties, in accordance with Article 48 [TEU];
> (e) by being notified of applications for accession to the Union, in accordance with Article 49 [TEU];
> (f) by taking part in the inter-parliamentary cooperation between national Parliaments and with the European Parliament, in accordance with the Protocol on the role of national Parliaments in the European Union.

A right of direct information from the EU institutions and a direct role in controlling respect for the principle of subsidiarity

Protocol no. 1 on the role of national parliaments in the EU and Protocol no. 2 on the application of the principles of subsidiarity and proportionality provide for direct relationships between EU institutions and national parliaments. Such a direct link is an innovation as compared with the past situation, where information had to go via national governments, as is the normal procedure in all 'classic' international organisations.[25] Not only all draft EU legislative acts, but also EU legislative programmes, as well as consultative documents from the Commission on legislative matters, Council minutes of its deliberations on legislative acts and the annual report of the Court of Auditors are now forwarded directly by the EU institutions concerned to the national parliaments for scrutiny and comments.

As mentioned above, before the Lisbon Treaty legislative acts could not be adopted by the EU institutions before a six-week period had elapsed from the transmission of the draft act to the EU Legislature. The transmission has now to take place in all official languages directly to national parliaments and on the same date as the transmission to the European Parliament and to the Council. And the period has now been increased to eight weeks. This increase to eight weeks is an improvement,

25 Already before the entry into force of the Lisbon Treaty, Mr Barroso, President of the Commission, took the initiative, in May 2006, to further enhance links with the national parliaments (see Commission Communication, 'A Citizen's Agenda – Delivering Results for Europe', COM(2006) 211 of 10 May 2006). This consisted, in particular, of sending information directly from the Commission to national parliaments. After three years this initiative has allowed the Commission to receive 525 opinions from national parliaments on Commission proposals. In addition, members of the Barroso Commission held over 550 meetings with national parliaments during the period 2005–9 (see the 2008 Annual Report from the Commission, COM(2009) 343 final).

but probably does not go far enough, especially as, in order to be effective, national parliaments will have to organise concertation between them (see Articles 9 and 10 of Protocol no. 1), which will obviously be time-consuming.[26]

A national parliament[27] may send, within eight weeks from such transmission, a reasoned opinion to the EU institutions stating why it considers that the draft legislative act does not comply with the principle of subsidiarity.[28] Such reasoned opinion must be taken into account by the authors of the draft legislative act.

The important role given to the national parliaments by the Lisbon Treaty obliged France to amend its Constitution, following the decision of its Conseil Constitutionnel.[29]

It remains to be seen whether national parliaments will try and organise co-operation among themselves in order to exercise their new powers better. COSAC, already in 2008, initiated a reflection in this direction. It has established a working group mandated to consider arrangements for the implementation of the new provisions of the Treaty.

The 'yellow card'

The Constitutional Treaty included a further step, nicknamed the 'yellow card' system, after soccer vocabulary.[30] This system, which was taken over in the Lisbon Treaty, provides that, if a reasoned opinion is issued

26 In its judgment of 30 June 2009, the German Constitutional Court notes that 'the effectiveness of this mechanism depends on the extent to which the national parliaments will be able to make organisational arrangements that place them in a position to make appropriate use of the mechanism within the short period of eight weeks' (para. 305).

27 In Declaration no. 51 to the Final Act of the IGC, Belgium stated that 'where the national parliamentary system is not unicameral, the provisions apply to the component chambers' in accordance with its constitutional law. According to the Constitution of Belgium, it is not only parliament chambers at the federal level which are component chambers, but also parliamentary assemblies of the Communities and of the Regions.

28 See Art. 6 of Protocol no. 2 on the application of the principles of subsidiarity and proportionality. On the control of subsidiarity by the national parliaments, see G. A. Bermann, 'The Lisbon Treaty: The Irish "No": National Parliament and Subsidiarity: An Outsider's View' (2008) 4 *European Constitutional Law Review* 453; J.-V. Louis, 'National Parliaments and the Principle of Subsidiarity: Legal Options and Practical Limits' (2008) 4 *European Constitutional Law Review* 429.

29 Decision of the Conseil Constitutionnel Nr. 2007–560 DC, 20 December 2007 and Constitutional law N. 2008–103, 4 February 2008 (new Arts. 88-6 and 88-7 of the 1958 French Constitution).

30 As opposed to a 'red card' system which would have allowed national parliaments to put a halt directly to the EU legislative process.

representing one-third of the total number of votes allocated to national parliaments (eighteen votes out of a total of fifty-four votes) for such purposes,[31] 'the draft must be reviewed'. Each national parliament is allocated two votes, which gives a total of fifty-four votes for an EU of twenty-seven Member States.[32] This system was considered insufficient by the Netherlands. During the 2007 German Presidency, in particular at the end of the negotiation of the IGC mandate at the European Council of June 2007, the Netherlands negotiated and obtained an additional specific mechanism, the 'orange card', which is applicable only to the codecision procedure.

The 'orange card'

Under this additional mechanism, where a reasoned opinion on the non-compliance of a codecision proposal with the principle of subsidiarity represents at least a simple majority of the votes allocated to the national parliaments (i.e. twenty-eight votes out of fifty-four), 'the proposal must be reviewed. After such review, the Commission may decide to maintain, amend or withdraw the proposal.'[33] If the Commission maintains its proposal, it must justify this by a reasoned opinion which, together with the reasoned opinions of the national parliaments, are to be submitted to the European Parliament and the Council for consideration. In that case, if by a majority of 55 per cent of the members of the Council *or* a majority of the votes cast in the European Parliament, at least one branch of the EU legislature is of the opinion that the proposal is not compatible with the principle of subsidiarity, 'the legislative proposal shall not be given further consideration'.[34]

Therefore, to follow the soccer vocabulary, we are close to a 'red card', but not quite. This is why some, also taking into account the fact that the national colour of the Netherlands is orange, christened this complicated system with the name of 'orange card'. Whatever the legal limits of this 'orange card', it would be politically difficult for the Commission, if the case arises, to continue with the procedure for the adoption of a given proposal when a significant number of national parliaments consider it to be contrary to the principle of subsidiarity.

---

31 Or a quarter of the total votes in the FSJ Area – that is, fourteen votes out of fifty-four.
32 See Art. 7(2) of Protocol no. 2.
33 Art. 7(3), 1st subpara., of Protocol no. 2.
34 Art. 7(3), 2nd subpara. of Protocol no. 2.

The right to bring an action for annulment of an EU act in case of infringement of the subsidiarity principle

The jurisdiction of the Court of Justice to review the legality of EU legislative acts on grounds of infringement of the principle of subsidiarity in an action for annulment brought by a Member State is explicitly confirmed. Protocol no. 2 on the application of the principle of subsidiarity even adds new rights to bring actions in the EU Court of Justice.

Article 8 of Protocol no. 2 gives national parliaments access to the EU Court of Justice. It allows actions for annulment to be brought by Member States 'or notified by them in accordance with their legal order on behalf of their national parliament or a chamber thereof' on grounds of infringement of the principle of subsidiarity by a legislative act.[35]

This new right is a real novelty compared with previous Treaties. Each Member State of course has to determine whether, and if so how, to give this possibility to its parliament, a possibility which may be almost a direct right, the Member State limiting itself to notifying the action brought by its national parliament.

Scrutiny of activities in the area of Freedom, Security and Justice (FSJ)

In the field of FSJ, national parliaments have to be informed, as is also the case for the European Parliament, of the content and results of the evaluation system of the implementation of FSJ policies by Member States. This system is to be put in place by the Council (Article 70 TFEU). National parliaments will also participate, together with the European Parliament, in a scrutiny procedure of Europol's activities to be laid down by a regulation adopted by codecision (Article 88(2), 3rd subparagraph, TFEU). The same will apply to their involvement in the evaluation of Eurojust's activities (Article 85(1), 3rd subparagraph, TFEU).

As regards these new provisions, some national parliaments have begun to reflect on the way they could be implemented.[36] How better to organise the 'association' of national parliaments with the control of the activities

---

35 In its judgment of 30 June 2009, the German Constitutional Court notes that 'it will . . . be decisive whether the right of national parliaments . . . to bring action will be extended to the question, which precedes the monitoring of the principle of subsidiarity, of whether the [EU] has competence for the specific lawmaking project' (para. 305).

36 See French Senate, Meeting of the EU Delegation, 11 June 2008, Internet site of the French Senate.

of Europol and Eurojust by the European Parliament? Should it entail the establishment of mixed committees between the European Parliament and the national parliaments? What would be the scope of the activities of these mixed committees?

In addition, as regards measures concerning family law with cross-border implications, which the Council can adopt by unanimity, the Treaty contains a *passerelle* which allows the Council to decide unanimously that, on some aspects, acts could be adopted by QMV (in co-decision). National parliaments have to be notified of any Commission proposal to make use of this *passerelle*, and any national parliament will have the right to object to this decision being taken within six months (Article 81(3), 3rd subparagraph, TFEU).[37]

Potential role in the area of CFSP, including ESDP

Protocol no. 1 on the role of national parliaments in the EU provides in Article 10 that COSAC

> may submit any contribution it deems appropriate for the attention of the [EP], the Council and the Commission. [COSAC] shall in addition promote the exchange of information and best practice between national Parliaments and the [EP], including their special committees. It may also organise interparliamentary conferences on specific topics, in particular to debate matters of [CFSP], including [ESDP].

This provision could lead to the involvement of national parliaments in the scrutiny of the EU's action in the area of CFSP, including ESDP. On this issue, it is worth recalling that a follow-up to the ESDP activities of the EU is already organised by the WEU Parliamentary Assembly (composed of delegations from national parliaments). However, it is clear that the European Parliament would like to win a 'monopoly' of control over these activities in the future. On this point, the European Parliament will have to confront not only the WEU Parliamentary Assembly, but also national parliaments, which consider that they have more legitimacy to play this role than the European Parliament.

---

37 This right of the national parliaments is new as compared with the previous version of this *passerelle*, which had been inserted in the TEC by the Amsterdam Treaty. It empowered the Council, acting unanimously after consulting the European Parliament, to switch any of the provisions from Title IV of Part III of the TEC to codecision, without giving any role to the national parliaments (see Art. 67(2), 2nd indent, TEC).

An active role in the simplified revision procedures of the Treaties

National parliaments will participate in the use of the general *passerelle* (Article 48(7) TEU). This procedure allows the European Council to decide by unanimity, with the consent of the European Parliament, to switch a legal basis from unanimity to QMV (with the exception of decisions with military implications or in the area of defence) or from a special legislative procedure to the ordinary legislative procedure (i.e. codecision). The European Council must notify its intention to the national parliaments, which will have six months to voice any opposition. It is a 'silence procedure': if no objection is made, the decision may be adopted. Therefore each national parliament will have a right of veto.[38]

In the other simplified revision procedure provided for in Article 48(6) TEU, national parliaments have the same role as they already had in the ordinary revision procedure – that is, ratification rights 'in accordance with [the] respective constitutional requirements' of the Member States.

Other issues on which national parliaments have a specific role

National parliaments are, moreover, given the right:

- to be notified of applications for accession to the Union (Article 49, 1st subparagraph, TEU);
- to take part in the inter-parliamentary co-operation between national parliaments and with the European Parliament, in accordance with Protocol no. 1;
- to be informed by the Commission on proposals based on the 'flexibility clause' (Article 352(2) TFEU, ex-308 TEC).

*

The various measures introduced by the Lisbon Treaty in order to increase the role of national parliaments in the EU political game, so as to strengthen further the democratic decision-making process and the democratic control of the EU institutions, are quite innovative. On this basis, it can be affirmed that national parliaments now appear as

---

38 In its judgment of 30 June 2009, the German Constitutional Court considered this veto power not to be 'sufficient to the requirement of ratification', and requested that the German law on the powers of the German parliament be amended so as to provide for a prior authorisation to be given by the German parliament to the government before it would agree on the use of such a *passerelle* (see para. 319).

potentially being real actors in the process of European integration.[39] It is up to them to organise themselves effectively in order to transform this potential into reality.

These measures might also have some 'collateral' consequences, at least in certain Member States, on the relationship between the two chambers of the national parliament (where such chambers exist), and also between the parliament and the government (particularly in the case of a minority government).

Section 16 The citizens' initiative and other possibilities for citizens to influence decisions of the EU

The citizens' initiative

As is solemnly confirmed in Article 10(1) TEU, the fundamental principle governing the functioning of the EU is that 'it shall be founded on representative democracy'.

For the first time, the Lisbon Treaty gives EU citizens, in addition to the other rights they already have to influence the EU decision-making process, a direct right to bring a so-called 'citizens' initiative' signed by 'not less than one million citizens who are nationals of a significant number of Member States'. Through such an initiative, they will be able to invite the Commission, within the limits of its powers, to submit appropriate proposals on matters for which they consider that a legal act of the EU should be adopted (Article 11(4) TEU). The details of this new right, such as the minimum number of Member States from which such a citizens' initiative must emanate, the minimum number of signatories per Member State, what definition is to be given to the word 'citizen' in this context, the procedures to be followed, the arrangements for checking the signatures

---

39 See report by H. Haenel, President of the EU Delegation of the French Senate, 11 June 2008, Internet site of the French Senate. See also report 'on the development of the relations between the European Parliament and national Parliaments under the Lisbon Treaty', European Parliament Committee on Constitutional Affairs, 2009, doc. A6–0133/2009.

For its part, the German Constitutional Court, in its judgment of 30 June 2009, considered that 'the institutional recognition of the Member States' Parliaments by the Treaty of Lisbon cannot compensate for the deficit in the direct track of legitimisation of the European public authority that is based on the election of the [MEPs]. The status of national parliaments is considerably curtailed by the reduction of decisions requiring unanimity' (para. 293). It adds that 'without democratically originating in the Member States, the action of the [EU] lacks a sufficient basis of legitimisation' (para. 297).

and so on, will have to be provided for in a regulation to be adopted in codecision (Article 24, 1st subparagraph, TFEU).

This provision is very innovative and symbolic.[40] One million signatures out of 500 million people is a rather easy target to reach. Different groups and non-governmental organisations are already preparing such draft 'citizens' initiatives'. The Commission will not be legally obliged to follow up on any such initiative, which is quite right, since the Commission will retain its responsibility for deciding whether to take an initiative or not. It has always been the case that the Commission has retained this responsibility when the European Parliament (Article 225 TFEU) or the Council (Article 241 TFEU) requests it to submit a proposal. The Commission will have to check, in particular, whether requests made through the initiative fall within the limits of the powers conferred on it by the Treaties – that is, whether these requests do not encroach on competences which remain within the remit of the Member States or would entail an amendment to the Treaties. But it is clear that, within this framework, the political impact of such an initiative will, in practice, force the Commission to engage in serious work following its receipt.

However, such initiatives would not be well informed, well prepared and effectively launched if a proactive policy is not vigorously undertaken to ensure that citizens, or more generally civil society, are properly informed. This is why, in order also to facilitate the taking of such 'citizens' initiatives' as provided for in Article 11(4) TEU, three other paragraphs in the same Article request:

- the EU institutions to give, by appropriate means, citizens and representative associations the opportunity to make known and publicly exchange their views in all areas of Union action (paragraph 1);
- the EU institutions to maintain an open, transparent and regular dialogue with representative associations and civil society (paragraph 2);
- the Commission in particular that it carry out broad consultations with parties concerned in order to ensure that the Union's actions are coherent and transparent (paragraph 3).

---

40 According to the 30 June 2009 judgment of the German Constitutional Court, 'The elements of participative democracy, such as the precept of providing, in a suitable manner, the citizens of the Union and "representative" associations with the possibility of making their views heard, as well as the elements of associative and direct democracy, can only have a complementary and not a central function when it comes to legitimising European public authority' (para. 295).

Openness and transparency

A number of Articles of the Treaties insist on openness, transparency and information to the citizens, to the point that these provisions sometimes appear as being excessively repetitive:

- as previously, Article 1, 2nd subparagraph, TEU states that EU decisions should be 'taken as openly as possible and as closely as possible to the citizens';
- Article 10(3) TEU, which is new, states that 'every citizen shall have the right to participate in the democratic life of the Union' and repeats that 'decisions shall be taken as openly and as closely as possible to the citizens';
- as part of the 'provisions having general application' (Title II of the TFEU), Article 15 lists different measures on openness. It provides that 'in order to promote good governance and ensure the participation of civil society, the Union institutions, bodies, offices and agencies shall conduct their work as openly as possible' (paragraph 1). It also provides that 'the [EP] shall meet in public, as shall the Council when considering and voting on a draft legislative act' (paragraph 2).[41] Finally, paragraph 3 provides for a right of access to documents of all the EU institutions, bodies, offices and agencies (whereas, previously, this access was provided for only to European Parliament, Council and Commission documents). In addition, 'each institution, body, office or agency shall ensure that its proceedings are transparent and shall elaborate in its own Rules of Procedure specific provisions regarding access to its documents' and the European Parliament and the Council 'shall ensure publication of the documents relating to the legislative procedures';
- Article 17(3) TFEU, which concerns churches and religious associations or communities as well as philosophical and non-confessional organisations, states that 'the Union shall maintain an open, transparent and regular dialogue with these churches and organisations';
- Article 20(2) TFEU, which lists the different rights of EU citizens, mentions 'the right to petition the [EP], to apply to the European Ombudsman, and to address the institutions and advisory bodies of the Union in

---

41 This publicity rule is also to be found in Art. 16(8) TEU: 'The Council shall meet in public when it deliberates and votes on a draft legislative act. To this end, each Council meeting shall be divided into two parts, dealing respectively with deliberations on Union legislative acts and non-legislative activities.'

any of the Treaty languages and to obtain a reply in the same language' (point d). These rights are reiterated in Article 24 TFEU, and Articles 227 and 228 TFEU set out the details of the procedure regarding respectively the right to petition and the right to apply to the Ombudsman.

These reiterations (even without taking into account other relevant provisions contained in the Charter of Fundamental Rights) show how much ground has been gained towards more information, openness and transparency since the period which preceded the Maastricht Treaty.

Finally, a second paragraph has been introduced in Article 55 TEU on the languages into which the Treaties may be translated (in addition to the usual provision on the twenty-three languages in which the text is authentic). Under this new paragraph,[42] the Treaty 'may also be translated into any other languages as determined by Member States among those which, in accordance with their constitutional order, enjoy official status in all or part of their territory. A certified copy of such translations shall be provided by the Member States concerned to be deposited in the archives of the Council.' The translations into these languages would therefore not be 'authentic texts' within the meaning of the first paragraph of Article 55 TEU, which concerns only the official languages of the EU, but rather unofficial translations for the information of those EU citizens who use these languages.[43]

The IGC added a Declaration no. 16 on this provision, stressing that it 'contributes to the objective of respecting the Union's rich cultural and linguistic diversity' and confirming 'the attachment of the Union to the cultural diversity of Europe'.

Other possibilities for the citizens to influence decisions of the Union

Other features of the Lisbon Treaty may be stressed which go in the direction of giving more opportunities for the citizens to influence decisions of the Union.

---

42 This paragraph had already been introduced in the failed Constitutional Treaty (see Art. IV-448(2)).

43 As regards languages whose status is recognised by the Constitution of a Member State on all or part of its territory or the use of which as a national language is authorised by law, the Council may, through an administrative arrangement with the Member State concerned and upon request from that State, authorise the use of such languages under certain conditions (e.g. that the costs incurred be borne by the requesting State) (see Conclusions of the General Affairs Council of 13 June 2005 (press release no. 9499/05), accessible on the Internet site of the Council.

Election of the President of the Commission
by the European Parliament

When electing the MEPs, the citizens have a direct influence, of course, on the way the EU is governed, but, in future, the European elections will also have a very important by-product, because the Lisbon Treaty provides that the Commission President 'shall be *elected* by the [EP] by a majority of its component members' (Article 17(7), 1st subparagraph, TEU, emphasis added) – that is, by at least 376 MEPs when the European Parliament is composed of 751 members, as provided for by the Lisbon Treaty. It remains true that it is the European Council which, 'acting by a qualified majority, shall propose to the [EP] a candidate for President of the Commission'. But, in doing so, the European Council has the obligation to take into account the results of the European elections and is also obliged to '[hold] the appropriate consultations', which means, *inter alia*, consultations with the European Parliament in advance of proposing its candidate for Commission President.[44] Moreover, if the candidate proposed by the European Council to the European Parliament does not obtain the required majority in the European Parliament (a majority of its component members), a majority which is higher than that required before the Lisbon Treaty (a simple majority of the MEPs present and voting), the European Council 'shall within one month propose a new candidate who shall be elected by the [EP] following the same procedure' (Article 17(7), 1st subparagraph, TEU). Therefore nothing would prevent the political parties from organising themselves in order to have candidates for the office of President of the Commission.[45]

The Council will legislate in public

Again for the first time, the Lisbon Treaty provides that 'the Council shall meet in public when it deliberates and votes on a draft legislative act' (Article 16(8) TEU). Since the 1990s, what is called 'transparency' or 'openness' has made a lot of progress in the Union. Nevertheless, one can still hear or read that 'the EU is the only place in the world where legislation is not adopted in public'. This is obviously not true. It was already not the case before the Lisbon Treaty, because all votes on legislative acts in the Council have been made public since the beginning of the 1990s,

---

44 This consultation procedure is set out in more detail in Declaration no. 11 on Art. 17(6) and (7) TEU.

45 See on this point the interesting little book by S. Hix, *What's Wrong with the European Union and How to Fix It?* (Cambridge: Polity Press, 2008).

and because the Council was already obliged to deliberate publicly on codecision files.[46] This development is reflected notably in Regulation 1049/2001 on access to documents,[47] in the Council's Rules of Procedure[48] and in the annual Council reports on transparency and openness. The Council was the first EU institution to establish an electronic register where all its documents are listed and which are mostly public (i.e. almost 900,000 by the end of 2008).[49]

Nevertheless, the Council now has a clear legal obligation *always* to deliberate in public when discussing a legislative act, which allows for no possibility of derogation. This could help, if not the citizens directly, at least the political parties, the members of the European Parliament and of the national parliaments, lobbies and associations, the media and so on to be better informed about the progress of a particular legislative file and about the issues being discussed, thereby opening a possibility to influence this process through public debate.

The right to good administration

Article 298 TFEU requests that 'in carrying out their missions, the institutions . . . of the Union shall have the support of an open, efficient and independent European administration'. The author of this book is (of course!) convinced that this was already the case. It must be stressed that this issue is also reflected in Article 41 of EU Charter of Fundamental Rights, which is also more detailed.

The changes in favour of the Committee of the Regions

The Committee of the Regions is composed of representatives of regional and local bodies who hold local electoral mandates or are accountable to an elected assembly. The Lisbon Treaty gives to this Committee for the first time the right to bring actions before the Court of Justice for the annulment of EU legislative acts for infringement of the subsidiarity principle, in cases where the consultation of the Committee is mandatory under the relevant legal basis (Article 8, 2nd subparagraph, of Protocol

---

46 See Art. 8 of the Council's Rules of Procedure (Council Decision (2006/683/EC, Euratom) of 15 September 2006, adopting the Council's Rules of Procedure (OJ No. L285, 16 October 2006, 47).

47 Regulation (EC) No. 1049/2001 of the European Parliament and of the Council of 30 May 2001 regarding public access to European Parliament, Council and Commission documents (OJ No. L145, 31 May 2001, 43).

48 See the new Council's Rules of Procedure adopted on 1 December 2009 (OJ No. L325, 11 December 2009, 35).

49 See the 2008 Annual Report of the Council on Access to Documents, April 2009. See also under 'Documents' on the Internet site of the EU Council, www.consilium.europa.eu.

no. 2). The Committee of the Regions has also obtained the right to bring actions for annulment in order to protect its prerogatives (Article 263, 3rd subparagraph, TFEU).

*

It is difficult to assess a priori the actual effects of the changes made to the provisions of the Treaties, especially on such an issue as the democratic legitimacy of the Union.

One has to avoid referring to national models in order to try and evaluate the EU's political architecture.[50] With the Lisbon Treaty, the 'executive power' in the EU continues to be divided and shared between the European Council, the Council and the Commission, to which one should now add the President of the European Council and the HR. As regards the 'legislative power', it is essentially shared between the European Parliament and the Council, but one should also note that the Commission's monopoly on legislative initiative is strengthened, that the national parliaments have a strengthened role, and that this is also the case for citizens, who will be able to act through the 'citizen's initiative'.

One should also stress that there remains a large part of EU competences where the decision-making procedures leave significant power with the Member States' representatives.[51] This is the case in a number of provisions providing for unanimity in the Council (tax, foreign policy, some areas of social policy, of environment policy, of economic and monetary policy, of justice and home affairs, the flexibility clause in Article 352 TFEU, etc.), or even for the common accord of the Member States[52]

---

50 This is, however, exactly what the German Constitutional Court did in its judgment of 30 June 2009 (see Section 17): 'With the present status of integration, the European Union does, even upon the entry into force of the Treaty of Lisbon, not yet attain a shape that corresponds to the level of legitimisation of a democracy constituted as a State' (para. 276). '[W]ith the Treaty, the Member States follow the construction pattern of a federal state without being able to create the democratic basis for this under the Treaties' (para. 296).

51 According to A. Moravcsik, this would mean that there is no democratic deficit in the EU. If many voters are not interested in participating in the European elections, this is because 'the scope of EU regulatory activity tends to be inversely correlated with the importance of the issues in the minds of European voters'. Moravcsik stresses that the issues seen by voters as the most important are social security, health care, internal security and public order, employment, pensions and taxes, whereas the major activities of the EU concern the internal market, agricultural policy, technical regulations, urgent humanitarian aid and foreign policy. A. Moravcsik, 'The European Constitutional Settlement' (2008) 31(1) World Economy 158.

52 Unanimity of the Members of the Council allows for abstentions (Art. 238(4) TFEU), whereas the common accord of the Member States requires a positive agreement by all of them.

(revision of the Treaties, appointment of judges, decisions on the seat of the institutions, language regime, etc.).

Overall, the progress made by the Lisbon Treaty marks an important step towards greater legitimacy in the functioning of the EU institutions:

- simplifications and clarifications will provide a better understanding: the Treaties have been simplified; the EU and the EC have been merged into one entity; the pillars, the legal acts, the procedures have also been simplified; the division of powers and the basic legal principles governing the EU have been codified and clarified;
- the European Parliament has been given many new powers in the legislative field, in the budgetary field, in the conclusion of international agreements and in the procedure for the appointment of the Commission;
- the national parliaments have been given real powers of control over respect for the subsidiarity principle by the EU institutions;
- citizens have been given the right to trigger the initiation of a possible legislative procedure;
- openness and transparency have been improved;
- the Charter of Fundamental Rights has been given Treaty legal value;
- the Court of Justice is able to control respect for the Charter by the EU institutions and has full jurisdiction in the FSJ area;
- the new method for calculating QMV in the Council as from 2014 makes it more proportional to the population of the Member States;
- QMV in the Council is to be applied in an increased number of cases.[53]

Therefore the Lisbon Treaty addresses some of the concerns expressed. However, one has to recognise that EU citizens will probably continue to feel that they are not the masters of the game in the same way as in the national or regional political arenas. In the future, political control over the EU activities will continue to be exercised through national institutions as well as through the European Parliament. This issue needs to be discussed in an open way, much more than it has been discussed up to now.[54]

---

53 The German Constitutional Court, in its judgment of 30 June 2009, seemed to regard this move as going in the direction of less democracy. One could obviously argue in favour of the opposite point of view. Is there more democracy with unanimity in the Council, which means that the adoption of a legislative act may be blocked by a minority representing less than 1 per cent of the EU population?

54 The German Constitutional Court, in its judgment of 30 June 2009, is of the opinion that 'the Treaty of Lisbon does not lead to a new level of development of democracy'

This does not mean that the system that has been established and developed over the years in the EU was not democratic and that decisions were taken in an undemocratic way. EU decision-making has a very effective system of checks and balances. An American observer of EU life noted that

> [T]he EU as a vehicle for sharing power between national governments and an international institution has evolved into a complex but effective system of checks and balances. Policy can be made only by painstaking consensus. By the time 70 percent of the 25 member governments, a technocratic European Commission and a directly elected European Parliament agree to a law, it is almost certain to represent a stable compromise.[55]

It remains that if things do not change, it will be very difficult in the future, if not impossible, to obtain positive reactions from the citizens if one needed to amend the EU Treaties with the aim of conferring more competences on the EU in order to correct existing imbalances (see the Conclusion, below).

Section 17 The judgment of 30 June 2009 of the German Constitutional Court and the issue of the democratic legitimacy of the EU

While concluding that the Lisbon Treaty is compatible with the German Constitution, the German Constitutional Court judged that the German law of ratification had to be amended on a number of points in order to give significant additional powers to the German parliament. In its general analysis, the Court strengthened the views it had expressed in its

(para. 295). In its view, 'neither the additional rights of participation, which are strongly interlocked as regards the effects of their many levels of action and in view of the large number of national parliaments, nor rights of petition which are associative and have a direct effect vis-à-vis the Commission are suited to replace the majority rule which is established by an election' (para. 294).

55 A. Moravcsik, 'Europe's Slow Triumph', *Newsweek*, 21 June 2004, 41. See also A. Moravcsik, 'Ignore the Skeptics; EU Democracy Is Doing Just Fine', *Newsweek*, 29 June 2009, 20. See also Rifkin, *European Dream*, 230: 'But the important thing to remember is that the regulatory decisions made in Brussels are themselves the result of a polycentric process of negotiation, compromise and consensus, involving many parties at the regional, national, transnational and global levels.' See also C. Rumford, *The European Union: A Political Sociology* (Oxford: Blackwell, 2002); M. M. Dean, *Governmentality: Power and Rule in Modern Society* (London: Sage, 1999); and T. R. Reid, *The United States of Europe* (London: Penguin Press, 2005).

judgment on the Maastricht Treaty in October 1993.[56] The 2009 judgment, which can hardly be characterized as a blueprint for European federalism, repeatedly uses insistent, tough and clear language, referring a great deal to the issue of democracy (or lack of it) in the EU. It may be summarized as follows:

- the point of departure of the Court's reasoning is the right to vote, which must be equal for each citizen and which is inviolable;
- this right is not (and probably cannot be) fully respected in the political organisation of the EU, in particular since the weight of the votes of the citizens for elections to the European Parliament differs by a factor from one to twelve and as the composition of other EU institutions is based on equality of states;
- the Lisbon Treaty 'contains contradictions because with the Treaty, the Member States follow the construction pattern of a federal State, without being able to create the democratic basis for this under the Treaties in the form of the equal election of a representative body of the people and of a parliamentary European government that is based on the legitimising power of a people of the Union alone' (para. 296);
- a European people does not exist; it is rather the peoples of the Member States which exist;
- effective democracy is and remains at the level of each EU Member State, and the Lisbon Treaty does not lead to a new level of development of democracy;
- the EU is an intergovernmental association of states which are and remain sovereign;
- the Member States are and must remain the masters of the EU Treaties; through their national parliaments, they must continue to decide on any future transfer of competence to the EU;
- furthermore, the development of the EU must not and cannot prevent the Member States from exercising their essential functions in economic, budgetary, cultural, social and security issues;
- there is an essential inviolable core of the German Constitution which cannot be delegated ('eternity guarantee');
- the transfer of competences to the EU seems to be regarded by the Court as already excessive in some areas; the Court considers certain

---

56 BVerFG, 89, 155 (1993) (see also Annex 1). On this 1993 judgment, see Weiler, 'Does Europe Need a Constitution?', and J. Baquero Cruz, 'The Legacy of the Maastricht-Urteil and the Pluralist Movement' (2008) 14 *European Law Journal* 389.

competences attributed to the EU as being not precise enough and it requested that they must be interpreted in a restrictive way;

- Germany does not recognize an *absolute* primacy of EU law; in some cases, non-compliance with the EU is not excluded; it should even be obligatory for German authorities if and when EU law does not respect the German Constitution (para. 241);
- as a matter of principle, there should always be the possibility of control by the German Constitutional Court over the activities of the EU institutions (including those of the Court of Justice);
- in case European integration should ever go too far, the structural democratic deficit of the EU would become unacceptable; in such a case, Germany would have to work to prevent that from happening and, 'if the worst comes to the worst', unilaterally withdraw from the EU (para. 264).

*

This important judgment certainly deserves thorough discussion.

One of the findings of the Constitutional Court is that the EU, due to its structural democratic deficit, is not, and cannot become, a federal state. However, at the same time the judgment criticises the EU as it is now for not complying with rules which are intrinsically linked to the existence of a state, while affirming that the EU is not and cannot become a state.

One may note that the Court does not examine the question of whether the historic features of the classic nation state should remain for ever applicable to the EU, or if the EU is something different from a state and, therefore, whether one should not try and continue to imagine new and specific democratic controls over the EU's action, which would be suited to such a new entity insofar as it is not comparable to a state.[57]

---

57 In the EU, both the European Parliament's and the Council's voting procedures take into account not only the number of Member States (partly), thus giving an advantage to the smaller ones, but also the weight of their population. Moreover, the Lisbon Treaty has given powers to the national parliaments and has established the possibility of a 'citizen's initiative' to be tabled by one million EU citizens. In any case, it should be noted that one of the characteristics of a federal State is that it gives its component entities (cantons, states or Länder) a weight which is never fully proportional to their respective population. For instance, in Switzerland, amending the Constitution requires a double majority, of the total population and of the twenty-six cantons (see Art. 195 of the Swiss Constitution, according to which an amendment to the Constitution 'shall come into force when it is approved by the People and the Cantons'). Therefore there may be instances where the majority of the population votes in favour of a given amendment to the Constitution while the majority of the cantons, thanks to the smallest ones, votes against. A minority of the population may win against the majority, contrary to the rule 'one man, one vote'. This happened in a constitutional referendum in March 1955.

One might also wonder why the following conclusions of the Court were only reached in 2009, as though the situation were new and had become unacceptable, whereas they actually touch on issues which have been well known for a long time:

- The fact is not new that the European Parliament does not ensure the equal representation of the citizens because the number of MEPs does not reflect the size of the population of the Member State they represent.
- The fact is also not new that the composition of most EU institutions is based on a representation in favour of the smaller Member States, or even on an equal representation of Member States irrespective of their population.
- Article 352 TFEU had predecessors (Article 308 TEC, previously numbered 235); it now has a much narrower scope, as compared with those, and it is also subject to stricter procedures. Therefore why require a prior law by the German parliament in 2009 before any use of this Article, whereas it had not been previously necessary, for example in 1993, at a period when this Article was widely and boldly used?
- Why does the German Constitutional Court now insist on a stricter control of the acts of the EU institutions, at the very time when the Lisbon Treaty has given teeth to the national parliaments of the Member States for them to exercise control over respect for the principle of subsidiarity by the EU institutions?
- Whereas the Lisbon Treaty does not extend the competences of the EU by very much, why give the impression that the increase of competences has now gone too far and that we are close to a disruption of democratic control?
- Why, forty-five years after the *Costa* v. *ENEL* judgment of the EU Court of Justice, go so far as to take the risk of disrupting the uniformity of EU law, by stressing several times that Germany does not recognise the *absolute* primacy of EU law?
- And why go now so far as to evoke a possible (even if not plausible) withdrawal of Germany from the EU?

Was such dramatisation necessary?

It is quite certain that the Lisbon Treaty, as such, did not deserve this. On the contrary, it takes many steps in the direction which has been advocated by the German Constitutional Court since 1974 (see the *Solange I* judgment), including by giving the status of primary law to the EU Charter of Fundamental Rights. It is most probable that this avalanche of criticisms was not addressed only to the Lisbon Treaty as such. It looks rather like a *cri de coeur* – the result of an accumulation of irritation over the years, in the face of an undesired development of the EU. The German Constitutional Court criticised the expansion of competences with successive treaties. It criticised the existing democratic imbalances in the treaties (which do not respect the principle of one vote per citizen), imbalances which, in the view of the Court, have now been further increased (more QMV, more powers to the European Parliament). It further criticised the lax attitude of the EU institutions when interpreting the extent of their own powers. This is obviously above all a criticism addressed to the European Court of Justice, despite the fact that is not often explicitly mentioned in the judgment.

*

This judgment is a serious piece of work which deserves attention, reflection and action on the part of all EU institutions and of all European governments and parliaments. It should entail a discussion about the future of Europe and about ways to reach a better level of democratic legitimation of the acts and actions of the EU institutions and fuller knowledge by the citizens of all the means which are at their disposal in order to exercise their democratic control over these acts and actions.

The Court considered that the Member States have shown that they are unable to establish a real democracy at the level of the EU. According to the Court, such a real democracy cannot be established through something other than the election of a parliament on the basis of the democratic principle of 'one man, one vote', a parliament which should then be the basis for a European government.[58]

Discussion should start on this well-reasoned opinion, and should address the following questions:

- Is this last solution the only one? Or would it be possible to find other ways? Is it the sine qua non for further developing European integration in order to allow the EU to continue to enlarge its activities? Or are there other solutions?
- Otherwise, is the EU condemned to the status quo? Has it reached the limits of possible integration?

---

58 This does not mean that the German Constitutional Court is in favour of such a solution, which it judges impossible to realise.

IV

Fundamental rights

Section 18 The origins of the EU Charter of Fundamental Rights

The original EC Treaty did not make any reference to fundamental rights. It was the 1992 Maastricht Treaty which inserted Article 6(2) in the EU Treaty, providing that 'the Union shall respect fundamental rights, as guaranteed by the European Convention for the Protection of Human Rights and Fundamental Freedoms . . . and as they result from the constitutional traditions common to the Member States, as general principles of Community law'. Before that, the EU Court of Justice had, as early as in 1969,[1] stated that fundamental human rights are 'enshrined in the general principles of Community law and protected by the Court'. Thereafter, the Court continued strengthening this protection so that 'respect for human rights is . . . a condition of the lawfulness of Community acts'.[2]

Such a guarantee was a prerequisite for the acceptance by Member States of the principle that EU law has primacy over national law, a principle which the Court of Justice had already enunciated in 1964. Without a guarantee that fundamental rights were properly protected at EU level, the conferral by Member States of competences on the EU might have entailed a lowering of the level of protection of human rights. This link with primacy was made very clearly by the German Constitutional Court in its case law which became known as *Solange* (meaning 'as long as' in German). In a judgment of 1974 (known as *Solange I*),[3] the German Constitutional Court stated that it would review whether EU legislation

---

1 Judgment of 12 November 1969, case. 29/69, *Stauder* [1969] ECR 425, para. 7. Judgment of 17 December 1970, case 11/70, *Internationale Handelsgesellschaft* [1970] ECR 1125, para. 4.
2 See Opinion 2/94, *Accession of the EC to the ECHR*, paras. 33 and 34. For a summary of the protection of fundamental rights in the EU, see also paras. 73 to 81 of the judgment of 30 June 2005 of the Human Rights Court, case 45036/98, *Bosphorus Hava Yollari Turizm v. Ireland*.
3 Case *Solange I*, BVerfGE 37, 271 of 29 May 1974, which may be found translated into English at www.ucl.ac.uk.

respects fundamental rights 'as long as' the EU did not have a directly elected parliament, with legislative powers, and a catalogue of fundamental rights. Later on, the German Constitutional Court somewhat relaxed its case law, in 1986 (*Solange II*)[4] and in 2000,[5] by stating that, as long as the EU's case law guarantees an effective protection of fundamental rights, actions in the German Court against an EU legal act will be dismissed, unless the applicant shows that the development of EU law and EU case law falls below a proper level of protection of fundamental rights. The Italian Constitutional Court followed a similar line.[6]

In a judgment of 30 June 2005, the Human Rights Court of the Council of Europe in Strasbourg followed similar reasoning in a case where a Member State was sued for having allegedly violated property rights due to the application of an EC Regulation. The Court stated that, on the condition that the EU 'is considered to protect fundamental rights, as regards both the substantive guarantees offered and the mechanisms controlling their observance, in a manner which can be considered at least equivalent to that for which the [ECHR] provides', the Court will consider that there is a 'presumption... that a State has not departed from the requirements of the [ECHR] when it does no more than implement legal obligations flowing from its membership of the [EU]'. It added, however, that 'any such presumption can be rebutted if, in the circumstances of a particular case, it is considered that the protection of [ECHR] rights was manifestly deficient. In such cases, the interest of international co-operation would be outweighed by the [ECHR] role as a "constitutional instrument of European public order" in the field of human rights.'[7]

At the initiative of Germany during its Presidency in the first half of 1999, the European Council, meeting in Cologne in June 1999, decided that a 'Charter of fundamental rights of the EU'[8] should be adopted.

---

4 Case *Solange II*, BVerfGE 73, 339 of 22 October 1986, at www.ucl.ac.uk.

5 Case '*Bananenmarktordnung*', BVerfGE 102, 147 of 7 June 2000, at www.ucl.ac.uk.

6 Case *Frontini* no. 183/73 of 27 December 1973, I, 1974, 314, and case *Fragd* no. 232/89 of 21 April 1989, I, 1990, 1855.

7 See paras. 155 and 156 of the above-mentioned *Bosphorus* judgment. For an analysis of this judgment, see J.-P. Jacqué, 'L'arrêt *Bosphorus*, une jurisprudence "Solange II" de la Cour européenne des droits de l'homme?' (2005) 3 *Revue trimestrielle de droit européen* 756.

8 See 'European Council Decision on the drawing up of a Charter of Fundamental Rights of the European Union', in Annex IV to the Presidency Conclusions, 3 and 4 June 1999, available on the Internet site of the Council.

The European Council decided to entrust the task of preparing the draft Charter to a body composed of representatives of the national parliaments and of the European Parliament, as well as representatives of the governments of the Member States and of the Commission. This procedure was chosen in order to introduce more openness, more publicity and broader-based democratic participation in the drafting of the text. This body, which called itself a 'Convention', was chaired by Roman Herzog, a former president of Germany and a former president of the German Constitutional Court.[9]

The Charter of Fundamental Rights of the European Union proposed by the Convention was approved after a few modifications and solemnly proclaimed in Nice by the European Parliament, the Council and the Commission on 7 December 2000.[10] In order to make it easier for readers to know which sources were used in the drafting of the Charter and what interpretation should be given to its provisions, a set of 'Explanations relating to the Charter of Fundamental Rights' was prepared by the Secretariat,[11] under the authority of the Præsidium of the Convention which drafted the Charter.[12]

However, the Charter was not incorporated into the Treaties and was not given legally binding force. The question of the Charter's legal status was to be considered later and became the second of the four questions in the 2000 Nice Declaration (see Box 3).

Section 19 The Charter of Fundamental Rights as referred to in the Lisbon Treaty

One of the most important changes, at least symbolically, sought by the failed Constitutional Treaty was to incorporate the EU Charter of Fundamental Rights as an integral part of the Treaty. The legal status of the Charter would thus have changed from one of a political declaration, although of a very high value, to the status of 'primary law', or Treaty-level law.

---

9   The concept and the composition of the 'Convention' served as a model for the European Convention which prepared the draft Constitutional Treaty.
10 See OJ No. C364, 18 December 2000, 1.
11 The Secretariat of the Convention was ensured by the General Secretariat of the Council and headed by Jean-Paul Jacqué, at that time one of the directors of the Council Legal Service.
12 See doc. CHARTE 4473/00 which may be found on the Internet site of the Convention which drafted the Charter at www.europarl.europa.eu/charter.

This was the proposed answer to be given to one of the four questions put by the Nice Declaration of December 2000 (see Box 3): 'the Status to be given to the Charter of Fundamental Rights for the Union'. Linked to this was the decision to provide for the accession of the EU to the 1950 European Convention for the Protection of Human Rights and Fundamental Freedoms (ECHR) (Article 6(2) TEU; see Section 21). These two important moves were agreed upon in the Convention, and the 2003–4 IGC did not question them. Therefore the Charter was fully incorporated as Part II of the text of the failed Constitutional Treaty.

The Convention and the 2003–4 IGC had agreed to amend the original Charter of 2000 by including modifications aimed, in particular – although redundantly with existing provisions – at confirming that the Charter would not modify the delimitation of competences between the Union and the Member States, and that the limits of the competences of the Union were not extended by the Charter (see Article 51 of the Charter).

Another modification was to enlarge the right of access to documents so as to cover not only the institutions, but also bodies, offices and agencies (Article 42 of the Charter).[13]

The 2003–4 IGC also modified Article 52 of the Charter in order to clarify the distinction between 'rights' and 'principles'. Rights are directly enforceable in court, while principles define objectives which should be aimed at by the EU legislator. The Charter contains about fifty 'rights, freedoms and principles' and one of the criticisms addressed to it is that it does not identify with enough precision which of its provisions are rights, freedoms, or principles.

Another change, which, like most others, was requested by the UK government, concerned the 'Explanations relating to the Charter'. These Explanations, which had been prepared by the Secretariat of the Convention on the Charter, had already been slightly revised by the Convention on the Constitutional Treaty. The UK government requested, and obtained, that both the Preamble and Article 57(2) of the Charter make an explicit reference to those Explanations, which were to be published in the OJ.

The 2003–4 IGC settled one additional issue which was important for some Member States (notably Hungary) and which the Convention had not been able to solve. These Member States insisted that a reference should be made to 'the rights of minorities', but this request, formulated in such a way, was unacceptable to other Member States. Finally, the

---

13 The legal basis for access to documents is now in Art. 15(3) TFEU.

compromise was to refer to 'the rights of persons belonging to minorities', therefore excluding collective rights (Article 2 TEU).

After the failure of the Constitutional Treaty, the German Presidency, when preparing the 2007 IGC mandate for the Lisbon Treaty, had to confront a lot of difficulties with the content, and above all with the legal status to be given to the Charter. The views of the Member States were divergent.

A few Member States thought that some of the political difficulties they had experienced in trying to ratify the Constitutional Treaty were caused by the fact that the Charter had been incorporated in the Treaty. The Charter was criticised, in particular in the United Kingdom, as containing some obligations, notably in social matters, which either could have negative effects on the economy, or would be impossible properly to implement (in particular the 'principles').

On the opposite side, among the eighteen Member States which had already ratified the Constitutional Treaty before it was abandoned, there was a strong commitment to keep the Charter in the Treaty. For them, it was one of the most symbolic and important changes. It constituted proof that the EU was not exclusively interested in the economic side of its activities. For some of these Member States, purely and simply abandoning the Charter was, therefore, totally unacceptable.

Finally, as a compromise between these two positions, it was decided, in the IGC mandate adopted in June 2007, that the Charter would not become an integral part of the Treaties, but that there would be a cross-reference to the Charter in Article 6(1) TEU, which would, in addition, expressly state that the Charter 'shall have the same legal value as the Treaties' (i.e. that it would have the status of 'primary law').[14] In addition, it was decided to clarify again, repeating Article 51 of the Charter, that 'the provisions of the Charter shall not extend in any way the competences of the Union as defined in the Treaties'[15] and to insert a

14 The 2007 IGC mandate stated that the version of the Charter to be referred to was the one 'as agreed in the 2004 IGC' – that is, the version of the Charter which had been contained in Part II of the Constitutional Treaty and was an amended version of the Charter of 2000. This is made clear in a note at the very end of the Charter in which it is explained that 'the above text adapts the wording of the Charter proclaimed on 7 December 2000, and will replace it as from the date of entry into force of the Treaty of Lisbon' (see OJ No. C303, 14 December 2007, 14).

15 This was also confirmed, for the third time, in Declaration no. 1 according to which 'the Charter does not extend the field of application of Union law beyond the powers of the Union or establish any new power or task for the Union, or modify powers and tasks as defined by the Treaties'. However, some Member States felt that this was not clear enough.

reference' to the Explanations (see Article 6(1), 2nd and 3rd subparagraphs, TEU).[16]

Some more fine-tuning was carried out in the Group of Legal Experts and was agreed by all twenty-seven delegations in October 2007:

- the Charter would be approved and 'solemnly proclaimed' again, in its '2004 version', by the European Parliament, the Council and the Commission before the signature of the Lisbon Treaty, so that the date and place of this proclamation would be inserted in Article 6(1) TEU. The Charter was in fact proclaimed in Strasbourg on 12 December 2007, one day before the signature of the Treaty on 13 December 2007;
- the Charter and the explanations would be published together in the *Official Journal of the European Union*, but separately from the Lisbon Treaty. The Charter was published on 14 December and the Lisbon Treaty was published on 17 December 2007;
- as a consequence, the Charter and the explanations would not be contained in Declarations annexed to the Final Act of the IGC, as originally proposed in the draft texts submitted to the IGC by the Portuguese Presidency in July 2007.

The substantive content of the Charter of Fundamental Rights

As is stressed redundantly both in the TEU and in the Charter itself, the Charter of Fundamental Rights *does not increase the competences of the EU*. It does underline the importance for the EU and its institutions of respecting fundamental rights and of being 'based on the rule of law' (in

The Czech Republic, for instance, adopted a unilateral Declaration (no. 53) according to which 'The Czech Republic also emphasises that the Charter does not extend the field of application of Union law and does not establish any new power for the Union. It does not diminish the field of application of national law and does not restrain any current powers of the national authorities in this field.'

16 Compare with Art. I-9 of the Constitutional Treaty, which did not have these two subparagraphs. The last subparagraph of Art. 6(1) TEU reads: 'The rights, freedoms and principles in the Charter shall be interpreted in accordance with the general provisions in Title VII of the Charter governing its interpretation and application and with due regard to the explanations referred to in the Charter, that set out the sources of those provisions.' In this context, one may note that the 3rd recital of Protocol no. 30 on the application of the Charter to Poland and the United Kingdom, which refers to the Courts of Poland and of the United Kingdom, mentions that Art. 6 TEU requires the Charter to be applied and interpreted by their national courts '*strictly* in accordance with the explanations'. This is not a correct reproduction of what is actually in Art. 6(1) TEU, where the word 'strictly' is not mentioned.

States, like France, Spain or Portugal, were used to such distinctions and did not want to renounce the idea of including 'principles'.

As there is no list of which are rights and which are principles, it is the way in which a given provision is drafted that enables us to distinguish between a right or a principle, but one has to recognise that this is not always easy. Typical drafting for a right would be, for instance, 'everyone has the right...', while typical drafting for a principle would be, for instance, 'the Union recognises and respects the right of...'. A single Article sometimes contains one paragraph giving rights and another one setting out principles. The explanations are helpful in this regard.

Examples of social rights are equality between women and men (Article 23 Charter), the prohibition of child labour (Article 32 Charter), the right to engage in work (Article 15 Charter), the right to protection from dismissal for reasons connected with maternity and the right to paid maternity leave and to parental leave (Article 33 Charter), the right to protection in the event of unjustified dismissal (Article 30 Charter), the right to fair and just working conditions (Article 31 Charter), the worker's right to information and consultation within the undertaking (Article 27 Charter), the right of collective bargaining and action (Article 28 Charter) and the right of access to placement services (Article 29 Charter).

Examples of principles are the right of access to social security and social assistance (Article 34 Charter) and to health care (Article 35 Charter), the rights of the elderly (Article 25 Charter), the right of persons with disabilities to integration in the life of the community (Article 26 Charter), access to services of general economic interest (Article 36 Charter), a high level of environmental protection (Article 37 Charter) and a high level of consumer protection (Article 38 Charter).

Some of the provisions of the Charter gave rise to lively debates in some Member States. In France a discussion took place on the 'right to life' and on the 'freedom of religion'. In the United Kingdom a discussion took place on the 'right of access to healthcare' and on the 'right of collective bargaining and action'.

The cases of abortion and of freedom of religion

To take the *first example*, the two issues raised during the ratification debate of the failed Constitutional Treaty in France were whether Article 2 Charter on the right to life and Article 10 Charter on the freedom of thought, conscience and religion would contradict or impede national rules, respectively, on the right to abortion and on the principle of *laïcité* (secularism).

As to **the case of abortion**, this issue has been hotly debated both in France and in Ireland. In France, some argued that the Charter might lead to a prohibition of abortion in France. In Ireland, on the contrary, others argued that the Charter might lead to a legalisation of abortion in Ireland. None of this is true. Article 2(1) of the Charter, on the right to life, reads, 'Everyone has the right to life.' This paragraph is based on the first sentence of Article 2(1) of the ECHR, which reads, 'Everyone's right to life shall be protected by law.' Although the Human Rights Court had not, so far, had an opportunity to interpret this provision, the Human Rights Commission did so in part in 1980, by noting that neither the notion of 'everyone' nor the notion of 'life' was defined in the Convention. In the particular case under review, which related to a therapeutic abortion, the Human Rights Commission decided that Article 2(1) of the ECHR did not impede national legislation from authorising such an abortion.[24] Thus, neither the Human Rights Court nor the Human Rights Commission settled the issue of whether the 'unborn' benefit from Article 2(1) ECHR and one may doubt that they will ever do so. The fact is that a great majority of the states parties to the ECHR, and to the EU, have had abortion laws in force for several years, with varying conditions and limits, while some states, such as Ireland,[25] Malta and Poland, currently forbid abortion (sometimes with the sole exception of a risk to the mother's life).

In any case, it should be made absolutely clear, once again, that like all the other provisions of the EU Charter, Article 2(1) is solely addressed to the EU institutions and is addressed to the Member States 'only when they are implementing Union law', and 'does not . . . establish any new power or task for the Union' (Article 51(1) Charter, and also Article 6(1) TEU). As abortion is clearly a matter for national law, the EU has no competence

24 Decision of 13 May 1980, case *X v. UK*, no. 8416/79, DR 19, 244.
25 Art. 40, Section 3, 3rd subsection, of the Irish Constitution reads, 'The State acknowledges the right to life of the unborn and, with due regard to the equal right to life of the mother, guarantees in its laws to respect, and, as far as practicable, by its laws to defend and vindicate that right.' See also Protocol no. 35 to the TEU and to the TFEU, which had originally been adopted in 1992, as well as the so-called Guimarães Declaration of 1 May 1992, which stated that the Protocol would not limit freedom to travel between Member States or to obtain or make available information on services lawfully available in Member States. A similar text was inserted in the Irish Constitution later on. Despite these texts, debate was going on during the ratification process of the Lisbon Treaty and led to the adoption of further texts (see Section 4).

an integral part of the general principles of the Community law the observance of which the Court ensures'.[28] The Charter will not make any changes to the legal situation as it was before the entry into force of the Lisbon Treaty.

As to **the case of the right to a high level of health protection**, Article 35 Charter provides that 'everyone has the right of access to preventive health care and the right to benefit from medical treatment under the conditions established by national laws and practices'. In this case also, it is quite clear that the 'right' which is recognised is a principle, which is expressly and entirely subject to 'national laws and practices' (see explanations on this Article). This provision does not establish a right to a minimum threshold of medical treatment. This right might exist in some Member States due to their national legislation or to internal commitments, but the Charter would not establish such a right in a given Member State if it does not already exist.

The legal status of the Charter of Fundamental Rights

Both in the 2000 Nice Declaration and in the 2001 Laeken Declaration, it was agreed that the question of the legal status of the Charter should be re-examined. It is clear now that, under the Lisbon Treaty, the Charter has the same legal value as the Treaties (Article 6(1) TEU).

Some Member States feared that the Charter could be construed as conferring additional competences on the EU to legislate on the issues covered by it. They also feared that the Charter could influence their internal legal order, to the extent that a purely internal action, independent of the implementation of EU law, would nevertheless fall within the scope of the Charter. These are the reasons why the 2002–3 Convention and then the 2003–4 IGC agreed on amendments to the original 2000 Charter. The amendments clarified that the Charter would not extend the field of application of Union law beyond the competences conferred on the Union, and that the Member States will have to respect the Charter only when they are implementing Union law. As mentioned above, these amendments have been further enhanced and developed by the Lisbon IGC. It was already the case up to now that the EU Court of Justice reviews

---

28 See judgment of 11 December 2007, case C-438/05, *Viking Line*, [2007] ECR I-10806, paras. 43 and 44. See also judgment of 18 December 2007, case C-341/05, *Laval*, [2007] ECR I-11845, paras. 90 to 92.

the respect of fundamental rights by the Member States only when they implement EC law.[29]

In contrast to the 2000 version of the Charter, its 2007 version also stresses that fundamental rights recognised in the Charter which resulted from the constitutional traditions common to Member States should be interpreted in harmony with those traditions, and that full account should be taken of national laws and practices as specified in the Charter (Article 52(4) Charter).[30]

Paragraph 7 of the same Article 52 provides that 'The explanations drawn up as a way of providing guidance in the interpretation of this Charter shall be given due regard by the courts of the Union and of the Member States.' A reference to these Explanations has also been added in the Charter's preamble and, at the Lisbon IGC, in Article 6(1) TEU, as a new third subparagraph. These Explanations are reproduced in the same issue of the *Official Journal* in which the Charter was published on 14 December 2007.

Finally, the Charter of Fundamental Rights has become legally binding upon the EU institutions and upon the Member States when they are implementing Union law. One has to recognise that this has not fundamentally altered the pre-existing legal situation. The Court of Justice had already stated in 1969 that 'fundamental human rights [are] enshrined in the general principles of Community law and protected by the Court',[31] and that 'respect for human rights is . . . a condition of the lawfulness of Community acts'.[32] Nevertheless, first, the Charter's content is broader than what was applicable before and, second, giving it the same legal value as the Treaty was a very powerful symbol. This will make it more apparent to the citizens that the new EU is to be a 'Union based on the rule of law' and has to respect their rights. However, the downside of this is that the citizens might mistakenly be under the illusion that the Charter will always be obligatory for their national authorities, even when the latter are not implementing EU law.

*

Despite their number and their precision, the legal clarifications made on the status of the Charter might escape the attention of ordinary citizens.

---

29 See, for instance, judgment of 24 March 1994, case C-2/92, *Bostock*, [1994] ECR I-976, para. 16, and judgment of 18 March 2000, case C-107/97, *Rombi and Arkopharma*, [2000] ECR I-3392, para. 65.

30 See also Declaration no. 1 of the Lisbon IGC.

31 Case 29/69, *Stauder*, para. 7.

32 Opinion 2/94, *Accession of the EC to the ECHR*, paras. 33 and 34.

Citizens may think that, the Charter having been given the same legal value as the Treaties, the EU now has a proper 'Bill of Rights'. They might think that all its provisions are obligatory in full and protect them in all situations. How, then, can one explain that these rights do not apply directly and fully to them in order to protect them from any policy action by any public authority? How can one explain that these rights are an obligation only for the EU institutions and not for the national public authorities, except when they implement EU law? The symbolic importance of the Charter is powerful, but its actual legal effects have been exaggerated on both sides.

Section 20 The Protocol on the application of the Charter to Poland and the United Kingdom

At the very end of the negotiations on the IGC mandate, in June 2007, the United Kingdom requested that a Protocol be annexed to the Treaties, which under Article 51 TEU has the same legal value as the Treaties, on the application of the Charter in the United Kingdom.[33] Poland decided later on during the Lisbon IGC to join the United Kingdom in this Protocol.[34]

This Protocol no. 30 has often been presented as being an 'opt-out', the aim and result of which would be that the Charter would not be binding for Poland or the United Kingdom.[35]

One has to stress, to begin with, that the Preamble of the Protocol expresses the opinion of all twenty-seven parties to the Treaty on a number of points, for example in its second recital, according to which 'the Charter is to be applied in strict accordance with the provisions of the aforementioned Article 6 [TEU] and Title VII of the Charter itself'. This is also the case for the sixth recital, according to which 'the Charter reaffirms the rights, freedoms and principles recognised in the Union and makes

---

33 See, on the interpretation of this Protocol, the analysis made by the UK House of Lords, which the author of this book shares to a large extent (EU Committee, 10th Report of Session 2007–2008, *The Lisbon Treaty: An Impact Assessment*, published on 13 March 2008).

34 In order to allow for the Czech Republic finally to deposit its instrument of ratification of the Lisbon Treaty, the European Council of 29 and 30 October 2009 agreed that the name of the Czech Republic would be added to Protocol no. 30, through a Protocol to be adopted at the time of the conclusion of the next Accession Treaty.

35 See, for example, F.-X. Priollaud and D. Siritzky, *Le Traité de Lisbonne: Texte et commentaire article par article des nouveaux traités européens (TUE-TFUE)* (Paris : La Documentation française, 2008), 456: 'Le Royaume-Uni a obtenu . . . un opting out lui évitant, en pratique, d'être lié par la Charte.'

those rights more visible, but does not create new rights or principles'. Legally speaking, these recitals commit not only Poland and the United Kingdom, but all twenty-seven states, which have all accepted them. Other recitals, as well as the two short Articles of the Protocol, bind only Poland and the United Kingdom but, as far as the two recitals mentioned above are concerned, they have been accepted by all twenty-seven as the correct legal interpretation of the Charter. The eighth recital of the Preamble refers to the 'wish of Poland and the United Kingdom to clarify certain aspects of the application of the Charter', and the ninth recital explains that Member States are 'desirous therefore of clarifying the application of the Charter in relation to the laws and administrative action of Poland and the United Kingdom and of its justiciability within Poland and within the United Kingdom'. The twelfth recital reaffirms that the Charter is without prejudice to other obligations of the United Kingdom and Poland deriving from Union law generally.

Is this Protocol an opt-out from the Charter?

This question is debatable. A lot of commentators have considered that Protocol no. 30 constitutes an opt-out from the Charter. One can express the opinion that this is not legally the case. There is no provision in the Protocol stating clearly that the Charter will not be legally binding for the United Kingdom and Poland. In fact, the operative part of Protocol no. 30 is composed of only two short Articles:

- according to Article 1(1) of the Protocol, the Charter does not extend the ability of the European Court of Justice or any British or Polish court to find the laws and practices of the United Kingdom or Poland inconsistent with the Charter. According to paragraph 2 of the same Article 1, nothing in Title IV of the Charter (the 'Solidarity' rights) creates justiciable rights applicable to Poland or the United Kingdom, except insofar as such rights are provided for in their national laws;
- according to Article 2 of the Protocol, the Charter shall apply to the United Kingdom and Poland only to the extent that the rights or principles it contains are recognised by the laws and practices of the United Kingdom or Poland.

One thing is obvious: the legal effects of the Protocol are not easy to determine. The question of whether the Protocol departs from the Charter and sets out a different interpretation to be applied specifically in the United Kingdom and Poland is not easy to answer. The question is whether the Protocol is simply declaratory of the consequences of the Charter across the whole EU or whether it creates different legal effects of the Charter as regards the United Kingdom and Poland, as compared with the other Member States.

As for the Preamble, it makes references to the desire of Member States to 'clarify' – not prescribe – the application of the Charter and does not allow a possibility for Poland and the United Kingdom not to be bound by the Charter.

Article 1(1) of the Protocol reflects the fact that the Charter does not create new rights. If a national law is inconsistent with a provision of the Charter then it is also inconsistent with an EU or international norm. This also reflects Article 51 of the Charter.

Article 1(2) is in line with the references made in a number of Articles of Title IV of the Charter to national laws and practices. It also corresponds to Article 52(5) of the Charter, which sets out the interpretation of the concept of 'principles' in the Charter. Article 52(5) already says that 'principles' cannot be relied upon directly before Courts as being enforceable rights. The Protocol stresses this point. However, Title IV of the Charter reflects principles which could influence the interpretation of EU acts, as provided by the last sentence of Article 52(5) of the Charter, and so indirectly affect individual rights. That said, to the extent that the EU will legislate in areas which are within its competence, national legislators and Courts will in any case be subject to that legislation.

Article 2 of the Protocol simply confirms the interpretation to be given to all Articles of the Charter when they refer to national laws and practices and in particular of Article 52(6) of the Charter, which stipulates that 'full account' is to be taken of national laws and practices where there is a reference to them. However, Article 2 of the Protocol does not prevent the use, in relation to Poland and the United Kingdom, of any relevant Articles of the Charter as referred to by the last sentence of Article 52(5) of the Charter, when interpreting or ruling on the validity of EU acts on the basis of an EU competence not connected with the Charter.

One could tentatively conclude that Protocol no. 30 should not lead to a different application of the Charter in Poland and the United Kingdom as compared with the other Member States. It might be the case that, even in other Member States, national courts will refer to the Protocol in order to interpret the horizontal articles of the Charter.

Moreover, it is worth recalling that the Charter is not the only provider of protection of fundamental rights in the EU. Article 6(3) TEU, under which 'fundamental rights . . . constitute general principles of the Union's law', also provides a means for challenging, on the basis of a violation of fundamental rights, EU law and the way Member States implement EU legislation. This is obviously applicable in Poland and in the United Kingdom. The Protocol does not change this situation: the legally binding status of the Charter is irrelevant where a fundamental right does constitute a general principle. The Court's approach to this has been confirmed in recent rulings on the right to collective action.[36] The Court's interpretation was that its power to rule on violations of the Charter which at the time was not legally binding (and therefore on violations of rights which existed only under international treaties outside the EU or the ECHR context) already existed because the basic principles in the Charter simply reflect general principles common to the Member States.

Ultimately, the interpretation of Protocol no. 30 will be a matter both for the EU Court of Justice and for national courts. It is not possible at this stage to predict what they will decide when interpreting the Protocol. Clearly, EU and Member States' courts cannot ignore the text of the Protocol. It is also likely that the EU Court of Justice will develop a tendency to refer to the rights guaranteed in the Charter and their origins, as well as to the new Article 6(3) TEU on the general principles of EU law, and will develop its fundamental rights jurisprudence on that basis.

The political signal that the UK government wanted to send was probably addressed in the first instance to its internal opinion. The UK government might have been helped, during the national process of ratification of the Lisbon Treaty, by the Protocol, which might have reassured those having concerns about giving a legally binding status to the Charter. But it remains to be seen whether the EU Court of Justice will accept interpreting the Charter in a different way as far as the United Kingdom and Poland are concerned. This is not obvious.

Section 21 The accession of the EU to the European Convention for the Protection of Human Rights and Fundamental Freedoms

The Lisbon Treaty provides that 'the Union shall accede to the European Convention for the Protection of Human Rights and Fundamental Freedoms [ECHR]. Such accession shall not affect the Union's competences as defined in the Treaties' (Article 6(2) TEU).

As to the procedure to accede to the ECHR, Article 218(6)(a)(ii) TFEU provides that the conclusion of the agreement will require the consent of

---

36 See discussion of the 'right to strike', *supra*, in Section 19.

the European Parliament, and Article 218(8), 2nd subparagraph, TFEU provides that such accession will require unanimity in the Council as well as approval by the Member States 'in accordance with their respective constitutional requirements'. The two last requirements (unanimity and ratification by Member States) were agreed upon by the Lisbon IGC.[37]

The EU accession to the ECHR will further reinforce the protection of human rights and fundamental freedoms within the Union, by increasing the uniformity of such protection through a fuller integration of the two European systems, while preserving the specific features of both. This will close a long saga, which started thirty years ago and culminated in the Opinion of the Court of Justice in 1996,[38] which stated that the EC did not have the necessary powers to accede to the ECHR.

The saga started with the 1974 *Solange* case law of the German Constitutional Court (see Section 18). This case worried the Commission, which proposed in 1979 that the European Community accede to the ECHR. That proposal did not meet with the approval of the Council. The Commission renewed it in 1990. The European Parliament, over the years, adopted several resolutions in favour of the Community's accession.

Against this background the Council decided to ask the Court of Justice for an opinion as to whether accession by the Community to the ECHR would be compatible with the EC Treaty. The Court held in 1996 that such an accession would entail a substantial change in the Community system for the protection of human rights, in so far as it would entail the Community entering into a distinct international institutional system, as well as the integration of all the provisions of the Convention into the Community legal order. Such a modification would be of constitutional significance and could therefore be brought about only by way of an amendment to the Treaty.

The 2002–3 Convention was invited to consider the issue by the 2001 Laeken Declaration. This was linked to the idea of making the EU Charter of Fundamental Rights legally binding. This modification of the legal status of the Charter was considered to entail the risk of increasing the possibility of discrepancies between the case law of the two courts (the EU Court of Justice in Luxembourg and the Human Rights Court in

---

37 Compare with Art. III-325 of the Constitutional Treaty which did not provide for these conditions.
38 See Opinion 2/94, 28 March 1996, *Accession of the EC to the ECHR*, [1996] ECR I-1759, paras. 27 and 35.

Strasbourg).[39] Thus it was suggested that a specific legal basis should be inserted into the Constitutional Treaty which would enable the Union 'to seek accession' to the ECHR. The Convention suggested that the Council would act unanimously when deciding to seek such accession. This voting rule was changed during the 2003–4 IGC to provide instead for QMV. The text of the legal basis itself was changed, on a proposal from the Legal Experts Group, to state directly that the Union 'shall accede' to the ECHR.

The 2003–4 IGC also agreed on the text of a new Protocol (the present Protocol no. 8). This Protocol requires certain conditions to be respected when proceeding with the accession:

- the specific characteristics of the Union and of Union law must be preserved, particularly in relation to the arrangements for the Union's possible participation in the control bodies of the ECHR, and in relation to the mechanisms concerning proceedings by non-Member States and individual applications;
- the competences of the Union and the powers of its institutions must not be affected;
- it must be ensured that the accession does not affect the situation of Member States in relation to the ECHR (protocols, derogations and reservations);
- actions between the Union and its Member States would have to be excluded from the scope of the agreement on accession, in order to take account of the monopoly conferred on the EU Court of Justice in such matters by Article 344 TFEU.

Moreover, a Declaration no. 2 was annexed to the Final Act of the Lisbon IGC, in which the Conference stated that the Union's accession to the ECHR should be arranged in such a way as to preserve the specific features of Union law. The IGC considered, in this connection, that the regular dialogue between the EU Court of Justice and the European Court of Human Rights could be reinforced when the Union acceded to the ECHR.

As said above, the Lisbon IGC decided to revert to unanimity in the Council for the EU to accede to the ECHR and to provide for ratification by each Member State (Article 218(8) TFEU). This does not really change things, due to the fact that, in any case, since the twenty-seven EU Member

---

39 It should be noted that the Strasbourg Court considers that the EU does effectively protect human rights (see the above-mentioned judgment of 30 June 2005 of the Human Rights Court, case 45036/98, *Bosphorus Hava Yollari Turizm v. Ireland*).

States are all contracting parties to the ECHR, each of them will have to ratify the amendments that will have to be made to the ECHR, in the context of the Council of Europe, in order to allow for the EU to become a party to it. This might not be easy. A good sign is that Protocol no. 14 to the ECHR, which allows the EU to accede to the ECHR, has finally been ratified by all the States members of the Council of Europe.[40] However, further amendments will need to be negotiated, adopted and ratified in order to allow the accession of the EU. A number of issues, such as deciding by whom and when the EU will be represented in the Court and in the Committee of Ministers, will have to be resolved.

Some time will no doubt be needed before the EU's accession, which will have the result that the Court of Strasbourg will be recognised as the single final authority in the field of human rights in Europe. This will avoid any risk of conflict between the Court of Luxembourg and the Court of Strasbourg. It will also avoid Member States being considered responsible for possible violations of the ECHR by the EU institutions.[41] It is true that those risks, which were small, have been further diminished by Article 52(3) of the Charter, which states that 'in so far as [the] Charter contains rights which correspond to rights guaranteed by the [ECHR], the meaning and scope of those rights shall be the same as those laid down by the said Convention. This provision shall not prevent Union law providing more extensive protection.'

40 This Protocol amends Art. 59 of the ECHR to provide that 'the EU may accede to this Convention'.

41 See judgment of 18 February 1999 of the Human Rights Court, case 24833/94, *Matthews v. UK*, in which the Court held that 'the very essence of the applicant's right to vote, as guaranteed by Art. 3 of Protocol No. 1 [to the ECHR] was denied' and that 'there has been a violation of that provision'. The applicant had contested the fact that an Annex III to the 1976 Act concerning the election of MEPs by direct universal suffrage, which is a primary law Act and cannot therefore be challenged before the EU Court of Justice, provided that the 1976 Act applied only to the United Kingdom (and not to Gibraltar). The Strasbourg Court found that, in such a case, the United Kingdom, as well as all parties to the 1976 Act, were responsible *ratione materia* under the ECHR.

V

Freedom, security and justice

Section 22 A short history of Justice and Home Affairs in the EU

The 1957 Rome Treaty did not contain provisions conferring powers on the Community in the area of Justice and Home Affairs. Co-operation among Member States in this field was being developed in the larger framework of the Council of Europe. The only provision dealing with a judicial issue was Article 220 of the EC Treaty (later renumbered 293 and now repealed by the Lisbon Treaty), which requested the Member States to conclude conventions between themselves on, *inter alia*, 'the simplification of formalities governing the reciprocal recognition and enforcement of judgments of courts or tribunals and of arbitration awards'. The 1968 Brussels Convention on jurisdiction and the enforcement of judgments in civil and commercial matters was concluded on this basis.[1]

Co-operation between Member States in the field of Justice and Home Affairs began in the 1970s. It took place in the framework of European Political Co-operation, as well as in the margins of the Council, involving ministers for home affairs on issues such as terrorism and police co-operation, drugs or border controls. The so-called 'TREVI Group'[2] was established informally in June 1976, following a request from the

---

1 This Convention was signed on 27 September 1968 and entered into force on 1 February 1973 (OJ No. L299, 31 December 1972, 32). It has been replaced by a Council Regulation (No. 44/2001, so-called 'Brussels I'), which entered into force on 1 March 2002 (OJ No. L12, 16 January 2001, 1). One may also mention the Rome Convention on the law applicable to contractual obligations signed on 19 June 1980, which entered into force on 1 April 1991 (OJ No. L266, 9 October 1980, 1). It has also been replaced by a European Parliament and Council Regulation (No 593/2008, so-called 'Rome I') which entered into force on 24 July 2008 and became applicable on 17 December 2009 (OJ No. L177, 4 July 2008, 6).

2 TREVI is said either to refer to the Trevi Fountain in Rome or to be a French acronym for 'Terrorisme, Radicalisme, Extrémisme, Violence Internationale'. Gradually, this Group came to meet in different configurations: TREVI I on counter-terrorism, TREVI II on police training and exchange of information, TREVI III on the fight against organised crime, and TREVI 92 on the abolition of controls for persons at internal borders.

European Council meeting in Rome in December 1975. Discussions in the margins also began to involve justice ministers concerning judicial co-operation, although most developments in judicial matters continued to take place within the larger framework of the Council of Europe and the Hague Conference on private international law.

Over time, several Member States were convinced that establishing complete free movement of persons within the Community, in a way that would be more efficient and also more visible for the citizens, should entail the abolition of physical controls on all persons at internal borders. However, such a move would require 'compensatory measures', such as reinforced controls at external borders, a common visa policy and other measures regarding third-country nationals, enhanced police and judicial co-operation, information exchange, and so on. The purpose of these measures was to ensure that the free movement of persons would not also become a 'free movement of criminals'.

The Single European Act

In 1986 the Single European Act inserted a new Article 8a in the EC Treaty which stated that 'the internal market shall comprise an area without internal frontiers, in which the free movement of goods, persons, services and capital is ensured in accordance with the provisions of this Treaty'. A Declaration on this Article confirmed the right of Member States to continue to take measures on 'controlling immigration from third countries, and to combat terrorism, crime, the traffic in drugs and illicit trading in works of art and antiques'. Another Declaration 'on the free movement of persons' stated that 'in order to promote the free movement of persons, the Member States shall co-operate . . . in particular as regards the entry, movement and residence of nationals of third countries. They shall also co-operate in the combating of terrorism, crime, trafficking in drugs and illicit trading in works of art and antiques.'

Underpinning this was the wish of several Member States to move towards what was called at the time a 'People's Europe' or 'Citizens' Europe', a Europe which the citizens would see as being of benefit to them in a concrete way. To that end, a committee was created in June 1984 by the European Council in Fontainebleau, whose mandate included the task of making proposals on 'how all police and customs formalities on the movement of persons at borders within the Community could be abolished as quickly as possible'.

The Schengen Agreement

Steps toward achieving this goal began outside the legal framework of the Community; one year after the Fontainebleau meeting, on 14 June 1985, Belgium, France, the Federal Republic of Germany, Luxembourg and the Netherlands signed, in Schengen, a village in Luxembourg at the border with France and Germany, the Schengen Agreement, which set out short-term measures and long-term objectives on the gradual abolition of checks at their common borders. The Agreement entered into force on 2 March 1986, but the actual lifting of borders was conditional upon the adoption of 'compensatory measures' to the abolition of checks on persons at internal borders. Therefore, on 19 June 1990, the same states signed the 'Schengen Implementing Convention' on 'compensatory measures' which constituted the heart of the system. They were joined later, through the conclusion of accession protocols, by Italy (November 1990), Portugal and Spain (June 1991), Greece (November 1992), Austria (April 1995) and the Nordic countries – Denmark, Finland and Sweden (December 1996).[3] The 'Schengen area' entered into force on 26 March 1995 comprising the five original states plus Portugal and Spain. It entered into force in October 1997 for Italy, in December 1997 for Austria and, after the integration of the Schengen *acquis* into the framework of the Union under the Amsterdam Treaty, in January 2000 for Greece and in March 2001 for the five Nordic States (Denmark, Finland, Sweden, Iceland and Norway).

The Maastricht Treaty

In the meantime, on 1 November 1993, the Maastricht Treaty had introduced provisions on co-operation in the fields of Justice and Home Affairs in Title VI of the EU Treaty (the third pillar). These provisions were no longer merely a corollary to the development of the internal market, but aimed to foster more efficient co-operation against cross-border criminality and illegal immigration. Ten Articles set out the procedures for dealing with nine areas 'of common interest': asylum policy, rules on crossing by persons of the external borders of the Member States and the exercise of controls at such borders, immigration policy and policy regarding nationals of third countries, combating

---

3 In December 1996, an Agreement was also signed with two non-EU Member States, Iceland and Norway, which allowed them to join the Schengen area together with the other Nordic countries and thus preserve the Nordic Passport Union.

drug addiction, combating fraud on an international scale, judicial co-operation in civil matters, judicial co-operation in criminal matters, customs co-operation and police co-operation. Like the second pillar (CFSP–ESDP), the third pillar functioned on the basis of unanimity in the Council, the other institutions (the European Parliament, the Commission and the Court of Justice) having only a very limited role. The Maastricht Treaty also introduced in the EC Treaty a new Article 100c, enabling the Council to adopt, by QMV, measures relating to a uniform format for visas and to determine, first by unanimity and, as from 1 January 1996, by QMV, 'the third countries whose nationals must be in possession of a visa when crossing the external borders of the Member States'.[4]

The Amsterdam Treaty

With its entry into force on 1 May 1999, the Amsterdam Treaty represented a first important breakthrough in the facilitation of decision-making in the area. The JHA provisions were completely rewritten. Measures relating to external border controls on persons (including visa policy[5]), asylum, immigration and safeguarding the rights of nationals of third countries, as well as measures in the field of judicial co-operation in civil matters, were 'communitarised' – that is, they were transferred from the former EU Treaty to the EC Treaty (new Title IV in Part Three of the EC Treaty). The remaining provisions in Title VI of the former EU Treaty were limited to police and judicial co-operation in criminal matters. At the same time, the Amsterdam Treaty incorporated, through a Protocol, the Schengen Convention and its Protocols into the EU framework.

A number of provisions which were transferred into the EC Treaty were switched from unanimity to QMV. For judicial co-operation in civil matters (except family law), codecision and QMV applied immediately upon entry into force of the Amsterdam Treaty (1 May 1999).[6] For some

---

4 The Council adopted two Regulations on this basis: Council Regulation (EC) No. 1683/95 of 29 May 1995, laying down a uniform format for visas (OJ No. L164, 14 July 1995, 1), and Council Regulation (EC) No. 574/1999 of 12 March 1999, determining the third countries whose nationals must be in possession of visas when crossing the external borders of the Member States (OJ No. L72, 18 March 1999, 2).

5 Except for the two visa issues (a list of third countries whose nationals are required to have visas, and a uniform format for visas), which were already covered by Art. 100c TEC and submitted to QMV. This Article was repealed by the Amsterdam Treaty and its subject matter was inserted in Art. 62(2)(i) and (iii) TEC, which continued to provide for QMV in the Council (and consultation of the European Parliament).

6 See 2nd indent of Art. 67(5) TEC.

other matters, the Amsterdam Treaty contained a deadline of five years at the end of which (1 May 2004) certain legal bases automatically switched from unanimity to QMV.[7] The Treaty also requested the Council to make use, by that date, of the *passerelle* which enabled the switching to the codecision procedure and QMV and to 'normalise' the provisions on the powers of the Court of Justice. The Council did use the *passerelle* in December 2004 and decided to switch a number of matters from unanimity to codecision and QMV as from 1 January 2005.[8]

The Court of Justice became fully competent in respect of the 'communitarised' matters,[9] with the exception of two limits set out in Article 68 of the EC Treaty: a preliminary ruling may be requested only by last-instance national courts, which have the choice of whether or not to make the request,[10] and the Court of Justice 'shall not have jurisdiction to

---

7 See Art. 67(4) TEC. As from 1 May 2004, codecision and QMV became applicable for adopting:

- procedures and conditions for issuing visas (Art. 62(2)(b)(ii)) TEC; and
- rules on a uniform visa (Art. 62(2)(b)(iv) TEC).

8 See Art. 67(2), 2nd indent, TEC. The Council Decision making use of this *passerelle* was adopted on 22 December 2004 (see footnote 58 in Chapter II). It made codecision and QMV applicable as from 1 January 2005 for adopting:

- measures removing controls on persons at internal borders (Art. 62(1) TEC);
- measures setting out standards and procedures for checks on persons at external borders (Art. 62(2)(a) TEC);
- measures setting out conditions under which third-country nationals can travel within the EC for a maximum of three months (Art. 62(3) TEC);
- 'burden sharing' measures between Member States with regard to the receiving of refugees and displaced persons (Art. 63(2)(b) TEC);
- measures with regard to illegal immigration and illegal residence, including repatriation (Art. 63(3)(b) TEC).

   The Council did not touch on the powers of the Court of Justice, which therefore remained restricted in accordance with Art. 68 TEC.

   In addition, pursuant to Art. 67(5), 1st indent, TEC, the precondition for any switching to codecision and QMV on issues regarding refugees and temporary protection was that the Council should have first, by unanimity, defined 'common rules and basic principles' governing such issues, which it did through the adoption of successive legislative acts, culminating in the Asylum Procedures Directive (2005/85/EE) adopted on 1 December 2005.

9 I.e. the entire range of judicial proceedings provided for by the EC Treaty, such as infringement proceedings (Arts. 226, 227 and 228 TEC), actions for annulment (Art. 230 TEC), actions for failure to act (Art. 232 TEC), preliminary rulings (Art. 234 TEC, with certain limits), action for damages (Arts. 235 and 235 TEC) and plea of illegality (Art. 241 TEC).

10 Under the ordinary preliminary ruling procedure provided for in Art. 234 TEC, questions may be asked by any national court or tribunal and last-instance courts are obliged to ask interpretation or validity questions.

rule on any measure or decision taken pursuant to Article 62(1) [on the absence of controls of persons when crossing internal borders] relating to the maintenance of law and order and the safeguarding of internal security'.

By comparison, the jurisdiction of the Court of Justice in the third pillar remained somewhat more limited. According to Article 35 of the former EU Treaty, only actions for annulment, preliminary rulings and dispute settlement could be brought to the Court of Justice, with a number of limitations. Actions for annulment could be brought only by the Commission or a Member State (by neither the European Parliament nor individuals), preliminary rulings could be requested only by courts or tribunals from those Member States which had accepted, in a declaration, the jurisdiction of the Court of Justice.[11] In doing so, the Member States were allowed to choose to limit the preliminary ruling questions only to last-instance courts, without obliging them to request a ruling (while in such a case, Article 234 of the EC Treaty obliged the last-instance courts to bring the question before the Court of Justice).[12] Other types of actions (infringement proceedings, actions for failure to act, actions for damages and pleas of illegality) were not allowed in the third pillar.

In order to take into account the specific needs in the JHA area, the Statute of the Court of Justice (and the Rules of Procedure) were amended to introduce an urgent preliminary ruling procedure. This procedure entered into force on 1 March 2008, and enables the Court of Justice to give preliminary rulings in about two months instead of the average nineteen months that are required for a normal procedure.[13]

The enlargement of the Schengen area

On 25 March 2001, the Schengen area covered thirteen of the then fifteen Member States, the two Member States not covered being Ireland and the

---

11 Out of twenty-seven Member States, only nineteen had, by 1 December 2009, accepted the jurisdiction of the Court of Justice to give preliminary rulings (Germany, Austria, Belgium, Cyprus, Spain, Finland, France, Greece, Hungary, Italy, Latvia, Lithuania, Luxembourg, the Netherlands, Portugal, the Czech Republic, Romania, Slovenia and Sweden).

12 Of the nineteen Member States which had accepted the jurisdiction of the Court of Justice (see note 11), only Spain has used this possibility to limit preliminary ruling questions to last-instance courts only.

13 See Art. 23a of the Statute of the Court of Justice and 104b of its Rules of Procedure. On this procedure see B. Chevalier, 'Les nouveaux développements de la procédure préjudicielle dans le domaine de l'espace judiciaire européen: la procédure préjudicielle d'urgence et les réformes principales prévues par le traité de Lisbonne' (2009) 9 *ERA Forum* 591.

United Kingdom. Two third states, Iceland and Norway, were associated with the area, in accordance with an Agreement concluded in May 1999 on the basis of Article 6 of the Protocol integrating the Schengen *acquis* into the framework of the European Union.[14] Only Ireland and the United Kingdom, which, under the Amsterdam Treaty, obtained the right to opt out, continued to apply controls on persons at their borders with the other Member States. Denmark also obtained the right to opt out of participating in the adoption of Community measures based on the new Title IV of the EC Treaty, but still applied them when they were part of, or constituted a development of, the Schengen *acquis*, although only as 'an obligation under international law' (Article 5 of the Protocol on the position of Denmark). Following the EU enlargements on 1 May 2004 and on 1 January 2007, the process towards fully applying the Schengen rules to the new Member States has continued. In December 2007, the Schengen area was extended to the three Baltic states, Poland, the Czech Republic, Slovakia, Hungary, Slovenia and Malta. At the time of writing, the Schengen area covered twenty-two out of twenty-seven Member States (the exceptions being Ireland, the United Kingdom, Cyprus, Bulgaria and Romania).[15]

In addition to Iceland and Norway, the Schengen area covers one more third State (Switzerland, since 2008),[16] and will also cover Liechtenstein (possibly by summer 2010).[17]

---

14 Agreement with the Republic of Iceland and the Kingdom of Norway concerning the latter's association with the implementation, application and development of the Schengen *acquis* (OJ No. L176, 10 July 1999, 36).

15 The controls were lifted on 21 December 2007 for land and maritime borders and on 30 March 2008 for air borders with nine Member States (Estonia, Hungary, Latvia, Lithuania, Malta, Poland, Slovenia, Slovakia and the Czech Republic), Cyprus still maintaining border controls. As to Bulgaria and Romania, border controls will be lifted once the conditions are met, following completion of the usual 'Schengen evaluation' process.

16 See Agreement between the EU and the EC and Switzerland signed on 26 October 2004 (OJ No. L53, 27 February 2008, 52). The Swiss people accepted it by a majority of 54.6 per cent in a referendum on 5 June 2005 and the Agreement became applicable on 12 December 2008 with regard to land borders and on 29 March 2009 with regard to air borders. In addition, the Swiss people also accepted by a majority of 56 per cent in a referendum on 25 September 2005 to extend to the ten new EU Member States the scope of the EU–Switzerland agreement on free movement of persons. They did the same on 8 February 2009, by a majority of 59.6 per cent, with regard to Bulgaria and Romania.

17 See the Protocol to the Agreement with Switzerland signed on 28 February 2008 (Council doc. 16462/06).

More variable geometry

In the meantime, this 'Schengen technique' – that is, variable geometry developed first outside the Treaties and gradually introduced into the EU system – has continued to evolve. One can mention for instance the decision by four Member States (Belgium, France, Germany and Spain) to interconnect their criminal records as from 31 March 2006.[18] They were later joined by the Czech Republic and Luxembourg. The Commission then submitted a proposal for a Council framework decision on the organisation and content of the exchange between Member States of information extracted from criminal records, which was adopted by the Council on 26 February 2009.[19] It also adopted a Council Decision setting up the corresponding information technology system (ECRIS).[20] A pilot project of interconnection is already working between fourteen Member States.

Similarly, the Prüm Convention was signed in Prüm (a small German city close to the border with Belgium and Luxembourg) on 27 May 2005 by seven Member States (Austria, Belgium, France, Germany, Luxembourg, the Netherlands and Spain).[21] It concerned exchange of police data such as DNA profiles, fingerprints and vehicle number plates. This Convention was to a large extent taken over in two Council Decisions adopted on 23 June 2008.[22]

Finally, since 2003, in a move not very popular among the other Member States, the home affairs ministers from the five largest Member States (Italy, France, Germany, Spain and the United Kingdom), calling themselves 'G 5', and then 'G 6' when they were joined by Poland, decided to meet regularly to discuss issues of common interest.[23]

---

18 The four Member States considered insufficient the Council Decision on the exchange of information extracted from criminal records which had been adopted on 21 November 2005 (OJ No. L322, 9 December 2005, 33). This Decision was designed to improve the systems of the 1959 European Convention on Mutual Assistance in Criminal Matters, mainly by speeding up transmission times.

19 See COM(2005) 690 final, Council Framework Decision 2009/315/ JHA (OJ No. L93, 7 April 2009, 23).

20 Council Decision 2009/316/JHA of 6 April 2009 (OJ No. L93, 7 April 2009, 33).

21 This Convention is reproduced in Council doc. 10900/05 of 7 July 2005.

22 See Council Decision 2008/615/JHA of 23 June 2008 on the stepping-up of cross-border co-operation, particularly in combating terrorism and cross-border crime (OJ No. L210, 6 August 2008, 1) and its implementing Decision 2008/616/JHA (OJ No. L210, 6 August 2008, 12).

23 The first meeting took place in May 2003 in Jerez (Spain) and was followed by more than ten meetings.

From the 2002–3 Convention to the Lisbon IGC

The 2002–3 Convention which proposed the draft Constitutional Treaty was nearly unanimous in its wish to strengthen the third pillar and to make it subject to the ordinary Community procedures. There was a common view in the 2004 IGC that the Area of Freedom, Security and Justice (FSJ), the new name for JHA, constituted one of the most important matters for the future of the Union. The IGC therefore decided to follow the path suggested by the Convention.

The wish to improve decision-making as well as the standard of democratic and judicial control, in order to develop the Union into an 'area of freedom, security and justice', had been repeatedly proclaimed to be 'at the very top of the political agenda'.[24] Despite the five-year programme adopted by the European Council in October 1999 and the following five-year programme (called 'The Hague Programme') adopted by the European Council in November 2004,[25] substantive progress in this area had been hampered mainly by the requirement of unanimity in the Council. Before the entry into force of the Lisbon Treaty, unanimity was still required for the whole of Title VI of the EU Treaty (police and judicial co-operation in criminal matters).[26] Unanimity was also required for family law issues in the field of judicial co-operation in civil matters (Article 65 of the EC Treaty) and legal immigration (Article 63(3)(a) and (4) of the EC Treaty). Unanimity not only made discussions in the Council much more difficult and lengthy, but also diminished the level of ambition in the search for a common (often low) denominator among Member States.

In addition, the powers of the Court of Justice were limited[27] both in the third pillar and in the EC Title on Visas, Asylum and Immigration, and the types of legal instrument available in the third pillar (decisions and framework decisions without direct effect)[28] were considered less effective

24 See 3rd paragraph of the Presidency Conclusions, European Council, Tampere (Finland), 15–16 March 1999 (doc. SN 2001/1/99 REV 1).
25 See Annex 1 to Presidency Conclusions, European Council, 4–5 November 2004 (doc. 14292/1/04 REV 1).
26 With the exception of measures necessary to implement Decisions, see Art. 34(2)(c) former TEU.
27 See H. Labayle, 'Architecte ou spectatrice? La Cour de justice de l'Union dans l'Espace de liberté, sécurité et justice' (2006) 42(1) *Revue trimestrielle de droit européen* 1. See also J. Callewaert, 'The European Court of Human Rights and the Area of Freedom, Security and Justice' (2007) 8 *ERA Forum* 511; and D. Leczykiewicz, 'Constitutional Conflicts and the Third Pillar' (2008) 33 *European Law Review* 230.
28 However, the case law of the Court of Justice limited the negative impact that this 'no direct effect' rule could have had on the preliminary ruling procedures. In 2005, having

- the ordinary types of legal instrument[31] (regulations, directives and decisions as defined in Article 288 TFEU);
- the general and horizontal principles of EU law;
- the full powers of the EU institutions, notably the powers of control by the Commission and the Court of Justice over the proper implementation by Member States of the legislative acts, although with a five-year transitional period with regard to third pillar acts adopted before 1 December 2009.

The purpose of these changes is to allow an efficient decision-making process and for better implementation by the Member States of the EU measures while making them subject to a proper parliamentary and judicial control, in order to improve the balance between security and judicial protection of citizens. One may argue that since the '9/11' tragedy, the fight against terrorism has become such a priority for the EU that this balance has not always been respected.

QMV and codecision for asylum, immigration and external border controls

All provisions on border checks, asylum and immigration (Chapter 2 of Title V of the TFEU) are now submitted to QMV and codecision. The situation in force before the Lisbon Treaty was that border checks and illegal immigration had been switched to QMV (now covered by Article 77 TFEU), as well as asylum and temporary protection in respect of which the EC acts defining the 'common rules and basic principles' had been adopted unanimously (as required by Article 67(5) TEC).[32] With the Lisbon Treaty, the remaining issue which was still subject to unanimity – that is, legal immigration – is now submitted to QMV and codecision (Article 79 TFEU).

In addition, these policies are made subject to the principle of solidarity and fair sharing of responsibility, including its financial implications.

---

31 However, Art. 9 of Protocol no. 36 on transitional provisions preserves the legal effects of third pillar acts (i.e. the absence of direct effects) adopted under the TEU prior to the entry into force of the Lisbon Treaty until those acts are repealed, annulled or amended under the Treaties as amended by the Lisbon Treaty.

32 Regulation 2725/2000 (Eurodac); Regulation 343/2003 (Dublin II); Directive 2003/09 (Reception); Directive 2004/83 (Qualification); Directive 2005/85 (Procedures); Directive 2001/55 (Temporary Protection) and Decision 2000/596 (Refugee Fund).

Specific provisions giving effect to this principle can be inserted in the acts adopted under Chapter 2 (Article 80 TFEU).

A more precise provision on judicial co-operation in civil matters

As had already been the case since 1 May 1999, judicial co-operation in civil matters remains subject to QMV in the Council and to codecision. Only 'measures concerning family law with cross-border implications' remain submitted to unanimity.[33] Article 81 TFEU reproduces the provisions of Article 65 TEC. The conditions remain the same: 'judicial co-operation', 'cross-border implication'[34] and 'necessary for the proper functioning of the internal market', although the latter condition has been mitigated (with the addition of the word 'particularly'). Some elements are added, such as the principle of mutual recognition of judicial and extrajudicial decisions and the possibility of adopting measures for effective access to justice, alternative methods of dispute settlement and training measures, but, in essence, the scope of the legal basis is not extended. It is even made more precise than in the EC Treaty and, more importantly, the list of areas in which EU measures may be adopted is made exhaustive.[35]

A restriction has been added by the Lisbon IGC with regard to the *passerelle* concerning family law matters. While under the EC Treaty[36] the *passerelle* enabled the Council, by unanimity and after consulting the European Parliament, to switch family law issues to QMV and codecision (see Article 67(2), 2nd indent, TEC), the Lisbon Treaty has added a new requirement for the use of this *passerelle*. A proposal to switch aspects of family law from unanimity to QMV and codecision will, in addition, have to be notified to national parliaments; the opposition of one, within

33 See Art. 81(3) TFEU. It remains to be seen whether it will always be easy to determine whether a given proposed measure constitutes such 'measure concerning family law'.

34 As to the condition of 'cross-border implications', the Commission has sometimes made a rather 'generous' interpretation of this condition and has proposed, for instance in the Regulation on a European Small Claims Procedure, to regulate also purely internal situations when they were not ancillary to the cross-border situation. The cross-border element must be a real and present one, not only theoretically and vaguely possible.

35 In Art. 65 TEC, the list of issues was clearly non-exhaustive ('measures... shall include'). In Art. 81 TFEU, the introductory paragraph says 'measures... aimed at ensuring', and then sets out the list of issues. In spite of that, the German Constitutional Court, in its judgment of 30 June 2009, was of the opinion that 'the Treaty of Lisbon... extends the European Union's existing possibilities of action in the area of judicial co-operation in civil matters' (para. 367).

36 And also in the failed Constitutional Treaty (see Art. III-269(3), 2nd subparagraph).

six months, will suffice to prevent the proposal from being adopted by the Council (see Article 81(3), 2nd and 3rd subparagraphs, TFEU).[37] It remains to be seen whether it will always be straightforward to determine whether a given proposed measure constitutes a measure concerning family law.

QMV and codecision for most provisions on criminal matters

With some exceptions, the Lisbon Treaty has switched most of the legal bases of the former third pillar on judicial co-operation in criminal matters (Chapter 4 of Title V of the TFEU) and police co-operation (Chapter 5 of Title V of the TFEU) to QMV and codecision. Thus the EU legislator is now empowered to adopt in codecision:

- provisions in the field of mutual assistance (recognition of judgments,[38] prevention and settlement of conflicts of jurisdiction, co-operation in proceedings, enforcement of decisions), including, where necessary for facilitating mutual recognition, approximation of specific national procedural laws through the adoption of minimum rules (Article 82 TFEU);
- provisions in the field of substantive criminal law setting out minimum rules concerning the definition of criminal offences and sanctions in a number of areas of serious crime with a cross-border dimension (Article 83 TFEU);
- supporting measures for helping Member States in the field of crime prevention (Article 84 TFEU);
- specific provisions on police co-operation (collection, storage, processing, analysis and exchange of information, co-operation in training and exchange of staff, on equipment and on research into crime-detection, common investigative techniques) (Article 87(2) TFEU);

---

37 Despite this new requirement the German Constitutional Court, in its judgment of 30 June 2009, ruled that the German parliament should adopt a law before the German representative in the Council could accept an extension of the EU competences for family law measures (para. 369).

38 The principle of 'mutual recognition of judgments and judicial decisions' being the underlying principle of the whole area of judicial co-operation in criminal matters (Art. 82(1), 1st subparagraph, TFEU). On the debate about the link between mutual recognition and approximation of national legislations in order to create mutual trust between Member States, see I. Bantekas, 'The Principle of Mutual Recognition in EU Criminal Law' (2007) 32 *European Law Review* 365.

- provisions setting out the structure, operation, field of action and tasks of Eurojust[39] (Article 85 TFEU) and Europol[40] (Article 88 TFEU) (on these two agencies see Box 23).

Such a major switch from unanimity to QMV and codecision was made acceptable to those Member States most sensitive about it because of the following measures:

- there is now a better delimitation of the scope of the legal bases compared with those in the former third pillar;
- a new procedural 'brake–accelerator' device has been provided for;
- more democratic control is ensured through new powers granted to the European Parliament and to the national parliaments (see below under 'Specific procedures for improving the functioning and democratic control of the FSJ Area');
- the 'mutual evaluation' mechanism has been extended;
- powers of initiative for the Member States have been kept in some areas (see below under 'Keeping the right of initiative of the Member States, extending the "mutual evaluation" system and adding some specific national concerns').

The redrafting of the legal bases on criminal procedure and substantive criminal law resulted in a more precisely defined scope and therefore a more limited competence for the Union.[41] While Article 31 of the former TEU on judicial co-operation in criminal matters began with the words 'common action . . . shall include', thus making non-exhaustive the list which followed, Articles 82, 83 and 87 TFEU are drafted in a limitative way, making the list of issues where competences are conferred on the

39 Eurojust was established by Council Decision 2002/187/JHA of 28 February 2002 (OJ No. L63, 6 March 2002, 1). This Decision has been substantially amended by Council Decision 2009/426/JHA of 16 December 2008 (OJ No. L138, 4 June 2009, 14).
40 Europol was established by a Convention signed on 26 July 1995 (the substantive legal basis of which was Art. K.1(9) of the TEU, which later on became Art. 30(2) TEU) (OJ No. C316, 27 November 1995, 2). It entered into force on 1 October 1998. On 6 April 2009, the Council decided to transform the Europol Convention into a Council Decision (doc. 8706/3/08 REV 3). This Decision became applicable on 1 January 2010. Europol therefore became subject to normal EU Staff Rules and to EU budget financing.
41 In spite of that, the German Constitutional Court, in its judgment of 30 June 2009, was of the opinion that 'the Treaty of Lisbon considerably extends the European Union's competences in the area of the administration of criminal law' (para. 352). It also said that 'the corresponding foundations of competence in the Treaties must be interpreted strictly – on no account extensively – , and their use requires particular justification' (para. 358).

BOX 23. EUROPOL AND EUROJUST

Europol was first mentioned in Article K.1(9) of the EU Treaty (Maastricht Treaty of 1992) as a 'Union-wide system for exchanging police information'. Based in The Hague, it was established in 1993 by a Ministerial Agreement in order to fight drug trafficking. This Agreement was replaced in 1995 by a Joint Action taken on the basis of Article K.3 of the EU Treaty* to establish the 'Europol Drug Unit' with a mandate wider than only drug trafficking, as it also covered trafficking in radioactive and nuclear substances, clandestine immigration networks and vehicle trafficking. This Joint Action was replaced by the 1995 Convention which entered into force in 1998. Europol is now regulated by a Council Decision adopted on 6 April 2009, which became applicable on 1 January 2010.**

The objective of Europol is 'to support and strengthen action by the competent authorities of the Member States and their mutual cooperation in preventing and combating organised crime, terrorism and other forms of serious crime affecting two or more Member States' (Article 3 of the 2009 Council Decision). Its tasks cover a wide range of criminal offences which are listed in an annex to the Decision. Its main task is the collection and exchange of information and the co-ordination of investigations carried out by national authorities.

These tasks correspond to those listed, in a non-exhaustive fashion, by Article 88 TFEU, which also provides that Europol's structure, operation, field of action and tasks should be determined by a regulation to be adopted in codecision by the European Parliament and the Council (acting by QMV). Until this is adopted, the present Council Decision, as adopted in April 2009, will continue to form the basis for the operation of Europol.

Eurojust was established in 2002 by a Council Decision,*** following a request from the European Council in Tampere in October 1999. Its legal basis was first inserted in the Amsterdam Treaty (Article 31(2) former EU Treaty). It was preceded by a Provisional Judicial Co-operation Unit. It is composed of one national member seconded from each Member State (prosecutor, judge or police officer with equivalent competence). Its main tasks are to support and improve co-ordination

---

* Joint Action of 10 March 1995 adopted by the Council on the basis of Article K.3 of the Treaty on European Union concerning the Europol Drugs Unit (OJ No. L62, 20 March 1995, p. 1).

** Council Decision of 6 April 2009 establishing the European Police Office (Europol) (OJ No. L121, 15 May 2009, 37). For more details see G. Roland and E. Buyssens, 'La transformation d'Europol en agence de l'Union – Regards sur un nouveau cadre juridique', *Revue du Marché commun et de l'Union européenne*, February 2009, 83.

*** Council Decision of 28 February 2002 setting up Eurojust with a view to reinforcing the fight against serious crime (OJ No. L63, 6 March 2002, 1), amended by Council Decision of 16 December 2008 (OJ No. L138, 4 June 2009, 14).

and co-operation between national investigating and prosecuting authorities in relation to serious crime and to facilitate the execution of judicial decisions during investigations. The list of offences concerned is essentially the same as that for Europol.

These tasks also correspond broadly to those listed, in a non-exhaustive fashion, by Article 85 TFEU. As for Europol, Eurojust's structure, operation, field of action and tasks should be determined by a regulation to be adopted in codecision by the European Parliament and the Council (acting by QMV). Until this is adopted, the present Council Decision, as amended in December 2008, will continue to form the basis for the operation of Eurojust.

Union an exhaustive one. In addition, the opening paragraphs of Articles 82 and 83 TFEU set out a new limitative condition for action – that is, the 'cross-border dimension'.[42] These limitations are balanced by specific provisions which enable the Council, by unanimity and with the consent of the European Parliament, to extend these lists of issues, thus offering the necessary flexibility in the future, should the need arise.[43] The provisions listing the tasks of Eurojust and Europol, on the other hand, are drafted in a non-exhaustive way ('these tasks may include: . . .', Articles 85(1) and 88(2) TFEU).

In addition, Article 83(2) TFEU clarifies a contentious issue which had emerged with the adoption, in 2003 and 2005 respectively, of two framework decisions which provided for criminal penalties in the field of environment protection.[44] This was contested by the Commission, which claimed that the Community legislator was competent to define, in a Community act, criminal offences when this was necessary to ensure the effective implementation of a Community measure. The Court of Justice annulled the two framework decisions.[45] Article 83(2) TFEU resolves this

---

42 On the 'cross-border' requirement, see *supra*, note 34. See also para. 363 of the judgment of 30 June 2009 of the German Constitutional Court.

43 See Art. 82(2)(d) TFEU on the possible extension of the list of criminal procedure issues on which minimum EU rules may be adopted, and Art. 83(1), 3rd subparagraph, TFEU on the possible extension of the areas of crime on which minimum EU rules on the definition of criminal offences and sanctions may be adopted.

44 Council Framework Decision 2003/80/JHA of 27 January 2003 on the protection of the environment through criminal law (OJ No. L29, 5 February 2003, 55) and Council Framework Decision 2005/667/JHA of 12 July 2005 to strengthen the criminal law framework for the enforcement of the law against ship-source pollution (OJ No. L255, 30 September 2005, 164).

45 The leading case on this issue is the judgment of 13 September 2005 (Case C-176/03, *Commission v. Council*, [2005] ECR I-7879). In point 48, the Court ruled that 'when the application of effective, proportionate and dissuasive criminal penalties by the competent

issue and expressly enables the EU legislator to adopt directives establishing 'minimum rules with regard to the definition of criminal offences and sanctions' if this 'proves essential to ensure the effective implementation of a Union policy in an area which has been subject to harmonisation measures'. In order to avoid the adoption of such a directive hampering the harmonisation measures in the EU policy area concerned, Article 83(2) TFEU provides that the directive will be adopted 'by the same ordinary or special legislative procedure as was followed for the adoption of the harmonisation measure in question'.

It should be noted that the 'brake–accelerator' mechanism (see below) will also apply to such a directive, which might pose problems for a measure which is considered 'essential to ensure the effective implementation of a Union policy' (e.g. related to the internal market). The same worry might arise as to the possible application to such a directive of the UK, Ireland and Denmark opt-out Protocols. Hence Declaration no. 26 provides that where a Member State opts not to participate in an FSJ measure, 'the Council will hold a full discussion on the possible implications and effects' of this non-participation and any Member State 'may ask the Commission to examine the situation on the basis of Article 116 [TFEU]'. Each Member State may also refer the matter to the European Council. Article 116 TFEU allows the adoption of directives to eliminate distortions of competition created by 'a difference between the provisions . . . in Member States'.

The Lisbon Treaty contains a new procedural device, nicknamed 'brake–accelerator' (see Box 24), which was inserted in two provisions:

- in Article 82(3) TFEU as regards the legal basis on approximation of certain aspects of criminal procedure provided for in Article 82(2);
- in Article 83(3) TFEU as regards the legal basis on approximation of criminal offences and sanctions in certain areas of criminal law provided for in Article 83(1) and (2).

---

national authorities is an essential measure for combating serious environmental offences, [the Community legislature can take] measures which relate to the criminal law of the Member States which it considers necessary in order to ensure that the rules which it lays down on environmental protection are fully effective'. In its judgment of 23 October 2007, the Court added that 'the determination of the type and level of the criminal penalties to be applied does not fall within the Community's sphere of competence' (point 70, Case C-440/05, *Commission v. Council*, [2007] ECR I-9097).

BOX 24. THE 'BRAKE–ACCELERATOR' MECHANISM

In order to make the switch to QMV acceptable in the sensitive area of criminal matters, the Lisbon IGC adopted a new procedure, with two elements:

- the first one is a so-called '**emergency brake**' system which allows a Member State which considers that a draft legislative act 'would affect fundamental aspects of its criminal justice system', to bring the matter to the European Council, in which case the codecision procedure is suspended. After discussion and in case of consensus, the European Council must, within four months, refer the draft back to the Council, which must terminate the suspension of the procedure (see Articles 82(3), 1st subparagraph, and 83(3), 1st subparagraph, TFEU);*
- the second element is a so-called '**accelerator**' designed to avoid a stalemate. If, within this four-month period, there is disagreement in the European Council and if at least nine Member States wish to establish an enhanced co-operation on the basis of the draft act in question, they will notify the European Parliament, the Council and the Commission accordingly and the enhanced co-operation will automatically apply between them, thus bypassing some of the preliminary steps which are normally required under the enhanced cooperation procedure and hence 'accelerating' the procedure (see Articles 82(3), 2nd subparagraph, and 83(3), 2nd subparagraph, TFEU).**

  * The failed Constitutional Treaty provided for a possible other intermediary step – that is, a request to the Commission or to the group of Member States from which the draft originated to submit a new draft, in which case the act originally proposed was deemed not to have been adopted – but the Lisbon IGC removed this option. Therefore, in case of disagreement in the European Council, the only option is the 'accelerator' (enhanced co-operation among a group of Member States).
  ** The failed Constitutional Treaty provided for a twelve-month period during which the above-mentioned new draft from the Commission or from the group of Member States could have been transmitted. This was removed by the Lisbon IGC.

The adoption of this mechanism was decisive in order to make the switch to QMV and codecision in these sensitive matters acceptable to all Member States.[46] The mechanism has been improved in comparison with the one provided for by the Constitutional Treaty.

---

46 On both provisions (Arts. 82(3) and 83(3) TFEU), the German Constitutional Court, in its judgment of 30 June 2009, decided that 'from the perspective of German constitutional law, the necessary degree of democratic legitimisation via the national parliaments can only be guaranteed by the German representative in the Council exercising the Member States' rights set out in Art. 82.3 and Art. 83.3 TFEU only on the instruction of the German Bundestag and, to the extent that this is required by the provisions on legislation, the Bundesrat' (para. 365). This means that in using the 'brake–accelerator' procedure, the German government will need most probably an instruction from the German parliament (see Appendix 1).

Finally, the Lisbon IGC decided that the legal basis enabling the Council to adopt by QMV measures on the freezing of assets to fight terrorism and related activities was to be inserted into the general provisions of the FSJ Title (Article 75 TFEU) instead of the Chapter on capital and payment. As a consequence, this provision falls under the two opt-out Protocols, that for the United Kingdom and Ireland and that for Denmark.[47]

A European Public Prosecutor's Office to protect the EU's financial interests

A new legal basis empowers the Council to establish, by unanimity and with the consent of the European Parliament, a European Public Prosecutor's Office. After difficult discussions during the 2004 IGC, it had been agreed to limit the Prosecutor's tasks to the combating of offences against the EU's financial interests (Article 86 TFEU). However, a *passerelle* enables the European Council to adopt, by unanimity, with the consent of the European Parliament and after consulting the Commission, a decision extending the powers of the Public Prosecutor to include serious crime having a cross-border dimension.[48]

Compared with the Constitutional Treaty, the Lisbon Treaty adds in paragraph 1 of Article 86 TFEU an 'accelerator' mechanism which enables a group of Member States to move forward with the establishment of the European Public Prosecutor's Office in case unanimity cannot be reached (on this mechanism see Box 25).

The idea of creating a more efficient system to protect the financial interests of the EU was first raised in 1976 by the Commission, which proposed, without success, to insert a provision on this issue into the Treaty.[49] It was followed by the introduction by the Maastricht Treaty of a specific provision (Article 209A TEC) and a specific reference in Article K.1(5) former TEU to the fight against fraud. The latter provision became the basis for the conclusion of the PIF Convention in

47 In order to avoid giving unintended signals regarding the freezing of assets, the United Kingdom made a unilateral Declaration no. 65 where it states that 'it intends to exercise its right [to opt in] under Art. 3 of the [UK and Ireland] Protocol' with regard to proposals made on the basis of Art. 75 TFEU. For its part, Ireland expressly excluded this provision from the scope of its opt-out (see Art. 9 of Protocol no. 21).

48 In Germany such a decision will require a preliminary law to be adopted by the German parliament (see para. 419 of the judgment of 30 June 2009 of the German Constitutional Court). For more details on the European Prosecutor, see D. Flore, 'La perspective d'un procureur européen' (2008) 9 *ERA Forum* 229.

49 COM (76) 418 final (OJ No. C222, of 22 September 1976, 2).

BOX 25. THE 'ACCELERATOR' MECHANISM

A sub-category of the 'brake–accelerator' was added by the Lisbon IGC in the Lisbon Treaty in the form of an 'accelerator', designed to enable a group of at least nine Member States to move forward with the adoption of a new EU instrument when unanimity cannot be reached in the Council, thus bypassing some of the preliminary steps which are normally required under the enhanced co-operation procedure. This 'accelerator' was inserted in the provisions on the European Public Prosecutor and on operational police co-operation.* It is a combination of the two steps of the 'brake–accelerator' mechanism:

- the first element resembles the '**emergency brake**', but for the benefit of the group of Member States which wants to break the stalemate. In the absence of unanimity in the Council, a group of at least nine Member States may request the draft legal instrument to be referred to the European Council, in which case the decision-making procedure in the Council is suspended. After discussion and in case of consensus, the European Council must, within four months, refer the draft back to the Council, which must terminate the suspension of the procedure and adopt the act (see Articles 86(1), 2nd subparagraph, and 87(3), 2nd subparagraph, TFEU);
- the second element is the same '**accelerator**' as in the 'brake–accelerator' system (Box 24). If, within the four-month period, there is disagreement in the European Council and at least nine Member States wish to establish an enhanced co-operation on the basis of the draft act in question, they will notify the European Parliament, the Council and the Commission accordingly and the enhanced co-operation will automatically apply between them (see Articles 86(1), 3rd subparagraph, and 87(3), 3rd subparagraph, TFEU).

* In the field of police co-operation, it is specified that the mechanism may not be used for acts which constitute a development of the Schengen *acquis*. This is due to the fact that the Schengen area already constitutes a closer co-operation established by the Treaty itself and that creating a 'sub-enhanced co-operation' inside Schengen would be contrary to the coherence and operability of the Schengen *acquis*.

1995.[50] In 1999 (Amsterdam Treaty), Article 209A TEC was replaced by Article 280 TEC, which, while it did not allow the EC legislator to adopt criminal law measures, did lead to the establishment of OLAF in 1999.[51]

---

50 'PIF' is an acronym for 'Protection des Intérêts Financiers'. The Convention of 26 July 1995 on the protection of the European Communities' financial interests entered into force on 17 October 2002 (OJ C 316, 27 November 1995, 49).
51 Acronym from 'Office de Lutte Anti-Fraude', established by a Commission Decision of 28 April 1999 (OJ No. L136, 31 May 1999, 20). The Council and the European Parliament

Specific procedures for improving the functioning and democratic control of the FSJ Area

The Lisbon Treaty has introduced some specific institutional elements designed to improve the functioning of the FSJ Area, while recognising the responsibilities of the Member States in this sensitive area.

The role of the European Council to define 'strategic guidelines' (Article 68 TFEU) is confirmed, thus ensuring the perpetuation of the practice of the five-year programmes, such as the 1999 Tampere programme, the 2004 Hague programme and the 2009 Stockholm programme.

The Lisbon Treaty has also improved democratic control over FSJ matters by giving a specific, and reinforced,[52] role to national parliaments in assessing the observance of the subsidiarity principle in the areas of judicial co-operation in criminal matters and police co-operation (Article 69 TFEU), in evaluating the implementation of the Union's policies (Article 70 TFEU), in evaluating Eurojust's activities (Articles 85(1), 3rd subparagraph, TFEU) and in scrutinising Europol's activities (Article 88(2), 2nd subparagraph, TFEU). The European Parliament also participates in these evaluation and scrutiny procedures.

Full judicial control

The Lisbon Treaty gives full jurisdiction to the Court of Justice over the whole FSJ Area. This means that all judicial proceedings provided for in the TFEU are available in the FSJ Area, including with regard to Europol and Eurojust. There are no longer any limitations on the preliminary ruling proceedings. With regard to judicial co-operation in criminal matters and police co-operation, the Commission and Member States are allowed to bring infringement actions[53] and the European

---

also adopted various acts on OLAF (two Regulations and an Interinstitutional Agreement adopted on 25 May 1999).

52 Art. 7(2), 1st subparagraph, of Protocol no. 2 provides for a lower threshold (a quarter instead of one-third of the total number of votes allocated to national parliaments) for a reasoned opinion by national parliaments on subsidiarity to trigger a review of a legislative proposal in the fields of judicial co-operation in criminal matters and police co-operation.

53 It is recalled that before the entry into force of the Lisbon Treaty, the Commission had infringement procedure powers only with regard to Community law matters (visas, asylum, immigration and judicial co-operation in civil matters), not with regard to police and judicial co-operation in criminal matters (third pillar).

Parliament and individuals are allowed to bring actions for annulment. All the other types of actions are also allowed (such as actions for failure to act, actions for damages and pleas of illegality). The possibility for the Commission to bring infringement actions in the field of judicial co-operation in criminal matters and police co-operation, as formerly covered by the third pillar, includes the possibility provided for in Article 260(2) and (3) TFEU to condemn the failing Member State to pay lump sums and daily penalties.

In addition to ensuring a better protection of individuals' rights in FSJ matters, the full jurisdiction of the Court of Justice substantially improves the control of the implementation of EU legislation in these matters. This should help create mutual trust between Member States, which is essential if the principle of mutual recognition set out in Article 67(3) and (4) TFEU is to function effectively.

There is, however, an exception, provided for in Article 276 TFEU, as concerns Chapters 4 and 5 on judicial co-operation in criminal matters and police co-operation. The Court of Justice has 'no jurisdiction to review the validity or proportionality of operations carried out by the police and other law-enforcement services of a Member State or the exercise of the responsibilities incumbent upon Member States with regard to the maintenance of law and order and the safeguarding of internal security'.[54]

In addition, contrary to the failed Constitutional Treaty, the Lisbon Treaty contains a five-year transitional period during which, with regard to the third pillar *acquis* already in force on the day of entry into force of the Lisbon Treaty (i.e. *acquis* adopted on the basis of Title VI of the former TEU), the (limited) powers of control of the Court of Justice and of the Commission will remain the same as before, unless the act in question is replaced or amended by an act adopted after the entry into force of the Lisbon Treaty (Article 10(1) to (3) of Protocol no. 36 on transitional provisions). This restriction was added by the Lisbon IGC after the difficult negotiations which took place within the Group of Legal Experts over the extension of the UK and Ireland opt-out Protocol.

---

54 This means that the similar exception which existed in the TEC with regard to measures under Art. 62(1) TEC (absence of controls of persons when crossing internal borders) is no longer applicable.

Keeping unanimity in a few very sensitive cases

The requirement of unanimity in the Council is retained in a number of specific cases which have been considered as being particularly sensitive:

- provisions concerning passports, identity cards, residence permits or similar documents (Article 77(3) TFEU);
- measures concerning family law with cross-border implications, as well as the *passerelle* enabling the Council to switch to QMV and codecision (Article 81(3) TFEU);
- the addition of further issues to the list of those on which minimum rules in criminal procedure can be adopted by QMV and codecision (Article 82(2)(d) TFEU);
- the identification of further areas of crime on which minimum rules can adopted by QMV and codecision (Article 83(1), 3rd subparagraph, TFEU);
- the establishment of a European Public Prosecutor's Office and the extension of its powers to include serious crime having a cross-border dimension (Article 86(1) and (4) TFEU);
- measures on operational police co-operation, other than those covered by Article 87(2) TFEU (Article 87(3) TFEU);
- measures setting out the conditions and limitations under which the competent judicial and police authorities of a Member State may operate in the territory of another Member State in liaison and in agreement with that Member State (Article 89 TFEU).

In order to avoid stalemates and enable a group of Member States to go further ahead when others are not willing to adopt a given act, the Lisbon IGC decided to design, in two cases, a specific version of the 'brake–accelerator' device, of a more 'accelerator' variety, to deal with situations where unanimity cannot be reached (see Box 25). These two provisions are:

- in Article 86(1), 2nd and 3rd subparagraphs, TFEU as regards the legal basis on the establishment of the European Public Prosecutor's Office provided for in Article 86(1), 1st subparagraph;
- in Article 87(3), 2nd and 3rd subparagraphs, TFEU as regards the legal basis on the adoption of measures on operational police co-operation provided for in Article 87(3), 1st subparagraph.

These provisions helped the non-opt-out Member States to accept the extension of the scope of the opt-out for the United Kingdom and Ireland. This mechanism did not exist in the failed Constitutional Treaty.

Keeping the right of initiative of the Member States, extending the 'mutual evaluation' system and adding some specific national concerns

The Lisbon Treaty has retained the right of initiative of Member States in the areas of judicial co-operation in criminal matters and police co-operation, but has subjected it to more demanding conditions. An initiative will have to be made by at least a quarter of the Member States (i.e. seven) acting jointly (Article 76(b) TFEU), while under the former EU Treaty, each individual Member State was entitled to submit an initiative in the third pillar (Article 34(2) former TEU). Article 294(15) TFEU, on the codecision procedure, addresses this specific case, but leaves a number of details to be resolved in practice.

In addition, the Lisbon Treaty (as was the case in the failed Constitutional Treaty) maintains and extends the 'mutual evaluation' system which had been developed in the context of the creation of the Schengen area, but was also used in areas of the third pillar which are related to the Schengen area. Article 70 TFEU enables the Council to lay down 'arrangements whereby the Member States, in collaboration with the Commission, conduct objective and impartial evaluations of the implementation of the Union policies' under the FSJ Title.

The Lisbon Treaty also creates a new standing Committee (COSI)[55] within the Council. However, unlike the 'Article 36 Committee' under the former TEU, this Committee will not be responsible for preparing the legislative work of the Council. Rather, it will ensure that 'operational co-operation on internal security' is promoted and strengthened within the Union (Article 71 TFEU). The European Parliament and national parliaments shall be kept informed of the proceedings of the COSI.

In addition, the Lisbon IGC added a new provision (which was not in the failed Constitutional Treaty) allowing the Member States 'to organise between themselves and under their responsibility such forms of co-operation and co-ordination as they deem appropriate between the competent departments of their administrations responsible for safeguarding national security' (Article 73 TFEU). Similarly, the Lisbon IGC added a new sentence on national security in the general provisions in the EU Treaty about relations between the EU and Member States (Article 4(2) TEU, of which the last sentence reads, 'in particular, national security remains the sole responsibility of each Member State'). Both provisions respond to a specific request from the UK government.

---

55 Acronym for the French name of the Committee, 'Coopération Opérationnelle en matière de Sécurité Intérieure'. See Decision 2010/131/EU of 25 February 2010, OJ No. L52, 3 March 2010, 50.

Finally, by its Declaration no. 36, the IGC confirmed that Member States may negotiate and conclude agreements with third countries or international organisations in the areas of judicial co-operation in civil and criminal matters and police co-operation 'in so far as such agreements comply with Union law'.

Section 24 Variable geometry in the Area of Freedom, Security and Justice

The issues dealt with in the FSJ area lie close to the heart of the sovereignty of the states and have been influenced by centuries of history and culture.

This is the reason why there has been, and will continue to be after the entry into force of the Lisbon Treaty, a differentiation in the nature and geographical scope of the FSJ rules, which results from the need to accommodate the concerns of certain Member States, in particular certain common law states, while not preventing others from co-operating as they deem appropriate. This 'variable geometry' results, on one hand, from specific Protocols annexed to the Treaties and, on the other hand, from agreements with third countries. This makes the adoption and implementation of acts in the FSJ area very difficult and complex.

The Schengen area

As explained in Section 22, the Schengen area was initiated originally by five Member States in 1985 outside the Treaties. It became a reality ten years later, on 25 March 1995, between seven Member States (Belgium, France, Germany, Luxembourg, the Netherlands, Portugal and Spain). The area progressively enlarged, to include Austria and Italy in 1997, Greece in 2000, five Nordic countries (Denmark, Finland, Sweden, Iceland and Norway) in 2001, Estonia, Hungary, Latvia, Lithuania, Malta, Poland, Slovenia, Slovakia and the Czech Republic in 2007, Switzerland in 2008 and, in the near future, Liechtenstein.

The Schengen area therefore covers twenty-two of the twenty-seven EU Member States (i.e. without Bulgaria, Cyprus, Ireland, Romania and the United Kingdom) and three non-EU states (Iceland, Norway and Switzerland). Ireland and the United Kingdom obtained in 1999, when the Schengen *acquis* was integrated into the EU framework, the right to remain outside the Schengen area, and to participate, at their request, only in parts of the Schengen *acquis*. In accordance with their accession treaty, Bulgaria and Romania are only partially bound by the provisions of the Schengen *acquis*: the provisions on the lifting of checks on persons at common borders with other Member States will only become fully applicable to them at the end of the evaluation process. Cyprus applies the same part of the Schengen *acquis* as Bulgaria and Romania, but the unresolved situation of the island impedes the lifting of border checks and the application of the EU rules on the control of external borders for the time being.

While its development started outside the Treaties, the Schengen *acquis* and the further development of the Schengen area have been integrated into the Treaties since 1 May 1999 by the Amsterdam Treaty. This Treaty also formally organised Schengen as an 'inbuilt' enhanced co-operation. The Protocol integrating the Schengen *acquis* into the framework of the EU stated that the Member States listed in Article 1 of that Protocol 'are authorised to establish closer co-operation among themselves'. However, contrary to an ordinary enhanced co-operation (Article 44(1), 2nd sub-paragraph, of the former EU Treaty), the Schengen *acquis* belonged to the EU *acquis* which any new Member State acceding to the EU must accept (Article 8 of the former Schengen Protocol). The situation remains the same after the entry into force of the Lisbon Treaty (see Articles 20(4) EU Treaty and 7 of Protocol no. 19).

With regard to the three, soon to become four, non-EU states which are members of the Schengen area, the institutional arrangements provided for in the applicable agreements enable their representatives to participate actively in the 'shaping' of the measures which constitute a development of the Schengen *acquis*.[56] This takes place within a Mixed Committee ('Comix') which meets, in the Council building, at all levels: experts (relevant working groups), senior officials (ambassadors/Coreper II) and ministers (JHA Council). However, the actual decision-taking, the power to adopt Schengen legal instruments, belongs exclusively to the EU legislator (Council alone or with the European Parliament).[57] The non-EU partners must then accept and apply them (Article 2(3) of the Agreement). The Agreement allows them not to accept a particular legal instrument, but the consequence is the automatic termination of

---

56 See Arts. 3 to 6 of the Agreement with Iceland and Norway and the same provisions in the Agreement with Switzerland (for references of these Agreements, see, respectively, notes 14 and 16).

57 Art. 8(1) of the Agreement with Iceland and Norway reads, 'the adoption of new acts or measures related to [Schengen matters] shall be reserved to the competent institutions of the European Union . . . such acts or measures shall enter into force simultaneously for the European Union and its Member States concerned and for Iceland and Norway'.

the whole Agreement (save for the possibility of the Mixed Committee deciding otherwise within ninety days).[58]

The specific situation of Denmark

When the Amsterdam Treaty entered into force on 1 May 1999, a number of third pillar matters (asylum, immigration and judicial co-operation in civil matters) were 'communitarised'. As Denmark was not in a position to accept such a move, it was allowed to obtain an opt-out from these matters and, as from then, no longer took part in the adoption of such 'Community measures' (i.e. Denmark did not have the right to vote in the Council).[59] On the other hand, Denmark has continued to take full part in the third pillar (Title VI of the former EU Treaty on police and judicial co-operation in criminal matters).

However, among the matters 'communitarised' by the Amsterdam Treaty were issues belonging to the pre-existing Schengen *acquis*, already applicable to Denmark. Therefore, in order to enable Denmark to continue being part of the Schengen area, the opt-out Protocol allowed Denmark a special 'opting in' possibility. Within six months of the adoption of a Schengen-building measure, Denmark has to indicate whether it will implement the Schengen-building measure as 'an obligation under international law'. This particularity ('obligation under international law') did not make it a real 'opt-in', as compared with the 'opting in' system for the United Kingdom and Ireland which, when they opt in, accept the legislative act as EC *acquis*, not as an obligation under international law. If Denmark decided not to implement such a measure, the other Member States had to 'consider appropriate measures to be taken'.[60] This required identifying, in each case, whether the measure in question constitutes a 'development of the Schengen *acquis*', an identification which was not always obvious.

Such an 'opting-in' possibility did not exist for those 'Community measures' which did not constitute a development of the Schengen *acquis* (such as asylum policy or judicial co-operation in civil matters, for instance). The only way in which Denmark could apply these

---

58 Art. 8(4) of the Agreement with Iceland and Norway and Art. 7(4) of the Agreement with Switzerland.
59 Art. 1 of the former Protocol on the position of Denmark.
60 Art. 5 of the former Protocol on the position of Denmark.

non-Schengen measures was to conclude an international agreement with the EC covering the same subject matter.

Thus, the opt-out regime for Denmark was quite severe and excluded it from participating in important pieces of EC legislation, without any easy possibility of opting in at a later stage, the only opting-in option (apart from renouncing the Protocol) being the conclusion of an international agreement with the EC, which is a very cumbersome procedure. This has not been solved with the Lisbon Treaty: the scope of the opt-out Protocol of Denmark has been extended to cover the whole FSJ area, which makes the situation of Denmark even more difficult. Article 1 of Protocol no. 22 on the position of Denmark no longer refers only to matters formerly covered by Title IV of the EC Treaty (visas, asylum, immigration and other policies related to the free movement of persons), but to the whole Title V of Part Three of the TFEU 'on the area of freedom, security and justice'.[61] Therefore the (severe) opt-out system now applies also to the former third pillar provisions which the Lisbon Treaty has 'communitarised'. However, the opting-in possibility for Denmark is not extended. As in the past, it covers only the Schengen-building measures. Denmark requested the addition to its opt-out Protocol of an annex which, should Denmark so decide in accordance with its constitutional requirements, would replace its present opt-out Protocol. This annex reproduces, in substance, the UK and Ireland opt-out Protocol, including its wider opting-in possibilities, which do not feature in the Denmark Protocol.

The specific situation of the United Kingdom and Ireland
The situation before the Lisbon Treaty

The UK and Ireland opt-out Protocol was more flexible than the Danish one, as it allowed wider possibilities of opting in. As in the case of Denmark, the Amsterdam Treaty allowed the United Kingdom and Ireland to opt out of measures on matters which were then 'communitarised': visas, asylum, immigration and judicial co-operation in civil matters. However, unlike Denmark, the United Kingdom and Ireland were allowed

---

61 In its Declaration no. 48 concerning the Protocol on the position of Denmark, the IGC specifies that, when an Act will contain provisions which apply to Denmark as well as provisions which do not apply to Denmark, the latter will not use its voting right to prevent the adoption of the provisions which do not apply to Denmark. It also specifies, as regards the solidarity clause of Art. 222 TFEU, that Denmark will participate in actions under this clause (both in the fields of FSJ and defence) in accordance with its opt-out Protocol.

'to notify... within three months after a proposal or initiative has been presented to the Council... [of their wish] to take part in the adoption and application of any such proposed measure'. While Denmark could opt in only after the Council had adopted the act and only if this was a Schengen-building measure, the United Kingdom and Ireland could opt in at the beginning of the decision-making procedure and therefore influence its content and take part in the adoption of the act which they would apply.[62] The United Kingdom and Ireland also had the possibility of opting in after the adoption of a measure, without a time limit.[63]

Like Denmark, the United Kingdom and Ireland continued to take full part in the third pillar (Title VI of the former EU Treaty on police and judicial co-operation in criminal matters) which was not 'communitarised' by the Amsterdam Treaty, apart from those matters falling under the Schengen *acquis*.

With regard to the Schengen *acquis*, the opt-out/opt-in rules for the United Kingdom and Ireland were specifically provided for in the Schengen Protocol. The United Kingdom and Ireland were allowed to request to take part in some or all of the provisions of the Schengen *acquis*, but such participation was conditioned upon an authorisation from the Council to be given by unanimity of the 'Schengen in' members. The Council adopted two Decisions, one allowing the United Kingdom and the other allowing Ireland to take part in some of the provisions of the Schengen *acquis* which are listed in detail in the Decisions.[64] Under these Decisions, the United Kingdom and Ireland were deemed irrevocably to have notified their wish to take part in all subsequent proposals building upon the Schengen *acquis* in which they participate.[65] In addition, the Council recalled that 'the Schengen *acquis* was conceived and functions as a coherent ensemble' and that 'any partial participation [by the

---

62 Art. 3 of the Protocol on the position of the United Kingdom and Ireland.
63 Art. 4 of the Protocol on the position of the United Kingdom and Ireland.
64 See Council Decision of 29 May 2000, concerning the request of the United Kingdom to take part in some of the provisions of the Schengen *acquis* (OJ No. L131, 1 June 2000, 43), and Council Decision of 28 February 2002, concerning Ireland's request to take part in some of the provisions of the Schengen *acquis* (OJ No. L64, 7 March 2002, 20). The Schengen provisions concerned are put into effect after a Council Decision. For the United Kingdom, such Decision was adopted on 22 December 2004 (OJ No. L395, 31 December 2004, 70). At the time of writing, a similar Decision had not yet been adopted for Ireland.
65 See Art. 8(2) of the Decision on the United Kingdom and Art. 6(2) of the Decision on Ireland.

United Kingdom and Ireland] in the Schengen *acquis* must respect the coherence of the subject areas which constitute the ensemble of this *acquis*.

It should be noted that the UK government is often interested in participating to a greater extent in the Schengen *acquis* – that is, in restricting the interpretation given to the scope of the UK opt-out. In two cases it brought in 2005 before the Court of Justice, the United Kingdom claimed it had the right to take part in a development of the Schengen *acquis* even without having been allowed in advance by the Council to take part in the area in question. The United Kingdom wanted to take part in the Frontiers Agency[66] and in the passport Regulation,[67] both texts which the Council had considered to constitute a development of the Schengen *acquis* in which the United Kingdom did not participate since they concerned the crossing of external borders. In both cases the United Kingdom lost. The Court ruled that 'the participation of a Member State in the adoption of a measure pursuant to Article 5(1) of the Schengen Protocol is conceivable only to the extent that that State has accepted the area of the Schengen acquis which is the context of the measure or of which it is a development'.[68] As the United Kingdom did not participate in the area of external border crossing in accordance with Article 4 of the Schengen Protocol, it could not notify under Article 5 its wish to participate in a development of the Schengen *acquis* in this area.

In addition, a specific Protocol authorised the United Kingdom to continue exercising controls on persons at its borders and to continue applying with Ireland a 'common travel area' and therefore allowing Ireland also to keep checks at borders with other Member States. As a consequence, other Member States were also authorised to exercise such controls on persons travelling from the United Kingdom and Ireland.[69]

---

66 Called 'Frontex'. See Council Regulation (EC) No. 2007/2004 of 26 October 2004, establishing a European Agency for the Management of Operational Cooperation at the External Borders of the Member States of the European Union (OJ No. L349, 25 November 2004, 1).

67 See Council Regulation (EC) No. 2252/2004 of 13 December 2004 on standards for security features and biometrics in passports and travel documents issued by Member States (OJ No. L385, 29 December 2004, 1).

68 Point 62 of Case C-77/05. See judgments of 18 December 2007, Cases C-77/05 and 137/05, *UK v. Council*, [2007] ECR I-11459 and I-11593.

69 See Protocol on the application of certain aspects of Art. 14 of the Treaty establishing the European Community to the United Kingdom and to Ireland (now Protocol no. 20).

The situation after the Lisbon Treaty

The Lisbon Treaty has extended the scope of the opt-out Protocol of the United Kingdom and Ireland to cover the whole FSJ area. Specific procedural mechanisms have been added in three Protocols (i.e. in the Schengen Protocol no. 19, in the United Kingdom and Ireland opt-out Protocol no. 21 and in the Protocol on transitional provisions no. 36), after lengthy negotiations during the Lisbon IGC. The negotiations took place in the Group of Legal Experts.

Regarding those parts of the Schengen *acquis* in which the United Kingdom and Ireland take part, pursuant to the Council Decisions adopted on the basis of Article 4 of the Schengen Protocol, the Lisbon Treaty has added a new provision (Article 5(2) to (5) of Protocol no. 19). It allows the United Kingdom or Ireland, in spite of Article 8(2) of the said Decision,[70] nevertheless to opt out from a measure building on such *acquis*. However, in order to protect the 'practical operability of the various parts of the Schengen acquis' and 'their coherence', there will be a price to be paid for opting out from a Schengen-building measure. This price (a quid pro quo) will be that the whole part of the Schengen *acquis* in which the United Kingdom or Ireland previously took part will 'cease to apply [to the United Kingdom or to Ireland] to the extent considered necessary by the Council'. A complicated 'emergency' procedure involving the Council, the European Council and the Commission is provided for. The purpose of this complex procedure is to enable, on the one hand, the United Kingdom or Ireland to 'retain the widest possible measure of participation' in the Schengen *acquis* already applicable and, on the other hand, the members of the Schengen area to protect 'the operability of the various parts of the Schengen acquis' and its coherence. The procedure provides that if its different steps fail to find a solution, the Commission will have the power to decide the extent to which and the conditions under which the Schengen *acquis* concerned will cease to apply to the opting-out State.[71]

---

70 Art. 8(2) of the Council Decision of 2000 concerning the United Kingdom. In the 2002 Decision on Ireland, the same Art. is numbered 6(2). These Articles provide that the United Kingdom and Ireland are 'deemed irrevocably to have notified . . . that [they wish] to take part in all proposals and initiatives which build upon the Schengen acquis'.

71 Four Declarations linked to the functioning of this new emergency procedure were also added in order to clarify certain aspects of this procedure, such as the possibility for the United Kingdom or Ireland to withdraw an opt-out request at any moment before the adoption of the Schengen-building measure, the fact that the Council should have a 'full discussion' at one of the stages of the procedure, and so on (see Declarations 44, 45, 46 and 47 annexed to the Final Act of the Conference, OJ No. C115, 9 May 2008, 352).

This means that the 2007 case law of the Court of Justice which forbids the United Kingdom or Ireland to opt into a draft legislative act building upon Schengen *acquis* in which the United Kingdom or Ireland have not been allowed to participate (by the Council acting by unanimity of the Schengen members) will remain valid.[72]

As to the non-Schengen *acquis* (i.e. most of the third pillar, judicial co-operation in civil matters, asylum, migration), the Lisbon Treaty inserted in the UK and Ireland opt-out Protocol a new provision (Article 4a of Protocol no. 21). It allows the United Kingdom or Ireland to opt out of a proposed amendment to an existing piece of FSJ *acquis* by which the United Kingdom or Ireland was already bound. The Council will then have to determine if the non-participation of the State concerned in the amended version of the existing piece of *acquis* would make its application 'inoperable for other Member States or the Union'. If so, the Council may urge the State concerned to change its mind and opt in to the amendment. If the State concerned does not opt in, the underlying piece of *acquis* will 'no longer be binding upon or applicable to [that State], unless the Member State concerned has made a notification [of opt-in] before the entry into force of the amending measure'. The Council may also 'determine that [the United Kingdom or Ireland] shall bear the direct financial consequences, if any, necessarily and unavoidably incurred as a result of the cessation of its participation in the existing measure'.

In addition, Protocol no. 36 on transitional provisions contains specific rules which apply only to the United Kingdom (not to Ireland). These specific rules relate to the general transitional period of five years provided for in Article 10(1) to (3) of the Protocol, during which the Court of Justice and the Commission powers of control will remain as limited as they were in the former EU Treaty (see below under 'The transitional provisions on the third pillar *acquis*'). Six months before the end of that five-year period, the United Kingdom is allowed by Article 10(5) of the Protocol to notify that 'it does not accept ... the powers of the [Court of Justice and the Commission]' as they would apply under the Treaties after the five-year transitional period has elapsed. If the United Kingdom uses this possibility, the price to pay (quid pro quo) will be that the acts in question (which were applicable to the United Kingdom) will cease to apply to it. The Council, by QMV, without the United Kingdom being allowed to vote, will 'determine the necessary consequential and transitional arrangements'. Also by QMV, but this time with the United

---

72 See Cases C-77/07 and C-137/05 (note 68).

Kingdom being allowed to vote, the Council may determine that the United Kingdom 'shall bear the direct financial consequences' of this opting out. Following this 'block opt-out', the United Kingdom may request to take part again in this *acquis*, but will have to do so in accordance with the conditions set out in the applicable Protocols (Schengen Protocol or the Protocol on the position of the United Kingdom and Ireland), through a case-by-case procedure.

This complex and finely tuned mechanism allows the United Kingdom 'to keep its sovereignty' because it will not automatically be obliged to be subject to the control of the Commission and the Court of Justice after the five-year transitional period. However, if the United Kingdom chooses this route, it will, by the same token, deprive itself of participation in common policies which aim to ensure better protection for citizens. This is again balanced by the possibility which the United Kingdom will retain of 'opting back' in some of the measures which were covered by the 'block opt-out', subject to the agreement of the other Member States.

The transitional provisions on the third pillar acquis

Protocol no. 36 on transitional provisions contains two provisions dealing with third pillar *acquis*:

- Article 9 states that 'the legal effects of the acts . . . adopted on the basis of the [EU Treaty] prior to the entry into force of the Lisbon Treaty shall be preserved until those acts are repealed, annulled or amended in implementation of the Treaties'. This transitional mechanism is the same as the one which was provided for in Article IV-438(3) of the failed Constitutional Treaty. With regard to the third pillar *acquis*, it means that the legal effects of the decisions and framework decisions (i.e. absence of direct effect)[73] adopted pursuant to Title VI of the former EU Treaty will continue to apply, as long as these acts have not been 'repealed, annulled or amended' pursuant to the Treaties as in force after 1 December 2009;
- Article 10 is new compared with the Constitutional Treaty. Paragraphs 1 to 3 provide for a transitional period of five years applicable to all Member States. During this period, the powers of the Court of Justice and of the Commission will continue to be as limited as in the former EU Treaty (no infringement actions, no annulment actions by individuals,

---

73 As interpreted by the Court of Justice in its *Pupino* Case (see note 28).

no actions for damages, limited preliminary ruling possibilities, etc.). However, as with the legal effects of the third pillar acts in force before 1 December 2009, this freezing of powers will cease each time a third pillar act is amended pursuant to the Treaties as in force after 1 December 2009.[74] Despite the fact that this issue is subject to discussion, it seems clear that any amendment to a given act, however minor it may be, will bring the whole act 'amended' under the new Lisbon rules. The freezing will in any event, and for all legal acts, cease five years after the entry into force of the Lisbon Treaty (i.e. on 1 December 2014), even for acts which have not been amended before that date.

As has already been explained, Article 10(4) and (5) contains specific provisions enabling the United Kingdom to opt out from the application of the full powers of the Court of Justice and the Commission six months before the end of the five-year transitional period (i.e. by 1 May 2014). In that case, the *acquis* concerned will no longer apply to the United Kingdom.

*

The improvements made to the FSJ provisions by the Lisbon Treaty lie mainly in the 'communitarisation' of the former 'third pillar' through its incorporation into one Title covering the whole FSJ Area. This brings a more consistent and simple architecture. It also will allow a full parliamentary (European and national) and judicial control of measures which may directly affect every citizen, thus helping to guarantee a better protection of the rights of individuals. This means, in concrete terms, a more efficient decision-making procedure. More QMV in the Council and more

---

74 In order to limit the scope and duration of this transitional rule, the IGC invited, in its Declaration no. 50, the EU legislator 'to seek to adopt . . . legal acts amending or replacing the [third pillar] acts'. It is expected that the Commission will propose systematically, at least for the most important legislation, replacing existing texts by new ones, in order to make them fall within the full jurisdiction of the Court of Justice and within the Commission's control powers (to bring infringement actions). Such an amendment or replacement will also end the preservation of the old legal effects of the third pillar acts provided for by Art. 9 of Protocol no. 36.

This method of replacing 'old' acts by 'new' ones was already in use following the entry into force of the Amsterdam Treaty in 1999. The Council replaced both the 1968 Brussels Convention and the 1980 Rome Convention by regulations (see note 1 of this chapter). It did the same with the 1998 Convention on jurisdiction and the recognition and enforcement of judgments in matrimonial matters (see Council Regulation no. 1374/2000 of 29 May 2000 on jurisdiction and the recognition and enforcement of judgments in matrimonial matters and in matters of parental responsibility for children of both spouses, OJ No. L160, 30 June 2000, 19).

VI

Institutions

Adapting the institutions to an enlarged EU

Among the most visible changes brought about by the Lisbon Treaty are the reforms of the institutions: these reforms concern the number of the institutions and their respective powers, composition and internal functioning. The institutions will now have to cope with the increased rights given to other political actors, such as the national parliaments, the Committee of the Regions and the citizens themselves.

The Lisbon Treaty increases the number of the EU institutions from five to seven, by giving the European Council and the European Central Bank the status of institution. The respective powers of the institutions are somewhat reshuffled, most notably through a widening of the scope of the codecision procedure, an increase in the number of cases where a (redefined) QMV in the Council will apply, a reform of the budget decision-making procedure, the creation of the new offices of a full-time European Council President, elected for up to five years, and of a Union High Representative for Foreign Affairs and Security Policy, appointed for five years, who is the president of the Foreign Affairs Council as well as one of the vice-presidents of the Commission, a reference to the Eurogroup which is chaired by a president elected by his/her peers and an extension of the jurisdiction of the Court of Justice. The Treaty also envisaged a reduced number of Commissioners as from 2014; however, following the negative Irish referendum in June 2007, the political decision has been taken to revert to one Commissioner per Member State. This political decision will have to be implemented through a 'decision . . . , in accordance with the necessary legal procedures', as foreseen in the European Council Conclusions of December 2008.

Section 25 The European Council

Legal consequences of giving the European Council the status of an institution

By adding the European Council (and the European Central Bank) to the list of EU institutions,[1] the Lisbon Treaty brings them within the scope of all the general provisions and rules that are applicable to the EU institutions, including provisions concerning the review by the Court of Justice of the legality of their acts. Each time a Treaty provision uses the term 'institutions' without specifying an exception, it will also include these two new institutions.

With regard to the European Council, the change, while not revolutionary, is substantial. Until the Lisbon Treaty, the European Council, composed of the heads of state or government and of the President of the Commission, was mentioned in Article 4 of the former TEU as a body which, through political conclusions or declarations, 'shall provide the Union with the necessary impetus for its development and shall define the general political guidelines thereof'. It was not an institution, although it could, in some rare cases, take decisions.[2]

Under the Lisbon Treaty, the European Council continues to fulfil this 'impetus' role and, in doing so, it acts by consensus, which is not a voting rule (Article 15(4) TEU).[3]

Whenever it adopts legally binding acts (it has a decision-making power in about thirty cases), the European Council is obliged to respect the rules fixed by the relevant legal basis, which identifies in each case the relevant procedure to be followed (type of legal instrument to be adopted,

---

1 Until the Lisbon Treaty, there were five institutions: the European Parliament, the Council, the Commission, the Court of Justice and the Court of Auditors (Art. 7 TEC).
2 I.e. the 'common strategies' in CFSP (Art. 13(2) former TEU), the 'decision' on a common defence (Art. 17(1) former TEU) and the 'conclusion' on the broad economic guidelines (Art. 99(2) TEC). However, in all other cases where Members of the European Council could adopt legal acts, the former Treaties entrusted this power to the Council 'meeting in the composition of the Heads of State or Government' (e.g. Art. 7(2) former TEU on the determination of the existence of a serious and persistent breach of the founding EU principles, or Art. 214(2) TEC on the nomination of the person intended to be appointed as President of the Commission).
3 See the editorial comments in the *Common Market Law Review*: 'Who leads the EU? Looking at current practice, and certainly if and when the Lisbon Treaty enters into force, the answer is simple: the European Council' (2009) 46 *Common Market Law Review* 1383. See also J. Werts, *The European Council* (London: John Harper Publications, 2008).

applicable voting rule, etc.).[4] The Treaty specifies that the President of the European Council and the Commission's President do not have the right to vote (Article 235(1) TFEU). The European Council is barred from exercising 'legislative functions' (Article 15(1) TEU). In order to regulate its new functioning as an EU decision-making body, the European Council adopted its own Rules of Procedure upon entry into force of the Lisbon Treaty (Article 235(3) TFEU).[5]

Likewise, following the suggestion of the Working Party of Legal Experts of the 2003–4 IGC, the European Council has been expressly added to the list of institutions against which an action for annulment, or an action for failure to act, may be brought before the Court of Justice (Articles 263 and 265 TFEU). It has also been specifically included, albeit together with the Council, in the list of separate sections of the budget (Article 316 TFEU).

A full-time and more stable President of the European Council

Under Article 4, 2nd subparagraph, of the former TEU, the European Council was chaired by the head of state or government of the Member State holding the six-monthly rotating Presidency of the Council. This situation attracted the same criticisms from some quarters as those directed at the rotating system for the Council Presidency. These criticisms focused on the difficulties in ensuring consistency and continuity in the work of the European Council, the changes of priorities in the EU's work every six months, the lack of leadership and the lack of time of the President to prepare properly the meetings of the European Council, given that this task comes on top of his/her normal tasks as head of state or government.

Therefore, providing for a full-time and more stable President of the European Council soon appeared as one of the main institutional issues disputed during the Convention. The larger Member States were generally in favour of a President elected for a renewable period of two and a half years and playing a significant role. The Commission and a number of the smaller Member States, which often prefer the six-monthly

---

4 The types of decision which the European Council can take are important decisions concerning the institutions and appointments (see list in Appendix 6).
5 See OJ No. L315, 2 December 2009, 51. The European Council and its President are assisted by the General Secretariat of the Council (Art. 235(4) TFEU). This was important in order to avoid the creation of a new bureaucracy and to avoid divergences of opinion between the existing Council's Secretariat and another Secretariat which could have been established to serve the European Council.

rotating presidency as being more 'egalitarian', were opposed to this idea. They argued that it could undermine the position of the President of the Commission and that it could promote 'intergovernmentalism' at the expense of the 'Community method'. As a consequence, the debate concentrated on the definition of the role of the President of the European Council. Should he/she be a real 'president' with important powers or only a 'chairman' in charge of chairing the meetings but not having any substantial power?

In the end, those in favour of having a full-time President of the European Council elected for several years were obliged to give up on their wish of entrusting him/her with important powers. They abandoned, in particular, their desire to give him/her the task of chairing the General Affairs Council and of co-ordinating the work of the different configurations of the Council. They were obliged to accept, instead, a rather vague job description and, at the same time, the establishment of a new so-called 'double-hatted' High Representative of the Union for CFSP matters – that is, that the High Representative should be a member of the Commission. This delicate balance was obtained thanks to a compromise between France (which was in favour of a strong President of the European Council and not enthusiastic about the concept of a 'double-hatted' High Representative) and Germany (which was of the opposite view on both issues). This delicate balance will have to be kept in mind when implementing the relevant provisions of the Treaty.

Under the present TEU, the European Council elects its President, by QMV, for a term of two and a half years, renewable once. This possible five years' duration corresponds to the duration of the mandates of the European Parliament and of the Commission (including the High Representative) (Article 15(5) TEU).[6] The President may not hold a national office at the same time (Article 15(6) TEU).

The President's tasks are the following (Article 15(6) TEU):

- to chair the European Council and drive forward its work;
- to ensure the preparation and continuity of the work of the European Council in co-operation with the President of the Commission, and on the basis of the work of the General Affairs Council;

---

6 However, one has to remember that the European Parliament may adopt a motion of censure of the Commission as a whole (including the High Representative as far as his/her duties as a Commission Member are concerned), therefore affecting this correspondence in the mandates, although not the fixed duration of the mandates, as the replacing Commissioners are to be appointed for the remainder of the mandate (Art. 17(8) TEU and 234 TFEU).

- to endeavour to facilitate cohesion and consensus within the European Council;
- to present a report to the European Parliament after each of the meetings of the European Council;
- to ensure, at his/her level and in that capacity, the external representation of the Union on issues concerning its common foreign and security policy, without prejudice to the powers of the High Representative.

Although the role of the President of the European Council in ensuring the external representation of the Union at his/her level are 'without prejudice' to the powers of the High Representative, one may suppose that, in practice, it will not be easy to delimit their respective powers as well as those of the Commission in external affairs. It remains to be seen how the EU will be represented at the highest level in a meeting with a third State or a group of third States. The logical interpretation will be for it to be represented by the President of the European Council and the President of the Commission, and that the High Representative will accompany them in appropriate cases. The Treaty provisions no longer give the six-monthly Presidency any role to play in the external representation of the EU. This will not be easy to implement in practice.

After having first chosen him at its informal meeting on 19 November 2009, the European Council on 1 December 2009 formally elected Herman Van Rompuy, Prime Minister of Belgium, as its first full-time President.

As a whole, the Lisbon Treaty certainly strengthens the European Council by consecrating its role as the only institution which has overall political leadership on all EU affairs. This creates the potential for a more coherent, more visible and more efficient EU. Depending on the wisdom and capabilities of its first President, and in particular his capacity to have good working relationships with the other actors involved – that is, the Presidents of the Commission and of the European Parliament, the six-monthly Presidencies, and the High Representative as President of the Foreign Affairs Council, this potentiality will become reality. This would be a decisive move towards an EU better equipped to face the challenges it has to confront.[7] The European Council needed a full-time President. Whatever their abilities, the successive heads of state or government serving for six months on a very part-time basis could not generally offer

---

7 In his address to the College of Europe in Bruges, on 25 February 2010, Herman Van Rompuy declared, 'I believe that the two most important domains of the European Council are economic policy and foreign policy. Simply put: economic policy to be strong, foreign policy to be united' (see full text on the Internet site of the Council).

enough of their time, attention and energy for this job. It remains to be seen if the full-time President, who by definition has not been directly elected by citizens, will carry enough political legitimacy to impose himself on the political scene as well as on his colleagues in the European Council.

Section 26 The Council

A new Presidency system

An important innovation of the Lisbon Treaty, which has been introduced with the aim of increasing the effectiveness of the functioning of the Council, is the change made to its six-monthly rotating Presidency. The six-monthly Presidency no longer presides over all ten configurations of the Council. The High Representative, appointed for a five-year mandate, 'shall preside over the Foreign Affairs Council' (Article 18(3) TEU; for more details, see Section 32). Similarly, the Eurogroup, although not being transformed into a formal configuration of the Council, but remaining an informal meeting of the finance ministers of the euro zone, is chaired by a President elected by his/her peers, by a simple majority, for two and a half years.[8] Combined with an elected President of the European Council, these stabilising measures for the Presidency of the Council should increase the consistency and the effectiveness of the functioning of the Council.

The other nine Council configurations,[9] in effect, continue to be chaired by a system of six-monthly presidency. A Decision on the exercise of the Presidency of the Council, which had already been agreed during the 2003–4 IGC, was adopted upon entry into force of the Lisbon

---

8 See Art. 2 of Protocol no. 14 on the Eurogroup. At its meeting on 10 and 11 September 2004, the Eurogroup had chosen Jean-Claude Juncker, Prime Minister and Finance Minister of Luxembourg, as President of the Eurogroup for two years as from 1 January 2005. He was re-elected three times (2007, 2009 and 2010).

9 Before the Lisbon Treaty, the Council, although unique, met in nine different configurations, depending on the subjects on its agenda (General Affairs/External Relations, JHA, Economy/Finance/Budget, Environment, Agriculture/Fisheries, Competitiveness, Employment/Social Policy/Health/Consumer Affairs, Transport/ Telecommunications/Energy and Education/Youth/Culture). This pre-existing situation is acknowledged in Art. 16(6) TEU. Until the Lisbon Treaty, the number of these configurations could be amended by a simple majority decision of the 'General Affairs' Council (Art. 2(1) of the 2006 Council's Rules of Procedure). Since the entry into force of the Lisbon Treaty, the adoption and amendment of this list requires a decision of the European Council by QMV (Arts. 16(6) TEU and 236 TFEU). The list is in Annex I to the Council's Rules of Procedure.

Treaty. On the one hand, it provides that the Council Presidency is held by pre-established groups of three Member States ('team Presidencies' or 'trio-Presidency') for a period of eighteen months, constituted on the basis of equal rotation and co-operating on the basis of an eighteen-month programme (for the list of presidencies until 2020 see Box 26).[10] However, the Decision also provides that 'each member of the group shall in turn chair for a six-month period all configurations of the Council, with the exception of the Foreign Affairs configuration' (Article 1(2) of the Decision). It therefore keeps the six-monthly Presidency system, even if it enables other solutions.

BOX 26. THE ROTATION OF COUNCIL PRESIDENCIES
FROM 2007 TO 2020

In accordance with what the Lisbon IGC had agreed, the European Council adopted a Decision concerning the exercise of the Presidency of the Council.[1] Declaration no. 9 of the IGC also provided that the Council should adopt a Decision implementing the European Council decision, which would contain, *inter alia*, the list of the six-monthly rotating presidencies until 2020 divided into 'trio' presidencies:[2]

Country	Six-monthly period	Year
Germany	January–June	2007
Portugal	July–December	
Slovenia	January–June	2008
France	July–December	
Czech Republic	January–June	2009
Sweden	July–December	
Spain	January–June	2010
Belgium	July–December	
Hungary	January–June	2011
Poland	July–December	
Denmark	January–June	2012
Cyprus	July–December	

---

10 See the European Council Decision on the exercise of the Presidency of the Council, which was contained in Declaration no. 9 (OJ No. L315, 2 December 2009, 50). A system of eighteen-month programmes had already been put in place in 2006 (see Art. 2(4) of the 2006 Council's Rules of Procedure, OJ No. L285, 16 October 2006, 47).

Country	Six-monthly period	Year
Ireland	January–June	2013
Lithuania	July–December	
Greece	January–June	2014
Italy	July–December	
Latvia	January–June	2015
Luxembourg	July–December	
Netherlands	January–June	2016
Slovakia	July–December	
Malta	January–June	2017
United Kingdom	July–December	
Estonia	January–June	2018
Bulgaria	July–December	
Austria	January–June	2019
Romania	July–December	
Finland	January–June	2020

[1] See OJ No. L315, 2 December 2009, 50.
[2] See OJ No. L322, 9 December 2009, 28, corrected by OJ No. L344, 23 December 2009, 56. This Decision also contains a list of Council preparatory bodies, notably in the Foreign Affairs area, which will be chaired by a fixed chairperson (who will also be a member of the European External Action Service).

One of the flexibilities brought about by the Lisbon Treaty is that, contrary to the previous situation, where a formal amendment to Article 203 TEC, involving ratification by the Member States, was required to change the rotating presidency system for the Council, the European Council is now empowered to change the system directly, acting by QMV (Articles 16(9) TEU and 236 TFEU).[11] In that case, it will nevertheless have to respect the rule according to which 'the Presidency of Council

11 For Council preparatory bodies below the political decision-taking level, the 2006 version of Art. 19(4) of the Council's Rules of Procedure enabled the Council to decide, by simple majority, that a committee created by the Treaty (other than Coreper) be chaired by a president other than the ordinary six-monthly rotating presidency. Coreper could also take such a decision, by simple majority, with regard to the chairmanship of other committees and working groups of the Council. Since the entry into force of the Lisbon

configurations, other than that of Foreign Affairs, shall be held by Member State representatives in the Council on the basis of equal rotation' (Article 16(9) TEU).

It remains to be seen whether and how a proper co-ordination of all configurations of the Council will be effectively ensured. The EU Treaty provides that the General Affairs Council is in charge of ensuring 'consistency in the work of the different Council configurations'. It also provides that this Council is to 'prepare and ensure the follow-up to meetings of the European Council, in liaison with the President of the European Council and the Commission' (Article 16(6) TEU). The President of the European Council and the President of the Commission could indeed play important roles in that respect. One must also stress that a proper co-ordination, in the twenty-seven capitals, between all ministers representing their government in the different configurations of the Council would help a lot in that regard!

The voting system in the Council

The Lisbon Treaty includes provisions designed to improve effectiveness in the functioning of the Council. The main measure to improve its effectiveness is, of course, the increase in the number of legal bases where the Council acts by QMV instead of unanimity. This, being coupled with a new QMV system designed to make it more legitimate and, in principle, simpler, should facilitate decision-taking.

Extension of the coverage of qualified majority voting

The Lisbon Treaty extends the coverage of QMV to about twenty new cases, and contains about thirty new provisions which provide for QMV,[12] some of which are of minor importance. The most notable sectors of extension are the FSJ area, the co-ordination of social security for migrant workers, the establishment of permanent structured co-operation in defence and the definition of the EU Defence Agency's statute and seat and its operational rules, culture, the diplomatic and consular protection

---

Treaty, these same decisions require QMV in the Council (see Art. 19(4), 3rd subpara., of the 2009 Council's Rules of Procedure).

12 See in Appendix 7 the list of eighteen existing legal bases which are switched to QMV and in Appendix 5 the list of new legal bases, in thirty-one of which QMV in the Council applies.

of EU citizens abroad and the establishment at the EU level of intellectual property rights and other centralised regimes. The Council may also use QMV for concluding with a Member State an agreement of withdrawal from the EU, for amending the six-monthly rotation system of Council Presidency and for adopting, together with the European Parliament, the rules on 'comitology'.

However, it should be stressed that measures in a number of important sectors (about eighty cases) continue to be adopted by unanimity or by common agreement, such as taxation, social security and social policy, measures on passports and identity cards, some issues of operational police co-operation, the establishment of an EU Public Prosecutor, own resources of the EU and the multiannual financial framework, the conclusion of trade agreements in certain sensitive fields, as well as most of the measures in CFSP including defence.[13] These issues are obviously very important and this is precisely the reason why the Member States have decided that unanimity there will remain the rule.

A new method of calculation for qualified majority voting

A new method of calculation of the QMV had been agreed on by the 2003–4 IGC and was inserted in the failed Constitutional Treaty. It has been incorporated in the Lisbon Treaty. This method takes into account but modifies the approach which had been proposed by the Convention, on which the 'consensus' noted by its president had been rather weak, given, in particular, the strong opposition of the representatives of the governments of Poland and Spain. Under this new method, QMV will no longer be based on weighted votes attributed to each Member State, as had been the case since 1957. It will be based on a 'double majority' with two thresholds: at least 55 per cent of the number of Member States and at least 65 per cent of the Union's population (Article 16 TEU) (see Box 27). This new rule will enter into force on 1 November 2014, until which time the former QMV as defined by the Nice Treaty continues to apply. Moreover, Article 3(2) of Protocol no. 36 on transitional provisions provides that, 'between 1 November 2014 and 31 March 2017, when an

---

13 See in Appendixes 5 and 8 the list of sixty-one cases where unanimity or common accord applies or continues to apply in the Council. To these should be added about twenty cases where unanimity or consensus applies at the level of the European Council.

BOX 27. ARTICLE 16 TEU (DEFINITION OF QMV WITHIN THE
COUNCIL) AND ARTICLE 235(1), 2ND SUBPARAGRAPH, TFEU
(DEFINITION OF QMV WITHIN THE EUROPEAN COUNCIL)

Article 16 TEU

. . .

4. As from 1 November 2014, a qualified majority shall be defined as at least 55% of the members of the Council, comprising at least fifteen of them and representing Member States comprising at least 65% of the population of the Union.

   A blocking minority must include at least four Council members, failing which the qualified majority shall be deemed attained . . .

5. The transitional provisions relating to the definition of the qualified majority which shall be applicable until 31 October 2014 and those which shall be applicable from 1 November 2014 to 31 March 2017 are laid down in the Protocol on transitional provisions.

Article 235(1), 2nd subparagraph, TFEU

Article 16(4) [TEU] . . . shall apply to the European Council when it is acting by a qualified majority. Where the European Council decides by vote, its President and the President of the Commission shall not take part in the vote . . .

act is to be adopted by qualified majority, a member of the Council may request that it be adopted in accordance with the qualified majority as defined [by the Nice Treaty]', these rules being repeated in Article 3(3) of the Protocol. This means that the new QMV method will not produce its full effects before 1 April 2017.

The two main reasons for the choice of this double majority system were, first, because it was considered, rightly or wrongly, as easier for the public to understand and, second, because it was perceived as closer to the essential nature of the EU, as being both a union of states and a union of citizens. This was reflected in the first Article of the failed Constitutional Treaty, which started with the words 'Reflecting the will of the citizens and States of Europe to build a common future', a formula which has disappeared from the Lisbon Treaty. The other reason was to keep the QMV threshold low enough to facilitate the adoption of acts in an enlarged Council. This latter aim will be achieved, whereas the first one may be considered as having been missed.

The evolution of the method of calculation of QMV in the Council

One of the major elements of the political and institutional architecture of the Union, as it has been painstakingly built up and finely tuned over the years, and to which the Member States pay close attention, is the sharing and balance of powers. This concerns not only the share of powers between the different EU institutions, but also the respective weight given to each Member State or to their nationals in the decision-taking system within each of those institutions.

Member States are 'present' in the decision-taking system of each of the three political institutions of the EU. This is indirectly the case through the presence and the number of their nationals in the European Parliament and in the Commission. This is directly the case through the weight carried by the vote of the representatives of their government in the Council.

In the original EC of six Member States in 1957, the system of weighted votes in the Council was based implicitly on a rough balance of demographic, economic and political elements. As shown in Box 28, the system was characterised by three 'clusters' of Member States: the larger ones (with four votes each, regardless of the fact that Germany was more populous than France and Italy), the middle-sized ones (with two votes each, despite the fact that Belgium was less populous than the Netherlands) and the smallest one (Luxembourg, which had a symbolic single vote[14]). This was done for political reasons, to show that the building of a reconciled Europe was a common endeavour, based in particular on the equal weight given to Germany and to France within the European institutions.[15]

At that time, the three larger Member States (France, Germany and Italy) together could outvote the other three Member States, which together could not block a decision, but neither could a large Member State alone. This situation would last for the first fifteen years of existence of the Community, until its first enlargement, in 1973.

---

14 Symbolic because the single vote could not make a difference in voting.

15 It is interesting to note that, together, the Netherlands and Belgium had a voting weight identical to a large Member State. This particular feature had remained untouched until the Treaty of Nice gave one vote more to the Netherlands (thirteen) than to Belgium (twelve), which together no longer equalled a large Member State. Under the Nice Treaty, only the three Benelux countries together could reach the twenty-nine votes equivalent to that of a large State.

In the 1957 Rome Treaty, the relative weakness of the weight of the smaller Member States in the Council was regarded as compensated for by the direct and indirect powers which the Treaty gave to the Commission. This institution was established with the aim that it would act independently, in the sole interest of the Community, regardless of the power or influence of particular Member States. Therefore it was considered a reassuring and counterbalancing element for the smaller or less powerful Member States. The three 'counterbalancing' powers of the Commission were:

- first, its exclusive right of initiative;
- second, the requirement of unanimity within the Council to amend a Commission proposal against the latter's will; and
- third, the 'super qualified majority' required in the Council (twelve positive votes, including four members in favour) in the rare cases when it could act without a Commission proposal.

These original three 'counterbalancing' powers of the Commission continued to exist after the Nice Treaty and have been retained in the Lisbon Treaty. They are aimed at favouring the smaller Member States.

These 'counterbalancing' powers were themselves 'rebalanced' in favour of the larger Member States through the fact that these States had two of their nationals appointed as members of the Commission, whereas the smaller States had only one of their nationals appointed. In a body acting by a simple majority, this meant that, together, the Commissioners from the larger Member States could outvote the Commissioners from the smaller Member States. This particular feature would remain the same until the 1995 enlargement, when the ten Commissioners from the five larger Member States could no longer outvote the ten Commissioners from the other Member States.

As from the first enlargement in 1973 onwards, the larger Member States could no longer outvote the other ones in the Council. At each successive enlargement thereafter, the system of weighted votes in the Council was mathematically extrapolated so as to keep roughly the three following characteristics:

- three 'clusters' of Member States (the cluster of large ones, in the range of ten and eight votes, the cluster of middle-sized ones, with five and four votes, and the cluster of small ones, with three and two votes);
- a QMV threshold of about 70–71 per cent of the votes;

- the simple majority of Council members automatically 'contained' in any given qualified majority.

However, this 'mathematical automaticity' had a very important political consequence. At each enlargement there was a significant change in the share of the total votes given to the larger Member States, which eroded from 70 per cent in 1954 to 55 per cent in 1995, although they represented about 80 per cent of the total EU population in 1995 (75 per cent after the last 2004 enlargement). The wide difference between these two figures (55 per cent of the votes and 80 per cent of the citizens) was considered excessive by the most populated States. They stressed that democracy requires that the principle of 'one citizen – one vote' should be better reflected, even in the Council (as compared with the European Parliament, where it is obvious that this principle applies more naturally although not quite perfectly).[16]

The biggest of the Member States, Germany, which had been reunified on 3 October 1990, started during the Amsterdam IGC to request that the increase in its population be reflected in its weight in the institutions. This is why the 1995 Accession Act gave Germany ninety-nine MEPs, while the three other large Member States were only given eighty-seven each. Previously, the four large Member States had an equal number of MEPs – that is, eighty-one each.

This, and the constant erosion of the share of the large Member States in the total of the votes of the government representatives in the Council, explains why the population criterion became such a contentious issue. It also explains why, during the Amsterdam IGC, the issues both of the weighting of votes in the Council and of the composition of the Commission were so inextricably linked, in view of the coming waves of enlargement. This remained the case during the Nice IGC, the 2003–4 IGC and the Lisbon IGC (see Box 28).

These issues are indeed at the heart of the sui generis *nature of the EU, between classic international organisations – which tend to recognise, as a principle, the equality of their Member States – and federations of states, where the democratic principle of the equality of citizens plays a bigger role.*

For the larger Member States, and particularly for Spain, renouncing 'their' second Commissioner meant they had to be 'compensated' by an

---

16 In its judgment of 30 June 2009, the German Constitutional Court attaches great importance to the principle of democratic equality of all citizens ('one man – one vote') (paras. 279, 282).

BOX 28. EVOLUTION OF THE WEIGHT OF COUNCIL MEMBERS' VOTES SINCE 1957

Member States	EU-6	EU-9	EU-10	EU-12	EU-15	EU-25	EU-27*	Population** × 1,000	Share of EU population*** %
	votes + % of votes								
Germany	4 23.5%	10 17.2%	10 15.9%	10 13.2%	10 11.5%	29 9%	29 8.4%	82,002.4	16.41
France	4 23.5%	10 17.2%	10 15.9%	10 13.2%	10 11.5%	29 9%	29 8.4%	64,350.8	12.88
UK		10 17.2%	10 15.9%	10 13.2%	10 11.5%	29 9%	29 8.4%	61,576.1	12.32
Italy	4 23.5%	10 17.2%	10 15.9%	10 13.2%	10 11.5%	29 9%	29 8.4%	60,045.1	12.02
Spain				8 10.5%	8 9.2%	27 8.4%	27 7.8%	45,828.2	9.17
Poland						27 8.4%	27 7.8%	38,135.9	7.63
Romania							14 4.1%	21,498.6	4.30
Netherlands	2 11.8%	5 8.6%	5 7.9%	5 6.6%	5 5.7%	13 4%	13 3.8%	16,485.8	3.30
Greece			5 7.9%	5 6.6%	5 5.7%	12 3.7%	12 3.5%	11,260.4	2.25
Belgium	2 11.8%	5 8.6%	5 7.9%	5 6.6%	5 5.7%	12 3.7%	12 3.5%	10,750.0	2.15
Portugal				5 6.6%	5 5.7%	12 3.7%	12 3.5%	10,627.3	2.13
Czech Rep.						12 3.7%	12 3.5%	10,467.5	2.09
Hungary						12 3.7%	12 3.5%	10,031.0	2.01
Sweden					4 4.6%	10 3.1%	10 2.9%	9,256.3	1.85
Austria					4 4.6%	10 3.1%	10 2.9%	8,355.3	1.67
Bulgaria							10 2.9%	7,606.6	1.52
Denmark		3 5.2%	3 4.8%	3 3.9%	3 3.4%	7 2.2%	7 2.0%	5,511.5	1.10
Slovakia						7 2.2%	7 2.0%	5,412.3	1.08
Finland					3 3.4%	7 2.2%	7 2.0%	5,326.3	1.07
Ireland		3 5.2%	3 4.8%	3 3.9%	3 3.4%	7 2.2%	7 2.0%	4,450.0	0.89

	17	58	63	76	87	321	345	Population	%
Lithuania						7 2.2%	7 2.0%	3,349.9	0.67
Latvia						4 1.2%	4 1.2%	2,261.3	0.45
Slovenia						4 1.2%	4 1.2%	2,032.4	0.41
Estonia						4 1.2%	4 1.2%	1,340.4	0.27
Cyprus						4 1.2%	4 1.2%	796.9	0.16
Luxembourg	1 5.9%	2 3.4%	2 3.2%	2 2.6%	2 2.3%	4 1.2%	4 1.2%	493.5	0.10
Malta						3 0.9%	3 0.9%	413.6	0.08
Total	**17**	**58**	**63**	**76**	**87**	**321**	**345**	499 665.1	**100.00**
QMV	12	41	45	54	62	232	255	until 31.10.2014: check that = 62% pop. (upon request)	
QMV threshold	70.6% of votes	70.7%	71.4%	71%	71.3%	72.3%	73.9%	from 1.11.2014: 15 MS + at least 65% pop.	
Blocking min.	6	18	19	23	26	90	91	1.11.2014: 13 MS or more than 35% pop.+ at least 4 MS	
Share of large Member States	70.5% of votes	68.8% of votes	63.6% of votes	63.3% of votes	55.2% of votes	52.8% of votes	49.3% of votes	6 out of 27 i.e. 22.2% of the number of MS	70.4% of the EU population

* Pursuant to Art. 3 of Protocol no. 36 on transitional provisions, these weighted votes will continue to apply until 31 October 2014.

** As applicable for the year 2010, pursuant to Annex I of the Council's Rules of Procedure (see OJ No. L325, 11 December 2009, 35). The population figures are updated each year.

*** To be used until 31 October 2014 for the calculation of the 62% threshold (62% of 499,665.1 is 309,792.4). As from 1 November 2014, it will be used for the second threshold of the voting system (at least 65% of EU population) under Art. 16(4) TEU.

increased voting weight in the Council. Moreover, Germany argued that democratic legitimacy required that the size of its population should be properly reflected in the institutions (following reunification, the population of Germany had increased by about 16 million to more than 80 million).

The Nice Treaty constituted a first step towards giving more importance to the demographic element. A double majority system (50 per cent of Member States and 50 per cent of population at the time) had been advocated during the Nice IGC by the smaller Member States, Germany and the Commission, but had been opposed by the other large Member States, particularly France and Spain. In the end, the Nice Treaty retained the system of weighted votes, with four 'clusters' of Member States. As a result, Germany and France still had (at least in appearance) the same number of votes each (twenty-nine), while Spain got twenty-seven votes – generous, and hard-fought-for, 'compensation' for the loss of 'its' second Commissioner. Germany requested and obtained an additional procedure, called 'the population safety net'. Under this new procedure, a Council member 'may request verification that the Member States constituting the qualified majority represent at least 62 per cent of the total population of the Union' (Article 205(4) TEC). Thanks to this procedure, Germany has in effect obtained more weight as compared with the other larger Member States, due to its larger population. These new QMV rules have been applicable since 1 November 2004 and will continue to be so at least until 31 October 2014 (for an overview see Box 28).

During the IGCs, the demographic element has always given rise to fierce opposition between the larger and the smaller Member States. It should, however, be underlined that, in real life, a coalition of 'big' versus 'small' never occurs in the Council (nor, it seems, within the Commission). Majorities vary very much, because they change according to specific subject matters, depending on the 'like-minded' Council members in each case: net contributors to or recipients from the EU budget, those that are in favour of rules more protective of the environment, those that are producers of wine, sugar or textiles, those that are exporters or importers of a given product and so on.

Each time a new method of calculating QMV is being negotiated, Member States try their best to keep maximum power to protect their national interests. All of them try to imagine every possible scenario in which they could be outvoted, and try to calculate their blocking power in such situations. They also study all theoretical possibilities available for constructing qualified majorities or blocking minorities through alliances with 'like-minded' Member States. Diplomats try to turn themselves into mathematicians.[17]

The debate on QMV during the Convention, in the 2003–4 IGC and in the Lisbon IGC

During the 2002–3 Convention, the debate focused on introducing a new system, which would depart from the traditional one of weighted votes, because the latter had been criticised as being too complicated to be understood by ordinary people. The Convention therefore recommended the whole discussion about the so-called 'double majority' system which had already taken place during the Nice IGC.

The double majority thresholds finally proposed by the Convention (50 per cent of the number of Member States and 60 per cent of the EU population) were satisfactory neither for the smaller Member States nor for Poland and Spain. The smaller Member States argued that the population threshold was too high when compared with the States threshold. Poland and Spain opposed the population method as such and argued that, especially when compared with the voting weight they had obtained in the Nice Treaty, the population threshold was in any case too low.

As a consequence, the 2003–4 IGC had to renegotiate the figures suggested by the Convention in order to make them acceptable both for Poland and Spain and for the smaller Member States. The resistance from Poland and Spain to the new QMV method was one of the main reasons for the failure of the IGC in December 2003. Then, following its change of government in March 2004, Spain agreed to continue the discussion on the basis of the new QMV method, but requested a population threshold of two-thirds (66.66 per cent), in order to keep a blocking power comparable to that which it had obtained under the Nice Treaty. This new (and clever) position resulted in the isolation of Poland, which concentrated its efforts on obtaining, in addition, a 'Ioannina-like' mechanism (see Box 29 on the 1994 'Ioannina decision').

17 In June 2004, a group of mathematicians argued that the 'clearest' way of ensuring respect for the basic democratic principle would have been to give each Member State a voting weight equivalent to the square root of its population (see paper by 'Scientists for a democratic Europe', available at www.ruhr-uni-bochum.de/mathphys/politik/eu/open-letter.htm. This was again proposed by Poland during the Lisbon IGC in June 2007. See K. Zyczkowski and W. Slomczynski, 'Voting in the European Union: The Square Root System of Penrose and a Critical Point', available at http://arxiv.org/ftp/cond-mat/papers/0405/0405396.pdf.

At the end of the IGC, in June 2004, as one could have foreseen, in order to achieve unanimity in the IGC it was necessary to increase both thresholds: 55 per cent for the Member States threshold and 65 per cent for the population threshold. A first collateral damage of that decision was a raising of the QMV threshold, thus making the adoption of acts in the Council more difficult. In addition, the result would have allowed any three of the four largest Member States to form a blocking minority; this was unacceptable, not only for the smaller Member States, but also for Spain, which would no longer have been instrumental in any such combinations of large Member States to form a blocking minority.

For these reasons, the 2003–4 IGC added a further requirement, according to which a blocking minority must include at least four Council members, otherwise a QMV would be deemed to have been attained. This was a small facilitating mechanism for decision making,[18] as well as a reassurance to Spain. At the last minute, at the request of Austria, the IGC also added a requirement that the 55 per cent threshold of Member States should comprise at least fifteen of them. This was appreciated by the small Member States, because it reduced the gap between the two percentages, which they always claimed should be as narrow as possible so as to keep a form of parity between the two thresholds. Since, in a Union of twenty-five, fifteen States represent 60 per cent of the Member States, this requirement had effectively resulted in increasing the threshold of States to 60 per cent. In an EU of twenty-seven, however, following the accession of Bulgaria and Romania in 2007, this requirement has lost its significance, as it corresponds to the 55 per cent threshold of Member States.

The 'Ioannina' mechanism

In order to accommodate the concerns of Poland, it was decided, at the end of the Lisbon IGC, that a Decision which had been negotiated during the 2003–4 IGC would be adopted by the Council on the same day as the signature of the Lisbon Treaty, although its entry into force

---

18 Another effective facilitating mechanism had been proposed during the IGC. It would have consisted in not counting abstentions any more: 'Abstentions shall not be taken into account when counting the total number of Council members and of population' (document CIG 83/04, 18 June 2004, 7). However, due to the opposition of Germany (because of the complex balance of powers between the Federation and the Länder which would have been disturbed by such a change), this proposal was not retained. Consequently, as was the case previously, an abstention still continues to have the same effects as a negative vote in a QMV (but not for vote by unanimity, where an abstention does not prevent adoption; see Art. 238(4) TFEU).

BOX 29. THE 'IOANNINA DECISION' OF 1994

At the end of the accession negotiations with Austria, Finland and Sweden in 1994, the issue of the adaptation of the weight of votes attributed to each member of the Council and of the QMV threshold in the Council was a very acute problem, which blocked the finalisation of the negotiations. The simple extrapolation of the number of votes attributed to each Member State, as had been done for the previous accessions, appeared to give more weight to the States with less population and to reduce the proportion of population represented by a qualified majority. Two Member States in particular (the United Kingdom and Spain) denounced that as being unacceptable.

After very difficult negotiations, a solution was finally found at an informal meeting of the twelve foreign ministers in Ioannina (Greece). This solution took the form of a Decision of the Council.* Pursuant to that Decision, if members of the Council representing twenty-three to twenty-five votes (i.e. close to the threshold of twenty-six votes required to form a blocking minority), indicated their intention to vote against the adoption by the Council of an act by a qualified majority, the Council would do its utmost to reach a satisfactory solution that could be adopted by at least sixty-five votes (instead of the sixty-two votes which were legally sufficient for the adoption).

However, the Decision makes it legally clear that, during that period, the Council's Rules of Procedure would always have to be respected. As these Rules provide that a simple majority of the Council may ask for a vote to take place, this explains why the application of this compromise has very rarely been invoked, and why it has never involved a delay of more than one day for the act at issue to be adopted.

* Council Decision of 29 March 1994 concerning the taking of decisions by qualified majority by the Council (OJ No. C105, 13 April 1994), amended on 1 January 1995 (OJ No. C1, 1 January 1995, 1).

---

was conditional upon the entry into force of the Treaty.[19] This Decision 'relating to the implementation of Article 16(4) [TEU]' and inspired by the 'Ioannina Decision' of 1994 (see Box 29), was contained in Declaration no. 7 to the Final Act of the Lisbon IGC.

The Decision adopted on 13 December 2007 ('the 2009 Ioannina-bis mechanism'; see Box 30) goes much further. As such, it could lead to

---

19 The commitment to adopt the Decision 'on the date of the signature of the Treaty of Lisbon' was contained in the introductory paragraph of Declaration no. 7. The Council effectively adopted this 'Ioannina-bis' Decision on 13 December 2007 by written procedure (doc. 16013/07).

BOX 30. THE 2009 'IOANNINA-BIS' MECHANISM

The Decision provides that, even when a qualified majority is reached in the Council on a given vote, a member of the Council may ask for the matter to be discussed further when the minority is close to the blocking minority provided for in the Treaty, as defined in the following way:*

(a) for the period from 1 November 2014 to 31 March 2017, when the minority represents three-quarters of the minority required by the Treaty for the EU population (i.e. 35.01 per cent of the population) or three-quarters of the minority required by the Treaty for the number of States (i.e. 45.01 per cent of the States);

(b) as from 1 April 2017, when the minority represents at least 55 per cent of the EU population or at least 55 per cent of the number of Member States necessary to constitute a blocking minority resulting from Article 16(4) TEU or Article 238(2) TFEU.

This decision makes it look as if the two thresholds in the double majority would have been increased to 66 per cent of States and 74 per cent of the EU population respectively for the period 2014–17 and even significantly more as from 1 April 2017:

• 55 per cent of the blocking minority as far as the number of Member States is concerned means $(55 \times 45)/100 = 24.75$ per cent of the Member States (with an EU of twenty-seven Member States, this means only six Member States);

• 55 per cent of the blocking minority as far as the population is concerned means $(55 \times 35)/100 = 19.25$ per cent of the EU population (easily reached with two large Member States).

---

* Art. 1 of the Decision reads:

From 1 November 2014 to 31 March 2017, if members of the Council, representing:

(a) at least three quarters of the population, or
(b) at least three quarters of the number of Member States

necessary to constitute a blocking minority resulting from the application of Article 16(4), 1st subparagraph, [TEU] or Article 238(2) [TFEU] indicate their opposition to the Council adopting an act by a qualified majority, the Council shall discuss the issue.

Art. 4 of the Decision reads:

As from 1 April 2017, if members of the Council, representing:

(a) at least 55% of the population, or
(b) at least 55% of the number of Member States

necessary to constitute a blocking minority resulting from the application of Article 16(4), 1st subparagraph, [TEU] or Article 238(2) [TFEU], indicate their opposition to the Council adopting an act by a qualified majority, the Council shall discuss the issue (OJ No. L314, 1 December 2009, 73).

a blockade of the decision-making process in the Council. However, it expressly retains, in its Article 6, the legal rule according to which the Council's Rules of Procedure must always be respected during the period when the Ioannina mechanism is invoked. As these Rules of Procedure provide in their Article 11(1) that a simple majority of the Council may request that a vote (according to the normal Treaty rules) take place, and as a qualified majority (which by definition exists in the given case) always contains a simple majority, this is not to be feared. Therefore, the result should be the same as that of the 1994 Ioannina Decision.

Of course, the Council's Rules of Procedure may be modified by the Council acting by a simple majority of its members. However, Protocol no. 9 adopted by the Lisbon IGC provides in its sole Article that 'before the examination by the Council of any draft which would aim either at amending or abrogating the Decision or any of its provisions, or at modifying indirectly its scope or its meaning through the modification of another legal act of the Union, the European Council shall hold a preliminary deliberation on the said draft, acting by consensus in accordance with Article 15(4) [TEU]'. This means that any amendment to the provisions according to which the 'Ioannina-bis' Decision must be implemented 'in compliance with the Rules of Procedure of the Council', as well as any amendment to the provisions of the said Rules of Procedures according to which a simple majority may at any time request the Council to proceed to a vote, will require a consensus in the European Council before they may be adopted. This is a safeguard for everybody: Poland, which can be assured that consensus will be required to amend the 'Ioannina-bis' Decision, and the other Member States, which can be assured that amending the 'linked' provisions in the Council's Rules of Procedure will also require consensus.

Section 27 The Commission

The powers of the Commission have been increased by the Lisbon Treaty. This is the case with the 'communitarisation' of the former third pillar (role of making proposals, role of ensuring the application of EU law by the Member States). It is also a consequence of the number of legal bases which are switched from unanimity in the Council to QMV. In such cases, the increased power of the Commission stems from the rule in Article 293 TFEU which requires unanimity in the Council for amending a Commission proposal when the Commission does not agree with the amendment.

This, clearly, significantly increases the influence of the Commission in the decision-making process.

Together with the new system of calculation of QMV, the issue of the size and composition of the Commission was one of the most passionately debated in all IGCs since the Maastricht IGC.

The most important measure of the Lisbon Treaty designed to increase the effectiveness of the Commission was the reduction of the number of Commissioners from one per Member State to two-thirds of the number of Member States, with a system of equal rotation. The Treaty provides that this measure should be applied as from 1 November 2014 (Article 17(5) TEU). In the meantime (i.e. until 31 October 2014), Article 17(4) TEU provides that the Commission is composed of one national per Member State. After the failure of the Irish referendum in June 2008, the European Council decided in December 2008 to abandon the planned reduction of the number of Commissioners, in order to facilitate the success of the second referendum. This political decision will have to be implemented through a 'decision . . . in accordance with the necessary legal procedures'.[20]

Some Member States feared that such a composition (one Commissioner per Member State) runs the risk of the Commission falling into a sort of intergovernmentalism. Why? Because Member States have a tendency to identify 'their' Commissioner as 'their representative' in the Commission, who would be there to defend their national interests. This runs contrary to the spirit and the letter of the Treaties, which mandate the independence of the Commission members from governments.[21] It is recalled that all decisions of the Commission are adopted by a simple majority, with one vote per Commissioner. Therefore, this 'intergovernmentalist' tendency could jeopardise the legitimacy of the Commission's decisions, since these decisions could be taken by a simple majority of fourteen Commissioners 'representing' only 11.32 per cent of the EU population on a purely theoretical calculation, reached by adding the population of the fourteen smallest Member States. Such a majority could easily outvote the six Commissioners who are nationals of the largest Member States having 70.4 per cent of the EU population. This, of course, is completely theoretical. However, the argument might be used in order to weaken the legitimacy of the Commission's decisions when it deals with

---

20 See para. 2 of the Presidency Conclusions (doc. 17271/1/08 REV 1), repeated in the Conclusions at the June 2009 European Council (see Box 12). See also note 23, *infra*.
21 Art. 17(3), 2nd and 3rd subpara., TEU.

politically sensitive dossiers (notably in the field of competition, merger control or state aid).

The truth is that the argument of legitimacy may also be used, and is actually used, in the other direction. As public opinion of the Member States tends to regard the EU as a classic international organisation, they might feel 'unprotected' without one of the members of the Commission being of their nationality.

It should be recalled that, as the Lisbon Treaty did not enter into force on or before 1 November 2009 (i.e. before the end of the term of office of the 'Barroso I' Commission), the Nice Treaty was to apply to the Commission which should have been appointed as from 1 November 2009 (i.e. the 'Barroso II' Commission). The Nice Treaty[22] had amended Article 213(1) TEC by providing that 'the number of Members of the Commission shall be less than the number of Member States'. This had entered into force on 1 January 2007 (i.e. as of when the EU consisted of twenty-seven Member States) and could not be derogated from. The Nice Treaty provided that 'as from the date on which the first Commission following the date of accession of the 27th Member State of the Union takes up its duties' – that is, on 1 November 2009 – the rule on the reduced Commission would apply. The Council would have been obliged to adopt, acting unanimously, a decision setting out the number of Commissioners and other 'implementation arrangements'.[23] The Council would have needed to adopt this difficult decision before 1 November 2009 – that is, before the beginning of the mandate of the 'Barroso II' Commission. One might have thought that the solution found in Article 17(5) TEU (i.e. two-thirds of the number of Member States) might have helped in that respect, but it would actually have been very difficult to adopt it. In any case, this issue did not arise, as the Council decided to wait the short period necessary for the Lisbon Treaty to enter into force. For the future, before the end of the term of office of the 'Barroso II' Commission (i.e. before 31 October 2014), a legal decision will have to be adopted in order to provide that, in accordance with what was decided in December 2008 and in June 2009 by the European Council, the Commission will continue to be composed of one member per Member State.[24]

---

22 Art. 4(2) of the Protocol on the enlargement of the EU, adopted at Nice.
23 The Commissioners were to be chosen 'according to a rotation system based on the principle of equality', see Art. 4(3) of the enlargement Protocol.
24 See Presidency Conclusions, European Council of 11–12 December 2008 (para. 2, doc. 17271/1/08 REV 1) and Presidency Conclusions, European Council of 18–19 June 2009 (para. 2, doc. 11225/1/09 REV 1). Some are of the opinion that a decision of the European

The debate on the size and composition of the Commission
in the Convention and in the 2003–4 IGC

As mentioned above, the smaller Member States have always insisted on the need to be 'represented' by one of their nationals in the Commission in order for the Commission to be more legitimate. Not without reason, they argue that, even if one of the larger Member States did not have one of its nationals as a member of the Commission, its interests would not be ignored, but that the same would not be necessarily true for the smaller Member States.[25] The larger Member States, for their part, insisted that the size of the Commission should be reduced, arguing that a Commission with twenty-seven and more members would not function effectively, that its members are not there to represent the interests of the Member States and that a Commission reduced in size would be more efficient and more collegial.

This is why, trying to square the circle, the Convention had suggested a strange and complicated formula. According to that formula, one national from each Member State would have been a 'member of the Commission'. However, only some of these 'members' (then to be called 'the European Commissioners') would have had the right to vote in the Commission. The other 'members' (then to be called 'the Commissioners') would have participated in Commission meetings, but without the right to vote.[26]

This formula was rejected by all Member States during the 2003–4 IGC.

After long discussions, a compromise was finally found, based on three elements:

Council would be sufficient, because of the clause at the end of Art. 17(5), 1st subpara., TEU (see phrase with emphasis added): 'the Commission shall consist of a number of members ... corresponding to two thirds of the number of Member States, *unless the European Council, acting unanimously, decides to alter this number*'. According to others this interpretation would be legally wrong, as this phrase has to be read in its context, and particularly together with the next subparagraph which sets out the conditions governing the principle of a reduced Commission (establishment of a strictly equal rotation system, reflecting the demographic and geographical range of all the Member States, which are developed in more detail in Art. 244 TFEU). According to them, this phrase therefore does not allow the European Council to change the principle itself of a reduced Commission, as its purpose is to enable the European Council to reduce further the number of Commissioners when the EU is enlarged to include more Member States, so as to be able to keep to a reasonable number of Commissioners.

25 Declaration no. 10 of the Lisbon IGC was meant to address these concerns.

26 See Art. 25(3) of the draft text as submitted by the Convention to the President of the European Council on 18 July 2003.

- equality between Member States: the rotation between the Commissioners would apply on a strictly equal footing, regardless of the size of the population of the Member States. Each Member State would have one of its nationals appointed as a Commissioner for two out of three mandates of the Commission. This system of equal rotation would be established by a unanimous decision of the European Council. Each successive Commission would be composed so as to reflect satisfactorily the demographic and geographical range of all the Member States;
- progressivity: the new system would only start to apply with the Commission which would be appointed on 1 November 2014;
- package deal with the composition of the European Parliament: the less populated Member States obtained the guarantee that each State, whatever its population, would have a minimum of six seats in the European Parliament.

However, this compromise was set aside in December 2008, following the need to find an arrangement required by the Irish authorities in order to present the Lisbon Treaty for a second ratification by referendum.

Additional powers conferred on the President of the Commission

The President of the Commission is politically more powerful when the Commission is larger rather than smaller. Moreover, the Lisbon Treaty confers on him additional legal powers.

Due to the fact that the High Representative is also a Vice-President of the Commission, the agreement of the President of the Commission is required before his/her appointment by the European Council (Article 18(1) TEU). The President of the Commission, the High Representative and the other members of the Commission are subject, as a body, to a vote of consent by the European Parliament (Article 17(7), 3rd subparagraph, TEU). Conversely, if a motion of censure on the Commission is tabled before the European Parliament and adopted, the members of the Commission will have to resign as a body and the High Representative will 'resign from the duties that he carries out in the Commission' (Articles 17(8) and 234 TFEU).

According to Article 17(6) TEU, 'a member of the Commission shall resign if the President so requests'. Therefore, the President no longer needs the approval of the College to ask a Commissioner to resign, as was previously the case (Article 217(4) TEC). However, if the President of the Commission asks the High Representative to resign, as a member of the

Commission the High Representative will have to resign 'in accordance with the procedure set out in Article 18', which states that the European Council may end the High Representative mandate by QMV, with the agreement of the Commission's President. As was the case before, the President may appoint Vice-Presidents (other than the High Representative) from among the members of the Commission.

The Commission's general role in ensuring the Union's external representation, except for CFSP

The Lisbon Treaty provides for a general rule according to which the Commission 'with the exception of [CFSP], and other cases provided for in the Treaties... shall ensure the Union's external representation' (Article 17(1) TEU). This codifies the general practice before the Lisbon Treaty, under which the Commission represented the EC when there is EC competence and when there is no obstacle to do so in the forum where the negotiation takes place.[27]

Section 28 The Court of Justice

The amendments concerning the Court of Justice which had been foreseen in the failed Constitutional Treaty were neither opposed nor criticised by any Member State. Therefore they were integrated in the Lisbon Treaty. The major change is that the jurisdiction of the Court of Justice has been increased in three ways:

- first, the Court's jurisdiction now covers the whole area of FSJ, while this area was, before the Lisbon Treaty, partially excluded from its competence. This is good news for the rule of law, for the uniform application of EU law and for the protection of individual rights. The only exception is that the Court, in the areas of judicial co-operation in criminal matters and police co-operation, cannot review the validity or proportionality of operations carried out by the police or other

27 There may be cases where, due to the fact that the EC (or the Commission on behalf of the EC), had no seat or no right to speak in an international organisation, the six-monthly Presidency would, instead, express the position of the EC. There also could be cases where, because a negotiation concerned both EC competences and Member State competences (so-called 'mixed agreements') and the Member States do not want to mandate the Commission to negotiate on their behalf on matters belonging to their competences, there would be two 'negotiators': the Commission with regard to EC competences and, if the Member States so decide, the six-monthly Presidency with regard to the competences of the Member States.

law enforcement services of a Member State or of measures taken by them in order to safeguard their internal security (Article 276 TFEU). In addition, the Lisbon Treaty provides for a limitation, although temporary, on the jurisdiction of the Court in the area of FSJ. Under this transitional rule, the limited jurisdiction of the Court regarding the former third pillar *acquis* (i.e. Title VI of the former TEU), adopted before the entry into force of the Lisbon Treaty, will continue for five years after its entry into force. This is one of the tricky issues which have been negotiated in the Legal Experts Group of the Lisbon IGC (see Sections 3 and 23);

- second, despite the fact that the CFSP remains outside the Court's jurisdiction,[28] the Court has been given the power to review the legality of decisions providing for restrictive measures against natural or legal persons (Article 275 TFEU);

- third, the scope of actions for annulment brought by individuals (and companies) against EU regulatory acts has been increased, by removing the condition that the act in question should be of individual concern to the individual.[29] Pursuant to Article 263, 4th paragraph, TFEU, it is now sufficient that the EU regulatory act 'is of *direct* concern [to him] and does not entail implementing measures', whereas Article 230, 4th paragraph, TEC required that the act be 'of *direct and individual* concern' to the individual (emphasis added).[30]

---

28 One may note that, not long before the Lisbon Treaty, the Court of Justice seems to have considerably expanded the possibility for the EC to act concerning matters one could consider as pertaining to the domain of CFSP (see judgment of 20 May 2008, case C-91/05, *Commission v. Council (small arms-ECOWAS)* [2008] ECR I-3651).

29 On this issue see T. Tridimas and S. Poli, 'Locus Standi of Individuals under Article 230(4): The Return of Euridice?', in P. Moser and K. Sawyer (eds.), *Making Community Law: The Legacy of Advocate General Jacobs at the European Court of Justice* (Cheltenham: Edward Elgar Publishing, 2008), 70. During the review of the drafting of the text in the Working Party of Legal Experts of the 2003–4 IGC, it was suggested that the words 'a regulatory act', which occur only in Art. 263 TFEU and are not defined, be replaced by the words 'a regulation or decision having no addressees', thus making it clear that the act in question is a non legislative one and, if it is a decision, that it is the normative type of decision (i.e. without addressees) and not the individual type. This suggestion was not retained by the Working Party.

30 The new wording in the Lisbon Treaty responds to the 2002 case law of the Court of Justice which interpreted the limits of Art. 230 TEC: 'according to the system for judicial review of legality established by the Treaty, a natural or legal person can bring an action challenging a regulation only if it is concerned both directly and individually. Although this last condition must be interpreted in the light of the principle of effective judicial protection by taking account of the various circumstances that may distinguish an applicant individually . . . such an interpretation cannot have the effect of setting aside the condition in question, expressly laid down in the Treaty, without going beyond the

In addition, the Lisbon Treaty provides expressly that actions for annulment may also be brought against acts of the European Council, as well as against 'acts of bodies, offices or agencies of the Union intended to produce legal effects vis-à-vis third parties' (Article 263, 1st paragraph, TFEU). This is an improvement as compared with the scope of actions for annulment under Article 230 TEC.

It might also be noted that the stages of the procedure for the Commission to request the Court of Justice to impose a fine on a Member State have been reduced. The Commission no longer needs to submit to the Member State concerned a 'reasoned opinion' to inform it in detail of its wrongdoing (Article 260(2) TFEU).

Finally, Article 267 TFEU contains a new provision under which the Court will have to act 'with the minimum of delay' when a preliminary ruling is requested in a case concerning a person in custody. The proposal made by the Court for an urgent procedure has already been approved by the Council.[31]

Besides, the name of the EU judicial institution as a whole becomes 'Court of Justice of the European Union', which 'shall include the Court of Justice, the General Court and specialised courts' (Article 19(1) TEU). Therefore the Court of Justice of the European Union will comprise several bodies, each with its own area of jurisdiction: the Court of Justice, the General Court (instead of the previous Court of First Instance) and specialised courts attached to the General Court (instead of the previous judicial panels).

The Lisbon Treaty has improved the procedure for appointing judges as compared with the previous system, whereby each Member State's government communicated the name of the candidate of its choice,[32] who, in practice, was then automatically appointed. Pursuant to Article

---

jurisdiction conferred by the Treaty on the Community Courts. . . . While it is, admittedly, possible to envisage a system of judicial review of the legality of Community measures of general application different from that established by the founding Treaty and never amended as to its principles, it is for the Member States, if necessary, in accordance with Art. 48 EU, to reform the system currently in force' (see judgment of 25 July 2002, case 50/00 P, *Union de Pequeños agricultores*, [2002] ECR I-6719, paras. 44, 45).

31 See Council Decision 2008/79/EC of 20 December 2007 amending the Protocol on the Statute of the Court of Justice (OJ No. L24, 29 January 2008, 42) and amendments to the Rules of Procedure of the Court of Justice adopted by the Court of Justice on 15 January 2008 (OJ No. L24, 29 January 2008, 39).

32 In a few Member States this choice is subject to an internal selection procedure. The German Law of September 2009 related to the Lisbon Treaty provides that German candidates for the Court of Justice and the General Court will have to be selected in the same way as for the German Supreme Courts.

255 TFEU, there will be a panel of seven persons chosen from among former judges from the Court of Justice and the General Court, from national supreme courts and lawyers of recognised competence, who will give an opinion on the candidates' suitability to perform the duties of judge and advocate-general. On the basis of this opinion, the judges will then be appointed by common accord of the governments of the Member States.[33]

The number of judges has not been changed. The Court of Justice consists of one judge from each Member State,[34] while the General Court includes 'at least' one judge per Member State (Article 19(2) TEU). As for the advocates-general of the Court of Justice, their number is still eight. As was previously the case in Article 222 TEC, Article 252 TFEU provides that 'should the Court of Justice so request, the Council acting unanimously, may increase' the number of advocates-general. At the end of the Lisbon IGC, Poland succeeded in obtaining the adoption by the IGC of Declaration no. 38, according to which 'if . . . the Court of Justice requests that the number of Advocates-General be increased by three (eleven instead of eight), the Council will . . . agree on this increase . . . In that case . . . Poland will, as is already the case for Germany, France, Italy, Spain and the United Kingdom, have a permanent Advocate-General'. The purpose was to put Poland on a par with the other larger Member States. The Court of Justice might not be very keen on such an increase in the number of advocates-general. In any case, it is up to it to request the increase.

Finally, the procedure for amending the Statute of the Court is modified: instead of unanimity, it may now be modified in codecision with QMV in the Council. This will make it easier for the Court of Justice to adapt itself to new challenges (Article 281 TFEU).[35] However, this

33 See Council Decision of 25 February 2010 on the operating rules of the panel (OJ No. L50, 27 February 2010, 18) and Council Decision of 25 February 2010 appointing the members of the panel (OJ No. L50, 27 February 2010, 20). A similar procedure, with a Selection Committee, has already been used for the appointment of the Judges to the EU Civil Service Tribunal (see Council Decision of 2 November 2004 establishing the European Union Civil Service Tribunal, OJ No. L333, 9 November 2004, 7; Council Decision of 18 January 2005, OJ No. L50, 23 February 2005, 7; and Council Decision of 22 July 2005, OJ No. L197, 28 July 2005, 28).

34 On this point see the opinion of the German Constitutional Court in its judgment of 30 June 2009: 'Also after the entry into force of the Treaty of Lisbon, the Court of Justice, for instance, must always be staffed according to the principle "one State, one judge" and under the determining influence of the Member States regardless of their number of inhabitants' (para. 288).

35 For a more detailed analysis see L. W. Gormley, 'The Judicial Architecture of the European Union in the Constitution', in P. G. Xuereb (ed.), *The Constitution for Europe: An*

possibility will not apply for Title I of the Statute (on the judges and advocates-general) which will still require a change of the Treaty in order to be modified, and for Article 64 of the Statute (on the language arrangements), which will require unanimity in the Council.

Section 29 Changes to other institutions and bodies

The European Central Bank

The European Central Bank (ECB) is now one institution of the EU among the others. The Bank was reluctant concerning this change, probably because of fear for its independence. As an institution, it is brought within the scope of all the general provisions and of the rules that are applicable to 'the institutions'.

This includes, for instance, the requirements to respect the principles of subsidiarity and proportionality (Article 5(3), 2nd subparagraph, TEU), to give equal attention to EU citizens (Article 9 TEU), to give citizens and representative associations the opportunity to make known and publicly exchange their views in all areas of EU action (Article 11(1) TEU), to keep national parliaments informed (Article 12(a) TEU), to 'practice mutual sincere co-operation' with the other EU institutions (Article 13(2) TEU), and to conduct its work 'as openly as possible' (Article 15(1) TFEU).[36]

In any case, for the ECB, becoming an institution will not really change its political or legal situation, as its independence is still guaranteed (Article 130 and 282(3) TFEU and Article 7 of Protocol no. 4 on the Statute of the ESCB and of the ECB). As to the jurisdiction of the Court of Justice to review the legality of the ECB acts, this was already provided for in the TEC and in the Protocol on the Statute of the ECB.[37]

Evaluation (Malta: EDRC, Medial Centre Print, 2005), 57. See also F. De Witte, 'The European Judiciary after Lisbon' (2008) 15 *Maastricht Journal of European and Comparative Law* 43.

36 However, with regard to the ECB, the Court of Justice and the EIB, Art. 15(3), 4th subparagraph, TFEU provides that the rules on access to documents apply 'only when exercising their administrative tasks'.

37 Arts. 230, 232, 237(d) and 241 TEC and Art. 35 of the ECB Statute. On the question of whether or not, before the Lisbon Treaty, the ECB was part of the Community structure and fell within the remit of EC law, see R. Torrent, 'Whom is the European Central Bank the Central Bank of? Reaction to Zilioli and Selmayr' (1999) 36 *Common Market Law Review* 1229. See also C. Zilioli and M. Selmayr, 'The External Relations of the Euro Area: Legal Aspects' (1999) 36 *Common Market Law Review* 273, as well as Zilioli and Selmayr, 'The European Central Bank: An Independent Specialized Organization of Community Law' (2000) 37 *Common Market Law Review* 591. The issue has been clarified

The Committee of the Regions

The Committee of the Regions is a consultative body composed of representatives of regional and local bodies who hold local electoral mandates or are accountable to an elected assembly (Article 300(3) TFEU). With the Lisbon Treaty, the Committee gains the right to bring actions before the Court of Justice for the annulment of EU legislative acts for infringement of the subsidiarity principle, in cases where its consultation is mandatory under the relevant legal basis.[38] The Committee of Regions also obtained the right to bring actions for annulment in order to protect its own prerogatives (Article 263, 3rd paragraph, TFEU).

In addition, a specific cross-reference to the advisory role of the Committee of the Regions (and of the Economic and Social Committee) was inserted in Article 13(4) TEU (paragraph 1 of which lists the seven EU institutions).

Section 30 Relations between institutions and the interinstitutional balance

It would be difficult to draw conclusions at this stage on which of the three political institutions is or is not a winner as a result of the Lisbon Treaty. One has to wait for the implementation of the Treaty before trying to draw any such conclusions.

For most observers, the European Parliament is regarded as the major winner. The European Parliament has gained legal powers in all areas, external and internal policies, participation in the adoption of the budget and in legislative power, and even a role to play in the procedure which may lead to a revision of the Treaties. However, despite the resistance of the European Parliament, the national parliaments do, for the first time, appear in the political landscape of the EU. This should be taken seriously by the European Parliament. Should the turn-out in the European

by the Court of Justice in its judgment of 10 July 2003, Case C-11/00, *Commission v. ECB* (on OLAF Regulation) [2003] ECR I-7147, paras. 91, 135: '91. ... the fact that a body, office or agency owes its existence to the EC Treaty suggests that it was intended to contribute towards the attainment of the European Community's objectives and places it within the framework of the Community... 135. ... recognition that the ECB has such independence does not have the consequence of separating it entirely from the European Community and exempting it from every rule of Community law... Finally, it is evident that it was not the intention of the Treaty draftsmen to shield the ECB from any kind of legislative action taken by the Community legislature.'

38 See Art. 8, 2nd paragraph, of Protocol no. 2 on subsidiarity and proportionality.

elections remain weak, or become even weaker, in the future, and should the 'democratic malaise' continue, despite the huge powers given to the directly elected European Parliament, pressure would grow to review the present system in the future. Most governments have already given more powers to their national parliament, either of their own will or through being 'forced' to do so by their constitutional court.[39]

On the side of the direct representation of the governments of the Member States, there are now two institutions instead of one, the European Council having become an institution alongside or, to put it better, above the Council. The increasing powers and influence gained over the years by the European Council were not due to legal provisions of a given Treaty, but to political reality. However, they are now legally recognised and strengthened by the Treaty. The fact that the European Council has a full-time and fixed President will, no doubt, increase its effectiveness and leadership in the Union's political life. Some hope that it might be supported in its task by the General Affairs Council. However, this will remain difficult, given the fact that this configuration of the Council is not composed of twenty-seven ministers able to impose co-ordination on their own national colleagues participating in the other configurations of the Council. As for the Foreign Affairs Council, it might play a decisive role if its members allow their fixed and full-time president, the High Representative, to represent in an authoritative and visible way the foreign policy of the Union. If one adds to those elements the fact that the Council will be able to decide by QMV on more issues than in the past, one could certainly conclude that the European Council and the Council are also big winners of the Lisbon reform.

The same can be said about the Commission, which, with the communitarisation of the former third pillar, has now gained a quasi-monopoly in all legislative proposals, taking into account the fact that no legislative act can be adopted in the area of CFSP. Its President sees his authority on the College enhanced. One should note also that the powers of the Commission to ensure the Union's external representation, except for the CFSP, are now legally recognised by the Treaty. However, one has also to recognise that, at least since 1999, the trend has not been in favour of strengthening the political authority of the Commission. The pressures exercised on it, sometimes by the most powerful Member States, often

---

39 This is the case in Germany after the judgment of 30 June 2009 of the German Constitutional Court, which obliged the government to submit a new law to its parliament in order to increase the powers of the German parliament in a number of instances.

by the European Parliament (e.g. through the conclusion of 'framework agreements' imposed on the Commission) are not foreign to this regrettable trend.

*

Over the years, through the successive modifications of the founding Treaties, the Member States have clearly demonstrated their will not to establish any single EU institution as politically too powerful. They have always imposed a balance between EU institutions. Therefore it is not by chance or by mistake that, in the present Union, several figures emerge as 'would-be rivals' in the future, be it the President of the European Council, the President of the Commission or the High Representative. In addition, for his/her part, the prime minister (or president) of the Member State exercising the six-monthly Presidency of the Council will make sure that he/she is not forgotten, through his/her political leadership over the presidents of all configurations of the Council, except Foreign Affairs.

How will that work in the future? Will the external EU representation become more efficient and visible, or on the contrary more messy than before, with the four above-mentioned figures fighting each other to appear at the forefront on the international scene? Will the co-ordination of the work of the different configurations of the Council improve with the strengthened role of the President of the European Council, or will it become totally disorganised, because of the rivalry between this president and the six-monthly Presidency? Will the centre (in Brussels), personified by the fixed and full-time Presidents of the European Parliament, of the European Council, of the Commission and of the Foreign Affairs Council, work in a coherent way and act in a decisive manner to develop further the integration of the Union? Or will these personalities fight each other and open the way to a 're-intergovernmentalisation' of the Union?

All these questions are open. Answers depend both on the personalities involved and on the economic and political situation of Europe. The future is difficult to foresee. It will be fascinating to observe where the new provisions of the Treaties will lead us.

VII

External affairs

Both in the 2002–3 Convention and in the 2003–4 IGC, the ambition was to take a major qualitative step forward in the field of external affairs. The aim was to make the Union more 'present in the world', as the European Council had requested in the 2001 Laeken Declaration. This was to be achieved by improving the functioning of the CFSP, as well as the consistency between the different areas of EU external policy: CFSP, trade, development, humanitarian aid and other sectoral external policies in environment, transport and so on, essentially through the establishment of new institutional tools.

Section 31 External affairs before the Lisbon Treaty

The origins and scope of the external competence of the Community

In the 1957 Rome Treaty, the EC competence in external affairs was purely economic, and in particular linked to the fact that the EC was first created as a customs union, with a common customs tariff. As international trade developed, and the EC progressively liberalised its internal trade and made use of its internal competences to create its internal market, with free movement of goods, services, capital and persons and harmonised internal rules, the corresponding external competences also developed. This was necessary to avoid the possibility that, by concluding international agreements on matters covered by internal EC rules, Member States would affect these rules or impede their development.[1]

---

1 See in particular judgment of 31 March 1971, Case 22/70, *AETR*, [1971] ECR 263. In this case the Court ruled that '28. Although it is true that articles 74 and 75 [i.e. the provisions on transport] do not expressly confer on the Community authority to enter into international agreements, nevertheless the bringing into force, on 25 March 1969, of Regulation no. 543/69 . . . necessarily vested in the Community power to enter into any agreements with third countries relating to the subject-matter governed by that Regulation . . . 30. Since the subject-matter of the AETR falls within the scope of Regulation no 543/69, the Community has been empowered to negotiate and conclude the agreement in question since the entry

The original Rome Treaty gave legal personality to the EC (Article 281 TEC). It provided that agreements concluded by the EC were binding on the EC institutions and on Member States (Article 300(7) TEC). It contained three Articles on external relations (Articles 131 to 133 TEC on common commercial policy) and one on the procedure for concluding international agreements (Article 300 TEC). Successive amendments to the TEC added new provisions and modified the procedure for nego-tiating and concluding international agreements. The Single European Act inserted provisions on external relations in specific policy chapters (such as environment and research, see Articles 174(4) and 170 TEC). The Maastricht Treaty added development co-operation (Articles 177 to 181 TEC) and the external representation of the single currency (Article 111 TEC). The Nice Treaty added economic, financial and technical co-operation with third countries (Article 181A TEC). The case law of the EC Court of Justice also contributed to the development of the principles governing EC competence in external affairs.

External trade policy was considered essentially as an exclusive compe-tence of the EC. However, this competence has never covered all areas of trade policy.[2]

The institutional framework of this policy was set out in Article 133 TEC (originally numbered 113). The Council acted, in principle, by QMV, on the basis of a proposal from the Commission, and without an obli-gation to consult the European Parliament. This was the case both for concluding international agreements and for adopting trade legislation. The Commission was in charge of representing the EC externally and negotiating on its behalf.

It is worth recalling that, in the area of trade, the EC is the most impor-tant power in the world. It is one of the most powerful actors in the World Trade Organization (WTO) and in international negotiations conducted in its framework, including the Doha Round, which was initiated in 2001 and is still in progress at the time of writing.

---

into force of the said Regulation. 31. These Community powers exclude the possibility of concurrent powers on the part of Member States, since any steps taken outside the framework of the Community institutions would be incompatible with the unity of the common market and the uniform application of Community law' (paras. 28, 30 and 31).

2 See Section 36. See Opinion 1/94 of 15 November 1994, *WTO*, [1994] ECR I-5267. In that opinion, the Court of Justice ruled that the Treaty excluded from EC competence the sectors of services (except cross-border services) and of intellectual property. For a clear description of EC powers before the Lisbon Treaty see the Conclusions of Advocate General Juliane Kokott on 26 March 2009, in Case C-13/07, *Commission v. Council* (accession of Vietnam to the WTO) [not yet published].

The origins and development of CFSP

The 1957 Rome Treaty focused on economic aspects and did not contain any provisions on foreign policy in a classic sense. Two rather ambitious attempts to add a political and defence dimension failed, these being the European Defence Community, and the associated European Political Community, which failed in 1954, and the so-called 'Fouchet plan', concerning political co-operation and defence policy, which failed in 1962.

From October 1970 and the Davignon Report,[3] the Member States endeavoured to consult one another on major international policy problems, in a purely intergovernmental manner, outside the existing EC institutions, through what was then called 'European political co-operation'. In 1973, the COREU (acronym of *Correspondance européenne*) network, allowing the exchange of encrypted telegrams between the Member States, was established. In 1986, the Single European Act (Article 30) formalised this political co-operation, according to which the high contracting parties endeavoured jointly 'to formulate and implement a European foreign policy'. At that time, when 'common positions' were adopted, they only constituted 'a point of reference' for the policies of the Member States. This co-operation had its own structures, and took place under the cover of special meetings of the foreign ministers of the Member States, separate from the EU Council. It was organised and served by the six-monthly rotating Presidency with the help of a small Secretariat, which was based in Brussels and composed of a few diplomats seconded from the Member States. The Commission was 'fully associated with the proceedings of Political Co-operation'.

It was in 1993, with the entry into force of the Maastricht Treaty,[4] that the European Union as such, and more particularly the Council, was given the power to define a Common Foreign and Security Policy (CFSP, the second pillar) in Title V of the former TEU. The Council was empowered to adopt, by unanimity, legal acts called 'common positions' and 'joint actions', which bound the Member States. The CFSP was still led by the Council's six-monthly Presidency, and the Commission remained, as under 'political co-operation', 'fully associated with the work'. The European Parliament was to be consulted by the Presidency 'on the main aspects and the basic choices of the [CFSP]' and to be 'kept regularly

---

3 'Rapport sur les problèmes de l'unification politique', adopted by the Foreign Ministers of the Six, known as 'Rapport Davignon', Luxembourg, 27 October 1970.
4 See Arts. J to J.11 of the Maastricht Treaty (on European Union).

Council in CFSP matters (Article 24(1) former TEU) and consulted the European Parliament on CFSP matters (Article 21 former TEU).

The main purpose of the creation of this new 'triple-hatted' office is to inject more visibility and more stability into the external representation of the EU on CFSP matters and more consistency between the different sectors of the EU's external action. The High Representative conducts the Union's CFSP. As Vice-President of the Commission, he/she ensures the consistency of the EU's external action, and is responsible within the Commission for the latter's responsibilities in external relations for co-ordinating other aspects of the EU's external action. As President of the Foreign Affairs Council,[11] he/she oversees the dossiers of external relations in all sectors. In addition, he/she may rely on the European External Action Service, including the 130 or so Union delegations abroad, which are placed under his/her authority.

The High Representative is appointed by the European Council, acting by QMV, with the agreement of the President of the Commission (Article 18(1) TEU). The President of the Commission, the High Representative and the other members of the Commission are subject, as a body, to a vote of consent by the European Parliament (Article 17(7) TEU). After having chosen her at its informal meeting on 19 November 2009, the European Council, with the agreement of the President of the Commission, formally appointed on 1 December 2009 Catherine Ashton, who was the Commissioner for trade, as the first High Representative under the Lisbon Treaty.

If the European Parliament votes on a motion of censure of the Commission, 'the members of the Commission shall resign as a body and the High Representative shall resign from the duties that he carries out in the Commission' (Article 17(8) TEU). This means that the High Representative would continue exercising his/her other functions, including as President of the Foreign Affairs Council.

The President of the Commission may request all members of the Commission to resign; however, if the President of the Commission requests the resignation of the High Representative, the High Representative shall resign 'in accordance with the procedure set out in Article 18(1) [TEU]', which gives to the European Council the power to end the term of office

---

11 The Foreign Affairs Council 'shall elaborate the Union's external action on the basis of strategic guidelines laid down by the European Council and ensure that the Union's action is consistent' (Art. 16(6), 3rd subparagraph, TEU).

of the High Representative (acting, in the same way as for his/her appointment, by QMV, with the agreement of the President of the Commission). Therefore the President of the Commission will need the agreement of the European Council to obtain the resignation of the High Representative.[12]

The High Representative's functions cover a wide range of activities. He/she is in charge of:

- presiding over the Foreign Affairs Council (Articles 18(3) and 27(1) TEU);
- taking part in the work of the European Council (Articles 15(2) TEU);
- ensuring the consistency of the Union's external action, which comprises the whole field of external action, not only CFSP (Article 18(4) TEU);
- as Vice-President of the Commission, being 'responsible within the Commission for responsibilities incumbent on it in external relations and for co-ordinating other aspects of the Union's external action. In exercising these responsibilities within the Commission, and only for these responsibilities, the [HR] shall be bound by Commission procedures to the extent that this is consistent with [his/her role in CFSP under Article 18(2) and (3)]' (Article 18(4) TEU);
- conducting the Union's CFSP (including ESDP), which he/she will 'carry out as mandated by the Council' (Article 18(2) TEU);
- ensuring, together with the Council, 'the unity, consistency and effectiveness of action by the Union' in CFSP (Article 26(2) TEU);
- exercising the right of initiative and making proposals in the field of CFSP (Articles 18(2), 27(1) and (3), 30(1), 42(4) TEU, and Articles 218(3) and (9) and 331(2) TFEU), in some cases jointly with, or with the support of, the Commission (e.g. Articles 22(2), 30(1) and 42(4) TEU and Article 222(3) TFEU);
- negotiating international agreements relating exclusively or principally to CFSP matters on behalf of the Union (Article 218(3) TFEU);
- representing the Union on matters relating to CFSP, which includes conducting political dialogue with third parties, expressing the Union's position in international organisations and international conferences

---

12 The High Representative is submitted, like all Members of the Commission, to the compulsory retirement procedure of Art. 247 TFEU: 'If any Member of the Commission no longer fulfils the conditions required for the performance of his duties or if he has been guilty of serious misconduct, the Court of Justice may, on application by the Council acting by a simple majority or the Commission, compulsorily retire him.'

and presenting the Union's position in the UN Security Council when the Union has defined a position (Article 27(2) and 34(2) TEU);

- putting into effect the CFSP and ensuring the implementation of CFSP decisions adopted by the European Council and the Council (Article 26(3) and 24(1) TEU), including organising the co-ordination of the Member States' action in international organisations and at international conferences (Article 34(1) TEU);
- regularly consulting the European Parliament 'on the main aspects and basic choices of the [CFSP and ESDP]', informing it 'on how those policies evolve' and ensuring that the Parliament's views 'are duly taken into consideration' (Article 36 TEU);
- exercising authority over the EU special representatives appointed by the Council on his/her proposal (Article 33 TEU);
- exercising authority over the European External Action Service which will assist him/her (Article 27(3) TEU), including the 130 or so Union delegations in third countries and at international organisations (Article 221(2) TFEU).

An important tool for the High Representative will be his/her direct links with the Political and Security Committee (PSC). The PSC was established in 2001 and formalised in the Nice Treaty (Article 25 former TEU). The members of the PSC are at ambassador level and are permanently based in Brussels. The PSC is responsible for monitoring the international situation, contributing to the definition of policies by delivering opinions to the Council, monitoring the implementation of agreed policies and exercising the political control and strategic direction of crisis management operations, including through taking decisions where authorised to do so by the Council.

The Lisbon Treaty introduces a few amendments to the previous provisions on the PSC, the main purpose of which is to increase the responsibility of the High Representative (Article 38 TEU):

- like the Council, the High Representative can request opinions from the PSC;
- the monitoring role of the PSC on the implementation of agreed policies is to be done 'without prejudice to the powers of the [HR]';
- the role of the PSC in the political control and strategic direction of the crisis management operations is to be exercised 'under the responsibility of the Council and of the [HR]'.

Finally, Article 2 of the Decision of the European Council on the exercise of the Presidency of the Council provides that 'the Chair of the [PSC] shall be held by a representative of the [HR]'.[13]

*

The relationships between the High Representative, the President of the European Council and the President of the Commission in ensuring the external representation of the EU in the outside world are difficult to foresee on the basis of the Treaty's provisions. They will be largely determined by practice and by the personalities who exercise these functions. The High Representative will also have to co-operate closely with the six-monthly rotating Presidency, which continues to chair nine of the ten configurations of the Council, and also with the foreign affairs minister of the Member State holding the six-monthly Presidency (who may replace her in chairing the Foreign Affairs Council; see Article 2(5) of the 2009 Council's Rules of Procedure).

At the level of heads of state or government, the Treaty provides that the EU's external representation is shared between the President of the European Council (for CFSP–CSDP, under Article 15(6) TEU, 'without prejudice to the powers of the [HR]') and the President of the Commission (for other matters see Article 17(1) TEU). The other members of the Commission keep the task of negotiating international agreements and representing the Union at their level, within their own area of responsibility (trade, agriculture, transport, FSJ, economic and monetary affairs, environment, etc.). The President of the European Council might also play a role of representation of the 27 Member States in areas outside the EU competences.

The Treaty gives the High Representative a co-ordinating role in the Commission (Article 18(4) TEU), but it does not give him/her, *ipso facto*, the legal power to impose his/her decisions on his/her colleagues in the College. Moreover, the President of the Commission might also wish to play a role in co-ordinating the external policies of the College, for example by deciding to chair himself the group of external affairs Commissioners (trade, development, enlargement, and external relations).

The 'triple hat' of the High Representative means that his/her tasks are very heavy, while he/she has to travel a lot and also to exercise his/her mandates both as a member of the Commission (weekly meetings) and as

13 This draft Decision had already been agreed upon during the IGC and inserted in Declaration no. 9. The Decision was adopted on 1 December 2009 (OJ No. L315, 2 December 2009, 50).

President of the Foreign Affairs Council (monthly meetings). The Treaty does not provide for deputies having the same extraordinary 'triple-hatted' responsibilities. Therefore, the High Representative will have to request ad hoc help from other colleagues for each of his/her 'hats', either from fellow Commissioners or from foreign affairs ministers of the Member States, on a case-by-case basis, in addition to the assistance provided by the External Action Service. The new office of 'triple-hatted' High Representative has created a lot of expectations: more coherence, more effectiveness and more visibility. It is evident that, in order to play this role in an efficient manner, the High Representative needs the support of an effective European External Action Service.

Section 33 The European External Action Service

With the creation of the European External Action Service (EEAS), the Lisbon Treaty brings about an important innovation in the organisational structures of the institutions in order to render the EU's external action more consistent and visible.

The Council has always been assisted by a General Secretariat, under the responsibility of a Secretary-General. Before the Lisbon Treaty, and since the entry into force of the Amsterdam Treaty in 1999, Javier Solana, the Secretary-General of the Council, was also the High Representative for the CFSP (SG/HR). He was assisted by a Deputy Secretary-General. Within the General Secretariat, there are different Directorates-General (DG). Before the Lisbon Treaty, there was one, DG E, in charge of External Relations (CFSP–ESDP, enlargement, trade and development), as well as the Policy Unit,[14] the Situation Centre[15] and the EU Military Staff.[16]

---

14 The Policy Planning and Early Warning Unit was created in 1998 as a consequence of the Amsterdam Treaty which had created the office of High Representative for CFSP and in accordance with Declaration no. 6 to the Final Act of the Amsterdam IGC. In this Declaration, the Conference had agreed to establish in the General Secretariat of the Council a unit whose task would be, *inter alia*, to monitor and analyse developments in areas relevant to the CFSP, to provide assessments of the Union's CFSP and identify areas where it could focus and to provide assessments and early warning of events or situations which may have significant repercussions on CFSP, including potential crises.

15 The Joint Situation Centre or 'SitCen' was created by the SG/HR. Initially within the Policy Unit, it was later turned into a separate unit where intelligence is exchanged between relevant services from the Member States. It produces daily assessments for the use of the Political and Security Committee and the SG/HR. Its attributions have also been expanded to cover criminal justice matters.

16 The EU Military Staff (EUMS) was established in 2001 (OJ No. L27, 30 January 2001, 7) and employs about 220 persons, of whom about 200 are military officers seconded by Member States. It provides military expertise to the Council and its bodies and

For its part, the Commission had, among its twenty-three DGs, six DGs dealing directly with external relations matters (DG External Relations, DG Trade, DG Development, DG Enlargement, DG Humanitarian Aid Office (ECHO) and DG EuropeAid Co-operation Office).

During the 2002–3 Convention, the idea emerged of a single unified service which would deal with all matters in the area of external relations of the Union, encompassing both CFSP (including ESDP), which was under the responsibility of services of the General Secretariat of the Council, and other sectors, such as external trade or development co-operation, which were the responsibility of services of the Commission. The creation of an EU diplomatic academy and of an EU diplomatic service was also contemplated. Some ideas about transforming the EU delegations abroad into 'EU embassies' were also discussed. The text of the Constitutional Treaty was less far-reaching than that.

In accordance with the June 2007 mandate, the Lisbon IGC took over the framework retained by the 2003–4 IGC. Therefore the Lisbon Treaty establishes the EEAS (Article 27(3) TEU) and contains a legal basis which enables the Council to establish the organisation and functioning of this service. The EEAS will have the task of assisting the High Representative. It will work 'in co-operation with the diplomatic services of the Member States and shall comprise officials from relevant departments of the General Secretariat of the Council and of the Commission as well as staff seconded from national diplomatic services of the Member States' (Article 27(3) TEU). One may note that this provision is placed in the Chapter on CFSP, within the Title on the EU's external action, although the role of the EEAS will not be limited to purely CFSP matters (see the assessment below).

The organisation and functioning of the EEAS have to be laid down by a decision of the Council, acting by unanimity on a proposal from the High Representative, after consulting the European Parliament and obtaining the consent of the Commission. Thus the Treaty leaves most of the details on the structure, organisation and functioning to be decided. The EEAS will include a central administration as well as the 130 or so former Commission and Council delegations abroad,[17] which have become

---

to the SG/HR. It also provides an early warning capability; plans, assesses and makes recommendations on the concept of crisis management and the general military strategy; supports the Military Committee regarding situation assessment and military aspects of strategic planning for EU-led operations; and so on.

17 Most of these delegations represented the Commission. The Council had only two delegations abroad, one at the UN in Geneva and one at the UN in New York.

'Union delegations' placed under the authority of the High Representative (Article 221(2) TFEU).[18] In accordance with Article 221(1) TFEU, 'Union delegations in third countries and at international organisations shall represent the Union'.

As to the scope of its activity and the services to be incorporated in the EEAS, it will probably integrate most, if not all, of DG External Relations of the Commission and most of DG E of the Council Secretariat (its CFSP–ESDP part),[19] as well as the Policy Unit of the Council. However, nothing is certain as regards other services of the Commission (DG Development, DG Humanitarian Aid Office (ECHO) and DG EuropeAid Co-operation Office), which might have to be split. There is much nervousness in the Commission about such a hypothesis. Many other questions need to be answered. Will the High Representative have his/her main office in the Commission's main building (the Berlaymont building), in the Council's seat (the Justus Lipsius building), in both, or in the EEAS (which will have its own building)?

According to Declaration no. 15 to the Final Act of the Lisbon IGC: 'as soon as the Lisbon Treaty is signed, the Secretary-General of the Council, High Representative for the Common Foreign and Security Policy, the Commission and the Member States should begin preparatory work on the European External Action Service'.

The same Declaration was contained in the Final Act of the 2003–4 IGC (Declaration no. 24). Thus Javier Solana, the High Representative for CFSP, and José Manuel Barroso, President of the Commission, submitted in March 2005 an 'Issues Paper on the European External Action Service' as a preparatory step towards another report for the European Council in June 2005, as requested by the European Council in December 2004. They then submitted to the European Council in June 2005 a 'Joint Progress Report' on the European External Action Service.[20] After the negative referendums in France and in the Netherlands, preparatory work stopped in June 2005.

---

18 Art. 1(39) of the Lisbon Treaty itself – that is, the Treaty which amends the TEU and TEC – expressly replaces, in Art. 20 former TEU, the words 'Commission delegations' by 'Union delegations'.

19 A smaller service remains within the Council General Secretariat to ensure, as other DGs do, its role of servicing the Council (Foreign Affairs) and its preparatory bodies and to continue to deal with trade, enlargement, development co-operation and other matters which will not fall within the sphere of activity of the EEAS.

20 See doc. 9956/05 of 9 June 2005, accessible on the Internet site of the Council. It contains as Annex II the March 'Issues Paper'.

It resumed after the signature of the Lisbon Treaty in December 2007. However, this work, which took place in the first half of 2008, during the Slovenian Presidency, remained discreet and not of an intensive nature, due to the fact that the ratification process was in progress. Work stopped again with the negative referendum in Ireland in June 2008. The Slovenian Presidency issued a report on the work done during its six months in office.[21] As for the EEAS, the report stated certain general principles such as the *sui generis* nature of the EEAS – being separate from both the Council and the Commission, but with close links to both. First indications were also given of the scope of the EEAS (single geographical and thematic desks, the Council Policy Unit and the relevant services of DG External Relations of the Commission and of DG E of the Council, but not trade, or enlargement as such), on its staffing (Member States' diplomats should be temporary agents) and its autonomy for the High Representative in management, budgetary and staff matters.

Preparatory work resumed again during the Swedish Presidency in the second half of 2009. In October 2009 the Presidency issued a report on this work, with guidelines for the High Representative in the preparation of the draft Council Decision on the organisation and functioning of the EEAS.[22] This report was endorsed by the European Council at its October 2009 meeting.[23] The European Council also invited the High Representative 'to present a proposal for the organisation and functioning of the EEAS as soon as possible after the entry into force of the Lisbon Treaty with a view to its adoption by the Council at the latest by the end of April 2010'.

Thus at the time of writing the Decision of the Council has not yet been adopted. The issues at stake were already clearly identified in the 2009 Presidency Report and may be summarised as follows.

Scope

- The EEAS should be composed of single geographical (covering all regions and countries) and thematic desks which would continue to perform, under the authority of the High Representative, the tasks

---

21 See Progress report from the Presidency to the European Council – Preparatory work in view of the entry into force of the Lisbon Treaty (doc. 10650/08 of 13 June 2008; see para. 12).

22 See Presidency report to the European Council on the European External Action Service (doc. 14930/09).

23 See Presidency Conclusions, European Council, 29–30 October 2009 (doc. 15265/09, para. 3).

carried out by the relevant parts of the Commission and the Council Secretariat before the entry into force of the Lisbon Treaty;

- some of the geographical desks will deal with the candidate countries from the overall foreign policy perspective, but preparation of enlargement negotiations will remain the responsibility of the Commission;

- management of trade policy will remain the responsibility of the Commission;

- development will still have to be discussed, notably as to the division of tasks between the EEAS and the Commission in programming of financial instruments, but the preparation and implementation of the policy will mostly remain the responsibility of the Commissioner concerned;

- ESDP structures[24] will be part of the EEAS, 'while taking full account of the specificities of these structures and preserving their particular functions, procedures and staffing conditions'. These structures will form an entity placed under the direct authority and responsibility of the High Representative (and in this capacity) and will respect Declaration no. 14 of the Lisbon IGC;

- on the programming of financing instruments in the area of external relations, the EEAS will 'play a leading role in the strategic decision-making'. The specific division of labour for programming the geographical and thematic instruments[25] between the EEAS and the Commission services was to be determined later. However, it was already agreed in the report that 'throughout the whole programming and implementation cycle, there should be very close co-operation and consultation between the High Representative and the EEAS and the relevant Commissioners and their services. The decisions concerning programming will be prepared jointly by the High Representative and the Commissioner

---

24 I.e. the Crisis Management and Planning Directorate (CMPD), the Civilian Planning and Conduct Capability (CPCC) and the Military Staff (EUMS), which were all in the Council General Secretariat. The Situation Centre (SitCen) will also be part of the EEAS, while putting in place the necessary arrangements to continue to provide other relevant services (notably in the field of Justice and Home Affairs) to the European Council, the Council and the Commission.

25 These instruments are the European Neighbourhood and Partnership Instrument, the Development Cooperation Instrument, the European Development Fund, the Instrument for Cooperation with Industrialised Countries, the European Instrument for Democracy and Human Rights, the Instrument for Nuclear Safety Cooperation and the Instrument for Stability.

responsible. The final proposals in this respect will continue to be adopted by the College of Commissioners';
- consultation procedures will be established between the EEAS and the services of the Commission with external responsibilities, including those in charge of internal policies with significant external dimensions;
- the EU Special Representatives or their tasks will be integrated into the EEAS.

Legal status, budget and staffing

- The EEAS will be a service of a *sui generis* nature separated from the Commission and the Council Secretariat, with autonomy in terms of administrative budget and management of staff. It will be treated as if it were an institution, in accordance with Article 1 of the Financial Regulation and Article 1b of the Staff Regulations;[26]
- the EEAS budget will be a separate section of the EU budget (under Heading V), to which the usual budgetary rules will apply (i.e. with control by the European Parliament and the Court of Auditors) and the High Representative will perform the duties of authorising officer and implement the EEAS administrative budget;
- the establishment of the EEAS will be guided by the principle of cost-efficiency aiming towards budget neutrality, although a limited number of additional posts for Member States' temporary agents will be necessary, which will have to be financed within the framework of the Financial Perspectives;
- the High Representative will act as appointing authority for EEAS staff, which will come from three sources: relevant departments of the General Secretariat of the Council and of the Commission, and staff seconded from national diplomatic services of the Member States (Article 27(3) TEU);
- all three categories of personnel will be treated equally, including as concerns their eligibility to assume all positions under equivalent conditions. Staff from Member States will therefore have the status of temporary agents which, under the conditions of employment for other servants,[27] grants them the same opportunities, rights and obligations as EU officials;

---

26 For the purposes of both the Financial Regulation (1605/2002, OJ No. L248, 16 September 2002, 1) and the Staff Regulations (723/2004, OJ No. L124, 27 April 2004, 1), the Economic and Social Committee, the Committee of the Regions, the Ombudsman and the European Data-Protection Supervisor are treated as an EU institution.
27 See Regulation 723/2004 (OJ No. L124, 27 April 2004, 1).

- recruitment will take place through a transparent procedure based on merit with the objective of securing the services of staff of the highest standard of ability, effectiveness and integrity while ensuring adequate geographical balance, a need for a meaningful presence of nationals from all EU Member States in the EEAS and aiming towards gender balance;
- appropriate arrangements will be made to ensure staff mobility, through rotation inside the EEAS (i.e. between headquarters and EU delegations and between services at the headquarters), rotation between the EEAS and national diplomatic services and, to the extent possible, mobility between the EEAS and the Commission and the General Secretariat of the Council for staff coming from these institutions.

EU delegations

- On 1 December 2009, the Commission delegations became EU delegations under the authority of the High Representative;
- the EU delegations will be part of the EEAS structure. They will contain both EEAS staff (including the head of delegation) and staff from relevant Commission services (for trade, development and other matters which will remain within the Commission). All staff will be under the authority of the head of delegation, while taking instructions from and reporting to the High Representative and the EEAS, as well as the relevant Commission services, depending on whether the subject matter falls within the remit of the EEAS or the Commission;
- the EU delegations will be progressively upgraded to be able to perform fully their co-ordination and representation role. In the meantime, the diplomatic representations of the six-monthly rotating Presidency will help the High Representative to perform these tasks. These questions, and in particular the issue of EU delegations accredited to international organisations, were not yet fully settled at the time of writing;
- EU delegations will also play a supporting role as regards diplomatic and consular protection of Union citizens in third countries. This was requested more particularly by the smaller Member States which do not have a large diplomatic network.[28]

---

28 It is recalled that, as part of the EU citizens' rights, every EU citizen has 'the right to enjoy, in the territory of a third country in which the Member State of which they are nationals is not represented, the protection of the diplomatic and consular authorities of any Member State on the same conditions as the nationals of that State' (see Arts. 20(2)(c) and 23

The October 2009 report identified three stages for the setting
up of the EEAS:

- a first stage, between 1 December 2009 and the adoption of the EEAS
  Decision (foreseen at the end of April 2010), during which the draft
  Decision will be officially tabled and discussed and the High Representative will have at her disposal both a small preparatory team and the
  support of the pre-existing external relations structures of the Commission and of the Council General Secretariat;
- a second stage, from the adoption of the EEAS Decision to 'full cruising
  speed', at the end of which a first status report should be made by the
  High Representative (in 2012);
- a third stage, between 2012 and before the end of the term of office
  of the High Representative on 31 October 2014, at the end of which a
  review of the functioning and of the organisation of the EEAS should
  be made, possibly with adjustments to the EEAS Decision.

*

The establishment of a single European External Service is expected
to help to ensure greater consistency in the EU's positions and actions
in external policies. It was always strange, and for historical reasons
only, that the services dealing with the EU's external relations were
totally separate and not always sufficiently co-ordinated. Therefore this
merger was absolutely unavoidable, albeit difficult. It will help to prepare and implement more coherent and efficient foreign policy actions
and will allow the High Representative to exercise better his/her different
functions.

Section 34 The Common Foreign and Security Policy

The possibility for the EU to progress towards a Common Foreign and
Security Policy (CFSP) has been strengthened by the Lisbon Treaty, with
the addition of new possibilities for EU action and with the introduction of more efficient structures and decision-making procedures.
The Treaty provides legal and institutional tools which, if used with
the necessary political will, could improve the functioning of CFSP,
greatly enhance the political visibility and effectiveness of the EU on

---

TFEU). This right had been introduced already in 1993, by the Maastricht Treaty (see
Art. 20 TEC, ex-Art. 8c). It is therefore primarily for the other Member States' diplomatic
authorities to help EU citizens whose Member State has no diplomatic representation in
a given third country.

the world stage, and improve the general coherence of its external action.

The innovations brought about by the Lisbon Treaty

The provisions of the EU Treaty, as amended by the Lisbon Treaty, while building on the language of the former EU Treaty in the area of CFSP, offer a better perspective for a more effective policy.

A stable and unified representation and leadership

As seen in Section 32, one of the main innovations of the Lisbon Treaty is that all functions previously entrusted to the six-monthly rotating Presidency (and to the former SG/HR)[29] in the area of CFSP are now entrusted to the new High Representative of the Union for Foreign Affairs and Security Policy.[30] The new High Representative ensures the consistency of the Union's external action (Articles 26(2) and 18(4) TEU), and conducts the Union's CFSP, including the common security and defence policy (Article 18(2) TEU). He/she contributes through his/her proposals to the development of this policy, which he/she carries out as mandated by the Council (Article 18(2) TEU). He/she presides over the Foreign Affairs Council (Article 18(3) TEU). The CFSP is put into effect by the High Representative and by the Member States, using national and Union resources (Article 26(3) TEU).

In particular, the High Representative contributes through his/her proposals to the development of the CFSP and ensures implementation of the decisions adopted by the European Council and the Council (Article 27(1) TEU). He/she represents the Union for matters relating to the CFSP, conducts political dialogue with third parties on the Union's behalf and expresses the Union's position in international organisations and at international conferences (Article 27(2) TEU).

As one of the Vice-Presidents of the Commission, the High Representative must ensure the consistency of the Union's external action, which includes external areas other than CFSP, such as development and

---

29 Including the power which the Commission had, in addition to the Member States, to submit proposals in CFSP matters to the Council (Art. 22(1) former TEU).

30 As well as to the President of the European Council, who, in accordance with Art. 15(6), 2nd subpara., TEU, 'shall, at his level and in that capacity, ensure the external representation of the Union on issues concerning its [CFSP], without prejudice to the powers of the [HR]'.

technical co-operation with third countries, humanitarian aid and trade policy.

The replacement of the six-monthly rotating Presidency by the High Representative should bring about more consistency and effectiveness in CFSP. This replacement will also bring about some changes in the organisation of the work of certain preparatory bodies of the Foreign Affairs Council. In particular, as stated in Article 2 of the European Council decision on the exercise of the Presidency of the Council,[31] the Political and Security Committee will be chaired by a representative of the High Representative. By contrast, the chair of the preparatory bodies of the various other Council configurations will continue to be chaired by the six-monthly rotating Presidency 'with the exception of the [preparatory bodies of the] Foreign Affairs configuration' and 'unless decided otherwise'.

The Council, in an implementing Decision, organised the chairmanship of forty or so Council preparatory bodies, dividing them into four categories: the first category (trade and development) would continue to be chaired by the six-monthly rotating Presidency and the three other categories (geographic, horizontal CFSP and ESDP) would be chaired by a stable chairperson chosen by the High Representative. The situation will be reviewed in 2012.[32]

As stated in Article 16(6) TEU, the Foreign Affairs Council 'shall elaborate the Union's external action on the basis of strategic guidelines laid down by the European Council and ensure that the Union's action is consistent'. Given that Titles and Chapters of the TEU and TFEU dealing with 'the EU's external action' cover not only CFSP (Chapter 2 of Title V TEU), but also other sectors such as trade, development, economic, financial and technical co-operation, humanitarian aid or restrictive measures (Part Five TFEU), this means that the Foreign Affairs Council's remit is rather wide. More generally, pursuant to Article 21(3) TEU, the Council and the Commission, assisted by the High Representative, must ensure consistency between the different areas of the Union's external action and between these and its other policies.

---

31 Adopted on 1 December 2009 (OJ No. L315, 2 December 2009, 50).
32 See Council Decision laying down measures for the implementation of the European Council Decision on the exercise of the Presidency of the Council adopted on 1 December 2009 (OJ No. L322, 9 December 2009, 28, corrected by OJ No. L344, 23 December 2009, 56).

A single procedure for negotiating and concluding international agreements

Given that (at last!) 'the Union shall have a legal personality' (Article 47 TEU)[33] and that 'the Union may conclude agreements with one or more States or international organisations in areas covered by [the CFSP Chapter]' (Article 37 TEU), there can no longer be any possible controversy on the capacity of the EU to conclude international agreements in the area of CFSP.

All international agreements concluded by the EU, whether in the CFSP or in other areas (the former first and second pillars), are now submitted to the procedures for negotiation and conclusion which are set out in a single Article, Article 218 TFEU. Article 24 former TEU, which provided for a specific procedure for negotiating and concluding international agreements in the second pillar (a procedure which applied also for the third pillar) has been repealed and replaced by the new procedure.

Under Article 218(3) TFEU, it is the Commission or the High Representative, 'where the agreement envisaged relates exclusively or principally to the [CFSP]' who will 'submit recommendations to the Council, which shall adopt a decision authorising the opening of negotiations and, depending on the subject of the agreement envisaged, nominating the Union negotiator or the head of the Union's negotiating team'. It is therefore for the Council to choose the 'Union negotiator', depending on the subject of the agreement.

In accordance with Articles 24(1) and 31(1) TEU, which provide for unanimity in CFSP matters, combined with Article 218(8) TFEU under which 'the Council shall act unanimously when the agreement covers a field for which unanimity is required for the action of a Union act', all decisions relating to agreements in the area of CFSP will be taken by the Council acting unanimously. The 'constructive abstention' by a Member State remains possible (Article 31(1), 2nd subparagraph, TEU). The possibility for a member of the Council to state that his/her government 'has to comply with the requirements of its own constitutional procedure'

---

33 Art. 1, 3rd para., TEU states that 'the Union shall replace and succeed the European Community'. *Notes verbales* were sent on behalf of the Council and the Commission to third States and international organisations notifying this legal succession and also the fact the Commission delegations became Union delegations on 1 December 2009. In Declaration no. 24, the IGC confirmed that 'the fact that the [EU] has legal personality will not in any way authorise [it] to legislate or to act beyond the competences conferred upon it by the Member States in the Treaties'.

(i.e. a possibly long ratification procedure, see Article 24(5) of the former TEU) has now disappeared.[34]

Finally, it is now explicitly stated that international agreements concluded by the EU in the area of CFSP are legally binding for the Member States as well as for the EU institutions (Articles 37 TEU and 216(2) TFEU, to be compared with the Article 24(6) of the former TEU).

For the rest, the rules and procedures are largely the same as previously, with a few improvements

During the discussions leading to the adoption of the June 2007 IGC mandate, the UK delegation, in particular, was keen to obtain language demonstrating that nothing in the Treaty would change the CFSP decision-making process or the (weak) powers conferred on the European Parliament, the Commission and the Court of Justice in that area. As a consequence of the United Kingdom's insistence, Title V containing CFSP provisions remained located in the TEU and was not transferred to the TFEU with the other external action provisions, and a new subparagraph underlining the specificity of CFSP was inserted in Article 24(1) TEU. For the same reasons, the United Kingdom obtained two IGC declarations, Declarations no. 13 and no. 14, with the same title ('Declaration concerning the common foreign and security policy'), which are quite repetitive, especially in stressing that the CFSP does not affect the responsibility of the Member States in the formulation and conduct of their national foreign policy.

Therefore, apart from its innovations as to the role of the High Representative, the Lisbon Treaty confirms that CFSP remains clearly subject to different rules and procedures from the other activities of the EU. It therefore remains a second pillar as it was before, largely in the hands of the Council, and of its members, the representatives of the governments of the Member States. The new second subparagraph of Article 24(1) TEU makes it clear that:

---

34 Before the entry into force of the Lisbon Treaty, under Art. 24(5) former TEU the representative of a Member State could state in the Council that an international agreement to be concluded under Art. 24 (or Arts. 24 and 38) former TEU would not be binding on his/her State before the completion of its constitutional requirements. Since the entry into force of the Lisbon Treaty on 1 December 2009, this possibility has disappeared and statements of this kind made in the past have lost their legal basis and become obsolete. Since that date, the procedure for the conclusion of all international agreements, whether signed before or after that date, is governed by Art. 218(6) TFEU. This new procedure, including the fact that the European Parliament has to give its consent in a good number of cases, applies to all international agreements.

- 'The [CFSP] is subject to specific rules and procedures. It shall be defined and implemented by the European Council and the Council acting unanimously, except where the Treaties provide otherwise.'
- 'The specific role of the European Parliament and of the Commission in this area is defined by the Treaties.'
- 'The Court of Justice of the European Union shall not have jurisdiction with respect to these provisions, with the exception of its jurisdiction to monitor compliance with Article 40 of [the TEU] and to review the legality of certain decisions as provided for by the second paragraph of Article 275 of the [TFEU].'

With regard to the unanimity rule, the cases where 'the treaties provide otherwise' – that is, than the usual unanimity rule – are notably the following:

- Article 31(1) TEU, like Article 23 of the former TEU, retains the possibility for any Member State to make a so-called 'constructive abstention' – that is, the possibility, when abstaining in a vote, to qualify its abstention by making a formal declaration which will result in the Member State in question not being obliged to apply the decision, although the decision will nevertheless commit the EU. However, if such 'constructive abstentions' represent at least one-third of the Member States comprising at least one-third of the EU population, 'the decision shall not be adopted';[35]
- the Lisbon Treaty slightly enlarges the cases where QMV could already be used in CFSP:[36]
  - decisions taken on the basis of a proposal which the High Representative has presented 'following a specific request from the European Council, made on its own initiative or that of the High Representative' (Article 31(2), 2nd indent, TEU). QMV is therefore not automatic,

---

35 Compare with Art. 23(1) former TEU: under this system, Council members representing one-third of the weighted votes (used for calculating QMV) could block a CFSP decision. Now, a double threshold will be necessary (one-third of the Member States, representing at least one-third of the EU population).

36 Compare with Art. 23(2) former TEU: under its 1st indent, QMV applied when adopting CFSP acts 'on the basis of a common strategy' (Art. 31(2), 1st indent, present TEU remains similar); under its 2nd indent, QMV applied when adopting decisions implementing CFSP acts (Art. 31(2), 3rd indent, present TEU remains similar); under its 3rd indent, when appointing an EU special representative (Art. 31(2), 4th indent, present TEU, remains similar). As before the Lisbon Treaty, procedural decisions are to be taken by a simple majority (compare Art. 31(5) present TEU with Art. 23(3) former TEU).

but applies only if there has been a prior specific request made by the European Council, this request having been adopted by unanimity;
- the decisions relating to the new start-up fund, in order to guarantee rapid access to appropriations in the EU budget for urgent financing of initiatives in the framework of the ESDP (Article 41(3), 3rd subparagraph, TEU);
- the decisions defining the European Defence Agency's statute, seat and operational rules (Article 45 TEU);
- some of the decisions concerning the Permanent Structured Co-operation in ESDP (Article 46(2) to (5) TEU);
• Article 31(2) TEU, like Article 23(2) of the former TEU retains in a slightly modified version the possibility that a CFSP decision submitted to QMV may be opposed by any Member State for 'vital and stated reasons of national policy' which will trigger an 'emergency brake' mechanism, under which the High Representative will search for a solution acceptable to the Member State concerned, and, if this does not succeed, the Council may, by QMV, refer the matter to the European Council for decision by unanimity.

The Lisbon Treaty also inserts a new *passerelle* in Article 31(3) TEU which enables the European Council, by unanimity, to transfer more cases to QMV than those listed in Article 31(2) TEU, with the exception of decisions having military or defence implications. In some Member States (e.g. the United Kingdom and Germany), the government will not be able to agree to the use of this *passerelle* without prior approval by its parliament.

With regard to the (limited) powers of the European Parliament in CFSP, they remain largely the same as they were before the Lisbon Treaty. The European Parliament may ask questions and make recommendations to the Council and to the High Representative. It shall hold a debate on CFSP twice a year (instead of once), including on ESDP (Article 36 TEU). Furthermore, as previously, the European Parliament shall certainly exercise political control through its powers over the EU budget, when an action of the EU is charged to that budget. The European Parliament has already announced its intention to control closely the organisation and action of the EEAS through its budgetary powers.

With regard to the (limited) powers of the Commission in CFSP, the Commission no longer has an autonomous right of initiative, as it had before the Lisbon Treaty under Article 22(1) of the former TEU. The present TEU provides that the Commission may support the High

Representative initiatives, and sometimes submit joint proposals with the High Representative, but not alone.[37] In addition, Article 27 former TEU, which provided that 'the Commission shall be fully associated with the work carried out in the [CFSP]' has been repealed by the Lisbon Treaty, as it was felt that the new office of 'triple-hatted' High Representative (i.e. also a Vice-President of the Commission) would take care of this 'full association'. The fact that the High Representative is a member of the Commission will no doubt give more political power to the Commission in the area of CFSP.

With regard to the (limited) powers of the EU Court of Justice in CFSP, they have been slightly enlarged, notably in the interest of ensuring better protection of the rights of individuals. The general rule remains that 'the [EU] Court of Justice shall have no jurisdiction with respect to provisions relating to [CFSP] nor with respect to acts adopted on the basis of those provisions' (Article 275, 1st subparagraph, TFEU, repeated in Article 24(1), 2nd subparagraph, TEU). However, in its new formulation, Article 40 TEU, which protects the areas where the EU institutions exercise their full powers (i.e. the areas covered by the ex-EC or first pillar) from possible encroachment through CFSP decisions, also protects CFSP from possible encroachments of acts adopted under the former first pillar.[38] This means that the jurisdiction of the EU Court of Justice to 'monitor compliance' with Article 40 TEU is extended to the control of the latter aspect (Article 275, 2nd paragraph, TEU). In addition, this same 2nd paragraph of Article 275 TFEU confers jurisdiction on the EU Court of Justice to review 'the legality of decisions providing for restrictive measures against natural or legal persons adopted by the Council on the basis of [the CFSP Chapter]' – that is, in the context of action against terrorism and against country-specific sanctions regimes.

---

37 Art. 22(1) former TEU read: 'Any Member State or the Commission may refer to the Council any question relating to the common foreign and security policy and may submit proposals to the Council.'

    Compare with the present Art. 30(1) TEU, which reads: 'Any Member State, the [HR], or the [HR] with the Commission's support, may refer any question relating to the common foreign and security policy to the Council and may submit to it, respectively, initiatives or proposals.'

38 Compare Art. 40 TEU with ex-Art. 47 former TEU, to which was added a new 2nd subparagraph: 'Similarly, the implementation of the policies listed [in Arts. 3 to 6 TFEU] shall not affect the application of the procedures and the extent of the powers of the institutions laid down by the Treaties for the exercise of the Union competences under this Chapter [i.e. the Chapter on CFSP]'.

Finally, **the five types of CFSP legal instruments have been reduced to one type**. Instead of 'principles and general guidelines', 'common strategies', 'joint actions', 'common positions' or 'decisions' (see Articles 12 and 13 former TEU), the European Council and the Council now adopt only one type of legal act for all CFSP actions – that is, decisions (see Articles 26(1) and (2) and 31(1) TEU).[39] Articles 24(1), 2nd subparagraph, and 31(1) 1st subparagraph, TEU, expressly exclude the adoption of legislative acts in the field of CFSP. The decisions concerning 'operational actions' 'shall commit the Member States in the positions they adopt and in the conduct of their activity' (Article 28(2) TEU).

However, it remains that there is no provision empowering the Commission to verify the correct implementation of CFSP decisions, and the EU Court of Justice has no jurisdiction, in case of non-implementation by a Member State of a CFSP decision, to condemn it for infringement or impose penalties on it.

Therefore, as was the case under the former TEU, this task of ensuring that the legally binding CFSP decisions are properly implemented is largely left to the goodwill of Member States, to their obligation of loyalty and thus to mutual peer pressure. Article 24(3) TEU provides that 'the Member States shall support the Union's external and security policy actively and unreservedly in a spirit of loyalty and mutual solidarity' and that 'they shall refrain from any action which is contrary to the interests of the Union or likely to impair its effectiveness as a cohesive force in international relations'. In the same spirit, various provisions refer to the duty of Member States to implement CFSP decisions.[40]

Article 24(3), 3rd subparagraph, TEU entrusts the Council and the High Representative with '[ensuring] compliance with [the] principles [of loyalty and mutual solidarity set out in the preceding subparagraphs]'. More specifically, Article 27(1) entrusts the High Representative with the task of '[ensuring] implementation of the decisions adopted by the European Council and the Council' in the field of CFSP.

---

39 The 'decision' is defined in Art. 288, 4th para., TFEU: 'A decision shall be binding in its entirety. A decision which specifies those to whom it is addressed shall be binding only on them.'

40 See e.g. Art. 29 TEU, which states that 'Member States shall ensure that their national policies conform to the Union positions'; Art. 32 provides that 'Member States shall ensure, through the convergence of their actions, that the Union is able to assert its interests and values on the international scene [and] shall show mutual solidarity'; Art. 35 states that the diplomatic representations (of Member States and of the EU) 'shall cooperate in ensuring that [EU] decisions [on CFSP] are complied with and implemented'.

Finally, a specific legal basis for the adoption by the Council, by unanimity, of 'rules relating to the protection of individuals with regard to the processing of personal data by the Member States when carrying out activities which fall within the scope of [the CFSP Chapter], and the rules relating to the free movement of such data' was added during the Lisbon IGC (Article 39 TEU). This provision derogates from the general legal basis provided for in Article 16 TFEU, in that it applies to the processing of data *by the Member States*, and not by the EU institutions, which remain subject to the general rule in Article 16 TFEU (including data in the field of CFSP).

Section 35 Security and Defence

The Lisbon Treaty has significantly modified the provisions of the TEU on European Security and Defence Policy (ESDP). The modifications give the Council and the Member States a wider choice of flexible solutions in order to conduct efficiently a whole range of civil and military operations and, accordingly, to improve the specific added value of the EU in the field of crisis management.

A short history of Security and Defence in the EU framework

ESDP is often presented as one of the recent success stories of the EU, the other being the single currency, although ESDP would have a very long way to go to reach a level of integration comparable to the euro (if ever). But, like the euro, ESDP is the result of a long maturing process.[41]

A first attempt on defence policy was the Treaty establishing the European Defence Community, signed in May 1952, one year after the Treaty establishing the Coal and Steel Community (ECSC), but it was rejected by the French parliament in August 1954. This Treaty was very ambitious. It aimed to establish a supranational Community with common armed

---

41 See R. A. Wessel, 'The State of Affairs in EU Security and Defence Policy: The Breakthrough in the Treaty of Nice', (2003) 8 *Journal of Conflict and Security Law* 265; G. Andréani, C. Bertram and C. Grant, *Europe's Military Revolution* (London: Centre for European Reform, 2001), available at www.cer.org.uk/pdf/p22x_military_revolution.pdf; P. de Schoutheete, *La cohérence par la défense: une autre lecture de la PESD*, Cahiers de Chaillot 71 (Paris: EU Institute for Security Studies, 2004); and N. Gnesotto (ed.), *EU Security and Defence Policy: The First Five Years (1999–2004)*, pref. by J. Solana (Paris: EU Institute for Security Studies, 2004), available at www.iss-eu.org/books/5esdpen.pdf.

forces, its own budget and institutions comparable to those of the newly created ECSC. Another attempt which failed was the so-called 'Fouchet plan' in 1962. In parallel, the less ambitious Western European Union had been established in 1948, and was enlarged to include (West) Germany and Italy in 1954.

Article 30(6) of the Single European Act in 1986 was the first Treaty provision binding the EU's Member States ever to mention the words 'European security'. The word 'defence', however, was not mentioned, because European security was seen only from its 'political and economic aspects' on which the 'High Contracting Parties' were to co-ordinate their positions. This was the lowest common denominator at that time.

The words 'common defence policy, which might in time lead to a common defence' appeared for the first time in the Maastricht Treaty in 1992. However, this stated ambition remained largely ineffective. The Bosnian war, which broke out during that period (1992–5), was widely perceived as a failure for the EU.

The Amsterdam Treaty, signed in October 1997, added a provision to the former TEU listing the so-called 'Petersberg tasks'[42] which the EU could undertake. These were 'humanitarian and rescue tasks, peacekeeping tasks and tasks of combat forces in crisis management, including peace-making' (Article 17(2) former TEU). But the EU's weakness was about to become apparent again in Kosovo, when Serbian forces started their activities in August 1998. Public opinion as well as governments became frustrated at seeing the EU's incapacity to manage crises effectively, even on its own doorstep, so exposed.

In December 1998, the United Kingdom and France, the two EU Member States with the most significant 'power-projection' capabilities in military terms, held a summit in St-Malo in which they adopted an important Declaration.[43] This was to be the real start for the European Security and Defence Policy: 'The European Union needs to be in a position to play its full role on the international stage . . . This includes the responsibility of the European Council to decide on the progressive framing of a common defence policy in the framework of CFSP . . . To this end, the Union must have the capacity for autonomous action, backed up by credible military

---

42 Named after the place near Bonn where the ministers of foreign affairs of the Member States of the Western European Union (WEU) first defined these tasks in June 1992.

43 For a list of important documents on ESDP, see M. Rutten (compiler), *From St-Malo to Nice: European Defence: Core Documents*, Chaillot Paper 47 (Paris: EU Institute for Security Studies, 2001), which contains the St-Malo Joint Declaration.

forces, the means to decide to use them, and a readiness to do so, in order to respond to international crises . . . In order for the European Union to take decisions and approve military action where the Alliance as a whole is not engaged, the Union must be given appropriate structures and a capacity for analysis of situations, sources of intelligence, and a capability for relevant strategic planning, without unnecessary duplication, taking account of the existing assets of the WEU and the evolution of its relations with the EU.'

From then on, things developed very fast. In June 1999, the European Council in Cologne decided to establish new bodies within the Council: the Political and Security Committee (PSC), consisting of national representatives based in their respective Permanent Representations in Brussels (which would replace the 'Political Committee' in Article 25 former TEU), the EU Military Committee (EUMC), made up of national chiefs of defence staff or their deputies and an EU Military Staff (EUMS) attached to the General Secretariat of the Council. It also decided that the EU would take over from the WEU both the Institute for Security Studies, based in Paris, and the Satellite Centre, based in Torrejón, Spain.[44]

In December 1999, the European Council meeting in Helsinki decided to boost Europe's military capabilities by setting a 'headline goal'. According to this headline goal, by 2003 the Member States should have been able to deploy, in the field, and within sixty days, up to 60,000 self-sustaining troops for a year (which, with rotations, would have implied a total pool of at least 200,000 available troops and three mobile corps headquarters). This too-ambitious goal has not been achieved.[45]

In December 2002, after difficult negotiations, the EU and NATO finally hammered out the so-called 'Berlin plus' Agreement, an arrangement allowing the Union to have recourse to NATO's assets and capabilities for an EU-led operation.

In parallel, and in order to complement the military side with a civilian side, which adds significant value to the EU's crisis management actions, the European Council had decided to set up a Committee for Civilian Aspects of Crisis Management.[46] It also defined civilian headline goals for crisis management, such as the deployment of policemen (5,000 persons),

---

44 See the two Council Joint Actions of 20 July 2001 (OJ No. L200; 25 July 2001, 1, 5).
45 In June 2004 a new headline goal was agreed, with aims to be reached in 2010 (see below).
46 Council Decision no. 2000/354/CFSP of 22 May 2000 (OJ No. L127, 27 May 2000, 1).

Resolution no. 1778. Intended as a bridging operation, it was launched in early 2008, reached initial operating capability in March 2008; when fully deployed, it involved around 3,700 troops; the operation ceased in mid-March 2009; it has been followed by a UN force (MINURCAT II);

- 'Atalanta' (EU NAVFOR Somalia) is an autonomous EU-led operation launched in 2008, as a result of deep concerns with regard to the outbreak of acts of piracy and armed robbery off the Somali coast. This operation is conducted in support of UNSC Resolutions no. 1814, 1816, 1838 and 1846 in order to contribute to the protection of vessels of the World Food Programme (WFP) delivering food aid to displaced persons in Somalia, to the protection of vulnerable vessels cruising off the Somali coast, and to the deterrence, prevention and repression of acts of piracy and armed robbery off the Somali coast. The operation reached its initial operational capability on 13 December 2008. It is the first EU maritime operation to be conducted in the framework of ESDP.

Three mixed military–civilian operations:

- 'Eusec-RD Congo' is a small EU advisory and assistance mission for security reform in the Democratic Republic of the Congo launched in June 2005. The mission provides advice and assistance to the Congolese authorities in charge of security while ensuring the promotion of policies that are compatible with human rights and international humanitarian law, democratic standards, principles of good public management, transparency and observance of the rule of law;
- The 'AMIS EU Supporting Action' was a civilian–military supporting action to the African Union (AU) mission in the Darfur region of Sudan (AMIS II). The purpose of the EU's supporting action was to ensure effective and timely EU assistance to the AU's enhanced AMIS II mission and to back the AU and its political, military and police efforts aimed at addressing the crisis in Darfur. The operation comprised both a civilian and a military component. It made available equipment and assets, provided planning and technical assistance and sent out military observers. It trained African troops, helped with tactical and strategic transportation and provided police assistance and training. Several dozen military and civilian personnel were deployed. The operation lasted from July 2005 until 31 December 2007, when AMIS handed over to the AU-UN hybrid operation in Darfur (UNAMID);
- 'EU SSR Guinea-Bissau', the EU Mission in support of security sector reform in the Republic of Guinea-Bissau, aims at providing local authorities with advice and assistance on security sector reform in the Republic of Guinea-Bissau, in order to contribute to creating the conditions for implementation of the National Security Sector Reform Strategy, in close co-operation with other actors, and with a view to facilitating subsequent donor engagement. It was launched in June 2008 and was extended until the end of May 2010. It counts some fifteen military and civilian advisors.

Fourteen civilian operations:

- 'EUPM' is the first EU-led police mission. It is taking place in Bosnia-Herzegovina, where it started on 1 January 2003, following on from the UN's International Police Task Force. It was welcomed by UNSC Resolution no. 1396. It is composed of some 500 police officers from about thirty countries and is aimed at establishing sustainable policing arrangements under BiH ownership in accordance with best European and international practice;
- 'Eupol Proxima' was an EU-led police mission in the FYROM which was launched in December 2003 (after operation Concordia) and lasted until December 2005. Police experts (i.e. around 200 personnel from EU Member States and other countries, uniformed police personnel and civilian internationals) monitored, mentored and advised the country's police, thus helping to fight organised crime as well as promoting European policing standards;
- 'Eujust Themis' was the first EU rule of law operation. It took place in Georgia and was launched in July 2004 for a period of one year. Some ten senior and highly qualified experts supported, mentored and advised ministers, senior officials and appropriate bodies at the level of the central government;
- 'Eupol Kinshasa' was an EU-led police mission in the Democratic Republic of the Congo launched in January 2005 and ending in mid 2007. It counted some thirty staff and aimed at assisting in the setting up of an Integrated Police Unit in order to contribute to ensuring the protection of the State institutions and reinforcing the internal security apparatus. In addition, it played a role in supporting police co-ordination during the 2006–7 electoral period;
- 'Eujust Lex' is an EU rule of law mission in Iraq which was launched in July 2005. It aims at improving the Iraqi criminal justice system by providing training (mainly outside Iraq) for officials in senior management and criminal investigation, primarily from the police, judiciary and penitentiary services, and improving skills and procedures in criminal investigation while ensuring full respect for the rule of law and human rights;
- The 'Aceh Monitoring Mission', conducted by the EU and five ASEAN countries, became operational in September 2005 and monitored the commitments undertaken by the government of Indonesia and the Free Aceh Movement (GAM) in the framework of their peace agreement, in particular decommissioning of weapons, relocation of non-organic military forces and so on. It also ruled on disputed amnesty cases. The mission ended in December 2006;
- 'EUPOL COPPS', the EU Coordinating Office for Palestinian Police Support, aims at contributing to the establishment of sustainable and effective policing arrangements under Palestinian ownership in accordance with best international standards, in co-operation with the EC's institution building programmes as well as other international efforts in the wider context of the Security Sector including Criminal Justice Reform. The mission's operational phase started in January 2006, with a staff of about thirty;

- 'EUPAT', the EU Police Advisory Team in the FYROM, was a follow-on mission in the FYROM after Concordia and Proxima, which aimed at further supporting the development of an efficient and professional police service based on European standards of policing; it consisted of some thirty police advisors from December 2005 until June 2006;
- 'EUBAM Moldova – Ukraine' is an EU support for border management, including the border between Ukraine and the separatist Transnistrian region of the Republic of Moldova. A Memorandum of Understanding was signed in October 2005. The operation was to end in November 2009;
- 'EU BAM Rafah', the EU Border Assistance Mission at Rafah, aims at providing a third-party presence at the Rafah Crossing Point between Egypt and the Palestinian Territories in order to contribute to the opening of the Rafah Crossing Point and to build confidence between the government of Israel and the Palestinian Authority. The mission started in November 2005, with a staff of about twenty;
- 'EUPOL Afghanistan', the EU Police Mission in Afghanistan, was launched in June 2007 and was established for an initial period of three years. It aims at contributing to the establishment of sustainable and effective civilian policing arrangements under Afghan ownership and in accordance with international standards. More particularly, the mission will monitor, mentor, advise and train at the level of the Afghan Ministry of Interior, regions and provinces. The mission counts some 230 staff;
- 'EUPOL RD Congo', the EU Police Mission undertaken in the framework of reform of the security sector and its interface with the system of justice in the Democratic Republic of the Congo, succeeded EUPOL Kinshasa. The aim of this mission is to provide advice and assistance for security sector reform in the Democratic Republic of the Congo, with the aim of contributing to Congolese efforts to reform and restructure the National Congolese Police and its interaction with the judicial system, while taking care to promote policies compatible with human rights and international humanitarian law, democratic standards and the principles of good governance, transparency and respect for the rule of law. It counts thirty-nine international staff, was launched in July 2007 and ended on 30 June 2009;
- 'EULEX Kosovo', the EU Rule of Law Mission in Kosovo, is to assist the local institutions, judicial authorities and law enforcement agencies in their progress towards sustainability and accountability and in further developing and strengthening an independent multi-ethnic justice system and a multi-ethnic police and customs service, ensuring that these institutions are free from political interference and adhere to internationally recognised standards and European best practices. It monitors, mentors and advises, but also has certain executive responsibilities. The Council decided to launch EULEX Kosovo on 16 February 2008. After having reached initial operational capability the mission reached full deployment by the

end of 2009. The legal basis for the Mission is UNSC Resolution no. 1244 and the UN Secretary-General's authority under this Resolution;

- 'EUMM Georgia' is a civilian monitoring mission in Georgia adopted on 15 September 2008 and deployed on 1 October. Its objectives are to contribute to stability throughout Georgia and the surrounding region and, in the short term, to contribute to the stabilisation of the situation, in accordance with the six-point Agreement of September 2008 and the subsequent implementing measures.

* Further details may be found on the Internet site of the Council, http://consilium.europa.eu under 'Policies' > 'Security and Defence' > 'EU operations'. The number of staff/forces is indicative only and may (have) evolve(d) in the course of an operation.

The Nice Treaty, which entered into force in 2003, brought about more innovations, in particular by enhancing the role of the Political and Security Committee in crisis management operations through giving it the right to adopt decisions upon delegation from the Council. Moreover, the European Council decided in December 2003 to establish a 'Civil Military Cell' designed, *inter alia*, to enhance the EU's capacity for crisis management planning and to generate the capacity to plan and run autonomous EU operations.[49]

The modifications brought about by the Lisbon Treaty

There was a strong will to make ESDP more effective during the 2002–3 Convention. While taking over the existing Treaty provisions, the Convention proposed several innovations, such as the updating of the Petersberg tasks[50] and the possibility of entrusting a crisis management task to a group of willing Member States, as well as 'structured co-operation' between those Member States fulfilling higher criteria in military capabilities, closer co-operation between willing Member States on mutual defence, the establishment of a defence agency, the possibility of having closer co-operation in defence and a legal basis to create a start-up fund for financing crisis management operations. But some of its suggestions, such as the 'structured co-operation' between 'the able' and closer co-operation in mutual defence between 'the willing', did not have unanimous support among the Member States.

49 See Presidency Conclusions of the European Council, 12–13 December 2003, 23 and doc. 10580/1/04 REV 1 of 8 September 2005, 'Civil Military Cell – Terms of Reference'.
50 As laid down in Art. 17(2) former TEU: 'Questions referred to in this Article shall include humanitarian and rescue tasks, peacekeeping tasks and tasks of combat forces in crisis management, including peacemaking.'

Thanks to preparatory talks held between France, Germany and the United Kingdom in autumn 2003, it was possible to reach informal agreement in the 2003–4 IGC fairly quickly during the Italian Presidency at the IGC meeting in Naples in November 2003, where the provisions on mutual defence and 'structured co-operation' proposed by the Convention were thoroughly redrafted and approved. They were then incorporated in the Constitutional Treaty.

In the June 2007 IGC mandate, it was decided to keep provisions on ESDP similar to those agreed during the 2004 IGC, although, like CFSP provisions, they were to be kept in the TEU instead of making them part of the TFEU. Thus,

- ESDP, which is now called 'Common Security and Defence Policy' (CSDP) continues to be an integral part of CFSP. The Union may use civilian and military assets on missions outside the Union for peace-keeping, conflict prevention and strengthening international security in accordance with the principles of the United Nations Charter;
- Member States are to make civilian and military capabilities available to the Union for the implementation of CSDP, in order to contribute to the objectives defined by the Council;
- the tasks to be performed in this respect will include joint disarmament operations, humanitarian and rescue tasks, military advice and assistance tasks, conflict prevention and peacekeeping tasks, and tasks of combat forces in crisis management, including peacemaking and post-conflict stabilisation;
- the use of QMV in the Council is possible in certain cases, such as the launching and the definition of the membership of 'permanent structured co-operation' (Article 46(2) TEU), the definition of the statute, seat and operational rules of the (already existing) Defence Agency (Article 45(2) TEU) and the establishment of a start-up fund for CSDP operations (Article 41(3), 3rd subparagraph, TEU);
- on a semantic level, one may note that, before the Lisbon Treaty, Article 17(1), 1st subparagraph, of the former TEU referred to 'the progressive framing of a common defence policy, which *might lead* to a common defence' (emphasis added), a wording which is also used by the present Article 24(1), 1st subparagraph, TEU ('the progressive framing of a common defence policy that might lead to a common defence'), whereas Article 42(2), 1st subparagraph, TEU, contains a slightly different wording: 'The common security and defence policy shall include the progressive framing of a common Union defence policy. This *will lead*

to a common defence . . . '. However, the political and legal requirements remain unchanged: any move to a common defence would require a unanimous decision of the European Council, and ratification by all Member States.

The clarification of the scope of EU crisis management tasks

The Lisbon Treaty has clarified the scope of the EU crisis management tasks by mentioning their two aspects, civilian and military, and by bringing the list of the Petersberg tasks up to date by explicitly including disarmament operations, military advice and assistance, conflict prevention and post-conflict stabilisation (Articles 42(1) and 43(1) TEU).

The mutual assistance and solidarity clauses

First, the Lisbon Treaty introduces, in Article 42(7) TEU, an obligation for all Member States to give aid and assistance by all the means in their power, in accordance with Article 51 of the UN Charter, to a Member State which has been the victim of armed aggression on its territory. In order to reassure those Member States which have a specific status with regard to such issues or which have adopted a policy of neutrality, it is made clear that this 'shall not prejudice the specific character of the security and defence policy of certain Member States'. Therefore this provision does not transform the EU into a military alliance. It also specifies that 'commitments and co-operation in this area shall be consistent with commitments under the [NATO Treaty] which, for those States which are members of it,[51] remains the foundation of their collective defence and the forum for its implementation'. This solidarity clause is of the utmost symbolic and political importance for the EU. However, it does not amount to a mutual defence clause and does not change anything in the respective position of each Member State vis-à-vis NATO.

Second, Article 222 TFEU contains another 'solidarity clause' according to which 'the Union and its Member States shall act jointly in a spirit of solidarity if a Member State is the object of a terrorist attack or the victim of a natural or man-made disaster'. They will assist it 'at the request of its political authorities'. It further provides that 'the Union shall mobilise all the instruments at its disposal, including the military resources made available by the Member States' for prevention, protection and assistance in case of terrorist threats or terrorist attacks. For that purpose, the Council will be assisted by the Political and Security Committee and

51 Twenty-one Member States of the EU are also members of NATO.

by the standing committee referred to in Article 71 TFEU (the COSI) in charge of ensuring that operational co-operation on internal security is promoted and strengthened within the Union. The significance of such a provision became more obvious following the terrible terrorist attacks on 11 March 2004 in Madrid and on 7 July 2005 in London.

The possibility of entrusting a group of Member States with a CSDP mission

The Lisbon Treaty has introduced the possibility for the Council to entrust a group of Member States, which are willing and have the necessary capability, with a CSDP mission having the aim of protecting EU values and serving its interests (Articles 42(5) and 44 TEU).

This is an innovation. It will provide the EU with greater flexibility in its reaction to certain crisis situations where a quick response is essential. Because, in practice, the larger Member States have a wider spectrum of capabilities than the smaller States, this possibility was seen by some small Member States as establishing a risky trend towards CSDP being taken over by the larger Member States. This explains why such a possibility had been resisted during the 2003–4 IGC. In any event, in practice most EU missions do not involve all twenty-seven Member States on the ground, but only those Member States, large or small, which decide to contribute to it, by providing personnel, transport and the support necessary to fulfil the aims of the mission. The possibility created by Articles 42(5) and 44 TEU will thus make certain operations easier to manage.

The 'permanent structured co-operation'

The Lisbon Treaty has created the possibility of 'permanent structured co-operation' between willing Member States 'whose military capabilities fulfil higher criteria' (Articles 42(6) and 46 TEU and Protocol no. 10 on permanent structured co-operation). This new grouping of Member States has been nicknamed 'the Schengen of Defence' or the 'eurozone of Defence'. Under these provisions, 'those Member States whose military capabilities fulfil higher criteria and which have made more binding commitments to one another in this area with a view to the most demanding missions shall establish permanent structured co-operation within the Union framework' (Article 42(6) TEU).[52]

---

52 On these new provisions see F. Santopinto, 'Bataille diplomatique sur fond de coopération structurée permanente', note d'analyse, Groupe de recherche et d'information sur la paix et la sécurité, 4 novembre 2009.

Protocol no. 10 provides that this co-operation 'shall be open to any Member State which undertakes, from the date of entry into force of the Treaty of Lisbon, to proceed more intensively to develop its defence capacities . . . and to have the capacity to supply by 2010 at the latest . . . targeted combat units' under specified conditions[53] (Article 1 of the Protocol). To that end, Member States participating in this co-operation will undertake, in particular, to 'take concrete measures to enhance the availability, interoperability, flexibility and deployability of their forces, in particular by identifying common objectives regarding the commitment of forces, including possibly reviewing their national decision-making procedures' (Article 2(c) of the Protocol). The able and willing Member States will notify their intention to the Council and to the High Representative. Within three months following that notification, the list of the Member States participating in this co-operation, which is not subject to a minimum number of participating States, will be adopted by the Council, acting by QMV after consulting the High Representative (Article 46(2) TEU). This swift and simple procedure is quite remarkable when compared with the conditions for launching an 'enhanced co-operation' in the field of CFSP–ESDP, which require unanimity (Articles 329(2) and 331(2) TFEU) and the participation of at least nine Member States (Article 20(2) TEU).

The 'permanent structured co-operation' is open to any Member State which fulfils the criteria and makes the required commitments. Likewise, any participating Member State may withdraw from the co-operation or be suspended from the co-operation when it no longer fulfils the criteria for participation. Pursuant to Article 46(3) TEU 'any Member State which, at a later stage, wishes to participate in [the] co-operation shall

---

53 Participating Member States must undertake to 'have the capacity to supply by 2010 at the latest, either at national level or as a component of multinational force groups, targeted combat units for the missions planned, structured at a tactical level as a battle group, with support elements including transport and logistics, capable of carrying out the tasks referred to in Art. 43 TEU, within a period of five to thirty days, in particular in response to requests from the UN, and which can be sustained for an initial period of 30 days and be extended up to at least 120 days' (Art. 1(b) of the Protocol).

The '2010 Headline Goal', agreed in June 2004, aimed at improving capabilities of the EU Member States so as to be able to respond to the whole spectrum of crisis management operations covered by the former TEU. It already comprised, as part of the rapid response capability, the 'battlegroups' formed among willing and capable Member States – that is, groups of at least 1,500 persons from one or more Member States with specific capabilities (ability to deploy abroad within ten days, ability to remain in the theatre of operations for a given period, etc.) (see doc. 6309/6/04 Rev 6, available in the Council's Register of documents on the Council's Internet site).

notify its intention to the Council and to the High Representative. The Council shall adopt a decision confirming the participation of the Member State concerned.' Conversely, 'if a participating Member State no longer fulfils the criteria or is no longer able to meet the commitments . . . the Council may adopt a decision suspending the participation of the Member State concerned', (Article 46(4) TEU) and 'any participating Member State which wishes to withdraw from [the co-operation] shall notify its intention to the Council' (Article 46(5) TEU). Again, in both cases (new participation or suspension of the participation of a Member State), the Council will decide by QMV.

The European Defence Agency

The Lisbon Treaty provides for the establishment by the Council, using QMV, of a European Defence Agency (EDA) in the field of defence capabilities development, research, acquisition and armaments (Articles 42(3) and 45 TEU). In fact, such an Agency had already been established by the Council in July 2004, acting unanimously on the basis of Article 14 of the former TEU, and is already functional.[54] The Lisbon Treaty enables the Council to amend the statute and operational rules of this Agency using QMV.

The mandate of the EDA is to identify operational requirements, to promote measures to satisfy those requirements, to contribute to identifying and implementing any measure needed to strengthen the industrial and technological base of the defence sector, to participate in defining a European capabilities and armament policy, and to assist the Council in evaluating the improvement of military capabilities. At the time of writing, the results of the work of the EDA have remained modest.

The participation of Member States in the EDA is optional: 'The [EDA] shall be open to all Member States wishing to be part of it' (Article 45(2) TEU). Member States are also free to participate in some or all of EDA projects and activities. Denmark does not participate. Ireland may also decide not to participate fully.

---

54 See Council Joint Action 2004/551/CFSP of 12 July 2004 on the establishment of the European Defence Agency (OJ No. L245, 17 July 2004, 17). The EDA employed about eighty persons at the time of writing. Its budget was 30 million euros in 2008 (22 million euros for functioning costs and 8 million euros of operational budget; see 2008 Financial Report, available on the Internet site of the EDA at www.eda.europa.eu).

The possibility of establishing a start-up fund for CSDP operations

The Lisbon Treaty facilitates the financing of EU military operations by allowing the Council to establish, by QMV, a start-up fund, made up of Member States' contributions, designed to finance preparatory activities of such operations quickly (Article 41(3), 3rd subparagraph, TEU). Again, the use of QMV for such a decision deserves to be noted.

*

From a political and institutional point of view, the two most important issues on the EU agenda for CSDP in the coming years are probably, on the one hand, how to improve the relationship of the EU with NATO[55] and, on the other hand, whether to establish an autonomous capacity to plan and command its crisis management missions.[56]

The fact that France decided in 2009 to return to the integrated military structure of NATO and that NATO, and thus also the United States, 'recognise the value that a stronger and more capable European defence brings'[57] may help in resolving these two issues. However, the first would require the acquiescence of Turkey and probably depends on the evolution of the situation with respect to Cyprus.

Section 36 Other sectors of external affairs, including trade policy

The Lisbon Treaty has added provisions on other sectors of external affairs and, more importantly, has made significant amendments to

---

55 See A. Toje, *The EU, NATO and European Defence: A Slow Train Coming*, Occasional Paper 74 (Paris: European Union Institute for Security Studies, 2008). See also D. Keohane and T. Valasek, *Willing and Able? EU Defence in 2020* (London: Centre for European Reform, 2008).

56 A small operation centre has already been established in Brussels, in 2007. A Council Decision of 10 May 2005 amending the 2001 Decision establishing the EU Military Staff (EUMS) provided that the EUMS would generate and maintain, at the time 'through the Civ/Mil Cell', the capacity within EUMS rapidly to set up an operation centre (or EU Ops Centre) (see OJ No. L132, 26 May 2005, 17). In April 2008, another Decision amending the EUMS Decision tasked it, as part of its role, to '[maintain] the capacity within EUMS rapidly to set up an operations centre for a specific operation, in particular where a joint civil/military response is required and where no national HQ is identified'. The 2008 Decision also mentions, among the EUMS tasks, the preparation of 'concepts and procedures for the EU Ops Centre' and also mentions that the EUMS 'contributes to the key nucleus reinforced, and to further augmentation, as required, of the EU Ops Centre' and 'provides the permanent key nucleus of the EU Ops Centre' (see OJ No. L102, 12 April 2008, 25, in particular 27, 28 and 29).

57 NATO Declaration adopted at the Bucharest Summit in 2008 (www.nato.int/docu).

ex-Article 133 TEC, renumbered Article 207 TFEU. The complex drafting of this Article has been improved by the Lisbon Treaty. The Treaty has extended the scope of the exclusive competence of the EU and has increased significantly the role of the European Parliament in trade policy.

Article 207 TFEU

The structure of Article 207 TFEU is more straightforward than the structure of Article 133 TEC, which, as a result of the Nice Treaty modifications in particular, contained complicated inter-paragraph references and derogations.

Article 207(1) TFEU defines the scope of the common commercial policy and thus of the Union's competences in this field. The exercise of the Union's competences in this field is further determined by paragraph 6, which sets certain limits in this regard. The last sentence of paragraph 1 provides that 'the common commercial policy shall be conducted in the context of the principles and objectives of the Union's external action'.[58] Similarly, Article 205 TFEU (which applies to all the EU's external action under the TFEU, and therefore also to trade policy) provides that 'the Union's action on the international scene . . . shall be guided by the principles, pursue the objectives and be conducted in accordance with the general provisions on the Union's external action laid down in Chapter I of Title V of the [TEU]' (i.e. the general provisions which apply to all the EU's external action, both CFSP and other sectors).

Article 207(2) TFEU lays down the procedure for the adoption of internal measures in the field of the common commercial policy and defines the form of such measures.

Article 207(3) to (5) TFEU lays down the procedures relating to the negotiation and conclusion of international agreements in the field of the common commercial policy.

---

58 It will need to be examined, on a case-by-case basis, whether the explicit insertion of the common commercial policy into the context of the principles and objectives of the Union's external action, as well as the new formulation of Art. 40 TEU (Art. 47 former TEU), may influence the interpretation of the scope and objectives of the common commercial policy under Art. 207 TFEU, in particular with respect to measures, such as the control of trade in dual use goods, where objectives of the CFSP and of the common commercial policy may be intertwined. Compare the principles laid down by the Court of Justice in its judgment of 20 May 2008, Case C-91/05, *Commission v. Council (small arms-ECOWAS)* [2008] ECR I-3651, concerning the objectives of the CFSP and development co-operation policy.

Scope of the EU competences in trade matters

Article 3(1)(e) TFEU lists 'common commercial policy' among the areas where the Union has an exclusive competence.

Article 207(1), first sentence, TFEU mentions areas which are covered by the common commercial policy. First, one notes that the use of the word 'particularly' means that the list of areas mentioned there is not exhaustive. Second, in addition to the areas which were mentioned in Article 133(1) TEC, the following areas have been added by the Lisbon Treaty: trade in services, the commercial aspects of intellectual property and foreign direct investment.

As concerns the areas of trade in services and the commercial aspects of intellectual property, for which the EC competence under Article 133(5) TEC was not exclusive, these areas have now become part of the exclusive competence of the EU. The determination of the scope of the sectors of 'trade in services' and of 'commercial aspects of intellectual property' is thus important. The interpretation of these areas would in principle include most, if not all, matters covered by the WTO's General Agreement on Trade in Services (GATS) and Agreement on Trade-Related Aspects of Intellectual Property Rights (TRIPS Agreement).

Foreign direct investment

As concerns foreign direct investment, while some aspects of foreign direct investment already fell under exclusive EC competence under Article 133(1) TEC, and other aspects under shared EC competence, pursuant to the internal market legal bases (such as Articles 71 and 80 TEC), other aspects relating in particular to post-establishment treatment of foreign investment, such as specific provisions on the rules and conditions for expropriation of foreign-controlled undertakings, generally remained within the competence of the Member States.

The inclusion of the area of foreign direct investment among the matters falling within the exclusive EU competence for the common commercial policy thus brings about a major modification of the previous delimitation of competences. In view of the fact that many Member States have concluded a large number of bilateral investment treaties, this is one of the most sensitive issues for the future. There are two important questions which will need to be clarified:

- Are some or all of the subject matters covered by these bilateral investment treaties, since the entry into force of the Lisbon Treaty, within exclusive EU competence?
- Must these bilateral treaties therefore be renegotiated or denounced?

The first question depends on the interpretation of the notion of 'foreign direct investment'. This notion would exclude portfolio investment, because such investment cannot be considered 'direct'. Furthermore, one might consider that post-establishment investment protection should be excluded from the scope of the notion of 'foreign direct investment'. Although Article 207(1) TFEU does not make an express distinction between pre-establishment (market access) aspects and post-establishment investment protection aspects, this thesis will deserve careful examination in the future.

To the extent that provisions of bilateral investment treaties contain provisions falling within the scope of Article 207 TFEU, the second question, relating to the future of such treaties, should be resolved pursuant to the principles set out in Article 351 TFEU (formerly Article 307 TEC). Similar considerations should apply with respect to multilateral treaties in this field.[59]

Limits of EU competences in trade matters

Article 207(1) TFEU must be read together with Article 207(6), which limits in two ways the exercise of the competences conferred on the EU in this Article.

First, Article 207(6) TFEU provides, in the first half of the sentence, that 'the exercise of the competences conferred by [Article 207] in the field of the common commercial policy shall not affect the delimitation of competences between the Union and the Member States'. It can be noted that this provision is not limited to the exercise of the Union's external competence. It differs in this respect from Article 133(6), 1st subparagraph, TEC, according to which 'an agreement may not be concluded by the Council if it includes provisions which would go beyond the Community's internal powers'. This new provision will have to be interpreted as excluding from the EU's exclusive competence subject matters for which the EU has no internal competence.[60]

Second, Article 207(6) TFEU provides, in the second half of the sentence, that 'the exercise of the competences conferred by [Article 207]

---

59 E.g. the Convention on the Settlement of Investment Disputes between States and Nationals of Other States (ICSID Convention), adopted within the World Bank, which entered into force on 14 October 1966.

60 One example could be limitations to market access for mode 3 hospital services, relating in particular to the requirement of an authorisation according to national health plans, and limitations to mode 3 and 4 services, referring to economic needs tests or nationality or citizenship requirements.

in the field of the common commercial policy... shall not lead to harmonisation of legislative or regulatory provisions of the Member States in so far as the Treaties exclude such harmonisation'. The objective of this limitation is clearly the same as that of Article 133(6), 1st subparagraph, TEC, which is to prevent the exclusion of harmonisation, for instance in the area of health (Article 168(5) TFEU), from being circumvented by the adoption of trade measures on the basis of Article 207 TFEU which would lead to such harmonisation.

Decision-making procedures for the adoption of internal acts

Article 207(2) TFEU lays down the procedure for the adoption of internal acts in the field of the common commercial policy, and determines the form of such acts. These acts will take the form of regulations and will be adopted under the ordinary legislative procedure (codecision).[61]

Article 207(2) TFEU appears to restrict the scope of the internal measures, to the extent that it applies to 'measures defining the framework for implementing the common commercial policy', whereas Article 133(2) TEC related to measures 'implementing the common commercial policy'. In principle, this new formulation could be interpreted as limiting the scope of internal measures to general framework measures, thereby excluding measures which laid down detailed rules or addressed specific situations. Such general framework measures would include, for instance, the Basic Trade Defence Instruments, the GSP Regulation, the Dual-Use Regulation and similar acts. This will probably give rise to discussions in the near future, as others may argue, on the contrary, that neither the other paragraphs of Article 207 TFEU nor other provisions in the TFEU provide for any other legal basis for the adoption of measures in the field of the common commercial policy. Therefore they may stress that Article 207(2) TFEU differs from legal bases in some other fields which distinguish between more general measures for which the ordinary legislative procedure applies and other, more specific measures for which a different procedure applies.[62] One interpretation is that such specific measures

---

61 Before the Lisbon Treaty the Council adopted internal measures under Art. 133(2) TEC by QMV on a proposal from the Commission, without any obligatory participation of the European Parliament, but the Council very often consulted it. Likewise, Art. 133(2) TEC did not determine the form of the act to be taken, but the vast majority of measures adopted under this provision were regulations.

62 See, e.g., on the one hand, Art. 43(2) TFEU concerning the establishment of the common organisation of agricultural markets and the other provisions necessary for the pursuit of the objectives of the common agricultural policy and the common fisheries policy (ordinary legislative procedure) and, on the other hand, Art. 43(3) TFEU concerning

would have to be adopted as delegated or implementing acts. Another interpretation would be to use the Treaty legal basis which provides for codecision, with the risk that the adoption of urgent trade measures would become more difficult in the future.

Decision-making procedures for the negotiation and conclusion of international agreements

According to Article 207(3), 1st subparagraph, TFEU, the procedure for the negotiation and conclusion of international agreements in the field of the common commercial policy is the one laid down in the general provisions of Article 218 TFEU, subject to the specific provisions of Article 207 TFEU. It is to be noted that Article 207(5) TFEU provides that the negotiation and conclusion of international agreements in the field of transport is subject to the provisions on the common transport policy.

As was the case before the Lisbon Treaty, when an international agreement is envisaged the Commission makes recommendations to the Council, which authorises it to open the necessary negotiations. The Commission conducts the negotiations in consultation with a special committee appointed by the Council to assist it in this task and within the framework of such directives as the Council may issue.

The new element introduced by the Lisbon Treaty is the requirement that the Commission has to report regularly not only to the special committee, but also to the European Parliament on the progress of negotiations (Article 207(3), 3rd subparagraph, last sentence, TFEU). Before the Lisbon Treaty, the European Parliament was informed on the negotiations as a matter of inter-institutional arrangements and practice. There is a distinction between the tasks of the special committee and the European Parliament, in that only the committee, but not the European Parliament, is consulted and assists the Commission. However, both the committee and the European Parliament are to be informed on the same footing about the progress of negotiations. It is possible that this obligation to inform the European Parliament will be accompanied by some kind of mechanism (which might take the form of an interinstitutional agreement) in order to avoid leaks to the third parties involved in the negotiations with the EU.

measures on fixing prices, levies, aid and quantitative limitations and on the fixing and allocation of fishing opportunities (Council, on a proposal from the Commission).

As was the case before the Lisbon Treaty, decisions authorising the signing of an agreement and, if necessary, its provisional application before entry into force are adopted by the Council on a proposal by the negotiator (Article 218(5) TFEU), which, in the field of the common commercial policy, is the Commission.

As previously, the decision concluding an agreement in the field of the common commercial policy is adopted by the Council on a proposal from the Commission (Article 218(6) TFEU). The new element introduced by the Lisbon Treaty concerns the participation of the European Parliament. According to Article 218(6)(a)(v) TFEU, the consent of the European Parliament is necessary for agreements covering fields to which, internally, codecision applies. Given that the legal basis for internal acts defining the framework for implementing the common commercial policy provides that such measures are to be adopted in codecision, agreements to implement these measures appear to require the consent of the European Parliament.

The voting rules for Council decisions for the negotiation and conclusion of agreements in the field of the common commercial policy are laid down in Article 207(4) TFEU, which applies also to decisions on the signing and on provisional application of agreements in this field. The general voting rule is QMV, subject to some exceptions.

The first exception is that, for agreements in the fields of trade in services and the commercial aspects of intellectual property, as well as foreign direct investment, Article 207(4), 2nd subparagraph, TFEU provides that the Council shall act unanimously where such agreements include provisions for which unanimity is required for the adoption of internal rules.

The second exception is that unanimity is required in accordance with Article 207(4), 3rd subparagraph, point (a), TFEU for agreements in the field of trade in cultural and audiovisual services, 'where these agreements risk prejudicing the Union's cultural and linguistic diversity'.

The third exception is that unanimity is also required in accordance with Article 207(4), 3rd subparagraph, point (b), TFEU for agreements in the field of trade in social, education and health services, 'where these agreements risk seriously disturbing the national organisation of such services and prejudicing the responsibility of Member States to deliver them'.

The interpretation of the scope of these qualifying conditions relating to the risk of a prejudice to the cultural and linguistic diversity of the EU and for the risk of a prejudice to the responsibility of Member States to deliver certain services will probably give rise to some interesting discussions in the future!

Amendments in other sectors of external affairs

The Lisbon Treaty also contains several modifications in the areas of development co-operation with third countries and of humanitarian aid (Articles 208 to 214 TFEU).

The EU development co-operation policy 'shall have as its primary objectives the reduction and, in the long term, the eradication of poverty' (Article 298(1), 2nd subparagraph, TFEU). One should stress that the EU is by far the largest donor of public aid to development in the world. Together, the EU and its Member States provided 60 per cent of total worldwide public aid to development in 2008 (49 billion euros).[63]

The Lisbon Treaty provides for a specific legal basis for the funding of humanitarian aid (Article 214 TFEC), which was, before the Lisbon Treaty, based on the provisions on development co-operation. These provisions provide also for the creation of a 'European Voluntary Humanitarian Aid Corps', the rules and procedures of which are to be set out by the ordinary legislative procedure (Article 214(5) TFEU).

*

The Lisbon Treaty has fundamentally modified the scope of EU exclusive competences and the decision-making procedures in the area of the common commercial policy.

The scope of the common commercial policy which falls under the exclusive competence of the Union has been expanded. It now includes trade in services and commercial aspects of intellectual property, as well as foreign direct investment. The scope for mixed agreements will, as a result, be limited in this area. However, the common transport policy remains excluded from the scope of the common commercial policy and, therefore, from exclusive EU competence.

QMV in the Council has been further extended. However, for the adoption of decisions relating to certain areas in the field of the common commercial policy, unanimity is still required.

The powers of the European Parliament have been considerably increased. EU internal measures in the field of common commercial policy will in principle be adopted by codecision, and the conclusion of

---

63 See Annual Report 2008 of the Commission on the Community policy in aid to development COM(2009) 296 final.

international agreements in this field will require the European Parliament's consent to the extent that they cover issues themselves falling under the codecision procedure. Furthermore, keeping the European Parliament 'immediately and fully informed at all stages of the procedure' of negotiation of such agreements has become a Treaty requirement, the purpose being to avoid surprises at the end of the negotiation of the agreement, when the European Parliament's consent will be required. The European Parliament is quite ready to make use of its right to reject an agreement, as it did for the EU–US 'SWIFT' Agreement in February 2010.

VIII

Financial, economic, social and other internal affairs

Section 37 The EU budget

A brief history of the EU budget

The rules governing the adoption of the EU budget have been modified a number of times. Originally, the 1957 Rome Treaty gave budgetary power exclusively to the Council (Article 203 of the original EEC Treaty). The European Parliament progressively obtained more powers.

For nearly thirty-five years, the procedure for the adoption of the annual budget has always respected the following lines: the European Parliament and the Council are seized by a draft budget tabled by the Commission. The procedure is subject to a timetable fixed by the Treaty. The budget is to be approved by the Council and to be finally decided by the European Parliament. The Council votes by a QMV specific to cases where the Council does not act on the basis of a proposal from the Commission, but on the basis of another act (a draft, a recommendation, etc.).[1] In such situations, unanimity is not required in the Council to change the proposal of the Commission (Article 250(1) TEC). Since the early 1970s, the European Parliament had obtained a right of codecision, and even the last word on so-called 'non-compulsory' expenditure. For its part, the Council kept the last word on the so-called 'compulsory' expenditure (mainly for the common agriculture policy).

On this basis, in the early years of the EC the negotiations between the European Parliament and the Council, or rather the fights about powers more than about figures, were taking place annually in lengthy sessions which frequently lasted overnight. The three EU institutions concerned (the European Parliament, the Council and the Commission) agreed in

---

1 This particular QMV was called 'budgetary majority' or 'double majority' because it required a double threshold to be fulfilled: not only the normal threshold for QMV of 255 positive votes out of a total of 345, but also a majority of two-thirds of the Council Members (i.e. eighteen in an EU of twenty-seven) (see Art. 205(2), 3rd subpara., TEC).

the 1980s to negotiate an agreement in order to make the procedure easier.

In any case, Member States, being the 'Masters of the Treaty', by the same token are the masters of the main rules of the budgetary game. This is the reason why the powers of the EU institutions in budgetary matters are strictly restricted, both on the revenue side and on the expenditure side.

On the revenue side

Until 1970, the EU was entirely financed, like most international organisations, by direct contributions from the Member States (Article 200 of the original EEC Treaty).

In 1970, on the basis of Article 203 of the original EEC Treaty (which later became Article 269 TEC), a Decision on the EU 'Own Resources' was adopted. The procedure to adopt this Decision is very heavy, as it requires (similarly to the adoption of the Treaties) unanimity in the Council and the ratification by all Member States according to their constitutional requirements; the European Parliament is only required to give a consultative opinion. There were three types of resources in 1970. The first two were the customs duties and the agricultural duties (including sugar duties) levied at the EC external borders. These two resources are levied on economic operators and collected by Member States on behalf of the EU.[2] The third one – that is, 'the VAT resource' – is levied on Member States' value-added tax bases, which are harmonised for this purpose in accordance with EC rules. The same percentage is levied on the harmonised base of each Member State, capped at 50 per cent of each Member State's gross national income (GNI). The VAT-based resource accounts for around 12 per cent of total EU resources. A fourth resource was added in 1988, which is based on the GNI and has become the most important. About three-quarters of the total EU revenue comes now from this fourth resource.

The Own Resources Decision[3] provides for a maximum limit: the total amount of resources available for the EU cannot exceed 1.24 per cent of the GNI of the EU (e.g. the 2010 budget: 1.04 per cent of the GNI, i.e. 122.9 billion euros payment appropriations). This figure is to be compared with the part of the GNI going on public expenditure (national, regional or

---

2 Member States keep 25 per cent as compensation for their collecting costs.
3 The last Decision (dated 7 June 2007) entered into force on 1 March 2009 and has been applicable retroactively since 1 January 2007 (OJ No. L163, 23 June 2007, 17).

BOX 32. PAYMENT APPROPRIATIONS AS A PERCENTAGE
OF GNI, 2000–13

Implemented budgets

2000	2001	2002	2003	2004	2005	2006	2007	2008
0.95	0.88	0.90	0.94	0.94	0.95	0.92	0.91	0.90

Forecasts in the Financial Perspectives

2009	2010	2011	2012	2012
0.97	1.00	0.96	0.97	0.94

local) in the Member States, which is about 45 per cent. Not only has this upper limit of 1.24 per cent never been reached by the EU but, as shown in Box 32, the percentage of GNI devoted to the EU budget has been in diminution for the last few years.

As can be seen from Box 32, despite the fact that the EU has expanded from fifteen to twenty-seven Member States since 2007, that most of the twelve States which became EU members in 2004/2007 have a lower level of wealth than the fifteen others, and that the areas of action of the EU have been enlarged, the percentage of the GNI devoted to the EU budget tends to decrease over the years.

The Own Resources Decision also includes a mechanism by which the United Kingdom gets a partial reimbursement of its due as it should be according to the normal rules of calculation of the Decision (see Box 33).

BOX 33. THE UK REBATE

The UK rebate is a specific mechanism which was first negotiated in 1984 by Prime Minister Margaret Thatcher ('I want my money back') and integrated in the Own Resources Decision. It was agreed, in order to correct the imbalance between the United Kingdom's payments to the EU budget (calculated with the normal rules of the Own Resources Decision) and the United Kingdom's 'returns' from the EU expenditure, which takes into account only the direct benefits drawn from the expenditure spent in the United Kingdom. The mechanism has been altered at the request of other Member States in order to limit the amount of the rebate. The correction oscillated between 5.2 and 5.7 billion euros between 2002 and 2007. It is borne by the other twenty-six Member States, which have expressed the strong wish to put an end to this derogation from the normal rules. Germany, the Netherlands,

Austria and Sweden obtained agreement to a reduction of their share of financing the UK rebate to a quarter of its normal value. The cost of this reduction is redistributed among the remaining twenty-two Member States. As a percentage of GNI, the United Kingdom in fact contributes less to the EU budget than do the Netherlands, Sweden, Germany, France, Italy, Austria or Denmark.

It has been agreed that the UK rebate mechanism should be re-examined in the framework of the comprehensive mid-term review of the Financial Perspectives for the period 2007–13.

On the expenditure side

First, the EU budget is not allowed to be in deficit (Article 268 TEC, now renumbered 310(1) TFEU).

Second, since 1988 the budget has had to respect a pluriannual financial framework, the Financial Perspectives. The Financial Perspectives constitute the programming of the expenses over several years, which reflect the political priorities of the EU (see the 2007–13 Financial Perspectives by type of expenditure, Box 34).

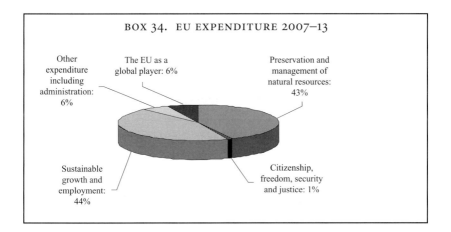

BOX 34. EU EXPENDITURE 2007–13

Other expenditure including administration: 6%

The EU as a global player: 6%

Preservation and management of natural resources: 43%

Sustainable growth and employment: 44%

Citizenship, freedom, security and justice: 1%

The discipline imposed by the Financial Perspectives has allowed the annual budgetary negotiation between the European Parliament and the Council to be much easier than it was before.

After the adoption of the budget, any expenditure authorised by the budget, in order to be implemented, also requires a 'legal basis' – that is, a legislative or administrative act adopted by the competent EU institution(s) in accordance with the conditions set out by the Treaties. Then, the Commission is responsible for the implementation of the budget. In reality, it shares most[4] of the management with the Member States, in particular for cohesion and structural expenses or for expenses in agriculture, research, networks and so on.

When implementing the budget, the Commission is bound by the rules of the Financial Regulation,[5] which were adopted by QMV by the Council, after consultation with the European Parliament and the Court of Auditors (Article 279(1) TEC). The implementation of the budget is audited both by the internal auditors of the Commission and by the European Court of Auditors, which is an EU institution. Both the annual internal report and the Court of Auditors report are sent to the European Parliament. Each year, under what is known as the 'discharge procedure' (Article 276 TEC), the Commission is accountable to the European Parliament for the use made of the resources at its disposal. The Treaty also provides for means to counter fraud affecting the financial interests of the Union (Article 280 TEC).

The Financial Perspectives

Since 1988 the EC annual budget has had to respect the Financial Perspectives, a financial framework valid for a period of five to seven years. This procedure, which was not foreseen in the Treaties, was created by an Interinstitutional Agreement (IIA) adopted in 1988 by the European Parliament, the Council and the Commission. The IIA must respect the overall ceiling of 1.24 per cent GNI resulting from the Own Resources Decision. Moreover, the IIA adds to this general ceiling for the maximum total expenditure possible, specific different sub-ceilings for each category of expenses during the same period of five to seven years. These sub-ceilings are binding for both arms of the budgetary authority (the European Parliament and the Council). The 1988 IIA has been modified several times, but its essential characteristics have not been changed.

The Financial Perspectives applicable at the time of writing covered the period 2007 to 2013. They were to be subject to a 'mid-term' review, which should have taken place in 2009 but has been left for later. Box 35 reproduces the ceilings set by the 2007–13 Financial Perspectives.

---

4 This is the case for 85 per cent of the expenses of the EU, according to J. O. Karlsson, former President of the Court of Auditors (*El País*, 14 March 1999).
5 See Financial Regulation of 25 June 2002, OJ No. L248, 16 September 2002, 1.

BOX 35. INTERINSTITUTIONAL AGREEMENT, FINANCIAL FRAMEWORK 2007–13[*]

Commitment appropriations	2007	2008	2009	2010	2011	2012	2013	Total 2007– 2013
	€million, 2004 prices							
1. Sustainable growth	51,267	52,415	53,616	54,294	55,368	56,876	58,303	382,139
1a. Competitiveness for Growth and Employment	8,404	9,097	9,754	10,434	11,295	12,153	12,961	74,098
1b. Cohesion for Growth and Employment	42,863	43,318	43,862	43,860	44,073	44,723	45,342	308,041
2. Preservation and Management of Natural Resources	54,985	54,322	53,666	53,035	52,400	51,775	51,161	371,344
of which market-related expenditure and direct payments	43,120	42,697	42,279	41,864	41,453	41,047	40,645	293,105
3. Citizenship, freedom, security and justice	1,199	1,258	1,380	1,503	1,645	1,797	1,988	10,770
3a. Freedom, Security and Justice	600	690	790	910	1,050	1,200	1,390	6,630
3b. Citizenship	599	568	590	593	595	597	598	4,140
4. EU as a global player	6,199	6,469	6,739	7,009	7,339	7,679	8,029	49,463
5. Administration	6,633	6,818	6,973	7,111	7,255	7,400	7,610	49,800
6. Compensations	419	191	190					800
Total commitment appropriations	120,702	121,473	122,564	122,952	124,007	125,527	127,091	864,316
as a percentage of GNI	1.10%	1.08%	1.07%	1.04%	1.03%	1.02%	1.01%	1.048% (average)
Total payment appropriations	116,650	119,620	111,990	118,280	115,860	119,410	118,970	820,780
as a percentage of GNI	1.06%	1.06%	0.97%	1.00%	0.96%	0.97%	0.94%	1.00% (average)
Margin available	0.18%	0.18%	0.27%	0.24%	0.28%	0.27%	0.30%	0.24% (average)
Own Resources Ceiling as a percentage of GNI	1.24%	1.24%	1.24%	1.24%	1.24%	1.24%	1.24%	1.24% (average)

[*] Interinstitutional Agreement, 17 May 2006, Annex I, OJ C139, 14 June 2006, 10.

The Financial Perspectives have been adopted for four successive periods (in 1988, 1993, 1999 and 2006). They have allowed a way out of the institutional conflicts, when the two arms of the budgetary authority were struggling about the precise limits of their respective powers. The Financial Perspectives have helped to offer predictability and order in the evolution of EC expenditure.

The Financial Perspectives are part of a series of understandings between institutions on budgetary matters. A first understanding settled the controversy on the classification of the expenditure as 'compulsory' and 'non-compulsory' in view of the implementation of Article 202 of the original EEC treaty (which later became Article 272 TEC) and the annual rate of increase of the non-compulsory expenditure. More generally, the limits were traced within which EC budgets could grow, thereby offering clear and predictable perspectives to Member States, which, at the end of the day, have to provide the necessary resources.

Over the years, other interinstitutional understandings have developed. Other elements were thus regulated, some directly related to the Financial Perspectives, others not: flexibility of the Financial Perspectives, budgeting rules, budgetary discipline, procedures to facilitate the annual budgetary process, clarifications on the role of the legislative authority as opposed to the budgetary authority, rules on the establishment of CFSP appropriations, overview of EC agencies and so on. The entire corpus was recast, acquiring more solemnity and visibility, in 1999, in the 'Interinstitutional agreement on budgetary discipline and sound financial management'.[6]

The Financial Perspectives were not a multiannual budget. They did not entail authorisation to spend, which is the main characteristic of a budget. They laid down the maximum limits (ceilings) up to which the budget of the EU could grow during a given period of several years. A budget for a given year established within the limits of the Financial Perspectives was deemed by the three institutions involved (Parliament, Council and Commission) to embody the annual rate of increase for the non-compulsory expenditure which was foreseen in Article 272(9) TEC.

Interinstitutional agreements, including the Financial Perspectives, hold a special place in the regulatory framework of the EC finances. Of course, they are subject to the Treaty, the Own Resources Decision and the Financial Regulation, but they entail legally binding effects between the three participating institutions.[7]

---

6 At the time of writing, the IIA in force was that dated 17 May 2006 (OJ No. C172, 16 June 1999, 1, and OJ No. C139, 14 June 2006, 1).

7 See judgment of 19 March 1996, Case C-25/94, *Commission v. Council (FAO fishery agreement)*, [1996] ECR I-01469. See Article 295 TFEU.

The main innovations brought about by the Lisbon Treaty

The Lisbon IGC took over the reforms which had been agreed during the 2003–4 IGC.[8] The main innovations brought about by the Lisbon Treaty are:

- the insertion into the TFEU of a specific primary law provision on the Financial Perspectives, which are now called the Multiannual Financial Framework;
- the substantial modifications made to the procedure for adopting the EU budget, by giving more powers to the European Parliament;[9]
- the introduction of codecision for the adoption of the Financial Regulation.

It should be noted that all these provisions (Own Resources, Multiannual Financial Framework, EU budget and Financial Regulation) now belong to the legislative field and will therefore have to be handled in public by the Council, as provided for by Article 16(8) TEU.

The Multiannual Financial Framework

The Lisbon Treaty has now enshrined the Multiannual Financial Framework (MFF) in primary law. Article 312 TFEU lays down the essential elements of the system (previously to be found in the IIA). The figures for a given period, which is now fixed at five years, as well as the provisions 'required for the annual budgetary procedure to run smoothly' are to be provided by a regulation adopted by unanimity in the Council and by the majority of the component members of the European Parliament. A *passerelle* allows the European Council, acting unanimously, to empower the Council to act by QMV when adopting (or modifying) the regulation.

The mechanics of the MFF remain unchanged compared with the Financial Perspectives. The figures to be laid down represent ceilings, as before, but compliance with those ceilings is mandatory by law, rather than voluntarily accepted and 'recognised' by agreement. The theoretical risk

---

8 See point 18 of the June 2007 IGC mandate under which 'the innovations as agreed in the 2004 IGC will be inserted into the Treaty...They concern...financial provisions (own resources, multiannual financial framework, new budgetary procedure)' (Presidency Conclusions, doc. 11177/1/07 REV 1).

9 However, some observers think that the new budgetary procedure is more favourable to the Council than to the European Parliament. See A. Potteau, 'Les finances publiques de l'Union européenne en 2007' (2009) 45(1) *Revue trimestrielle de Droit européen* 105.

of the past, following which a participating institution could denounce the IIA, and walk out of it, is therefore now excluded.

Two other issues are to be stressed.

- Stability in case of disagreement between the European Parliament and the Council as to the renewal of the MFF is guaranteed by the Treaty: Article 312(4) TFEU foresees that, when a regulation laying down a new MFF is not adopted by the time of the expiry of the previous one, the provisions concerning the last year of the old MFF will continue to apply.
- Conditions for decisions on the revision of the MFF have been made more stringent than under the IIA. Under the latter, the Council could decide a revision of the ceilings of the MFF up to 0.03 per cent of the EU GNI by qualified majority.[10] Now, the voting rule of Article 312(2) TFEU (unanimity) will prevail in all cases, unless the *passerelle* of Article 312(2), 2nd subparagraph, TFEU were to be (unanimously) enacted.[11]

Therefore, although changes brought about by the Lisbon Treaty show no substantial modification with respect to the provisions which were contained in the IIA, the shift in their legal nature will in practice result in the balance being tilted towards stability and predictability (rather than flexibility) with respect to the MFF.

The new annual budget procedure

The changes to the Treaty which had been proposed by the 2001–3 Convention (where the European Parliament played a particularly active role) were not completely followed by the 2003–4 IGC which drafted the Constitutional Treaty.

In particular, the IGC did not accept the suggestion of the Convention that the European Parliament be given a very dominant budgetary power. Therefore the 2003–4 IGC amended the draft provided by the Convention on a number of points, in order to share the budgetary powers between the European Parliament and the Council in a more balanced way.

The Lisbon IGC kept this balance, which is reflected in Article 314 TFEU. These provisions represent the first major change in the rules governing the adoption of the EU budget in thirty-five years. The main

---

10 See point 22 of the Interinstitutional agreement on budgetary discipline and sound financial management of 17 May 2006 (OJ No. C136, 14 June 2006, 1).

11 On this issue, see Declaration no. 59 made by the Netherlands.

characteristics of these changes are the simplification of the procedure and the increase in the European Parliament's powers.

The abolition of the distinction between compulsory and non-compulsory expenditure is the most significant and far-reaching change. The last word that each of the arms of the budgetary authority used to have on a part of the EU expenditure has now been replaced by a simplified codecision on all budget lines. It may be argued, even if this does not explicitly result from the provisions of the Treaty, that the same should prevail not only on the establishment of the budget, but also when adjusting the budgetary provisions in the course of the budgetary exercise (the transfers process). The Financial Regulation which was in force on 1 December 2009 will need to be amended in this respect.[12] This will, in principle, give more powers to the European Parliament, which will have a say on 100 per cent of the budget. However, this conclusion must be counterbalanced by the change in the procedure (see below).

The first stages of the annual budgetary process are not affected as compared with the pre-Lisbon era. However, after the – now single – reading of the draft budget by each of the two arms of the budgetary authority, typically in late October of year n-1, a new landscape opens up. Save for the (most improbable) cases where the European Parliament will approve without any amendment the Council common position, and/or where the Council approves all the European Parliament amendments, representatives of the European Parliament and of the Council will meet in a Conciliation Committee. That Committee then will have twenty-one days to produce a joint text. This will be a formidable challenge for the European Parliament and for the Council, both from a substantive and a logistics point of view. In the past practice, each institution focused on 'its' part of the budget, knowing that, as for the rest, the other branch had a decisive influence. Under the TFEU, the two arms of the budgetary authority will have to agree on each and every one of the (approximately) 1,700 budget lines, and settle several hundred EP amendments (480 in 2009). Moreover, agreement will have to be translated into a fully legal text in all EU languages, in view of the accomplishment of the procedure in the final stages. In the case where the Conciliation Committee is not be able to agree on such a joint text within the twenty-one-day time frame, the budgetary procedure will start all over again, with the Commission submitting a new draft budget.

12 See Art. 24 of the Financial Regulation 1605/2002 of 25 June 2002 (OJ No. L248, 16 September 2002, 1).

This will be a real challenge for all, which should begin with the organisation and planning for the Conciliation Committee, to be agreed upon, if possible in advance, by the European Parliament and the Council. Then, the twenty-one-day deadline and the number of persons involved (27 + 27 + the Commission + the General Secretariat of the Council) will necessarily entail the organisation of preliminary, informal but in-depth contacts between a few representatives of both deciding institutions, with the help of the Commission.

In the case where the Conciliation Committee produces a joint text, the final stages of the process are exhaustively regulated in Article 314(6) to (8) TFEU. The joint text is submitted to the Council and the European Parliament for approval, which has to come within fourteen days. All possible outcomes of the process are foreseen in detail by the Treaty, together with their consequences, the political balance of which has been finely tuned by the Treaty's authors:

- If both the European Parliament and the Council approve the joint text, or one approves it and the other fails to take a decision, the budget is deemed to have been approved;
- if both the European Parliament (by a majority of its component members) and the Council reject the joint text, or one rejects it and the other fails to act, the budget is deemed to have been rejected and the budgetary procedure starts all over again, the Commission having to submit a new draft budget;
- if the European Parliament (by a majority of its component members) rejects the joint text and the Council approves it, the result is the same: the budgetary procedure starts all over again, the Commission having to submit a new draft budget;
- if the European Parliament approves the joint text whilst the Council rejects it, the European Parliament may, within (an additional) fourteen days from the Council's rejection and by a reinforced majority (a majority of its component members and three-fifths of the votes cast) confirm its amendments on the draft budget. Should this happen, the budget is deemed to have been adopted on that basis. Where an amendment has not been confirmed under those circumstances, the joint text reached at the conciliation prevails.

Tight timelines, and tough consequences in case of failure, translate the strong will of the authors of the Treaty to bring more discipline into the EU annual budgetary process. Indeed, possible differences between the two arms of the budgetary authority, if not resolved quickly, can lead to a major upheaval. The restarting of the budgetary procedure in the final two months of the year would cause delays to and disruption of EU business, and almost certainly entail recourse to the 'provisional twelfths' (Article 315 TFEU). The two branches of the budgetary authority would probably think twice before going down that road. The TFEU offers only one case where such consequences can be staved off: this will happen when the Council rejects the joint text, and the European Parliament maintains its amendments on the draft budget by a reinforced majority (majority of the component members of the European Parliament *and* three-fifths of the votes cast),[13] thus 'saving' the budget. It should be noted, however, that this is a highly unlikely scenario: it would indeed be extraordinary that the Council rejects a text that its representatives have approved at the conciliation, given the cohesion and the hierarchical relationship between the latter and the former. More unpredictable is the vote of the Plenary of the European Parliament on the results that its representatives have achieved at the Conciliation Committee; if negative, such a vote leads to the rejection of the budget, as foreseen in Article 314(7)(c) TFEU.

Further formal changes have been brought to the budget by the Lisbon Treaty, compared with the provisions under the TEC. Under the TFEU, the budget is no longer a *sui generis* decision but a legislative act (see introductory part of Article 314 which refers to a 'special legislative procedure'),[14] established on a proposal by the Commission (Article 314(2) TFEU). The budget being a legislative act, the Council is obliged to meet in public when it deliberates and votes on it (Article 16(8) TEU). However, Protocol no. 2 on the application of the principles of subsidiarity and proportionality is not applicable because the budget is, by its very nature, an instrument which belongs to the exclusive competence of the EU, and to which, therefore, the principle of subsidiarity does not apply (Article 5(3) TEU).

Finally, the practice of 'budgetary trilogue', which had already existed for several years, has been 'officialised' through Article 324 TFEU into regular meetings between the three institutions involved in the budgetary procedure (the European Parliament, the Council and the Commission).

*

The balance of powers between the two arms of the budgetary authority has been modified by the Lisbon Treaty. The rule according to which there

---

13 See Art. 314(7)(d) TFEU.
14 In accordance with Art. 289(3) TFEU: 'legal act adopted by a legislative procedure shall constitute legislative acts'.

can be no EU budget without the European Parliament's support has been maintained, but the European Parliament now has full powers over the 'compulsory expenditure'. This, together with the codecision power the European Parliament has gained on agricultural legislative acts, will give the European Parliament much greater deciding power on the common agricultural policy than before.

This will also allow the European Parliament to play with its budgetary power in order to try to obtain powers that the Treaty has not conferred upon it. Over the years, the European Parliament has become quite a good player in this political game, where the legal rules, even of a primary law level, are sometimes ignored (see Box 36).

BOX 36. A PARTICULAR EXAMPLE OF THE EXTENSIVE USE BY THE EUROPEAN PARLIAMENT OF ITS BUDGETARY POWERS*

The expenses of the EU Council in the ESDP field

But the issue goes far deeper than mere presentation techniques; we can detect an underlying malaise within the European Parliament on this issue and, at the time of writing, it is uncertain how this will develop in a new legislature. Because of the 'gentlemen's agreement', Parliament would not normally see a droit de regard on the Council's budget, but there is a feeling there that this particular expenditure in the ESDP field, despite assurances that such expenditure is in no way 'operational', should in fact not be shielded from scrutiny by being incorporated in the Council's budget in this way, albeit transparently. Watch this space! This issue between Parliament and Council, which has so far mercifully not even developed into a major skirmish, is the perfect example perhaps of what this chapter has tried to demonstrate: that ongoing budget negotiations are not really about figures (the ESDP budget within the Council budget is microscopic) but about institutional prerogatives.

* W. Nicoll and M. Bryan-Kinns, 'The Budget Procedure', in Nicoll and Bryan-Kinns, *The Council of the European Union*, 3rd edn (London: John Harper Publishing, 2004), 111.

The Financial Regulation and other issues

In accordance with the modifications introduced by the Lisbon Treaty, the **Financial Regulation** is now adopted in codecision with the European Parliament, after consultation of the Court of Auditors, while it was in the past adopted only after consultation of the European Parliament (Article 322(1) TFEU). In addition, the unanimity requirement for the Council 'to determine the methods and procedure whereby the budget revenue provided under the EU's own resources shall be made available to the Commission' has been replaced by QMV (Article 322(2) TFEU).

The provisions on **own resources** remain largely the same as previously. The content of Article 6(4) former TEU, under which 'the Union shall provide itself with the means necessary to attain its objectives and carry through its policies' has been inserted at the beginning of Article 311 TFEU on own resources. Otherwise, the adoption of the Own Resources Decision remains submitted to unanimity and still requires the prior approval of Member States 'in accordance with their respective constitutional requirements' (Article 311, 3rd subparagraph, TEU). The Lisbon Treaty added a last subparagraph which enables the Council, by QMV and with the European Parliament's consent, to 'lay down implementing measures for the Union's own resources system in so far as this is provided for in the [Own Resources Decision]'.

As to the provision on **combating fraud** which affects the financial interests of the Union, it remains largely the same, save for the deletion of the last sentence in Article 280(4) TEC, which excluded a measure concerning the application of national criminal law or the national administration of justice (see Article 325(4) TFEU). It should also be recalled that the EU has the possibility to establish a European Public Prosecutor's Office designed 'to combat crimes affecting the financial interests of the Union' (Article 86 TFEU).

The '**discharge procedure**' remains the same as before the Lisbon Treaty (Article 319 TFEU).

Section 38 European monetary union and the euro zone

In substance, the EU and EC Treaties provisions on economic and monetary policy remain broadly unchanged. However, the Lisbon Treaty has added important provisions designed to strengthen what is sometimes named the 'economic governance' in the euro zone – that is, the ability of the Council to contribute to a better management of the euro zone.

A short history of economic and monetary issues in the EU

The original Rome Treaty addressed only briefly the issue of co-ordination of the economic and monetary policies of the Member States. Article 6(1) of the original EEC Treaty provided for a general obligation for Member

States to 'co-ordinate their respective economic policies to the extent necessary to attain the objectives of the Treaty'. Article 145 (later Article 202 TEC) stated that the Council was to 'ensure co-ordination of the general economic policies of the Member States'. Articles 103 to 109 of the original EEC Treaty dealt with conjunctural policy, exchange-rate policies of the Member States and assistance and safeguard procedures in case of balance-of-payment difficulties.

In 1964, the Commission recommended the strengthening of monetary co-operation in meetings of ministers of finance and within the Monetary Committee. A Committee of the Governors of the Central Banks was established. The six Member States agreed to consult each other before modifying exchange rates of their currency. At the end of 1968, the 'Barre Plan', named after the then Vice-President of the Commission, Raymond Barre, recommended a closer co-ordination of the economic policies of the Member States and the establishment of a Community arrangement for monetary co-operation.[15] The Barre Plan was highly contested, but it generated a lively debate. At the end of 1969, the six heads of state or government, at their summit in The Hague, stated that 'a plan in stages should be worked out during 1970 with a view to the creation of an economic and monetary union'.[16] That was the first time that the aim of an economic and monetary union (EMU) was agreed upon.

In 1970, the Werner Committee, named after its chairman who was then the Prime Minister and Finance Minister of Luxembourg, presented a report on the progressive realisation in three stages of an EMU.[17] The heads of state or government of the six Member States, meeting in Paris in 1972, agreed on the principle of this objective. From the very beginning, the reasons for the creation of the EMU were more political than economical. The EMU was intended to be one of the essential elements of European political integration.

In 1971–3, the implosion of the Bretton Woods system of fixed exchange rates, combined with the first oil crisis, created serious disturbances in the exchange rates between the Member States, which held up the move towards EMU.

---

15 'Commission Memorandum to the Council on the Coordination of Economic Policies and Monetary Cooperation within the Community' (Bulletin of the EC, No. 3-1969).
16 'Third General Report on the Activities of the Community' – 1969.
17 Rapport au Conseil et à la Commission concernant la réalisation par étapes de l'UEM dans la Communauté (OJ No. C136, 11 November 1970, 1).

In 1979, the European Monetary System (EMS) was established. It consisted of an exchange-rate mechanism (ERM), outside the Treaty, based on a non-legally binding instrument – that is, a Resolution of the European Council of 5 December 1978.[18] The Resolution left it to each Member State to decide whether or not to join the EMS. The EMS was based on the European Currency Unit (ECU), which was a basket currency, consisting of fixed amounts of each Member State currency. The central rates were used to establish a grid of bilateral exchange rates, with in principle 2.5 per cent margin fluctuations. The EMS lasted until the launch of the euro in 1999.

The 1986 Single European Act did not add much to that, apart from adding the words 'Economic and Monetary Union' in the title of the chapter on Co-operation in economic and monetary policy. Nevertheless, the liberalisation of capital movements triggered by the Single European Act boosted the idea of a fully fledged EMU. In June 1988, the European Council met in Hanover and established a Committee to study and propose concrete stages leading towards monetary union. The Delors Committee, chaired by the President of the Commission, sketched out in its 1989 Report the main aspects of the future EMU. This was the basis of the relevant provisions of the 1992 Maastricht Treaty.

The provisions of the Maastricht Treaty on EMU have not been modified in substance by the Amsterdam and Nice Treaties.

In three phases, the implementation of the Maastricht Treaty led to the introduction, on 1 January 1999, of a single currency, the euro,[19] in eleven Member States out of fifteen – that is, without Denmark and the United Kingdom, which had a derogation Protocol, and without Greece and Sweden, which did not fulfil the convergence criteria. Greece joined two years later, in January 2001, and the euro became a physical reality, in notes and coins, on 1 January 2002. Then Slovenia (2007), Cyprus and Malta (2008) and Slovakia (2009) later joined the euro zone.

Right from the beginning, the transfer of powers from the Member States concerned essentially their monetary powers, while their fiscal, budgetary and economic powers remained intact. This is why the European Council, building on Article 99 TEC, under which 'Member States shall regard their economic policies as a matter of common concern and

---

18 EC Bulletin No. 12.
19 The name 'euro' was chosen in 1995, at the Madrid European Council of 15–16 December 1995 (see doc. 400/95).

shall co-ordinate them within the Council', and on Article 104(1) TEC, under which 'Member States shall avoid excessive government deficits', adopted in Amsterdam in June 1997 the Stability and Growth Pact.[20] This Pact was modified, taking into account the difficulties in its implementation, by the European Council in March 2005: 'Improving the Implementation of the Stability and Growth Pact'.[21] However, the financial and economic crisis which began in 2008 again demonstrated the difficulties which Member Sates have in applying these rules.

The modifications brought about by the Lisbon Treaty

Both in the Convention and in the 2003–4 and Lisbon IGCs, particular emphasis was put on improving economic governance within the EU, particularly within the euro zone. This emphasis has been kept in the Lisbon Treaty. The Treaty confirms that the monetary policy is an exclusive competence of the EU for the Member States whose currency is the euro (Article 3(1)(c) TFEU).

On the drafting side, the provisions of Chapters 2 to 4 of the TEC on monetary matters, which had not been 'cleaned up' during the simplification exercise which had been carried out in the Amsterdam Treaty (in particular the deletion of obsolete provisions) have been reorganised, and the obsolete parts (i.e. the transitional provisions applicable only during the period before the putting into place of the euro and of the ECB) have been deleted. Therefore, although still complex, the reading is easier.

As part of this restructuring of the Chapters, a number of provisions 'specific to Member States whose currency is the euro' have been regrouped (in Chapter 4 of Title VIII on economic and monetary policy). The vocabulary used has been clarified: the 'euro-ins' are now, throughout, called 'Member States whose currency is the euro' (instead of 'Member States without a derogation' in the TEC), while the 'euro-outs' remain 'Member States with a derogation' and the provisions which concern them are now to be found mainly in the Chapter on transitional provisions (Chapter 5).

---

20 Presidency Conclusions, European Council, Amsterdam, 16–17 June 1997 (sn 150/97) (see OJ No. C236, 2 August 1997, 1. Regulations were adopted later on (nos. 1466/97 and 1467/97).

21 Presidency Conclusions, European Council, 22–23 March 2005 (doc. 7619/1/05 REV 1). Regulations were adopted in June 2005 (no. 1055/2005 and no. 1056/2005, OJ No. L174, 7 July 2005, 1).

Improved decision-making and representation for the euro zone

The legal basis contained in the penultimate sentence of Article 123(4) TEC (in the Chapter on transitional provisions) which enabled the Council, by QMV (of the 'euro-ins'), to 'take the . . . measures necessary for the rapid introduction of the ecu as the single currency of [the euro-in] Member States', was still being used after the introduction of the euro for all the measures needed afterwards. It has now been transformed into a proper legal basis for the future. It enables the European Parliament and the Council, by codecision, 'to lay down the measures necessary for the use of the euro as the single currency' (Article 133 TFEU).

Important powers are given to the Council, with only those Council members representing Member States whose currency is the euro (the 'euro-ins') having the right to vote, to strengthen co-ordination and surveillance of 'euro-ins' budget policies and set out economic policy guidelines for them (Article 136 TFEU).

The 'euro-ins' will have to give their prior acceptance to a new member joining the euro (Article 140(2), 2nd subparagraph, TFEU).

The existence of the Eurogroup, which consists of the 'euro-ins' finance ministers, is formally recognised. The Lisbon Treaty provides that it is chaired for two and a half years by a president elected by his/her peers (Article 137 TFEU and Protocol no. 14 on the Eurogroup).[22]

As for the international representation of the euro, there is not much change. The provisions enabling the Council to adopt by QMV (with only the 'euro-ins' voting) 'a decision establishing common positions on matters of particular interest for economic and monetary union within the competent international financial institutions and conferences' and to adopt 'appropriate measures to ensure a unified representation within the international financial institutions and conferences' (Article 138(1) TFEU) were already in existence (Article 111(4) TEC). They are not substantially modified. One may note the deletion, from Article 138(1) TFEU, of the introductory phrase which, in Article 111(4) TEC, made the use of the Council's powers 'subject to paragraph 1' of Article 111 TEC which empowered the Council to conclude, by unanimity, agreements on an exchange-rate system for the euro in relation to non-EC currencies.[23]

---

22 The Eurogroup has been chaired since 1 January 2005 by Jean-Claude Juncker, Prime Minister and Treasury Minister of Luxembourg.

23 The provisions on the conclusion of agreements in this field are now in the Title on international agreements, in Art. 219 TFEU, which takes over provisions from Art. 111(1) to (3) and (5) TEC.

Article 138(1) TFEU provides that the Council 'shall adopt a decision establishing common positions on matters of particular interest for EMU within the competent international financial institutions and conferences'. This provision is similar to Article 111(4) TEC, which used the words 'decide on the position of the Community at international level as regards issues of particular relevance to EMU and its representation'. Despite this legal obligation and the fact that it could act by QMV, the Council has never implemented this provision.

It is to be noted that, contrary to the previous rule, the measures to ensure the representation of EMU within the competent international institutions and conferences are not legally obligatory any more ('may' instead of 'shall').

The European Central Bank has formally become an 'institution' (Article 13(1) TEU), which will not affect its independence. The Lisbon Treaty enables the European Council to make appointments to the Executive Board of the European Central Bank by QMV instead of common accord (Article 283(2) TFEU). Moreover, amendments to the Statute of the European System of Central Banks and of the European Central Bank are now subject to adoption by codecision (i.e. QMV, instead of unanimity; see Article 129(3) TFEU) or by the Council alone, by QMV, also when proposed by the Commission (Article 129(4) TFEU), while, before, QMV applied only when such amendments were recommended by the Central Bank itself (Article 107(5) TEC).

Finally, the IGC adopted a Declaration to stress the importance of the Stability and Growth Pact (see Declaration no. 30 on Article 126 TFEU).

Improved decision-making in the area of economic and monetary policy

The Lisbon Treaty abolishes the so-called 'co-operation procedure' (the ancestor of codecision), which, in the EC Treaty, remained in use only in the field of EMU.

Despite the wish of the Commission and of some Member States, the Council acts in relation to the co-ordination of national economic policies and excessive government deficits will continue, as was the case before the Lisbon Treaty, to be taken mainly upon a Commission *recommendation*, rather than upon a Commission *proposal* (Articles 121 and 126 TFEU). The only exception is the first sentence of Article 126(6) TFEU on the existence of an excessive deficit in a Member State, where the Council will act on a proposal, instead of a recommendation from the Commission (as was the case under Article 104(6) TEC). The significance of this distinction is that Article 293(1) TFEU, pursuant to which the Council may amend Commission proposals only by acting unanimously, does not apply to recommendations (or other acts such as drafts, initiatives, etc.). The Council may therefore amend the latter as part of the process of adopting the act recommended by the Commission and by using the same QMV rule as provided for the adoption of the act.[24]

*

The creation of the euro was certainly a decisive moment in the history of the EU. The EMU is unique in history, as it is based on a single market and establishes a single currency for sovereign States, while they keep their powers in the budgetary and fiscal fields, albeit accepting a convergence of their economic policies. This situation, confronted with the effect of the financial and economic crisis which began in 2008, is expected to promote further economic and financial integration, at least in the euro zone. EMU is a work in progress. It has created an era of monetary stability, but it brings at the same time risks and responsibilities and, therefore, the need to improve further the co-ordination of budgetary and economic policies in the Member States of the euro zone. On this issue, one has to recognize that this budgetary and economic convergence has not improved over the years.[25]

Section 39 The internal market and free competition

In its Article 3(1)(g) on the means to be used by the Community to achieve its objectives, the EC Treaty included the following commitment to undistorted competition: 'For the purposes set out in Article 2 [on EC objectives], the activities of the Community shall include, as provided in this Treaty and in accordance with the timetable set out therein: ... (g) a

---

24 However, when the Council does not act on the basis of a Commission proposal, but on the basis of another act such as a recommendation, the type of QMV to be used will be the one with the higher threshold (see Art. 238(2) TFEU which provides in this case a threshold of at least 72 per cent of the Council Members, in addition to the threshold of at least 65 per cent of the EU population). This requirement of a more 'difficult' QMV when the Council does not act on the basis of a Commission proposal has always existed in the Treaties.

25 See D. H. Bearce, 'EMU: The Last Stand for the Policy Convergence Hypothesis?' (2009) *Journal of European Public Policy*, special issue on ten years of EMU, 582, in particular 597: 'economic policy convergence among the euro area countries has not continued after 1999 and may have reversed in certain dimensions. For policy-makers, the lack of policy convergence means that European monetary union rests on fragile foundations.'

The Lisbon Treaty brings a few modifications which will be described below, without modifying the fact that social policy remains essentially in the hands of the Member States authorities.

*

In its Article 2 on the **values** of the Union on which the Union is founded, the EU Treaty places among them 'human dignity', 'equality', 'the rights of persons belonging to minorities' and 'solidarity and equality between women and men'.[36] Moreover, among the objectives of the Union, listed by Article 3 TEU, are 'the well-being of its peoples' (paragraph 1), the establishment of a 'highly competitive social market economy, aiming at full employment and social progress' and its commitment to 'combat social exclusion and discrimination', to 'promote social justice and protection, equality between women and men, solidarity between generations and protection of the rights of the child' (paragraph 3).

The Lisbon Treaty adds a new **'horizontal' social clause**, Article 9 TFEU, according to which the EU must take into account, in the definition and implementation of all its policies and activities, the 'requirements linked to the promotion of a high level of employment, the guarantee of adequate social protection, the fight against social exclusion, and a high level of education, training and protection of human health.' The adoption of this clause was considered important by some delegations (Belgium and France in particular). It is a legally binding clause for the institutions and, as such, its respect by the EU institutions is subject to the control of the Court of Justice.

Moreover, measures in the field of **social security**, based on Article 48 TFEU, which are necessary to bring about freedom of movement for migrant workers and their dependants, have been switched to QMV and codecision and their scope has been extended to cover also self-employed workers. These concern technical measures such as the aggregation, for the purpose of acquiring and retaining the right to benefit and of calculating the amount of benefit, of the periods spent in different Member States, and the payment of benefits to persons residing in another Member State.

The procedure of the so-called 'emergency brake' will, however, be applicable in this case. According to this procedure, if a Member State considers that a draft legislative act 'would affect important aspects of

36 It is recalled that a 'risk of a serious breach by a Member State of the values referred to in Art. 2' might lead to the suspension procedure established by Art. 7 TEU and that the respect of (and the commitment to promote) these values is one of the conditions required to become a Member State of the Union (Art. 49, 1st subpara., TEU).

its social security system, including its scope, cost or financial structure, or would affect the financial balance of that system',[37] it can bring the matter to the European Council.[38] In that case, the codecision procedure is suspended for a duration of four months. After discussion, the European Council must either refer the draft back to the Council, which will terminate the suspension of the procedure, or request the Commission to submit a new proposal, in which case the act originally proposed is deemed not to have been adopted (see Article 48, 2nd subparagraph, TFEU).

This was one of the famous 'red lines' of the UK government. Therefore QMV will be the rule 'in principle' but, if one Member State insists, it may obtain a right of veto. However, to do that, the government of the Member State concerned will have to bring the matter to the European Council and that, probably, will happen only in the case of serious problems.

Apart from that, the provisions on social policy remain broadly the same as they were before the Lisbon Treaty. Article 153 TFEU on social policy is identical to Article 137 TEC. Therefore,

- as before, the European Parliament and the Council are empowered to adopt in codecision, the Council using QMV, 'minimum requirements' for certain matters. QMV thus continues to apply for adopting measures on the protection of workers' health and safety, working conditions, information and consultation of workers, integration of persons excluded from the labour market and equality between men and women with regard to labour market opportunities and treatment at work;
- as before, unanimity is still applicable in the Council for the adoption of 'minimum requirements' in the most sensitive matters, such as social security and social protection. Unanimity thus continues to apply for adopting measures on social security and social protection for workers, protection of workers where their employment contract is terminated, the representation and collective defence of the interests of workers and employers and conditions of employment of third-country nationals;[39]

---

37 See also Declaration no. 22 on Arts. 48 and 79 TFEU.
38 Declaration no. 23 recalls that in that case, in accordance with Art. 15(4) TEU, the European Council acts by consensus.
39 One could note that point (g) of Art. 153(1) TFEU on conditions of employment for third-country nationals legally resident in the Union appears to be redundant, as it is superseded by point (b) of Art. 79(2) TFEU on 'the definition of the rights of third-country nationals residing legally in a Member State' which can be regulated by QMV and codecision.

- as before, such minimum requirements 'shall not affect the right of Member States to define the fundamental principles of their social security systems and must not significantly affect the financial equilibrium of such systems' and 'shall not prevent any Member State from maintaining or introducing more stringent protective measures compatible with the Treaties' (Article 153(4) TFEU);
- as before, 'pay, the right of association, the right to strike or the right to impose lockouts' continue to be excluded from EU competence and remain a national competence (Article 153(5) TFEU).

The Lisbon Treaty has also retained the *passerelle* allowing for the Council, acting unanimously on a proposal from the Commission, after consulting the European Parliament, to decide to switch to QMV and codecision with regard to the adoption of minimum requirements on the list of matters which are now submitted to unanimity (see Article 153(2), 4th subparagraph, TFEU), with the exception of social security and social protection.

It has also retained the possibility for social partners, management and labour, to conclude at Union level agreements on matters covered by Article 153 TFEU, which, at their joint request, may be transformed into a decision of the Council binding throughout the EU (Article 155 TFEU, which is similar to Article 139 TEC).[40]

Article 152 TFEU has introduced a special reference to the **role of the social partners** at the level of the EU. It commits the EU to facilitate dialogue between the social partners and it refers to the fact that the 'Tripartite Social Summit for Growth and Employment'[41] shall contribute to this social dialogue.

One may also mention that Article 3 TEU makes a reference to the protection of the rights of the child as one of the objectives of the EU.

Finally, Article 6(1), 1st subparagraph, TEU, by conferring on the Charter of Fundamental Rights the same legal value as the Treaties, gives the

---

40 Four of those 'agreements' have been adopted by social partners and transformed into Council directives (Directive 96/34 on parental leave, Directive 1999/63 on the working time of seafarers, Directive 1999/70 on fixed-term work and Directive 2000/79 on the working time of mobile workers in civil aviation).

41 The Tripartite Social Summit for Growth and Employment takes place once a year, before the Spring European Council. It has been established by a Decision of the Council 2003/174/EC of 6 March 2003 (OJ No. L70, 14.3.2003, 31–33).

same legal value to the provisions of the Charter in the social field. However, it has to be stressed (see Section 19) that these provisions are essentially addressed to the EU institutions when they legislate and that the 'provisions of the Charter shall not extend in any way the competences of the Union as defined in the Treaties' (Article 6(1), 2nd subparagraph TEU).

*

The Lisbon Treaty has strengthened the commitment of the EU to social progress and to social rights. However, the fact remains that social policy is a competence which is shared between the EU and its Member States and that the EU has only a small share of that competence – that is, on the aspects defined in the TFEU (Article 4(2)(a) TFEU). The few cases in which progress has been made, such as the horizontal social clause and a very limited switch to QMV in the Council, should not hide the fact that social policy remains, essentially, within the competences of the Member States.[42] This corresponds to the political will of the majority of them.

Section 41 Services of general interest

Initially, European integration was about the establishment of an internal market and respect for free competition. Services of general interest which cannot operate according exclusively to market rules had been treated as exceptions.

It is only in the Amsterdam Treaty, in 1997, that an Article 16 was introduced in the TEC which recognised 'the place occupied by services of general economic interest in the shared values of the Union as well as their role in promoting social and territorial cohesion'. Article 16 TEC provided also that 'the Community and the Member States, each within their respective powers and within the scope of application of this Treaty, shall take care that such services operate on the basis of principles and conditions which enable them to fulfil their missions'. It is to be stressed

---

42 See Declaration no. 31 on Art. 156 TFEU under which 'the Conference confirms that the policies described in Art. 156 fall essentially within the competence of the Member States'. According to the German Constitutional Court in its 30 June 2009 judgment, 'the essential decisions in social policy must be made by the German legislative bodies' (para. 259). The Court otherwise gave a rather positive description and analysis of the social policy followed so far by the EU (see paras. 392 to 400). In particular, it said that the allegation made by the complainants according to which European economic policy would be purely market-oriented without any social-policy orientation is incorrect (para. 393). Even the case law of the EU Court of Justice was found to have shown a series of elements for a 'social Europe' (para. 398).

that Article 16 began with the terms, 'Without prejudice to Articles 73, 86 and 87 [TEC]', in order to preserve the application of Article 73 on public services in the area of transport and of Articles 86 and 87 on competition and on State aid.

The EU Charter of Fundamental Rights also contains a provision under which 'the Union recognises and respects access to services of general economic interest as provided for in national laws and practices, in accordance with the Treaties, in order to promote the social and territorial cohesion of the Union' (Article 36). As stressed in the Explanations relating to the Charter, this Article does not create any new right. It merely sets out the principle of respect by the EU for the access to services of general economic interest as provided for by national provisions, when those provisions are compatible with EU legislation.

Despite the fact that these provisions had an important political and symbolic impact, their legal effect was weak.

In 2002, the European Council

> [underlined] the importance for citizens, and for territorial and social cohesion, of access to services of general economic interest . . . [It asked] the Commission to . . . continue its examination with a view to consolidating and specifying the principles on services of general economic interest, which underline Article 16 of the Treaty, in a proposal for a framework directive, while respecting the specificities of the different sectors involved and taking into account the provisions of Article 86 of the Treaty. The Commission will present a report by the end of the year.[43]

Despite those conclusions, the Commission, in a 'White Book' of 2004, concluded that it was better not to make such a proposal for the time being.[44]

The issue was raised with some passion during the referendum campaign on the Constitutional Treaty, both in the Netherlands and in France. The situation was exacerbated in the Netherlands, following decisions taken by the Commission on the Dutch system of financial help to social housing. Therefore one of the prerequisites of the Dutch government, when negotiating the June 2007 IGC mandate, was to obtain Treaty provisions on this issue.

The Lisbon Treaty brought two important changes to the prevailing legal situation.

---

43 Presidency Conclusions, Barcelona European Council, 15 and 16 March 2002, para. 42.
44 COM (2004) 374 final.

First, as the failed Constitutional Treaty already had, it added to the provision on services of general economic interest a legal basis enabling the European Parliament and the Council, by codecision, to legislate on this matter by '[establishing] these principles and set these conditions without prejudice to the competence of Member States, in compliance with the Treaties, to provide, to commission and to fund such services' (Article 14 TFEU, which corresponds to Article 16 TEC). The preceding sentence stresses that the principles and conditions at issue are 'particularly economic and financial conditions'.

Second, the Lisbon IGC adopted, on the initiative of the Dutch government, a new Protocol on services of general interest (Box 38).

BOX 38. PROTOCOL NO. 26 ON SERVICES OF GENERAL INTEREST

THE HIGH CONTRACTING PARTIES,

WISHING to emphasise the importance of services of general interest,

HAVE AGREED UPON the following interpretative provisions, which shall be annexed to the [TEU] and to the [TFEU]:

Article 1

The shared values of the Union in respect of services of general economic interest within the meaning of Article 14 of the [TFEU] include in particular:

- the essential role and the wide discretion of national, regional and local authorities in providing, commissioning and organising services of general economic interest as closely as possible to the needs of the users;
- the diversity between various services of general economic interest and the differences in the needs and preferences of users that may result from different geographical, social or cultural situations;
- a high level of quality, safety and affordability, equal treatment and the promotion of universal access and of user rights.

Article 2

The provisions of the Treaties do not affect in any way the competence of Member States to provide, commission and organise non-economic services of general interest.

Therefore, notwithstanding the follow-up which might or not be given by the Commission to the new legal basis in Article 14 TFEU, Protocol no. 26 does in any case establish new and fundamental rules which have Treaty value.

*

The Commission has let it be known, in a 2007 Communication,[45] that it still has doubts on the opportunity to legislate on this matter. It seems to consider that the Protocol will be sufficient. Some Member States are of another opinion, and will probably insist in future that the Commission uses its power to propose a regulation on the basis of Article 14 TFEU.[46] Whatever might happen in the field of secondary law, Protocol no. 26, which has Treaty legal value, will probably have consequences in the way the Treaty has to be interpreted in this area.

Section 42 Agriculture, energy, health and other internal affairs

The Lisbon Treaty did not much change the extent of EU competences in the areas of activities mentioned in this section. However, some changes have been made concerning some of these activities, either on the exact definition of the EU competence or on the procedures to be followed to adopt decisions.

Agriculture and fisheries

The common agricultural policy (CAP) was one of the first Community policies and it still is one of the most integrated ones. It also represents an important part of the EU budget, albeit in constant decrease: it represented 60 per cent of the budget in the 1990s; it represented 42 per cent of the 2009 budget – that is, 56 billion euros, including 41 billion for the CAP expenses proper[47] and the rest for rural development, less than 1 billion being for fisheries. Expenses have been frozen until 2013 at their 2006 level. France is the main beneficiary of CAP (23 per cent of the total expenses, compared with 14.5 per cent for Spain, 13.1 per cent for Germany, 12.1 per cent for Italy and 8.9 per cent for the United Kingdom). The CAP has been under constant reform since the 1990s, in particular with regard to the decoupling of production and aids and the rural development policy.

---

45 Communication of 20 November 2007 on Services of General Interest (doc. COM [2007] 725 final).

46 See, e.g., in France, the Report of the Senate, 'Les services d'intérêt général après le Traité de Lisbonne', Délégation pour l'UE, Senate, no. 376, 4 June 2008.

47 Therefore expenses for cohesion (48.4 billion euros in 2009) are now more important.

The extent of the competences of the EU in this area has not been modified by the Lisbon Treaty. The only changes concern the decision-making procedure, but they are very important, because they greatly increase the European Parliament's powers.

The **decision-making procedure** which was previously applicable in all cases – that is, QMV in the Council and consultation of the European Parliament (Article 37 TEC) – has been replaced by two procedures, contained in Article 43(2) and (3) TFEU, which differ depending on the type of measures:

- the ordinary legislative procedure (codecision) now applies for establishing the common organisation of agriculture markets and other provisions necessary for the pursuit of the objectives of the common agricultural policy and the common fisheries policy (Article 43(2) TFEU, which provides also for the consultation of the Economic and Social Committee);
- QMV in the Council, on a proposal from the Commission (without consultation of the European Parliament) for adopting the measures on fixing prices, levies, aid and quantitative limitations, and on the fixing and allocation of fishing opportunities (Article 43(3) TFEU). Because the words 'legislative procedure' are not mentioned in the legal basis, the measures adopted on that basis are not legislative acts.

The **budgetary procedure** (see Section 37) has increased the European Parliament's powers in decisions on agriculture spending, with the abolition of the previous distinction between the 'compulsory expenditure' (which were mainly CAP expenses) and the 'non-compulsory expenditure' (Article 31(4) TFEU). Before the Lisbon Treaty, the European Parliament had only a consultative role as far as the compulsory expenditure was concerned. With the Lisbon Treaty, the Council and the European Parliament have to agree on this part of the budget as well.

The extension of the European Parliament's powers in the procedure to be followed for the conclusion of international agreements by the EU will also affect agreements concerning agriculture and fisheries (see Article 218(6) TFEU).

Therefore with the Lisbon Treaty the European Parliament has gained a very important role in the area of agriculture and fisheries, through both its legislative and its budgetary powers. The impact of this increased role will certainly be significant in the future.

Energy

Before the Lisbon Treaty, the EC already had a competence to adopt legal acts in the area of energy.[48] To do this, the EC institutions could make use of Article 175 TEC (environmental protection),[49] Article 95 TEC (internal market),[50] Articles 155 and 156 TEC (trans-European networks)[51] and Article 100 TEC (difficulties in supply).[52]

The Council could act by QMV under Articles 155 and 156, but projects adopted on this basis which related to the territory of a Member State required the approval of the Member State concerned (Article 156, 2nd subparagraph, TEC). Acts based on Article 95 TEC required QMV and codecision. Acts adopted under Article 175 TEC required QMV and co-decision, but a number of exceptions required unanimity, among them 'measures significantly affecting a Member State's choice between different energy sources and the general structure of its energy supply' (Article 175(2)(c) TEC).

With the Lisbon Treaty, Member States have decided to confer an explicit and general competence on the EU in the area of energy – that is, Article 194 TFEU (Box 39). Article 4(2)(i) TFEU lists energy among the areas in which competences are shared between the EU and the Member States.

Measures in this area will be adopted by QMV and in codecision. However, there are two caveats:

- Article 194(2):[53] 'Such measures shall not affect a Member State's right to determine the conditions for exploiting its energy resources, its choice

---

48 Not to mention the powers of the ECSC and of Euratom in their specific fields of action.
49 Directive 2009/28/EC of the European Parliament and of the Council of 23 April 2009 on the promotion of the use of energy from renewable sources and amending and subsequently repealing Directives 2001/77/EC and 2003/30/EC (OJ No. L140, 5 June 2009, 16).
50 Regulation (EC) No. 1228/2003 of the European Parliament and of the Council of 26 June 2003 on conditions for access to the network for cross-border exchanges in electricity (OJ No. L176, 15 July 2003, 1).
51 Decision 1364/2006 of the European Parliament and the Council laying down guidelines for trans-European energy networks and repealing Decision 96/391 and Decision 1229/2003 (OJ No. L262, 22 September 2006, 1).
52 Council Directive 2004/67/EC of 26 April 2004 concerning measures to safeguard security of natural gas supply (OJ No. L127, 29 April 2004, 92).
53 See also Declaration no. 35 on Art. 194 TFEU: 'The Conference believes that Article 194 does not affect the right of the Member States to take the necessary measures to ensure their energy supply under the conditions provided for in Article 347.'

BOX 39. ARTICLE 194(1) TFEU ON ENERGY

In the context of the establishment and functioning of the internal market and with regard for the need to preserve and improve the environment, Union policy on energy shall aim, in a spirit of solidarity between Member States, to:

(a) ensure the functioning of the energy market;
(b) ensure security of energy supply in the Union;
(c) promote energy efficiency and energy saving and the development of new and renewable forms of energy; and
(d) promote the interconnection of energy networks.

---

between different energy sources and the general structure of its energy supply, without prejudice to Article 192(2)(c)';[54]

- Article 194(3): unanimity is required for measures which are 'primarily of a fiscal nature'.

A lot of comments have presented Article 194 TFEU as a major innovation establishing a new competence of the EU allowing it to act in the area of energy. However, it is difficult to affirm that the competences of the EU have actually been increased in the area of energy, taking into account the possibilities the EC already had to act on the basis of Articles 95, 155, 156, 175 and 308 TEC. These competences have been made explicit and codified in a single Article.

One has also to note the new formulation of Article 122(1) TFEU, which does not change the scope of former Article 100(1) TEC but is more precise, in allowing the Council to decide 'in a spirit of solidarity between Member States, upon the measures appropriate to the economic situation, in particular if severe difficulties arise in the supply of certain products, notably in the area of energy'.

Altogether, it is not obvious that the changes made by the Lisbon Treaty in the area of energy are legally significant. The competence of the EU is made clearer and more explicit but, apparently, not wider. This symbolises the growing importance attached to this area by the EU. One has also to note that the solidarity between Member States in this area is stressed twice in the Treaty, due in particular to requests from Poland and the Baltic countries.

---

54 Under Art. 175(2)(c) EC Treaty, the EC could act in this case, with unanimity in the Council.

Public health

Protection of public health is one of the basic requirements which the EU will have to take into account in any of its policies or activities (Article 9 TFEU).

Article 4(2) TFEU lists an aspect of public health as one of the competences which the EU shares with its Member States: '(k) common safety concerns in public health matters, for the aspects defined in this Treaty'.

Article 6 TFEU lists among the fields where the EU is competent to support, co-ordinate or supplement the actions of the Member States 'the protection and improvement of human health'.

On substance, the TFEU deals with public health in its Article 168. This Article adds two new kinds of measures to the list of measures which could, before the Lisbon Treaty, already be adopted by the EU:

- in its paragraph 4(c): (legislative) 'measures setting high standards of quality and safety for medicinal products and devices for medical use'. However, the adoption of such measures was already possible on the basis of Article 95 TEC.[55] One has to note that the legislative action of the EU in the areas mentioned in paragraph 4 could be regarded as being restricted by the addition of the words 'in order to meet common safety concerns';
- in its paragraph 5: (incentive) 'measures concerning monitoring, early warning of and combating serious cross-border threats to health, and measures which have as their direct objective the protection of public health regarding tobacco and the abuse of alcohol, excluding any harmonisation of the laws and regulations of the Member States'. Such actions had already been undertaken before the Lisbon Treaty.[56]

One could also note that, under paragraph 7, the competence of the Member States looks more protected now than before the Lisbon Treaty. While the former Article 152(5) TEC stated that the EC action in this area 'shall fully respect the responsibilities of the Member States for the organisation and delivery of health services and medical care', the new Article 168(7) TFEU adds that 'the responsibilities of the Member States shall include the management of health services and medical care and

---

55 Council Directive 93/42/EEC of 14 June 1993 concerning medical devices (OJ No. L169, 12 July 1993, 1).

56 On alcohol: see 'An EU Strategy to Support Member States in Reducing Alcohol Related Harm' (COM (2006)625 final of 24 October 2006). On tobacco: see Green Paper entitled 'Towards a Europe Free from Tobacco Smoke: Policy Options at EU level' (COM(2007)27 final of 30 January 2007).

the allocation of the resources assigned to them', restricting further the possibility of EU action.

On the whole, the scope of competence of the EU in the field of public health will remain more or less unchanged after the Lisbon Treaty. The definition of national policies in this field remains clearly an exclusive competence of the Member States.

Space

The Lisbon Treaty gives to the EU an explicit legal basis to act in the field of space policy, by expressly including space in Article 189 TFEU, in its Title XIX on research and technological development.

Article 189(1) TFEU, in particular, requires the Union 'to draw up a European space policy'. It goes on by specifying that 'To this end, it may promote joint initiatives, support research and technological development and co-ordinate the efforts needed for the exploration and exploitation of space.'

Article 189(2) specifies that the procedure to be followed is the ordinary legislative procedure in order to establish the necessary measures, which may take the form of 'a European space programme'.[57] Any harmonisation of the laws and regulations of the Member States is excluded: this precision is new as compared with the failed Constitutional Treaty.

Article 189(3) provides for the establishment of 'any appropriate relations [of the EU] with the European Space Agency'.[58]

Article 189(4) states that 'this Article shall be without prejudice to the other provisions of this Title', as Articles 179 to 188 might also be used for a policy in the field of space.

The new provisions on space policy (Article 173 TFEU) therefore codify a competence that the EU could already exercise on the basis of the previous EC provisions in the area of research and technological development and industry, as it had done, for instance, by adopting the Galileo programme.[59]

---

57 See, in this area, the resolution adopted by the Council on 22 May 2007 (doc. 10037/07).
58 The European Space Agency is an international intergovernmental organisation established in 1975 and distinct from the EU. At the time of writing, it had eighteen Member States, a staff of around 2,000 and a budget of 3.6 billion euros. Its main 'spaceport' is in Kourou (French Guyana). The EU and the ESA have concluded a framework agreement which entered into force in 2004.
59 Council Regulation (EC) 1321/2004 of 12 July 2004 on the establishment of structures for the management of the European satellite radio-navigation programmes (OJ No. L246, 20 July 2004, 1) and Regulation (EC) 683/2008 of the European Parliament and of the

Sport

Article 165 TFEU gives to the EU an explicit legal basis for acting in the field of sport, along with its possible actions in the area of education, vocational training and youth.

The possible action of the EU in this field is limited to supporting, co-ordinating or supplementing the action of the Member States (Article 6(e) TFEU). Any harmonisation of the laws and regulations of the Member States is excluded (Article 165(4)). The specific nature of sport, its structures based on voluntary action and its social and educational function are emphasised (Article 165(1), 2nd subparagraph). The aims given to the EU by Article 165 TFEU are:

- to 'contribute to the promotion of European sporting issues' (paragraph 1);
- to develop 'the European dimension in sport, by promoting fairness and openness in sporting competitions and co-operation between bodies responsible for sports, and by protecting the physical and moral integrity of sportsmen and sportswomen, especially the youngest sportsmen and sportswomen' (paragraph 2, last indent);
- to 'foster cooperation with third countries and the competent international organisations in the field of education and sport' (paragraph 3).

EU action was already possible in the area of sport before the Lisbon Treaty (see Declaration no. 29 of the Amsterdam IGC on sport and Declaration of the December 2000 Nice European Council). The Commission issued a White Paper on Sport in July 2007.[60]

It is recalled that the Court of Justice has decided several times that sport, as an economic activity, must respect European law, for instance with respect to the free movement of workers.[61]

Changes for other sectoral activities

The decision-making procedures in other sectoral activities have been changed by the Lisbon Treaty. For instance, the vote in the Council has been switched from unanimity to QMV for:

Council of 9 July 2009 on the further implementation of the European satellite navigation programmes (EGNOS and Galileo) (OJ No. L196, 24 July 2008, 1).

60 COM(2007) 391, 11.7.2007.
61 See judgment of 24 October 1974, Case 36/74, *Walrave*, [1974] ECR 1405, and judgment of 15 December 1995, Case C-415/93, *Bosman*, [1995] ECR, I-4921.

- provisions concerning the principles of the regulatory system for transport (when their application would be liable to have a serious effect on the standard of living and level of employment in certain regions and on the operation of transport facilities (Article 91 TFEU);
- the establishment of 'measures for the creation of European intellectual property rights to provide uniform protection of intellectual property rights through the Union and for the setting up of centralised Union-wide authorisation, coordination and supervision arrangements' (Article 118 TFEU); however, the same Article provides that, as concerns the 'language arrangements for the European intellectual property rights', the Council shall act unanimously. In other words, as it is the case that such language arrangements will always be necessary, the decision-making in this field will still remain subject to unanimity, as it was before the Lisbon Treaty (when the EU could act only on the basis of Article 308 TEC);[62]
- incentive measures in the field of culture (Article 167 TFEU), tourism (Article 195 TFEU) and civil protection (Article 196 TFEU).
- With regard to policy on economic and social cohesion, the Lisbon Treaty added the word 'territorial', so that it now reads 'economic, social and territorial cohesion' (see Title XVIII of Part Three of the TFEU).[63]

---

62 See Opinion of the Court of Justice 1/94 of 15 November 1994, [1994] ECR I-5267, para. 32.

63 In the Financial Perspectives for 2007–13, the cohesion policy of the Union represents the most important policy in budgetary terms (308 billion euros, to be compared with the 293 billion for CAP). In the 2009 EU budget, expenses for cohesion amount to 48.4 billion euros, to be compared with the 41.1 billion euros for CAP. In this area of the EU policy, see also Protocol no. 28 on economic, social and territorial cohesion.

$\sim$

Conclusion: the Lisbon Treaty
and beyond

Knowing the history and the context of the negotiation and of the birth of a treaty is useful. Having a clear legal interpretation of its provisions is necessary. However, the real story of a treaty begins with its implementation. For the Lisbon Treaty, even more than for other treaties, this story is impossible to foresee.

This is more the case for the Lisbon Treaty than for any preceding European Treaty, because it was not negotiated in the same way. Its substance was negotiated mostly by politicians within the European Convention, and not by diplomats within an IGC. This partly explains why some of its provisions leave room for flexibility in the way they will be implemented in practice. This is the case for the way in which the High Representative, Catherine Ashton, will play her complex role as well being also, at the same time, President of the Foreign Affairs Council and Vice-President of the Commission. This is also the case for the way in which the President of the European Council, Herman Van Rompuy, the President of the Commission, José Manuel Barroso, and the six-monthly rotating Presidency of the Council will organise their relations, or for the role that the General Affairs Council and Coreper could play in those relations. Therefore the fate of the Lisbon Treaty will not only depend on its text. It will also depend on the persons who will have to develop its potentialities, as well as on the economic and political context in which it will be applied.

However, in order to clarify the point of departure of this future story, one should try and answer some questions:

- Does the Lisbon Treaty take over the reforms envisaged in the failed Treaty establishing a 'Constitution for Europe'?
- If the answer to that question is positive, does this mean that the Lisbon Treaty is a mere repackaging of the 'Constitution for Europe'?
- Does the Lisbon Treaty mark a leap towards the eventual establishment of a European federal entity?

- Does this Treaty put an end to the imbalances which affect the EU in some areas?

Does the Lisbon Treaty take over the reforms envisaged in the 'Constitution for Europe'?

The Lisbon Treaty does take on board the significant reforms to the Treaties which were foreseen in the Constitutional Treaty. The most important of these reforms, which aim at strengthening the Union, its effectiveness and its legitimacy, are as follows.

- The 'communitarisation' of the former third pillar: this means that the European Parliament, the Court of Justice and the Commission have been given the same important powers in this area as in the former first pillar. This allows the EU to act more efficiently in this area. It also provides for the possibility of deciding by QMV in the Council and, therefore, of aiming at more ambitious legislation. It entails an effective control of the correct implementation by the Member States of this legislation. It also entails democratic and judicial control of respect by the EU institutions of the law and fundamental freedoms.
- An increase in the powers of the European Parliament: this is the case in a number of fields. The European Parliament has gained more powers in the legislative, budgetary and international areas. It now even has the possibility of initiating amendments to the founding Treaties. The European Parliament now has much more power to influence EU policies. At the same time, the national parliaments of the Member States have been given the possibility of intervening directly in the EU legislative process.
- The establishment of two new functions: a full-time President of the European Council, Herman Van Rompuy, who was elected for two and a half years, renewable once; and a full-time High Representative for Foreign Affairs, Catherine Ashton, appointed for five years, who is, at the same time, President of the Foreign Affairs Council and a Vice-President of the Commission. If efficient and co-ordinated, these two new figures will strengthen considerably 'the centre' of the EU. They might, together with the other institutions and bodies which have 'federal' characteristics, become active actors in the development and progress of European policies. This should result in better visibility for the EU on the international scene.

- The new definition and method of calculation of QMV in the Council and the extension of its scope of application, which allow for going in the direction of an enhanced democratic legitimacy for the decisions taken by the Council.
- The Treaty also offers facilitated possibilities for enhanced co-operation among some Member States, especially in the area of security and defence ('permanent structured co-operation') and in the area of the former third pillar (Freedom, Security and Justice).

By taking on the reforms which were envisaged in the 'Constitution for Europe', the Lisbon Treaty contains potential improvements for the effectiveness and legitimacy of the Union. It allows the EU to adopt common policies and actions more easily and more democratically in certain areas. Although the EU does not gain many new competences, it obtains better tools, in particular for it to be more active and visible on the international scene.

Is the Lisbon Treaty a mere repackaging of the failed 'Constitution for Europe'?

On a number of issues, the Lisbon Treaty is different from the Constitutional Treaty. These differences are far from being insignificant.

The most important of the differences between the Constitutional Treaty and the Lisbon Treaty are political. All of them take the opposite direction to the federalist one:

- Not only has the term 'constitution' been abandoned, but the Lisbon IGC also abandoned the constitutional approach: 'the constitutional concept . . . is abandoned' (paragraph 1 of the IGC mandate). The Lisbon Treaty, contrary to what the Constitutional Treaty would have done, does not repeal all existing Treaties and replace them by a single text. It adds another layer to the many already existing layers of treaties and protocols. Moreover, even after having consolidated the texts which have been amended,[1] about twenty treaties, all having the same legal value, remain in force and govern the EU's activities.
- Abandoning the constitutional concept was accompanied by the disappearance of all terms which could have been seen as going in the

---

1 The consolidated versions of the Treaties which have been published (OJ No. C115, 9 May 2008) only help the reader to see the resulting picture of the puzzle, each piece being one of the numerous Treaties which are in force.

same direction as steps towards the establishment of a state. This is the case for the terms 'Minister for Foreign Affairs', 'law' and 'framework law', as well as for the reference to the EU anthem, the EU flag, the EU motto and the 'European Day'. The text of the Charter on Fundamental Rights[2] and the formal enshrining of the primacy of EU law have also been removed from the Treaty.

The Lisbon Treaty also contains a number of legal differences from the Constitutional Treaty, which equally go in a direction opposite to a federalist one:

- For the first time, powers are given to national parliaments to intervene in the EU legislative procedure. The provisions contained in the Constitutional Treaty on this issue have been significantly strengthened by the Lisbon Treaty. If national parliaments of the Member States coordinate themselves effectively, they may have a real influence on the European legislative process. This has been symbolically emphasised by the insertion of a new provision, devoted entirely to the role of the national parliaments in 'the good functioning of the Union' (Article 12 TEU).
- A number of provisions, strengthened by the Lisbon Treaty, emphasise the fact that the EU is an international organisation, whose masters are and remain the Member States:
- It is not the Treaty itself which establishes the EU, but its High Contracting Parties (Article 1 TEU; compare with Article I-1(1) Cst).
- The Union shall act '*only*' within the limits of the competences conferred upon it by the Member States (Article 5(2) TEU; compare with Article I-11(2) Cst).

The Lisbon Treaty is a different political animal,[3] as compared with the Constitutional Treaty; while that Treaty was an attempt to mark a historic step in a federalist direction, this ambition has been abandoned with the Lisbon Treaty.

---

2 However, the Lisbon Treaty gives the Charter Treaty legal valüe (Art. 6(1) TEU).
3 'A sheep in sheep's clothing', as the Lisbon Treaty has been described by Professor Alan Dashwood, in a Conference held in Dublin on 11 May 2009 in the Irish Centre for European Law.

Does the Lisbon Treaty change the nature of the European Union or mark a leap towards the eventual establishment of a European federal entity?

All the elements of the Constitutional Treaty which had been obtained by the more Euro-sceptic governments have been retained in the Lisbon Treaty:

- For the first time, the founding EU Treaties oblige the EU to respect the 'essential functions' of the Member States (Article 4(1) and (2) TEU):

    1. In accordance with Article 5 [TEU], competences not conferred upon the Union in the Treaties remain with the Member States.
    2. The Union shall respect the equality of Member States before the Treaties as well as their national identities, inherent in their fundamental structures, political and constitutional, inclusive of regional and local self-government. It shall respect their essential State functions, including ensuring the territorial integrity of the State, maintaining law and order and safeguarding national security. In particular, national security remains the sole responsibility of each Member State.

    This article limits the competences of the EU in a stricter way than before, especially as there is no legal definition of exactly what the 'essential functions' of a State are.
- Other provisions go in the same direction. This is the case of Articles 2 to 6 TFEU on the classification of the EU's competences. It is also the case of the mechanisms contained in Protocols no. 1 and no. 2, which give the national parliaments the power to control the EU institutions in their duty to respect the principle of subsidiarity (Article 5(3) TEU). The irruption of the national parliaments into the EU legislative process is especially important, at a time when the European Parliament has failed once again, in the June 2009 elections, to attract more voters and, therefore, more legitimacy. Some observers now question whether trying to increase the European Parliament's effective political legitimacy[4] should be abandoned, or if it is still a credible aim for the future.

4 As Chris Patten has written, 'We have created a political body that has the power to hold EU institutions to account but has no obvious European electorate to which it can itself be held accountable. A parliament without a people inevitably increases the sense of frustration that many European voters feel about the process of making Europe-wide policy choice in their name. If the Lisbon Treaty is ratified later this year, one of the changes should result in national parliaments becoming more involved in European decision making. But we need to look country-by-country at what else we can do to tie Europe's own parliament

- In the same vein, new limitations are imposed on the powers of the EU institutions. Thus some provisions give powers to external entities which, before the Lisbon Treaty, were a monopoly of the EU institutions. This is the case of the citizens' initiative which enables them to request the launching of a legislative proposal. This is also the case of the role given to national parliaments regarding control over Europol and Eurojust. The very aim of the EU Charter for Fundamental Rights is also to impose limits on the exercise of the powers of the EU institutions. In the future, when the EU becomes a party to the ECHR, the European Court of Strasbourg will control the compliance with the provisions of the ECHR by the EU institutions.[5] One could also mention the more precise limits of the EU's competences in the Freedom, Security and Justice area and in public health.

Moreover, the limits of the EU's competences are highlighted several times in the Treaty or in its Protocols:

- That is the case in the new Protocol no. 25 on the exercise of shared competences: 'when the Union has taken action in a certain area, the scope of this exercise of competence only covers those elements governed by the Union act in question and therefore does not cover the whole area'.
- It is also the case in the new Protocol no. 26 on services of general interest: 'The shared values of the Union in respect to services of general economic interest . . . include in particular . . . the essential role and the wide discretion of national, regional and local authorities in providing, commissioning and organising services of general economic interest as closely as possible to the needs of the users' (Article 1). 'The provisions of the Treaties do not affect in any way the competence of Member States to provide, commission and organise non-economic services of general interest' (Article 2).

One must add that, with Article 50 TEU, the right of any Member State to withdraw from the Union is recognised (see Section 13), a right which is not recognised in federal states. Moreover, despite the fact that they have

into national politics. Unless we do that better, fewer people will vote for MEPs' (*European Voice*, 4 June 2009).

5 In doing so, the EU takes a 'qualitative step', making itself subject to this external control, as is already the case with the national legal orders (see L. S. Rossi, 'Constitutionnalisation de l'UE et des droits fondamentaux' (2002) 38 *Revue trimestrielle de Droit européen* 27.

no legal value, a number of Declarations attached to the Final Act of the IGC which adopted the Lisbon Treaty go in the same direction, stressing the limits or the absence of EU powers in one field or another. This is in particular the case of:

- Declaration no. 1, which stresses that the Charter of Fundamental Rights does not extend or modify the powers and tasks of the Union;
- Declarations no. 13 and no. 14, which both underline that CFSP will not affect the responsibilities of the Member States to conduct foreign policy;
- Declaration no. 18, which recalls that 'competences not conferred upon the Union in the Treaties remain with the Member States' (a repetition of the last sentence of Article 5(2) TEU);
- Declaration no. 24, which confirms that the legal personality of the European Union does not allow the Union to legislate or act beyond the EU's competences;
- Declaration no. 31 on social policy, which stresses that this policy '[falls] essentially within the competence of the Member States';
- Declaration no. 42, which underlines that Article 352 TFEU 'cannot serve as a basis for widening the scope of Union powers beyond the general framework created by the provisions of the Treaties as a whole and, in particular, by those that define the tasks and the activities of the Union'.

Most, if not all, of these Declarations are redundant and legally inoperative. However, politically, it is significant that they all go in the same direction. They aim at stressing solemnly, and even doing so twice if need be, the limits of the powers of the Union. This is important politically, as it expresses a lack of enthusiasm, or maybe even of trust, of the Member States (it is recalled that all these Declarations were adopted by common agreement of the twenty-seven parties to the IGC). For instance, from this point of view, it is interesting to compare Declaration no. 42 on the 'flexibility clause' (Article 352 TFEU)[6] with a 1972 Declaration on the corresponding provision of the previous Treaty:[7] '[the Heads of State or government] agreed that in order to accomplish the tasks laid out in the different action programmes, it was advisable to use as widely

---

6 Art. 352 TFEU is the new version of the former Art. 308 TEC (formerly Art. 235 TEC, in force since 1958).

7 This Declaration was adopted by the Heads of State or government of the Member States, meeting in Paris on 19–21 October 1972.

as possible all the provisions of the Treaties including Article 235 of the EEC Treaty'. One cannot escape the conclusion that the spirit in 2007 was not the same as it was in 1972, even if, meanwhile, the provisions of the Treaties had been modified on a number of points and helped, through the establishment of new legal bases, to lessen the need for the 'flexibility clause'.

The Lisbon Treaty did not change the nature of the Union, which remains a **'partially federal entity'**.[8] This means that the EU is neither a classic international intergovernmental organisation, nor a State: it acts with federal powers in some fields (external trade and competition policy, for instance) and as a classic international organisation in other fields (notably foreign policy). There is no realistic prospect in the foreseeable future of the EU becoming a federal State. Therefore the EU's partial federalism will not replace the present European Nation States. Nobody is working today to build a European State. However, the fact that there will not be a European State does not mean that the EU cannot pursue political aims and that the EU cannot have a political dimension. It does not mean either that the EU cannot in future deepen the integration of its Member States in order to protect better their interests and those of their citizens.

As I have already written in 2003,

> The challenge is to continue to find the right balance between, on the one hand, the necessity for efficient, democratic, transparent central decision-making and the uniform application of the laws, which are needed in order to respond effectively to the economic, social, environmental and security challenges of this century, challenges which none of the Member States, whatever their size and importance, are able to answer on their own. This entity will be characterised by the fact that Member States will keep their external identity in the world and that their participation in decision making and implementation will continue to be much more preponderant than in existing federal States.[9]

The Treaty does not change the nature of the Union, which remains a 'partially federal entity'. Far from being a leap towards the establishment of a European federal entity, the Lisbon Treaty marks a halt to the ambitions of the federalists. It might even be seen as a 'containment' of the powers of the European Union.

---

8 See my article 'The European Union: Towards a New Form of Federalism?'.
9 Ibid., 86–7. The book was published in 2006, but the text of my article was written at the end of 2003 – that is, before the end of the Convention which drafted the Constitutional Treaty.

Does the Lisbon Treaty put an end to the 'imbalances' which affect the EU in some areas?

This being said, in order to judge whether or not the Lisbon Treaty represents a great leap forward, one of the essential issues is to ascertain whether it has put an end to some of the major imbalances which affect the Union. These imbalances, some of which are due to the fact that the EU remains a classic international organisation in some areas, whereas it works in a federal way in other areas, are at the very heart of the European project. They create uncertainty and may be a cause of instability; in any case, they make it difficult for the EU to continue to work efficiently[10] in a durable way.

1. The first of these imbalances concerns *economic and monetary union* (EMU): it affects the relationship between the two parts of this Union: economic and monetary. The euro is the single currency of sixteen Member States, and it will probably become the currency of more of them in the future. In economic terms, there is an obvious and unavoidable link between the economic and the monetary parts if one wants to be sure that the currency will remain stable while allowing reasonable economic growth. In the present EU, the euro – that is, the monetary part of EMU – is managed in a 'federal' way by the European Central Bank. However, the economic part of EMU – that is,

---

10 E. B. Haas (1924–2003) had already explained in 1958 how integration in a given policy area might create a need for further integration in another area (E. B. Haas, *The Uniting of Europe: Political, Social and Economic Forces 1950–1957* (Stanford University Press, 1958)). This situation ('spillover') refers to a situation where co-operation or integration in one area pushes towards (or is even seen as making necessary) more co-operation or integration in another area. This process might be more or less objectively pressing and more or less manipulated for political considerations. The question is whether economic integration leads from one step to another. In a schematic way, one could say that the internal market pushes to economic and monetary union, which pushes to budget/social/taxation common policies, which push to a political legitimacy imperative, which pushes to political integration.

   Other authors, e.g. A. Moravcsik, *The Choice for Europe: Social Purpose and State Power from Messina to Maastricht* (Ithaca: Cornell University Press, 1998), stress that the spillover thesis ignores the fact that the Nation State is and remains the core element, both as far as political legitimacy is concerned (for citizens) and as far as the international scene is concerned (in international relations). One may go even further down that road and argue that the progress of co-operation/integration in the EU will continue for as long as it serves the interests of the Nation States which are members of the EU. If and when these Nation States consider that this does not serve their interests any more, they will stop the delegation of powers and possibly request regaining control over specific areas of policy.

fiscal, budgetary and economic policies – remains almost completely in the hands of the Member States.[11] For this economic part, the powers of the centre are, de jure or de facto, limited to recommendations which are not effectively binding. This is for good reasons, as Angela Merkel, Federal Chancellor of Germany, stressed in her 'Humboldt Speech on Europe' in May 2009:[12] 'The powers regarding budget, tax and social policy are held by the Member States for good reasons.' It is certainly an inescapable fact that there is a necessity for a direct link between these powers and an effective political legitimacy (i.e. the link between the voters and those who decide). Therefore, resolving this asymmetry while keeping the present political features of the EU represents an almost impossible task. However, a monetary union which is based on loose rules on budget/fiscal/economic governance will remain regarded as incomplete and, therefore, not guaranteeing stability.

2. The second major imbalance concerns the *free movement of persons* – that is, the imbalance between the external and the internal movement of persons.[13] On the one hand, the EU allows the free movement of persons inside its borders, and the rules and instruments regulating this freedom are governed in a 'federal' way. However, on the other hand, Member States keep in its entirety their power to grant their nationality to non-EU citizens, or to allow them to immigrate for long-term stays, thus offering these new citizens or immigrants complete freedom to move to any other EU State. The asymmetry of these two sides is therefore clear. It is difficult to correct, however, because the issue in this case also touches the core sovereignty of the nation state.

---

11 This imbalance is all the more striking since, as the EU budget represents only around 1 per cent of the total GNI of the EU, as compared with approximately 45 per cent of the budget of the public authorities of its twenty-seven Member States, the EU does not have the budgetary means at its disposal which could help to deal with an economic and financial crisis.

12 Humboldt Speech on Europe, Humboldt University, 27 May 2009.

13 'L'année 2008 permet de mesurer nettement la distance qui sépare la circulation externe (entrée et immigration) de la circulation interne à l'Union (séjour et circulation). A l'extension de celle-ci, répond la limitation de celle-là, protégée par la souveraineté nationale. Les réactions de plusieurs Etats, à la suite de l'arrêt Metock, l'illustrent bien' (The year 2008 allows one to measure clearly the gap which separates external movement (entry and immigration) from internal movement within the Union (the right to stay and travel). The extension of the latter is countered by limitations on the former, which is protected by national sovereignty. The reactions of several States, following the *Metock* judgment, illustrate this well' (author's translation) (J.-Y. Carlier, 'La libre circulation des personnes dans l'UE 1.1/31.12.2008' (2009) *Journal de Droit Européen* 79. (See judgment of 25 July 2008, Case C-127/08, *Metock*, [2008] ECR I-6241).

3. The third imbalance concerns *the internal market*: the aim and effect of the internal market is to open the internal borders to a free flow of goods, services, capital and workers. This aim has more or less been achieved, with the corollary condition that there are no distortions of competition between the Member States. A number of directives and regulations have been adopted to avoid such distortions. However, differences in fiscal and social laws and conditions are not considered in the Treaty as being distortions of competition. The Treaty enables the EU to adopt common rules on direct taxation and minimum rules on social policy, but without making them necessary conditions for the internal market. Therefore these common rules are almost always subject to unanimity in the Council and they are minimal. As a result, Member States retain almost complete freedom in those fields, hence the tensions over what is characterised by some as 'social dumping' or 'fiscal dumping', and the reactions to certain judgments of the EU Court of Justice (such as *Viking* or *Laval*).[14] Again, this asymmetry – which is denied by others, who regard this situation as a normal area of competition between the Member States – is not easy to correct, as it also touches on the core sovereignty of the Member States.

4. A fourth imbalance concerns participation in *EU military operations*: the way it has been worked up to now is that the Member States which decide to participate with troops also have to pay their expenses.[15] Therefore they 'pay twice' (men and money), whereas the Member States which do not participate with troops in the operations do not contribute to their financing either, even though the military operations are carried out on behalf of the EU.

5. Last, but not least, the most important of the EU's imbalances concerns its *political legitimacy*: the more that competences to adopt legislation have been transferred by the Member States to the EU, the more this has reduced the powers of their national parliaments to adopt such legislation. Therefore voters have the feeling that they have less control over the political decisions which govern their life and their future. It is true that, in parallel, more powers have been given to the European Parliament. However, the MEPs are elected by fewer and

---

14 See judgment of 11 December 2007, Case C-438/05, *Viking*, [2007] ECR I-10806, and judgment of 18 December 2007, Case C-341/05, *Laval*, [2007] ECR I-11845.

15 A principle which comes from NATO, where it is expressed by the formula 'Costs lie where they fall.'

fewer voters (a turnout of only 43 per cent in the 2009 elections, in constant decline since the first European elections in 1979, when the turnout was 63 per cent). It is true that a number of new measures to enhance democratic legitimacy have been included in the Lisbon Treaty, but will that be enough? The truth is that there is no political game at the European level. The political game continues to be played out almost exclusively at the national level, in each of the twenty-seven Member States.[16] Do we need more than that? If yes, one could try to imagine finding a bold solution, for example through the direct election of the President of the Commission, who could be given the power to lead a European Executive, which would be responsible both to the European Parliament and to the European Council. However, given the present opposition of most Member States to the establishment of something which would look like a federal entity, such a 'simple' option cannot be envisaged. To quote again the May 2009 speech by Angela Merkel, **'The EU is not a State, and it is not meant to become one.'**

It is difficult to imagine any kind of institutional solution at EU level, which would require yet another modification to the Treaty, because this would not be accepted by those who are opposed to going in a federal direction. Another difficulty is that, even if it is recognised that the EU is not a State and cannot be ruled by a system appropriate to rule States, the 'democratic deficit' of the EU is more a question of perception than of reality, as demonstrated by G. Majone and A. Moravcsik. However, one could transpose here the remark made by André Gide in *Les Faux Monnayeurs* (The Counterfeiters): 'Dans le domaine des sentiments, le réel ne se distingue pas de l'imaginaire' (where feelings are concerned, the real is no different from the imaginary). It is a fact that the EU's decision-making is subject to many checks and balances, that it is more open than any national government, that it is submitted to scrutiny both by the European Parliament and by national parliaments, that it allows for a very active input by 'civil society' and by lobbies, and so on. However, it is also a fact that, despite all that, the citizens think that they do not have enough control over the way the EU's decisions and laws are made. Therefore the challenge is to find a way to convince them of the contrary.

16 As the German Constitutional Court stressed in its 30 June 2009 judgment, 'it cannot be overlooked, however, that the public perception of factual issues and of political leaders remains connected to a considerable extent to patterns of identification which are related to the Nation State, language, history and culture' (para. 251).

remain to be decided in what way such corrections would have to be made. Quite obviously, it could be done either by further delegations of competences to the centre (more powers to the EU), or by cutting back on delegations of competences made in the past (return of powers to the Member States). In the past, Member States have always settled this kind of issue by accepting more co-operation and more integration. However, the history of the Lisbon Treaty is a sign that, if placed in a situation where there was an absolute necessity to decide between these solutions, it is no longer certain that, in the future, the unanimous choice of the twenty-seven would always be in favour of deeper integration of the European Union.[19]

Moreover, it is probable that this choice will be even more difficult without public opinion having first successfully been convinced that the most important of the imbalances described above has been resolved. This means that the issue of the political legitimacy of the EU is the single priority on which efforts have to be concentrated in the future. If no improvement is possible on this crucial issue, the message given by the tumultuous story of the Lisbon Treaty might well be, 'All right for us to carry on, but do not forget that European integration is not irreversible.' This would mean that, despite the wording of the Preamble and of Article 1 TEU, the 'ever closer Union'[20] would not be without limits and that things could even go backwards.

The Lisbon Treaty has not corrected the major asymmetries which still characterise the EU's architecture, which might be a factor of instability in the future, in case of stormy weather. The absolute priority should now be to try and improve the EU's democratic legitimacy and its visibility for the citizens, especially through better control by each national parliament over the participation of their government in the decisions taken by the EU.

*

The very fact that the Lisbon Treaty has finally entered into force is a relief for the supporters of the European project. Moreover, the Treaty, by retaining most of the reforms envisaged by the Constitutional Treaty,

---

19 One may stress that the Treaties of Maastricht, Amsterdam and Nice contained 'left-overs' or promises for a next IGC. This is not the case for the Lisbon Treaty.

20 The Preamble of the TEU (penultimate paragraph) and Art. 1, 2nd subpara., TEU as modified by the Lisbon Treaty have retained the words 'creating an ever closer union', which had disappeared in the text of the Constitutional Treaty. This wording ('ever closer union') had been part of the Preamble (1st para.) of the TEC since 1957 ('Determined to lay down the foundations of an ever closer union among the peoples of Europe').

does provide useful tools for deepening and strengthening the European project, should the political will be there. However, that does not alter the fact that this Treaty does not represent a great leap forward. The truth is that it even marks a halt to the hopes of the 'federalists'.

Difficult debates and decisions will still be required in the years to come. As the EU is and will remain necessary in order to preserve peace, freedom and prosperity in Europe and meet the challenges of the future, there is no other way forward than to have the support of the European citizens. Therefore the ways and means must be found to show them that they have the power to exercise real democratic control over the EU's decisions, without transforming the EU into a federal State. This major issue will not be resolved without strong political will, as it implies a change of political culture. In the absence of such political will, one may expect a stagnation of the EU.

Such a stagnation would play against the interests of the Europeans, as none of the twenty-seven EU Member States is able to deal on its own with the challenges of today. Whatever those challenges, the contribution of the European Union is needed to help in tackling them. What could the influence of any single European State be, for example,

- in trying to plead for a policy of protecting the environment and/or for combating climate change?
- on acting in favour of better regulation of competition in the world and playing a significant role in world trade negotiations?
- on fighting against international crime, traffic in human beings, and the illegal drugs trade?
- on acting in order to promote peace, democracy, human rights, and equality between women and men in the world?
- on protecting minorities in the whole of Europe, thus avoiding tensions which could, as has often been the case in the past, give birth to violence and armed conflicts?

*

The European project is the most noble cause in history, as its primary and essential aim is reconciliation and peace among peoples who have fought each other for centuries.

Beyond this, common policies in some fields, co-operation in other fields, are a necessity today for European States in order to preserve and improve the way of life and the interests of their citizens.

In order to achieve these aims, the ways followed in the past – inter-governmental co-operation and classic international organisations – have proved to be less efficient and less democratic than the (imperfect) EU. The absolute priority should now be to enhance the EU's democratic legitimacy and improve its visibility.

Therefore Europeans have to work harder and be more innovative, either in strengthening the European Union by improving its political functioning, or in imagining a new and original way to organise the Europe of the future better.

Appendix 1

The judgment of 30 June 2009 of the Federal Constitutional Court of Germany on the Lisbon Treaty

In its judgment of 30 June 2009 (63 pages, 421 paragraphs), the Federal Constitutional Court of Germany found that the Act approving the Lisbon Treaty as well as the Act amending the German Basic Law (i.e. the German Constitution, *Grundgesetz* – hereinafter GG), are compatible with the GG. However, the Court found that the 'Act Extending and Strengthening the Rights of the Bundestag and the Bundesrat in EU Matters' infringes the GG, insofar as those bodies have not been accorded sufficient rights of participation in EU law-making and treaty amendment procedures. Following this judgment, an Act extending the parliament's rights was adopted on 8 (Bundestag) and 18 (Bundesrat) September 2009, which enabled Germany's instrument of ratification of the Lisbon Treaty to be finally signed and deposited on 25 September 2009.

While the Court's judgment opened the way for ratification of the Lisbon Treaty by Germany, the possibility that this judgment might affect the future development of the European integration process cannot be excluded.[1] In any case, the operation of the Treaties' provisions which aim to facilitate and accelerate the work of the EU, such as the 'flexibility clause' (Article 352 TFEU), the *passerelles* and simplified revision procedures, will certainly be slowed down.

---

1 See the (excessive) comment by A. Leparmentier: 'La Cour donne son feu vert au Traité de Lisbonne, s'empressent les plus optimistes. En réalité, elle vient de mettre un point final à l'intégration européenne' (A. Leparmentier, 'L'Allemagne apaisée enterre le rêve européen', *Le Monde*, 17 July 2009). See also the analysis of A.-L. Barrière and B. Rousel, *Le Traité de Lisbonne, étape ultime de l'intégration européenne? Le jugement du 30 juin 2009 de la Cour constitutionnelle allemande*, Note du Cerfa 66 (Paris: Institut français des relations internationales, 2009). The judgment has been criticised by a number of German politicians, such as Joschka Fischer (*Die Zeit*, 9 July 2009) and Carl-Otto Lenz (*Frankfurter Allgemeine Zeitung*, 8 August 2009), who noted that the Court had used the word 'sovereignty' thirty-three times in its judgment.

A brief summary of the Court's judgment

The main standard of review against which the Court measured the constitutionality of the Act approving the Lisbon Treaty is the relation between the requirements of the GG and the stage of development reached by European integration. In particular, the Court's judgment emphasises the following elements:

- The right to vote and the democratic principle of parliamentary representation 'as the source of State authority' (para. 209) requires that the will of the electorate be reflected as proportionally as possible in the allocation of seats in the Parliament, so that each citizen has an equal share in the exercise of State authority (para. 214). The democratic principle embodied in the right to vote is protected by the so-called 'eternity guarantee' of the identity of the free constitutional order (Article 79.3 GG) and cannot even be altered by amending the GG (para. 218).
- As regards the formal limits for the conferral of powers to the EU, the Court stressed that the transfer of sovereign powers to the EU must respect Germany's constitutional identity. The GG aims for Germany's integration in an association of sovereign national States (*Staatenverbund*), in which the German citizens remain the subjects of democratic legitimisation (para. 229).
- As for the nature and content of powers which may be transferred to the EU and as regards their exercise by the EU institutions, Germany must retain sufficient latitude for the shaping of essential elements of citizens' life – especially where political decisions 'particularly depend on the understanding of culture, history and language' – such as citizenship, the monopoly of the police and the military on the use of force, revenue and expenditure including external aspects, any intensive encroachments on fundamental rights such as the deprivation of liberty in criminal law, the use of the language, family life and education, freedom of opinion, of the press and of association and of religious belief or ideology (paras. 252–260).

In light of the above considerations, the Court found that the Lisbon Treaty complies with the constitutional requirements of the GG. It based its findings notably on the following considerations:

- *The level of democratic legitimacy of the EU should keep pace with the extent of the powers transferred to it.* An increase in integration can be unconstitutional if the level of democratic legitimacy is not commensurate with the extent and weight of supranational powers transferred.

At the present stage of its integration, the EU is not a State; it remains the creation of sovereign States under international law. It is therefore not required to develop its institutional system democratically in the same way as that of a State, which it indeed does not achieve. In spite of the reference in Article 14(2) TEU to the European Parliament being composed of representatives of the Union's citizens, and contrary to what the wording of Article 10(1) TEU suggests, the Court noted that 'the European Parliament is not a body of representation of a sovereign European people' (para. 280). It remains 'a representation of the peoples of the Member States' (para. 284), thus using the same wording as in Article 189, 1st subparagraph, TEC.[2] For the Court, this results from the fact that the constitutional principle of electoral equality ('one man, one vote') is counterbalanced by the international law principle of the equality of States (para. 279).[3] This construction is acceptable, since 'democracies of the Member States with their majorities and decisions on political direction are represented on the level of the European institutions in the Council and indeed in the Parliament' (para. 286).

- The distribution and delimitation of competences as they result from the Lisbon Treaty preserve the sovereign authority of Member States, insofar as the EU's competence is based on the principle of conferred powers. The Lisbon Treaty does not allow the EU to decide on its own powers (*Kompetenz-Kompetenz*). It does not lead to abandoning the sovereignty of Germany (as is also apparent from the right to withdraw from the EU). However, the approval of Treaty changes by means of a simplified procedure and the use of *passerelles* will require the previous adoption of a national law under Article 23(1) GG, except in areas sufficiently predetermined by the Treaty (see below).
- The German Bundestag still retains sufficient responsibility and competences of its own, in areas where new powers are transferred to the EU, such as co-operation in criminal matters, judicial co-operation in civil matters, common defence and social policy, but a restrictive interpretation of the Treaty is advocated.

---

2 Under Art. 189 TEC: 'the [EP] . . . shall consist of representatives of the peoples of the States brought together in the [EC]'.

3 As a result, 'the weight of the vote of a citizen from a Member State with a low number of inhabitants may be about twelve times the weight of the vote of a citizen from a Member State with a high number of inhabitants' (para. 284).

Immediate implications of the judgment

The attached table gives an overview of the Lisbon Treaty provisions whose application requires, according to the Court's ruling, the prior adoption of a law, or the prior approval, by the German Parliament.

As appears from this table, different forms of agreement by the German parliament will be needed, depending on the provision or the subject matter concerned:

- Prior adoption of a law by the Bundestag, with the consent of the Bundesrat (i.e. a law, pursuant to Article 23(1), 2nd sentence, GG, and, if necessary pursuant to the 3rd sentence GG, which may be challenged in the German Constitutional Court) for the following cases (paras. 414, 417 and 419):
  - use of the general *passerelle* (Article 48(7), 3rd subparagraph, TEU);
  - use of the specific *passerelle* in family law (Article 81(3), 3rd subparagraph, TFEU);
  - use of the specific simplified revision procedure for adding further aspects of criminal procedure on which minimum EU rules can be adopted (Article 82(2)(d) TFEU);
  - use of the specific simplified revision procedure for adding further areas of crime on which minimum EU rules can be adopted (Article 83(1), 3rd subparagraph, TFEU);
  - use of the specific simplified revision procedure for extending the powers of the European Public Prosecutor's Office (Article 86(4) TFEU);
  - use of the specific simplified revision procedure for amending the EIB statute (Article 308, 3rd subparagraph, TFEU);
  - use of the 'flexibility clause' (Article 352 TFEU). The Court underlines that, contrary to the former Article 308 TEC, Article 352 TFEU does not refer any more to 'the operation of the common market', which therefore, in its view, allows a broader application,[4] making it possible 'to substantially amend Treaty foundations' (para. 328).
- Explicit prior consent by the Bundestag, and, where necessary, by the Bundesrat, although not necessarily in the form of a law (but the silence

---

4 However, the modification of the wording of Art. 352 (formerly 308) is unlikely to change its use. The EU Court of Justice has long since allowed a broad application of Art. 308 TEC (formerly 235), linked to the objectives of the Treaties rather than to the completion of the internal market (see for instance Opinion 2/94 on the accession of the EC to the ECHR, para. 29). The German Court's judgment is actually and obviously an implicit criticism of the EU Court's case law.

of the Bundestag or the Bundesrat may not be construed as approval), for the use of the following specific *passerelles* (para. 416):
- CFSP (Article 31(3) TEU);
- social policy (Article 153(2), 4th subparagraph, TFEU);
- environment (Article 192(2), 2nd subparagraph, TFEU);
- multiannual financial framework (Article 312(2), 2nd subparagraph, TFEU);
- enhanced co-operation (Article 333(1) and (2) TFEU).
- Prior instruction to the government of the Bundestag and, where necessary, the Bundesrat in the following cases of emergency brake procedures (para. 418):
- social security (Article 48, 2nd subparagraph, TFEU);
- mutual assistance in criminal judicial matters (Article 82(3) TFEU);
- minimum rules in substantive criminal law (Article 83(3) TFEU).

The above conditions – as they have been set out in the amended Act Extending and Strengthening the Rights of the Bundestag and the Bundesrat in EU Matters[5] – might represent a burden, and a source of delay for the EU decision-making process, although, to a certain extent, this is already the case for a number of Member States, via the procedures of 'parliamentary scrutiny'.

Nevertheless, it is worth stressing that a certain number of cases where the Court's ruling requires the prior adoption of a law, or the prior approval, by the German parliament as a condition for the German member of the Council to vote positively:

- either fall under the classic Treaty provision which already provides that, for entering into force, the EU act in question had to be 'approved by the Member States in accordance with their respective constitutional requirements' (see below);
- or may be read in the context of the new Treaty provisions allowing national parliaments to have their say in EU decision-making (see in general Article 12 TEU); in this regard, the Court stresses the larger role

---

5 In addition, one may note that, with regard to common defence, the German legislation adopted in September 2009 provides that two acts will have to be adopted by the German parliament: first, it will have to authorise the German government to approve the European Council Decision and, second, it will have to adopt a law to approve this Decision. On another issue, this legislation provides that the German candidates for the EU Court of Justice and for the General Court will have to be selected in the same manner as a Supreme Court judge in Germany.

which national parliaments may be called to play, following not only the Lisbon Treaty, but also the Amsterdam and Nice Treaties.

The cases for which the Treaties already use the formula used for the ratification of amendments to the Treaties and for which, therefore, the requirement laid down by the Court for the adoption of a law by the German parliament (para. 412) does not appear to change the situation, are the following:

- use of the general simplified revision procedure (Article 48(6) TEU);
- decision to establish a common defence (Article 42(2), 1st subparagraph TEU);
- addition or strengthening of the rights of EU citizens (Article 25, 2nd subparagraph, TFEU);
- accession to the ECHR (Article 218(8), 2nd subparagraph, 2nd sentence, TFEU);
- uniform election procedure for the European Parliament (Article 223(1), 2nd subparagraph, TFEU);
- conferral on the EU Court of Justice of a specific jurisdiction in intellectual property rights (Article 262 TFEU);
- system of own resources for the EU (Article 311, 3rd subparagraph, TFEU).

Indirect implications of the judgment

The application of EU law by Germany will have to respect what the Court has defined as the 'unalienable constitutional identity' of Germany. The recognition by German jurisdictions of the primacy of EU law over national law might accordingly depend on whether this condition is deemed to be fulfilled in a given case. Furthermore, Germany might not be in a position to participate in further developments of EU integration, if this were to create an unacceptable imbalance between powers exercised at EU level and what the Court considers to be the EU's structural democratic deficit.

Primacy of EU law

The Court examines the relationship between German constitutional law and EU law along the lines of classic public international law. The linchpin of the Court's approach is its confirmation that EU law remains a 'derived fundamental order' (para. 231). According to the Court's ruling, EU law, including its primacy, applies in Germany by virtue (and within the limits) of constitutional empowerment – that is, legislation permitting the conferral of sovereign powers (paras. 240, 242, 332, 343).

By its very nature, this concept has consequences for the primacy of EU law in Germany. In the Court's view, 'the primacy of application of European law remains, even with the entry into force of the Lisbon Treaty, an institution conferred under an international agreement – that is, a derived institution which will have legal effect in Germany only with the order to apply the law given by the Act Approving the Lisbon Treaty' (para. 339). European law only affects the application of national law 'to the extent required by the Treaties and permitted by them pursuant to the order to apply the law given nationally by the Act approving the Treaty' (para. 335). The Member States 'permanently remain the masters of the Treaties' (para. 231).

There are inherent constitutional limits for the application of Union law in Germany. In the Court's view, 'the Federal Republic of Germany does not recognize an absolute primacy of application of Union law, which would be constitutionally objectionable' (para. 331), and 'the Basic Law . . . does not waive the sovereignty contained in the last instance in the German constitution' (para. 340). It does not, according to the Court, contradict 'openness to international law if the legislature, exceptionally, does not comply with the law of international agreements . . . provided this is the only way in which a violation of fundamental principles of the constitution can be averted'. The Court refers to the EU Court of Justice as adopting a similar line of reasoning in its *Kadi* judgment,[6] where it 'placed the assertion of its own identity as a legal community above the commitment that it otherwise respects' – that is, United Nations Security Council Resolutions (para. 340).[7]

---

6 Judgment of 3 September 2008, Joined Cases C-402/05 P and C-415/05 P, *Kadi v. Council and Commission*, [2008] ECR I-6351.

7 On this point see J.-P. Jacqué, 'Primauté du droit international versus protection des droits fondamentaux, note sur CJCE: arrêt du 3 septembre 2008, Kadi c/Conseil et Commission', (2009) 45 *Revue trimestrielle de droit européen* 161, particularly 178: 'Quel argument opposer à une Cour constitutionnelle nationale qui invoquerait sa propre constitution pour paralyser l'adoption de mesures de mise en œuvre du droit communautaire? En procédant à une affirmation aussi forte de l'indépendance de l'Union face aux contraintes de l'ordre international, ne fait-on pas naître le danger de détricoter l'édifice fragile de la primauté du droit communautaire sur le droit national?' (What argument could then be useful against a national constitutional court which wished to invoke its own national Constitution in order to prevent the adoption of measures implementing Community law? By expressing such a strong assertion of the autonomy of the Union against the constraints of the international legal order, has it not brought about the danger of dismantling the fragile construction of the primacy of Community law over national law? (author's translation))

The ruling does not regard primacy as an essential element of the Community legal order, but as something merely 'induced' by the German order to apply the Treaty and therefore constantly subject to a constitutionality review: 'in this respect, it is insignificant whether the primacy . . . is provided for in the Treaties themselves or in Declaration no. 17 annexed to the Final Act of the Lisbon Treaty. For in Germany, the primacy of Union law only applies by virtue of the order to apply the law issued by the Act approving the Treaties. As regards public authority exercised in Germany, the primacy of application only reaches as far as the Federal Republic of Germany approved this conflict of law rule and was permitted to do so' (para. 343). The Court confirmed that '*exceptionally, and under special and narrow conditions, the Federal Constitutional Court [may declare] European Union law inapplicable in Germany*' (para. 340, emphasis added).[8]

The Court's ruling is thus a possible source of conflict with long-standing EU Court of Justice case law on the primacy of EU law (including both the Treaties and secondary legislation adopted on the basis thereof) over national law (including constitutional law).[9]

Role of the German Constitutional Court

As a logical consequence of the role it gives the GG vis-à-vis EU law, the Court ultimately claims jurisdiction over acts of the Union's institutions affecting 'inalienable guarantees' under the GG. This 'reserve competence' (para. 341) of the Court results from the possibility that the EU Court of Justice might fail to preserve respect for the delimitation of powers between the EU and its Member States. In this respect, the Court does not address the issue of a possible conflict with the EU

---

8 The Court considered itself empowered to conduct two types of review of EU law:

   (1) an ultra vires review (the transfer of powers conferred on the EU is not respected);
   (2) identity review (the inviolable character of the German Constitutional identity is not respected).

9 See, in particular, as concerns the German Constitution, the EU Court's judgment of 11 January 2000, Case C–285/98, *Kreil*, [2000] ECR I-69. See also judgment of 17 December 1970, Case 11/70, *International Handelsgesellschaft*, [1970] ECR I-120, which is particularly clear: 'the validity of a Community measure or its effect within a Member State cannot be affected by allegations that it runs counter to either fundamental rights as formulated by the Constitution of that State or the principles of a national constitutional structure'.

Court's case law, except by recalling that it '[recognizes] the final character of the decisions of the [EU] Court of Justice only "in principle"' (para. 337).

As the Member States remain both sovereign States and the masters of the Treaty, they also retain, according to the Court, 'the right to review the adherence to the integration programme' (para. 334). Referring both to its own 1993 ruling concerning the Treaty of Maastricht and to the 2008 ruling of the Czech Constitutional Court on the Lisbon Treaty, the Court reiterates that it can 'review whether legal instruments of the European institutions and bodies remain within the limits of the sovereign powers conferred on them or if the Community jurisdiction interprets the Treaties in an extensive manner that is tantamount to an inadmissible autonomous Treaty amendment' (para. 338).

The Court considers itself obliged, 'within the limits of its competence' (para. 235),[10] to verify respect for the principle of limited conferred powers ('*ultra vires* review') and of constitutional identity ('identity review') (paras. 234, 235, 240) 'if legal protection cannot be obtained at the Union level' (para. 240). The ultimate outcome of such a review might, in the Court's judgment, be the inapplicability of parts of EU law in Germany: 'The *ultra vires* review as well as the identity review can result in Community law or Union law being declared inapplicable in Germany' (para. 241). In this regard, the Court even explicitly recommended that the legislature establish a specific category of proceedings to allow the Court to review EU law and ensure that it remains within the boundaries set.[11] This is hardly compatible with the Treaty, which provides that it is for the EU Court of Justice to 'ensure that in the interpretation and application of the Treaties the law is observed' (see Article 19(1) TEU, which replaced in substance Article 220, 1st subparagraph, TEC). What would happen if all Member States were to establish such a national mechanism?

In this respect also, the Court's ruling is a possible source of conflict with EU law and the EU Court, all the more so if it encouraged supreme jurisdictions in other Member States to take similar stances.

---

10 These limits are not enumerated in the judgment.
11 'What is also conceivable, however, is the creation by the legislature of an additional type of proceedings before the Federal Constitutional Court that is especially tailored to ultra vires review and identity review to safeguard the obligation of German bodies not to apply in Germany, in individual cases, legal instruments of the EU that transgress competences or that violate constitutional identity' (para. 241).

The future of EU integration

(i) De lege lata

A reading of the ruling leaves the impression that the Court only just accepted the conformity of the Lisbon Treaty with the GG, and that it only gave its clearance subject to a restrictive reading of the Treaty provisions. The following examples may be given to illustrate this:

- although the Court acknowledged the existence of 'mechanisms of protection' to 'preserve the Member States' responsibility', in particular the right of national parliaments to introduce an action before the EU Court of Justice for non-compliance with the subsidiarity principle, it noted, however, that it will 'be decisive whether [this right] will be extended to the question, which precedes the monitoring of the principle of subsidiarity, of whether the European Union has competence for the specific lawmaking project' (paras. 301 to 305);
- the Court stressed that, when exercising their (newly conferred) powers, the EU institutions must see to it that Member States keep 'tasks of a sufficient weight' at their level, which legally and practically are the preconditions of a living democracy. In this context, 'what is decisive for the constitutional assessment of the challenge is . . . whether the Federal Republic of Germany retains substantial national scope of action' in essential areas (para. 351).

The above-mentioned essential areas, which the Court also referred to as the democratic *Primärraum* (primary realm or area) (para. 360), are nationality or citizenship, monopoly of the police and military on the use of force, revenue and expenditure and particularly intrusive restrictions on fundamental rights (detention), cultural questions such as language, the shaping of conditions concerning the family and education, freedom of speech, press and association, and the approach taken with respect to religions and other ideology (para. 249). In the Court's view, it is particularly suitable to limit the Union's action in such areas to what is necessary for the co-ordination of cross-border situations (para. 251).

The field of *criminal law and criminal procedural law* is very sensitive, as 'by criminal law, a legal community gives itself a code of conduct that is anchored in its values' (para. 355) and 'with the decision on punishable conduct, the legislature takes the democratically legitimised responsibility for a form of sovereign action that counts among the most intensive encroachments on individual freedom in a modern constitutional State' (para. 356). The Court hardly hid its feeling that the transfer of competences has been too extensive in this field. The Union's powers 'must be interpreted strictly – on no account extensively – and their use requires particular justification' (para. 358). The Court acknowledged that the fight against particularly serious crime which takes advantage of the territorial limitation of criminal prosecution by a State, and the cross-border dimension of crimes 'can be a special justification for the transfer of sovereign powers also in this context'. The Court stressed that the cross-border dimension required by Article 83(1), 1st subparagraph, TFEU (on minimum rules defining criminal offences and sanctions) 'does not exist [merely because] the institutions have formed a corresponding political will' (para. 359).

The Court also required a restrictive interpretation of competences in the area of mutual recognition of judgments and in the general area of the law of criminal procedure (Article 82 (1) and (2) TFEU) (para. 360).

The Court closely examined the 'annex competence' of Article 83(2) TFEU, which enables the Union to approximate criminal law in policy areas which have been subject to harmonisation measures. According to the Court, this competence is potentially unlimited. Nevertheless, the Lisbon Treaty 'provides sufficient indications for an interpretation in conformity with the constitution'. The use of the 'annex competence' needs to be limited to situations where 'it is demonstrably established that a serious deficit as regards enforcement actually exists and it can only be remedied by the threat of a sanction'. According to the Court, these 'conditions also apply to the existence of an annex competence for criminal law that has already been assumed by the European jurisdiction' (para. 362).

In the same line of reasoning, the Court required that any use of the power under Article 83(1) TFEU to define criminal offences and sanctions be limited to the cross-border dimension of a specific criminal offence. This could be done, the Court suggested, by 'minimum rules not covering the complete area of a criminal offence . . . but merely part of the constituent elements of the offence' (para. 363). In addition, the competences of the Union in this field must be interpreted in a way which is compatible with the principle of guilt (notion of individual responsibility). This principle is part of the German inalienable constitutional identity (para. 364).

Another area in which the Court defined the limits of German participation is the *Common Foreign and Security Policy*. With the Lisbon

Treaty, the EU has not taken the step towards a system of mutual collective security (para. 390). The German requirement of parliamentary approval for the deployment of German soldiers for an EU operation continues to apply (para. 382). The Lisbon Treaty (and in particular Article 43(2) TEU) does not oblige Member States to provide national armed forces for military deployments of the EU. 'A possible political agreement by the Member States to deploy armed forces in the European alliance would not be capable of generating on the legal level an obligation to act which could overrule the mandatory requirement of parliamentary approval' (para. 388).

The Court also stated that, if the European Council decided on a *common defence* in accordance with Article 42(2), 1st subparagraph, TEU, Germany could not participate in an ordinary Treaty amendment (Article 48(2) to (5) TEU) which would replace the principle of unanimity by qualified majority voting in this field (para. 391).

The Court also interpreted Article 42(7), 1st subparagraph, TEU, which provides that, in case of armed aggression on the territory of a Member State 'the other Member States shall have towards it an obligation of aid and assistance by all the means in their power', in the sense that 'This obligation does not necessarily encompass the use of military means' (para. 386). This is in line with the June 2009 decision of the heads of state or government on the Irish concerns, which provides, in Section C (5th para.), that 'it will be for Member States . . . to determine the nature of aid or assistance to be provided' (see Box 13).

The Court further indicated limits for the development of rights derived under Article 25(2) TFEU from *Union citizenship*. Measures strengthening the citizenship of the EU must respect the derived and complementary nature of that citizenship and must preserve national citizenship: 'The German State people retains its existence as long as the citizenship of the Union does not replace the citizenships of the Member States or is superimposed on it. The derived status of the citizenship of the Union and the safeguarding of the national citizenship are the boundary of the development of the civic rights of the Union which is set out in Article 25.2 TFEU and the boundary of the Court of Justice of the European Union's case-law . . . Possibilities to differentiate on account of nationality continue to exist in the Member States' (para. 350).

(ii) De lege ferenda

The democratic deficit of the EU which the Court considered to exist but which is acceptable, at this stage of EU integration, would apparently not, in the Court's view, permit further substantive steps towards a deepening of this integration.

In the view of the Court – which assessed the EU structure by means of classic Nation State standards (para. 289) – the Union suffers from a structural democratic deficit, one of the reasons being the way the European Parliament is composed. The Court also referred to the fact that the principle of equality of States remains the rule for the composition of the European Council, of the Council, of the Commission and so on. It stressed that 'Also after the entry into force of the Lisbon Treaty, the Court of Justice, for instance, must always be staffed according to the principle "one State, one judge" and under the determining influence of the Member States regardless of their number of inhabitants' (para. 288).

This deficit cannot be compensated for by other provisions or elements of democracy, as these only have a complementary, and not an essential, democratic function. In particular, the double qualified majority in the Council 'counteracts excessive federalisation, without, however, complying with the democratic precept of electoral equality' (para. 292). In the Court's view, the parliaments of the Member States see their position 'considerably curtailed', in spite of their institutional recognition, since decisions by unanimity become rarer and police and judicial co-operation in criminal matters has been supranationalised (para. 293).

Overall, the Court found the present balance between the extent of EU powers and the EU democratic legitimacy still to be acceptable. The Court warned, however, about the consequences of a potential future imbalance between the nature and extent of the Union's competences and what the Court considered to be the level of the Union's democratic legitimacy.[12] Should such an imbalance occur,[13] it would be 'for

---

12 'European unification on the basis of a union of sovereign States under the Treaties may, however, not be realized in such a way that the Member States do not retain sufficient space for the political formation of the economic, cultural and social circumstances of life' (para. 249). 'An increase of integration can be unconstitutional if the level of democratic legitimisation is not commensurate to the extent and the weight of supranational power of rule' (para. 262).

13 According to the Court, it would in particular be impossible for the EU to become a federal State: 'a structural democratic deficit that would be unacceptable ... would exist if the extent of competences, the political freedom of action and the degree of independent formation of opinion on the part of the institutions of the Union reached a level corresponding to the federal level in a federal State – that is, a level analogous to that of a State' (para. 264).

the Federal Republic of Germany due to its responsibility for integration, to work towards a change, and if the worst comes to the worst, even to refuse to further participate in the European Union' (para. 264).

*

Lisbon Treaty provisions the application of which requires, according to the Court's ruling, the prior adoption of a law, or the prior approval, by the German parliament

Treaty provision	Voting rule	Procedure for approval pursuant to the GG[1]
(a) Simplified revision procedures		
Article 48(6) TEU simplified revision procedure for Part Three of the TFEU	unanimity in the European Council + approval by Member States in accordance with their respective constitutional requirements	**law** based on Article 23(1), 2nd sentence and, where applicable, Article 23(1) third sentence + Article 79(2)
Article 42(2), 1st subpara., TEU decision establishing a common defence	unanimity in the European Council + adoption of such a decision by Member States in accordance with their respective constitutional requirements	**law** based on Article 23(1), 2nd sentence and, where applicable, Article 23(1), 3rd sentence + Article 79(2)
Article 25(2) TFEU provisions to strengthen or to add to the rights linked to the Union citizenship listed in Article 20(2) TFEU	unanimity in the Council + consent of the EP + approval by Member States in accordance with their respective constitutional requirements	**law** based on Article 23(1), 2nd sentence and, where applicable, Article 23(1), 3rd sentence + Article 79(2)

Treaty provision	Voting rule	Procedure for approval pursuant to the GG
Article 83(1), 3rd subpara., TFEU identification of other areas of particularly serious crime with a cross-border dimension	unanimity in the Council + consent of the EP	**law** based on Article 23(1), 2nd sentence
Article 82(2)(d) TFEU identification of other specific aspects of criminal procedure for which minimum rules may be established	unanimity in the Council + consent of the EP	**law** based on Article 23(1), 2nd sentence
Article 86(4) TFEU extension of the powers of the European Public Prosecutor's Office	unanimity in the European Council + consent of the EP	**law** based on Article 23(1), 2nd sentence
Article 308 TFEU amendment of the EIB Statute	unanimity in the Council	**law** based on Article 23(1), 2nd sentence
Article 218(8), 2nd subpara., TFEU accession to the ECHR	unanimity in the Council + approval by Member States in accordance with their respective constitutional requirements	**law** based on Article 23(1), 2nd sentence and, where applicable, Article 23(1) third sentence + Article 79(2)
Article 223(1), 3rd subpara., TFEU uniform election procedure for the EP	unanimity in the Council + consent of the EP + approval by Member States in accordance with their respective constitutional requirements	**law** based on Article 23(1), 2nd sentence and, where applicable, Article 23(1), 3rd sentence + Article 79(2)

(*cont.*)

(cont.)

Treaty provision	Voting rule	Procedure for approval pursuant to the GG
Article 262 TFEU conferral of jurisdiction of the EU Court in disputes relating to intellectual property rights	unanimity in the Council + approval by Member States in accordance with their respective constitutional requirements	**law** based on Article 23(1), 2nd sentence and, where applicable, Article 23(1) 3rd sentence + Article 79(2)
Article 311, 3rd subpara., TFEU own resources decision	unanimity in the Council + approval by Member States in accordance with their respective constitutional requirements	**law** based on Article 23(1), 2nd sentence and, where applicable, Article 23(1), 3rd sentence + Article 79(2)
(b) General *passerelle*		
Article 48(7) TUE	unanimity in the European Council + consent of the EP by a majority of its members + absence of veto by a national parliament	**law** based on Article 23(1), 2nd sentence
(c) Specific *passerelles*		
Article 81(3) TFEU *passerelle* in the field of family law	unanimity in the Council + absence of veto by a national parliament	**law** based on Article 23(1), 2nd sentence
Article 31(3) TEU *passerelle* in the field of CFSP	unanimity in the European Council	**explicit approval** by the Bundestag and, where necessary, the Bundesrat
Article 153(2) TFEU *passerelle* in the field of social policy	unanimity in the Council	**explicit approval** by the Bundestag and, where necessary, the Bundesrat

Treaty provision	Voting rule	Procedure for approval pursuant to the GG
Article 192(2) TFEU *passerelle* in the field of environment	unanimity in the Council	**explicit approval** by the Bundestag and, where necessary, the Bundesrat
Article 312(2) TFEU *passerelle* as regards the multiannual financial framework	unanimity in the Council	**explicit approval** by the Bundestag and, where necessary, the Bundesrat
Article 333(1) and (2) TFEU *passerelle* in the context of enhanced co-operation	unanimity in the Council	**explicit approval** by the Bundestag and, where necessary, the Bundesrat
(d) Flexibility clause		
Article 352 TFEU flexibility clause	unanimity in the Council + consent of the EP + Commission shall draw national parliaments' attention to proposals based on this Article	**law** based on Article 23(1), 2nd sentence
(e) 'Emergency brake' clauses		
Article 48, 2nd subpara., TFEU emergency brake procedure in the field of social security	QMV in the Council (codecision); consensus in the European Council	**instruction** of the Bundestag and, where necessary, the Bundesrat
Article 82(3) TFEU emergency brake procedure in the field of criminal procedure	QMV in the Council (codecision); consensus in the European Council	**instruction** of the Bundestag and, where necessary, the Bundesrat

(cont.)

(cont.)

Treaty provision	Voting rule	Procedure for approval pursuant to the GG
Article 83(3) TFEU emergency brake procedure as regards the accessory competence for criminal law in harmonised areas	QMV in the Council (codecision) or special legislative procedure, as was followed for the adoption of the harmonisation measures in question; consensus in the European Council	**instruction** of the Bundestag and, where necessary, the Bundesrat

[1] Pursuant to Art. 23(1), second sentence, GG, the conferral of sovereign powers on the EU requires a law which is adopted by the majority of votes cast in the Bundestag. Pursuant to Art. 23(4), the Bundesrat participates in the forming of an opinion at federal level on matters of the European Union if it had to participate in the adoption of national measures on the subject matter concerned or if the matter fell within the competence of the *Länder*. Pursuant to Art. 23(1), third sentence, in connection with Art. 79(2) GG, modifications of the founding treaties of the European Union, as well as comparable rules which change or supplement the GG in its substance or which enable such changes or supplements, require a law to be approved by two-thirds of the members of the Bundestag and two-thirds of the votes in the Bundesrat. Pursuant to Art. 79(3) GG, modifications of the GG which touch upon, *inter alia*, the principles laid down in Arts. 1 to 20 of the GG are inadmissible.

Appendix 2

The judgment of 26 November 2008 of the Czech Constitutional Court on the Lisbon Treaty

In its judgment of 26 November 2008 (71 pages, 218 paragraphs), the Czech Constitutional Court concluded that the Lisbon Treaty and the EU Charter of Fundamental Rights are not in conflict with the Czech constitutional order.

It stressed that the Court had concentrated its review only on those provisions of the Treaty whose consistency with the Czech Constitutional order were expressly contested. Therefore it remained legally possible that a group of deputies or senators might submit a new petition on the constitutionality of other provisions of the Lisbon Treaty.[1]

The Court stressed that the transfer of powers from State organs of the Czech Republic to an international organisation cannot go as far as to violate the very essence of the Republic as a democratic State governed by the rule of law, founded on respect for the rights and freedoms of human beings and of citizens. A transfer to the EU of the competence to define its own competences (*Kompetenz-Kompetenz*) would also be inconsistent with the Czech Constitution. However, the Court noted that the Lisbon Treaty does not have such consequences and it concluded that the Lisbon Treaty, together with the EU Charter of Fundamental Rights, is consistent with the Czech constitutional order. The Court stressed that the transfer of certain competences of the State to the EU, which arises from the free will of the State and which will be exercised with its participation, is not a weakening of the sovereignty of the State.[2] On the contrary, it can lead to a strengthening of sovereignty through the joint actions of an integrated whole.

---

1 A second petition was made by seventeen Senators on 29 September 2009. In its judgment of 3 November 2009, the Court decided, unanimously, that the Lisbon Treaty, and the ratification of it, does not contravene the constitutional order of the Czech Republic.
2 'In a modern, democratic State, governed by the rule of law, State sovereignty is not an aim in and of itself, in isolation, but is a means for fulfilling the fundamental values on which the construction of a constitutional State, governed by the rule of law, stands' (para. 209).

It also stressed that amendments to the EU Treaties will continue to be possible only with the consent of all EU States, which thus remain 'the masters of the Treaties'. As to the 'flexibility clause' in Article 352 TFEU, it is sufficiently limited and is not a blanket provision which would be contrary to the Czech Constitution.

The Court recalled that, according to its case law,[3] if, even after the ratification, in exceptional cases, one could conclude that the Treaty was inconsistent with the Czech constitutional order, it is the Czech constitutional order, especially its substantial core, which 'must take precedence' (para. 85). The same applies to secondary law: 'should, therefore, these delegated powers [to the EU] be carried out by the EU organs in a manner that is regressive in relation to the existing conception of the essential attributes of a democratic law-based State, then such exercise of powers would be in conflict with the Czech Republic's constitutional order, which would require that these powers once again be assumed by the Czech Republic's national organs' (paras. 130, 216).

One can find some similarities between this judgment of the Czech Constitutional Court of November 2008 and the judgment of the German Constitutional Court of June 2009 (see Appendix 1).

---

3 In the 'Sugar quotas' case (Pl. US 50/04) and in the 'Arrest warrant' case (Pl. US 66/04).

Appendix 3

List of provisions on a simplified revision procedure and of *passerelles*

Provisions on a simplified revision procedure

These provisions allow for amending, in an easier way than the ordinary revisions procedure, one or several articles of the TEU or TFEU or of a protocol thereto. There are twelve such provisions:

Simplified revision of Treaty provisions

Article in the TEU/TFEU	Subject matter
48(6) TEU	**general provision** which allows for amending articles in Part Three of the TFEU on internal EU competences[1] by a unanimous decision of the European Council, followed by a ratification procedure within Member States, but without the need to convene a Convention and an Intergovernmental Conference
25, 2nd subpara., TFEU	enables the Council, by unanimity and with the EP's consent, to strengthen or add to the rights of the EU citizens, followed by a ratification procedure within Member States, but without the need to convene a Convention and an Intergovernmental Conference[2]
82(2)(d) TFEU	enables the Council, by unanimity and with the EP's consent, to identify other aspects of criminal procedure for which minimum rules may be established
83(1), 3rd subpara., TFEU	enables the Council, by unanimity and with the EP's consent, to extend the list of areas of crime which may be subject to minimum EU rules

(*cont.*)

Article in the TEU/TFEU	Subject matter
86(4) TFEU	enables the European Council, by unanimity and with the EP's consent, to extend the powers of the European Public Prosecutor's Office
98, 2nd sentence, TFEU	enables the Council, by QMV, to repeal a provision allowing aid to be granted to the economy of certain areas of Germany affected by its division (applicable as from 1 December 2014)
107(2)(c) TFEU	enables the Council, by QMV, to repeal a provision allowing aid to be granted to the economy of certain areas of Germany affected by its division (applicable as from 1 December 2014)
300(5) TFEU	enables the Council, by QMV, to review the nature of the composition of the Committee of the Regions and of the Economic and Social Committee

[1] The revision may not increase the competences conferred on the EU (Art. 48(6), 3rd subpara., TEU).
[2] This provision already existed in Art. 22, 2nd subpara., TEC.

Simplified revision of Protocols' provisions

Article in the TFEU	Subject matter
126(14), 2nd subpara., TFEU	enables the Council, by unanimity, to replace the whole Protocol on the excessive deficit procedure (consultation of the EP and ECB)[1]
129(3) and (4) TFEU	allows for amending certain articles of the ECB Protocol (some in codecision, others by the Council using QMV)[2]
281, 2nd subpara., TFEU	allows for amending certain articles of the Protocol on the EU Court of Justice (codecision)[3]
308, 3rd subpara., TFEU	allows for amending certain articles of the EIB Protocol (Council, by unanimity)[4]

[1] This provision already existed in Art. 104(14), 2nd subpara., TEC.
[2] This provision existed already in Art. 107(5) TEC.
[3] This provision already existed in Art. 245, 2nd subpara., TEC.
[4] This provision already existed in Art. 266, 3rd subpara., TEC.

Passerelles

A *passerelle* (or bridging clause) is a provision in the Treaties which enables passing from one procedure or voting rule to another (from unanimity to QMV in the Council or from a special legislative procedure to an ordinary legislative procedure (codecision)). There are eight *passerelles* in the TEU and TFEU:

Article in the TEU/TFEU	Subject matter
48(7), 1st subpara., TEU	general *passerelle* enabling the switching of legal bases in the TFEU or in Title V of the TEU (CFSP) from unanimity in the Council to QMV
48(7), 2nd subpara., TEU	general *passerelle* enabling the switching of legal bases in the TFEU from a special legislative procedure to the ordinary legislative procedure (codecision)
31(3) and (4) TEU	specific *passerelle* enabling the switching of legal bases in the CFSP Chapter from unanimity in the Council to QMV (except for decisions having military or defence implications)
81(3), 2nd subpara., TFEU	specific *passerelle* enabling the switching of aspects of family law with cross-border implications from a special legislative procedure (with unanimity) to the ordinary legislative procedure (codecision)[1]
153(2), 2nd subpara., TFEU	specific *passerelle* enabling the switching of certain matters of social policy from a special legislative procedure (with unanimity) to the ordinary legislative procedure (codecision)[2]
192(2), 2nd subpara., TFEU	specific *passerelle* enabling the switching of certain matters in the field of environment (fiscal measures, country planning, etc.) from a special legislative procedure (with unanimity) to the ordinary legislative procedure (codecision)[3]
312(2), 2nd subpara., TFEU	specific *passerelle* enabling the switching of the legal basis on multiannual financial framework from unanimity in the Council to QMV

(*cont.*)

(*cont.*)

Article in the TEU/TFEU	Subject matter
333 TFEU	general *passerelle* enabling the switching, within a reinforced co-operation, of unanimity in the Council to QMV (except for defence) or from a special legislative procedure (with unanimity) to the ordinary legislative procedure (codecision)

[1] This provision already existed in Art. 67(2), 2nd indent, TEC.

[2] This provision already existed in Art. 137(2), 2nd subpara., TEC.

[3] This provision already existed in Art. 175(2), 2nd subpara., TEC.

Appendix 4

Existing legal bases switched to the ordinary legislative procedure (codecision)

Article in TEU/TFEU	Subject matter	Procedure in former Treaties
1. 42, 1st subpara., TFEU	application of competition rules to production and trade in agricultural products (general rules)	QMV in Council + EP consultation (Art. 36 TEC)
2. 43(2) TFEU	common organisation of markets and general objectives in common agriculture and fisheries policy	QMV in Council + EP consultation (Art. 37(2) TEC)
3. 51, 2nd subpara., TFEU	exclusion in a Member State of certain activities (linked to the exercise of official authority) from the application of provisions on the freedom of establishment	QMV in Council, without EP participation (Art. 45, 2nd subpara. TEC)
4. 56, 2nd subpara., TFEU	extension of the benefit of the freedom to provide services to third-country nationals established within the EU	QMV in Council, without EP participation (Art. 45, 2nd subpara., TEC)
5. 59(1) TFEU	liberalisation of a specific service	QMV in Council + EP consultation (Art. 52(1) TEC)

(cont.)

(cont.)

Article in TEU/TFEU	Subject matter	Procedure in former Treaties
6. 64(2) TFEU	adoption of other measures on the movement of capital to or from third countries involving direct investments	QMV in Council, without EP participation (Art. 57(2) TEC)
7. 75, 1st subpara., TFEU	fight against terrorism – definition of a framework for administrative measures on freezing of assets, etc. of natural or legal persons, groups or non-State entities	QMV in Council, without EP participation (Art. 60 + 301 TEC)
8. 79(2)(a) + (b) TFEU	legal immigration[1]	**unanimity** in Council + EP consultation (Art. 63(3)(a) + (4) TEC)
9. 82(1) + (2) TFEU[2]	judicial co-operation in criminal matters (mutual recognition of judicial decisions, prevention of conflicts of jurisdiction, training, co-operation in criminal proceedings and enforcement, minimum rules in certain aspects of criminal procedure)	**unanimity** in Council + EP consultation (Art. 31(1)(a) to (d) TEU)
10. 83(1) + (possibly 2) TFEU[3]	minimum rules on definition of criminal offences and sanctions in a list of areas of serious crime	**unanimity** + EP consultation (Art. 31(1)(e) TEU)
11. 85(2) TFEU	Eurojust	**unanimity** + EP consultation (Art. 31(2) TEU)

Article in TEU/TFEU	Subject matter	Procedure in former Treaties
12. 87(2)	police co-operation (non-operational) (collection, storage, processing, analysis and exchange of information, support for the training of staff and common investigative techniques)	**unanimity** + EP consultation (Art. 30(1)(b) to (d) TEU)
13. 88(2) TFEU	Europol	**unanimity** + EP consultation (Art. 30(2)TEU)
14. 91(2) TFEU	provisions on principles of the transport regulatory system liable to have serious effects on the standard of living and employment in certain areas and on transport facilities	**unanimity** + EP consultation (Art. 71(2) TEC)
15. 116, 2nd subpara., TFEU	measures necessary to eliminate distortions in the internal market due to differences between national rules or action	QMV in Council, without EP participation (Art. 96 TEC)
16. 121(6)	detailed rules for the multilateral surveillance procedure	co-operation procedure (Art. 99 (5) TEC)
17. 129(3) TFEU	modification of certain provisions of the ESCB and ECB protocol	**unanimity** in Council + EP consultation (Art. 107(5) TEC)
18. 133 TFEU	measures necessary for use of the euro	QMV in Council, without EP participation (Art. 123(4), 3rd sentence, TEC)
19. 177(1), 1st subpara., TFEU	Structural Funds	QMV in Council + EP assent (Art. 161 TEC)

(*cont.*)

(cont.)

Article in TEU/TFEU	Subject matter	Procedure in former Treaties
20. 177(1), 2nd subpara., TFEU	Cohesion Fund	QMV in Council + EP assent (Art. 161 TEC)
21. 207(2) TFEU	definition of framework for implementing the common commercial policy	QMV in Council, without EP participation (Art. 133(2) TEC)
22. 212(2) TFEU	economic, financial and technical co-operation measures with third countries (other than developing countries)	QMV in Council + EP consultation (Art. 181A TEC)
23. 257 TFEU	establishment of specialised courts attached to the General Court	**unanimity** + EP consultation (Art. 225A TEC)
24. 281, 2nd subpara., TFEU	modification of the Statute of the EU Court of Justice, except Title I and Art. 64	**unanimity** in Council + EP consultation (Art. 245 TEC)
25. 291(3) TFEU	rules and general principles for controlling the exercise of implementing measures	**unanimity** in Council + EP consultation (Art. 202, 3rd indent, TEC)
26. 322(1) TFEU	financial rules	QMV in Council + EP consultation (Art. 279(1) TEC)
27. 336 TFEU	staff regulations for officials + employment conditions for other servants of the EU	QMV in Council + EP consultation (Art. 283 TEC)

[1] Illegal immigration has been subject to codecision since 1 January 2005 (Council Decision of Dec. 2004 making use of the *passerelle* in Art. 67(2), 2nd indent, TEC)

[2] Coupled with a 'brake-accelerator' procedure in para. 3.

[3] Coupled with a 'brake-accelerator' procedure in para. 3.

Appendix 5

New legal bases

New legal bases where QMV applies in the European Council

Article in TEU/TFEU	Subject matter	Act and procedure	EP role
1. 15(5) TEU	election of the European Council President	decision	
2. 16(6) TEU + 236(a) TFEU	list of Council configurations other than General and Foreign Affairs[1]	decision	
3. 18(1) TEU	appointment of the High Representative	– decision – with the agreement of the Commission President	

[1] Before the Lisbon Treaty, this list was established by the Council configuration on General Affairs by a simple majority (but in practice it had been established at the European Council).

New legal bases where unanimity applies in the European Council

Article in TEU/TFEU	Subject matter	Act and procedure	EP role
1. 14(2), 2nd subpara., TEU	composition of the EP	decision	initiative + consent

(cont.)

(cont.)

Article in TEU/TFEU	Subject matter	Act and procedure	EP role
2. 17(5), 1st subpara., TEU	modification of the number of Commissioners (from 2014)	decision	
3. 17(5), 2nd subpara., TEU + 244 TFEU	system of equal rotation between Commissioners (from 2014)	decision	
4. 22(1) TEU	identification of strategic interests and objectives of the EU in CFSP and other areas of external action	– decision – on a Council recommendation	
5. 31(2), 2nd subpara., TEU	decision following 'emergency brake' on the adoption of a CFSP decision	– decision – on request from Council acting by QMV	
6. 31(3) TEU	*passerelle* – switching to QMV in the field of CFSP (excluding defence)	decision	
7. 48(6) TEU	simplified revision procedure concerning Part Three of the TFEU (internal Union policies and action)	– decision – on a proposal from a Member State, the EP or the Commission – consultation of the Commission (and of the ECB in case of institutional changes to the monetary area) – approval by the Member States in accordance with their constitutional requirements	consultation

Article in TEU/TFEU	Subject matter	Act and procedure	EP role
8. 48(7), 1st subpara., TEU	*passerelle* – switching to QMV	– decision – non-opposition of national parliaments within six months	consent[1]
9. 48(7), 2nd subpara., TEU	*passerelle* – switching to codecision	– decision – non-opposition of national parliaments within six months	consent[2]
10. 50(3) TEU	extension of the period of two years before the withdrawal of a Member State	– decision – in agreement with the Member State concerned	
11. 86(4) TFEU	extension of the powers of the European Public Prosecutor's Office	– decision – consultation of the Commission	consent
12. 312(2), 2nd subpara., TFEU	*passerelle* – switching to QMV for the multiannual financial framework	decision	
13. 355(6) TFEU	modification of the status, with regard to the EU, of one of the Danish, French or Netherlands overseas countries or territories	– decision – on the initiative of the Member State concerned – consultation of the Commission	

[1] By a majority of its component members.
[2] By a majority of its component members.

New legal bases where consensus applies in the European Council

Article in TEU/TFEU	Subject matter	Act and procedure	EP role
1. 48, 2nd subpara., TFEU	co-ordination of social security for migrant workers (employed and self-employed) – *emergency brake* (referral back to Council or request to submit new draft)	no legal act	
2. 68 TFEU	strategic guidelines for legislative and operational planning within the area of freedom, security and justice	no legal act	
3. 82(3) TFEU	judiciary co-operation in criminal matters – *brake–accelerator* (referral back to Council or request to submit new draft + facilitated enhanced co-operation).	no legal act	
4. 83(3) TFEU	minimum rules on definition of criminal offences and sanctions – *brake–accelerator* (referral back to Council or request to submit new draft + facilitated enhanced co-operation)	no legal act	
5. 86(1), 2nd + 3rd subparas., TFEU	establishment of the European Public Prosecutor's Office – *accelerator* (referral back to Council or facilitated enhanced co-operation)	no legal act	
6. 87(3), 2nd + 3rd subparas., TFEU	measure on operational police co-operation – *accelerator* (referral back to Council or facilitated enhanced co-operation)[1]	no legal act	

[1] The 'accelerator' mechanism does not apply to acts which constitute a development of the Schengen *acquis* (see Art. 87(3), 4th subpara., TFEU).

New legal bases where QMV applies in the Council

Article in TEU/TFEU	Subject matter	Act and procedure	EP role
1. 11(4) TEU + 24 TFEU	establishment of procedures and conditions for citizens' initiatives	regulation	codecision
2. 31(2), 2nd indent, TEU	CFSP decision on a proposal from the HR following a request from the European Council adopted by consensus	decision	
3. 41(3), 3rd subpara., TEU	start-up fund for ESDP: – procedures for setting up and financing the fund – procedure for administering the fund – financial control procedures	– decision – proposal from HR	
4. 45(2) TEU	definition of the Defence Agency's statute, seat and operational rules	decision	
5. 46(2) TEU	establishment of permanent structured co-operation in the field of defence	– decision – consultation of HR	
6. 46(3) TEU	participation of a Member State in a permanent structured co-operation in defence	– decision – consultation of HR	
7. 46(4) TEU	suspension of the participation of a Member State in a permanent structured co-operation in defence	decision	
8. 50(2) TEU	agreement on the withdrawal of a Member State	– decision – recommendation or proposal from the EU negotiator (see Art. 218 TFEU)	consent

(*cont.*)

(cont.)

Article in TEU/TFEU	Subject matter	Act and procedure	EP role
9. 14, 2nd sentence, TFEU	principles and conditions for the functioning of the services of general economic interest	regulation	codecision
10. 23, 2nd subpara., TFEU	co-ordination and co-operation measures necessary to facilitate diplomatic and consular protection of EU citizens abroad	directive (special legislative procedure)	consultation
11. 70 TFEU	arrangements for the evaluation of implementation of FSJ *acquis* by Member States	– measures (any type of legal act) – proposal from Commission	
12. 84 TFEU	promotion and support of Member States' action in crime prevention	measures (any type of legal act, but no harmonisation)	codecision
13. 98, 2nd sentence, TFEU	repeal of a provision allowing aid to the economy of certain areas of Germany affected by its division (applicable as from 1 December 2014)	– decision – proposal from Commission	
14. 107(2)(c) TFEU	repeal of a provision allowing aid to the economy of certain areas of Germany affected by its division (applicable as from 1 December 2014)	– decision – proposal from Commission	
15. 118, 1st subpara., TFEU	creation of European intellectual property rights and setting up of a centralised Union-wide authorisation system	measures (any type of legal act)	codecision
16. 136(1) TFEU	specific measures for the 'euro-ins' to strengthen the co-ordination and surveillance of budgetary discipline and set out economic policy guidelines	– using the procedures in Arts. 121 and 126 TFEU (except 126(4)) – QMV of 'euro-ins'	

Article in TEU/TFEU	Subject matter	Act and procedure	EP role
17. 165(1), 2nd subpara. + (2), 7th indent, TFEU	sport	measures (any type of legal act, but no harmonisation)	codecision
18. 182(5) TFEU	implementing the European research area (as a complement to multiannual framework programmes)	measures	codecision
19. 189 TFEU	European space policy	measures (any type of legal act, but no harmonisation)	codecision
20. 194(2) TFEU	energy policy (non-fiscal measures)	measures (any type of legal act)	codecision
21. 195(2) TFEU	tourism	measures (any type of legal act, but no harmonisation)	codecision
22. 196(2) TFEU	civil protection	measures (any type of legal act, but no harmonisation)	codecision
23. 197(2) TFEU	administrative co-operation	regulation (but no harmonisation)	codecision
24. 214(3) TFEU	humanitarian aid (framework)	measures (any type of legal act)	codecision
25. 214(5) TFEU	European Voluntary Humanitarian Aid Corps	regulation	codecision
26. 222(3), 1st subpara., 1st sentence, TFEU	implementation of the solidarity clause (with no defence implications)	– decision – joint proposal from the Commission and the HR	information
27. 243 TFEU	setting out of salaries, allowances and pensions of the President of the European Council and of the High Representative	decision	
28. 255 TFEU	establishment and appointment of the consultative panel on appointment of judges and	– decision – initiative of the President of the Court of Justice	

(cont.)

(cont.)

Article in TEU/TFEU	Subject matter	Act and procedure	EP role
	advocates-general to the Court of Justice and the General Court		
29. 298(2) TFEU	European administration	regulation	codecision
30. 300(5) TFEU	revision of rules on the nature of the composition of the Committee of the Regions and of the Economic and Social Committee	– decision – Commission proposal	
31. 311, 4th subpara., TFEU	implementing measures of the Union's own resources system	regulation (special legislative procedure)	consent

New legal bases where unanimity applies in the Council

Article in TEU/TFEU	Subject matter	Act and procedure	EP role
1. 6(2) TEU (+ 218 TFEU)	accession of the EU to the ECHR	– conclusion by Council decision – approval by Member States in accordance with their constitutional requirements	consent
2. 8(2) TEU (+ 218 TFEU)	specific agreements with neighbouring countries	conclusion by Council decision (unanimity if considered to be an association agreement)	consent
3. 39 TEU	data protection (processing and free movement of data by Member States when carrying out CFSP activities)	decision	

Article in TEU/TFEU	Subject matter	Act and procedure	EP role
4. 41(3), 1st subpara., TEU	specific procedures for guaranteeing rapid access to appropriations in EU budget for urgent financing of CFSP initiatives	decision	consultation
5. 44 TEU	entrusting an ESDP mission to a group of willing Member States	decision	
6. 46(6) TEU	decisions on permanent structured co-operation in defence (other than its establishment or a Member State's accession or suspension)	decision	
7. 21(3) TFEU	social security or social protection measures necessary for attaining objective of free movement of EU citizens	decision (special legislative procedure)	consultation
8. 65(4) TFEU	decision on compatibility with the Treaties of a restrictive national tax measure concerning third countries	– decision – application by the Member State concerned	
9. 77(3) TFEU	measures on passports, ID cards, residence permits, etc. considered necessary for attaining objective of free movement of EU citizens	decision (special legislative procedure)	consultation
10. 82(2)(d) TFEU	extension of EU competence in criminal procedure	decision	consent
11. 83(1), 3rd subpara., TFEU	extension of the areas of crime that meet the criteria specified in the paragraph	decision[1]	consent
12. 86(1) TFEU	establishment of a European Public Prosecutor's Office	regulation (special legislative procedure)[2]	consent

(cont.)

(*cont.*)

Article in TEU/TFEU	Subject matter	Act and procedure	EP role
13. 118, 2nd subpara., TFEU	language arrangements for the European intellectual property rights	regulation (special legislative procedure)	consultation
14. 194(3) TFEU	measures in the field of energy policy which are primarily of fiscal nature	regulation (special legislative procedure)	consultation
15. 222(3), 1st subpara., 2nd sentence, TFEU	implementation of the solidarity clause (with defence implications)	– decision – joint proposal from the Commission and the HR	information
16. 301, 2nd subpara., TFEU	composition of the Economic and Social Committee	– decision – proposal from the Commission	
17. 305, 2nd subpara., TFEU	composition of the Committee of the Regions	– decision – proposal from the Commission	
18. 308, 3rd subpara., TFEU	modification of the EIB Statute	– decision (special legislative procedure) – request from EIB + consultation of Commission – proposal from Commission + consultation of EIB	consultation
19. 312(2), 1st subpara., TFEU	multiannual financial framework	regulation (special legislative procedure)	consent,[3]
20. 333(1) TFEU	switching to QMV within an enhanced co-operation (excluding in defence)	decision	
21. 333(2) TFEU	switching to codecision within an enhanced co-operation (excluding in defence)	decision	consultation

[1] Coupled with an 'accelerator' procedure in the 2nd and 3rd subparas.

[2] Coupled with an 'accelerator' procedure in the 2nd and 3rd subparas.

[3] By a majority of its component members.

Appendix 6

List of articles in the TEU and in the TFEU which enable the European Council to take decisions having legal effects

Article in TEU/TFEU	Subject matter	Procedure
7(2) TEU	determination of the existence of a serious and persistent breach of the EU values by a Member States	– unanimity – proposal of one-third of Member States or from Commission – EP consent
14(2), 2nd subpara., TEU	establishment of European Parliament's composition	– unanimity – EP initiative and consent
15(5) TEU	election of the European Council President	QMV
15(5) TEU	ending of the term of office of the European Council President	QMV
17(5), 1st subpara., TEU	modification of the number of Commissioners	unanimity
17(7), 1st subpara., TEU	proposal to the European Parliament of a candidate for President of the Commission	QMV
17(7), 3rd subpara., TEU	appointment of the Commission	– QMV – prior EP consent
18(1) TEU	appointment of the High Representative	– QMV – with the agreement of Commission President
18(1) TEU	ending the High Representative's term of office	– QMV – with the agreement of Commission President

(cont.)

(*cont.*)

Article in TEU/TFEU	Subject matter	Procedure
22(1) TEU	identification of strategic interests and objectives of the EU in CFSP and other areas of external action	– unanimity – on a recommendation from the Council
26(1), 1st subpara. + 31(1) TEU	identification of strategic interests, objectives and general guidelines for CFSP	unanimity
31(2), 2nd subpara., TEU	decision following 'emergency brake' on the adoption of a CFSP decision	– unanimity – on request from the Council acting by QMV
31(3) TEU	triggering of the *passerelle* in CFSP	unanimity
42(2), 1st subpara., TEU	establishment of a common defence	– unanimity – approval by Member States in accordance with their constitutional requirements
48(3), 1st subpara., TEU	decision in favour of examining amendments to the Treaties	– simple majority – consultation of EP + Commission (and of ECB if institutional changes in monetary area)
48(3), 2nd subpara., 1st sentence, TEU	decision not to convene a Convention	– simple majority – EP consent
48(6), 2nd sub., TEU	amendments to the provisions of Part Three (internal EU competences) of the TFEU (simplified revision procedure, no increase of EU competences)	– unanimity – consultation of EP and Commission (and ECB if institutional changes in monetary area) – approval by Member States in accordance with their constitutional requirements

Article in TEU/TFEU	Subject matter	Procedure
48(7), 1st and 4th subpara., TEU	triggering of the general *passerelle* (QMV)	– unanimity – EP consent – non-opposition from national parliaments within six months
48(7), 2nd and 4th subpara. TEU	triggering of the general *passerelle* (codecision)	– unanimity – EP consent – non-opposition from national parliaments within six months
50(3) TEU	extension of the period after which the Treaties cease to apply to a withdrawing State	– unanimity – in agreement with Member State concerned
86(4) TFEU	extension of powers of the European Public Prosecutor	– unanimity – EP consent – consultation of Commission
235(3) TFEU	adoption of the European Council's Rules of Procedure	simple majority
236(a) TFEU	list of Council configurations other than General Affairs Council and the Foreign Affairs Council	QMV
236(b) TFEU	Presidency of Council configurations other than Foreign Affairs Council	QMV
244 TFEU	rotation system for Commissioners	unanimity
283(2) TFEU	appointment of the members of the ECB executive board	– QMV – recommendation from the Council – after consultation with EP and ECB Governing Council

(*cont.*)

(*cont.*)

Article in TEU/TFEU	Subject matter	Procedure
312(2), 2nd subpara., TFEU	triggering of the *passerelle* for the multi-annual financial framework	unanimity
355(6) TFEU	amendment of the status with regard to the EU of one of the Danish, French or Dutch overseas territories	– unanimity – initiative from Member State concerned – consultation of Commission

Appendix 7

Existing legal bases switched from unanimity to qualified majority voting

Article in TEU/TFEU	Subject matter	Act and procedure	Article in former Treaties
1. 16(9) TEU	organisation of the Presidency of the Council	European Council decision	203 TEC
2. 23, 2nd subpara., TFEU	measures to facilitate diplomatic and consular protection	– Council regulation (special legislative procedure) – consultation of EP	20 TEC
3. 48, 1st subpara., TFEU	co-ordination of social security for migrant workers (employed and self-employed)	**codecision**[1]	42 TEC
4. 53(1) TFEU	provisions on the taking-up and pursuit of self-employed activities even if they entail amendments of existing principles laid down by law in Member States	**codecision**	47(2) TEC

(*cont.*)

(cont.)

Article in TEU/TFEU	Subject matter	Act and procedure	Article in former Treaties
5. 74 TFEU	administrative co-operation in the area of freedom, security and justice	– Council measures (non-legislative) – on a Commission proposal or initiative from Member States (minimum one-quarter) – consultation of EP	66 TEC + 34(1) TEU
6. 79(2)(a)+(b) TFEU	legal immigration	**codecision**	63(3)(a)+(4) TEC
7. 82(1)+(2) TFEU	judicial co-operation in criminal matters	**codecision**[2]	31(1)(a) to (d) TEU
8. 83(1)+(2) TFEU	minimum rules on definition of criminal offences and sanctions in a list of areas of serious crime	**codecision**[3]	31(1)(e) TEU
9. 855é° TFEU	Eurojust	**codecision**	31(2) TEU
10. 87(2) TFEU	police co-operation (non-operational)	**codecision**	30(1)(b) to (d) TEU
11. 88(2) TFEU	Europol	**codecision**	30(2) TEU
12. 91(2) TFEU	provisions on principles of the transport regulatory system liable to have serious effects on the standard of living and employment in certain areas and on transport facilities	**codecision**	71(2) TEC

Article in TEU/TFEU	Subject matter	Act and procedure	Article in former Treaties
13. 129(3) TFEU	modifications of certain provisions of the ESBC and ECB Statute	– **codecision** – on a proposal from the Commission, or – on a recommendation from the ECB	107(5) TEC
14. 167(5) TFEU	incentive measures in the field of culture	**codecision**	151(5) TEC
15. 283(2), 2nd subpara., TFEU	appointment of members of ECB executive board	– European Council decision – on a recommendation from the Council – consultation of EP and ECB Governing Council	112(2)(b) TEC
16. 257 TFEU	establishment of specialised courts attached to the General Court	**codecision**	225A TEC
17. 281, 2nd subpara., TFEU	modification of the Statute of the EU Court of Justice, except Title I and Art. 64	**codecision**	245 TEC
18. 291(3) TFEU	rules and general principles concerning mechanism for control by Member States of the Commission's exercise of implementing powers	**codecision**	202 TEC

[1] Coupled with a 'brake' procedure in the 2nd subpara.

[2] Coupled with a 'brake–accelerator' procedure in para. 3.

[3] Coupled with a 'brake–accelerator' procedure in para. 3.

Appendix 8

Pre-existing legal bases where unanimity, common accord or consensus continues to apply

Pre-existing legal bases where unanimity in the European Council continues to apply

Article in TEU/TFEU	Subject matter	Act and procedure	Article in former Treaties
1. 7(2) TEU	existence of a serious and persistent breach by a Member State of the EU's values	– decision – initiative of one-third of the Member States or Commission proposal – EP consent	7(2) TEU
2. 26(1), 1st subpara. + 31(1) TEU	identification of strategic interests, objectives and general guidelines for CFSP	decision	13(2) TEU
3. 42(2), 1st subpara., TEU	establishment of a common EU defence	– decision – adoption of the decision by the Member States in accordance with their respective constitutional requirements	17(1) TEU

Pre-existing legal bases where unanimity in the Council continues to apply

Article in TEU/TFEU	Subject matter	Act and procedure	Article in former Treaties
4. 24(1), 2nd subpara., 1st sentence, + 31(1) TEU	CFSP (ordinary framework)	– decision – HR proposal or initiative from a Member State	23(1) TEU
5. 41(2) TEU	not charging on the EU budget operating expenditure for CFSP	decision	28(3) TEU
6. 42(4) TEU	CSDP (ordinary framework)	– decision – HR proposal or initiative from a Member State	23(1) TEU
7. 19(1) TFEU	measures to combat discrimination based on sex, racial or ethnic origin, religion or belief, disability, age or sexual orientation	– measure (any legal act, special legislative procedure) – EP consent	13(1) TEC
8. 22 TFEU	arrangements for exercising the right to vote and to stand as a candidate in municipal elections and EP elections in the Member State of residence without being a national of that State	– measure (any legal act, special legislative procedure) – EP consultation	19 TEC

(*cont.*)

(*cont.*)

Article in TEU/TFEU	Subject matter	Act and procedure	Article in former Treaties
9. 64(3) TFEU	step backwards in Union law as regards liberalisation of movement of capital to or from third countries	– measure (any legal act, special legislative procedure) – EP consultation	57(2) TEC
10. 81(3), 1st subpara., TFEU	measures concerning family law with cross-border implications	– measure (any legal act, special legislative procedure) – EP consultation	65 + 67(5), 2nd indent, TEC
11. 87(3), 1st subpara., TFEU	operational police co-operation	– measure (any legal act, special legislative procedure)[1] – EP consultation	30(1) TEU
12. 89 TFEU	conditions and limitations under which the competent authorities of the Member States may operate in the territory of another Member State	– measure (any legal act, special legislative procedure) – EP consultation	32 TEU
13. 92 TFEU	derogation from the obligation of non-discrimination based on nationality in the field of transport	measure (any legal act)	72 TEC

Article in TEU/TFEU	Subject matter	Act and procedure	Article in former Treaties
14. 108(2), 3rd subpara., TFEU	compatibility with the internal market of an aid granted by a Member State or through state resources (derogation from Art. 107 TFEU or from regulations based on Art. 109)	– decision – application by a Member State	88(2), 3rd subpara., TEC
15. 113 TFEU	harmonisation of legislation concerning turnover taxes, excise duties and other forms of indirect taxes	– measure (any legal act, special legislative procedure) – EP consultation	93 TEC
16. 115 TFEU	approximation of legislation which directly affects the establishment or functioning of the internal market (in cases other than covered by Art. 114 TFEU)	– measure (any legal act, special legislative procedure) – EP consultation	94 TEC
17. 126(14), 2nd subpara., TFEU	modification/ replacement of the Protocol on the excessive deficit procedure	– measure (any legal act, special legislative procedure) – EP and ECB consultation	104(14), 2nd subpara., TEC
18. 127(6) TFEU	specific tasks for the ECB concerning policies relating to prudential supervision	– regulation (special legislative procedure) – EP and ECB consultation	105(6) TEC

(cont.)

(*cont.*)

Article in TEU/TFEU	Subject matter	Act and procedure	Article in former Treaties
19. 140(3) TFEU	fixing of the rate a which the euro is to be substituted for the currency of the Member State(s) concerned	– measure (any legal act) – with the agreement of the Council member representing the Member State(s) concerned – ECB consultation	123(5) TEC
20. 153(2), 3rd subpara., TFEU	– social security and social protection of workers – protection of workers where their employment contract is terminated – representation and collective defence of the interests of workers and employers, including co-determination – conditions of employment for third-country nationals legally residing in Union territory	– measure (any legal act, special legislative procedure) – EP consultation	137(2), 2nd subpara., TEC
21. 155(2), 2nd subpara., TFEU	implementation of agreements between management and labour in the fields of Art. 153(2) where unanimity is required	– measure – request of the signatory parties – Commission proposal – information of EP	139(2) TEC

Article in TEU/TFEU	Subject matter	Act and procedure	Article in former Treaties
22. 192(2), 1st subpara., TFEU	environment: – provisions primarily of a fiscal nature – measures affecting town and country planning, quantitative management of water, land use – measures significantly affecting a Member State's choice between different energy sources and the general structure of its energy supply	– measure (any legal act, special legislative procedure) – EP consultation	175(2), 1st subpara., TEC
23. 203 TFEU	association of the countries and territories of the Union	– measure (any legal act, special legislative procedure or not) – Commission proposal – EP consultation if special legislative procedure	187 TEC
24. 207(4), 2nd subpara., TFEU	common commercial policy – exceptions to QMV for agreements on: – trade in services; commercial aspects of intellectual property and foreign direct investment, when unanimity is required for the adoption of an internal EU act	– conclusion by a Council decision – EP consent if agreement covers fields to which codecision applies or in which the Council adopts legislative acts with the EP consent – EP consultation in other cases	133(5)+(6) TEC

(cont.)

(cont.)

Article in TEU/TFEU	Subject matter	Act and procedure	Article in former Treaties
	– trade in cultural and audiovisual services, where these agreements risk prejudicing the Union's cultural and linguistic diversity; – trade in social, education and health services, where these agreements risk seriously disturbing the national organisation of such services and prejudicing the responsibility of Member States to deliver them		
25. 218(8), 2nd subpara., TFEU	international agreements: – agreements covering a field for which unanimity is required for the adoption of an internal EU act – association agreements – agreements on economic and financial co-operation (Art. 212 TFEU) with candidates for accession – EU accession to the ECHR	– conclusion by a Council decision – EP consent if association agreement or if covers fields to which codecision applies or in which the Council adopts legislative acts with EP consent – EP consultation in other cases	300 TEC

Article in TEU/TFEU	Subject matter	Act and procedure	Article in former Treaties
26. 219(1) TFEU	agreements on an exchange-rate system for the euro in relation to third States' currencies	– decision – recommendation from ECB + Commission consultation, or – Commission recommendation + ECB consultation – EP consultation	111(1) TEC
27. 223(2), 2nd sentence, TFEU	rules or conditions relating to the taxation of MEPs or former MEPs	– EP regulation (special legislative procedure) – on EP initiative – Commission opinion – Council consent	190(5) TEC
28. 252, 1st subpara., TFEU	increasing the number of advocates-general	– decision – request from the Court	222 TEC
29. 257, 4th subpara., TFEU	appointment of the members of the specialised courts	decision	225a TEC
30. 332 TFEU	derogation to normal rule on expenditure resulting from implementation of enhanced co-operation	– decision – EP consultation	44 TEU
31. 342 TFEU	rules governing the language regime of the Union's institutions	regulation	290 TEC

(*cont.*)

(*cont.*)

Article in TEU/TFEU	Subject matter	Act and procedure	Article in former Treaties
32. 346(2) TFEU	changes to the list of arms, munitions and war material	– decision – Commission proposal	296(2) TEC
33. 352 TFEU	flexibility clause	– measure (any legal act, special legislative procedure or not) – Commission proposal – EP consent	308 TEC

[1] Coupled with an 'accelerator' mechanism.

Pre-existing legal basis switched from QMV to unanimity in the Council

Article in TEU/TFEU	Subject matter	Act and procedure	Article in former Treaties
34. 329(2), 2nd subpara., TFEU	authorisation to proceed with enhanced co-operation in CFSP	– decision – request of the Member States concerned (at least nine) – HR and Commission consultation – EP information	27c TEU
35. 331(2), 3rd subpara., TFEU	acceptance of the participation of a Member State in an existing enhanced co-operation in CFSP	– Council decision – request from the Member State concerned – HR consultation	27e TEU

Pre-existing *passerelles* where unanimity in the Council continues to apply

Article in TEU/TFEU	Subject matter	Act and procedure	Article in former Treaties
36. 81(3), 2nd subpara., TFEU	family law – switching to codecision aspects with cross-border implications	– decision – Commission proposal – EP consultation – non-opposition of national parliaments within six months	67(2), 2nd indent, TEC
37. 153(2), 4th subpara., TFEU	social policy – switching to codecision for: – protection of workers where their employment contract is terminated – representation and collective defence of the interests of workers and employers (but does not apply to pay, right of association, right to strike or to lock-outs) – conditions of employment for third-country nationals legally resident	– decision – Commission proposal – EP consultation	137(2), 2nd subpara., TEC
38. 192(2), 2nd subpara., TFEU	environment – switching to codecision in matters mentioned in Art. 192(2), 1st subpara., TFEU	– decision – Commission proposal – EP consultation	175(2), 2nd subpara., TEC

Pre-existing legal bases where unanimity in the Council continues to apply, followed by approval or adoption by Member States, in accordance with their constitutional requirements

Article in TEU/TFEU	Subject matter	Act and procedure	Article in former Treaties
39. 49 TEU	Council acting upon an application for accession to the EU received from a European State	– EP consent – Commission consultation – accession agreement to be ratified by each Contracting Party, in accordance with its respective constitutional requirements	49 TEU
40. 25, 2nd subpara., TFEU	addition of new rights for EU citizens	– measures (special legislative procedure) – EP consultation – approval by the Member States in accordance with their constitutional requirements	22 TEC
41. 223(1), 2nd subpara., TFEU	measures for the election of MEPs by direct universal suffrage	– measures (special legislative procedure) – on initiative from, and after obtaining consent of, EP – approval by the Member States in accordance with their constitutional requirements	190(4) TEC
42. 262 TFEU	conferral of jurisdiction on the EU Court of Justice	– measures (special legislative procedure) – EP consultation	229A TEC

(*cont.*)

Article in TEU/TFEU	Subject matter	Act and procedure	Article in former Treaties
	in disputes relating to the application of EU acts creating European intellectual property rights	– approval by the Member States in accordance with their constitutional requirements	
43. 311, 3rd subpara., TFEU	system of own resources	– decision (special legislative procedure) – EP consultation – approval by the Member States in accordance with their constitutional requirements	269 TEC

Pre-existing legal bases where common accord of the Member States continues to apply

Article in TEU/TFEU	Subject matter	Act and procedure	Article in former Treaties
44. 19(2), 3rd subpara., TEU	appointment of judges and advocates-general of the Court of Justice and of the General Court	– common accord of the governments of the Member States – after consulting the Art. 255 panel	223+224 TEC
45. 48(2) to (5) TEU	ordinary revision of the Treaties	– common accord of the IGC in the form of an international agreement – ratification by all the Member States in accordance with their constitutional requirements	48 EU
46. 341 TFEU	determining the seats of the institutions	common accord of the governments of the Member States	289 TEC

REFERENCES

Andréani, G., C. Bertram and C. Grant. *Europe's Military Revolution* (London: Centre for European Reform, March 2001, available at www.cer.org.uk/pdf/p22x_military_revolution.pdf)

Bantekas, I. 'The Principle of Mutual Recognition in EU Criminal Law' (2007) 32 *European Law Review* 365

Baquero Cruz, J. 'The Legacy of the Maastricht-Urteil and the Pluralist Movement' (2008) 14 *European Law Journal* 389

Barrett, G. 'Building a Swiss Chalet in an Irish Landscape? Referendums on European Union Treaties in Ireland and the Impact of Supreme Court Jurisprudence' (2009) 5 *European Constitutional Law Review* 32

Barrière, A.-L. and B. Rousel. *Le Traité de Lisbonne, étape ultime de l'intégration européenne? Le jugement du 30 juin 2009 de la Cour constitutionnelle allemande*, Note du Cerfa 66 (Paris: Institut français des relations internationales, 2009)

Barrington R. 'Was Holding a Referendum on Lisbon Treaty Really Necessary?', *Irish Times*, 11 July 2008

Bearce, D. H. 'EMU: The Last Stand for the Policy Convergence Hypothesis?' (2009) 16 *Journal of European Public Policy*, special issue on ten years of EMU, 582

Benoît-Rohmer, F. 'La Charte des droits fondamentaux de l'Union européenne' (2001) II (160) *Juris-Classeur* and (2001) 19 *Dalloz* 1483

Bermann, G. A. 'The Lisbon Treaty: The Irish "No": National Parliament and Subsidiarity: An Outsider's View' (2008) 4 *European Constitutional Law Review* 453

Callewaert, J. 'The European Court of Human Rights and the Area of Freedom, Security and Justice' (2007) 8 *ERA Forum* 511

Carlier, J.-Y. 'La libre circulation des personnes dans l'UE 1.1/31.12.2008', (2009) *Journal de Droit Européen* 79

Charlemagne, *The Economist*, 13–19 June 2009, 34

Chevalier, B. 'Les nouveaux développements de la procédure préjudicielle dans le domaine de l'espace judiciaire européen: la procédure préjudicielle d'urgence et les réformes principales prévues par le traité de Lisbonne' (2009) 9 *ERA Forum* 591

398

Cini, M. *European Union Politic*, 2nd edn (Oxford University Press, 2007)

de Ruyt, J. *A Minister for a European Foreign Policy* (Florence: Schuman Centre, European University Institute, 2005)

de Schoutheete, P. *La cohérence par la défense: une autre lecture de la PESD*, Cahiers de Chaillot 71 (Paris: EU Institute for Security Studies, 2004)

Dean, M. M. *Governmentality: Power and Rule in Modern Society* (London: Sage, 1999)

De Witte, F. 'The European Judiciary after Lisbon', (2008) 15 *Maastricht Journal of European and Comparative Law* 43

Editorial comment. 'Who Leads the EU?' (2009) 46 *Common Market Law Review*, 1383

Fischer, J. *Die Zeit*, 9 July 2009

Flore, D. 'La perspective d'un procureur européen' (2008) 9 *ERA Forum* 229

Follesdal, A. and S. Hix. 'Why There Is a Democratic Deficit in the EU: A Response to Majone and Moravcsik' (2006) 44 *Journal of Common Market Studies* 537

Fried, R. J. 'Providing a Constitutional Framework for Withdrawal from the EU: Article 59 of the Draft European Constitution' (2004) 53 *International and Comparative Law Quartely* 407

  'Secession from the European Union: Checking Out of the Proverbial "Cockroach Motel"' (2004) 27 *Fordham Law Journal* 590

Gnesotto, N. (ed.). *EU Security and Defence Policy: The First Five Years (1999–2004)*, pref. by J. Solana (Paris: EU Institute for Security Studies, 2004, available at www.iss-eu.org/books/5esdpen.pdf)

Gormley, L. W. 'The Judicial Architecture of the European Union in the Constitution', in Peter G. Xuereb (ed.), *The Constitution for Europe: An Evaluation* (Malta: EDRC, Medial Centre Print, 2005), 57–72

Haas, E. B. *The Uniting of Europe: Political, Social and Economic Forces 1950–1957* (Stanford University Press, 1958)

Hegeland, H. 'The European Union in National Parliaments: Domestic or Foreign Policy? A Study of Nordic Parliamentary Systems', in J. O'Brennan and T. Raunio (eds.), *National Parliaments within the Enlarged European Union: From 'Victims' of Integration to Competitive Actors* (New York: Routledge, 2007), 95–115

Herma, C. 'Intergovernmental Conference on the Lisbon Treaty', in *Treaty of Lisbon – Provisions, Evaluation, Implications*, UKIE Analytical Paper Series 20 (Office of the Committee for European Integration, Department of Analyses and Strategies, 2008, available at www.ukie.gov.pl), 38–76

Hix, S. *What's Wrong with the European Union and How to Fix It?* (Cambridge: Polity, 2008)

House of Lords (UK). *The Lisbon Treaty: An Impact Assessment* (13 March 2008), Vol. I 10th Report of Session 2007–08 (HL Paper 62-I)

House of the Oireachtas (Ireland). *Ireland's Future in the European Union: Challenges, Issues and Options*, Report, Sub-Committee on Ireland's Future in the European Union (2008)

Jacqué, J.-P. *Droit institutionnel de l'Union européenne*, 5th edn (Paris: Dalloz, 2009)

'L'arrêt Bosphorus, une jurisprudence "Solange II" de la Cour européenne des droits de l'homme?' (2005) 3 *Revue trimestrielle de droit européen* 756

'Primauté du droit international versus protection des droits fondamentaux, note sur CJCE: arrêt du 3 septembre 2008, Kadi c/Conseil et Commission' (2009) 45 (1) *Revue trimestrielle de droit européen* 161

'Une vision réaliste de la procédure de codécision', in *Mélanges en hommage à Georges Vandersanden – Promenades au sein du droit européen* (Brussels: Bruylant, 2008), 183–202

Jarlebring, J. 'Taking Stock of the European Convention: What Added Value Does the Convention Bring to the Process of Treaty Revision?' (2003) 4 *German Law Journal* 785

Kaddous, C. 'Role and Position of the High Representative of the Union for Foreign Affairs and Security Policy under the Lisbon Treaty', in S. Griller and J. Ziller (eds.), *The Lisbon Treaty – EU Constitutionalism without a Constitutional Treaty* (Vienna: Springer Verlag, 2008), 205–21

Keohane D. and T. Valasek, *Willing and Able? EU Defence in 2020* (London: Centre for European Reform, 2008)

Kuijper, P. J. 'The Second Second Irish Referendum: Finally a Fair Choice' (2009) 36(2) *Legal Issues of Economic Integration* 101

Labayle, H. 'Architecte ou spectatrice? La Cour de justice de l'Union dans l'Espace de liberté, sécurité et justice' (2006) 42(1) *Revue trimestrielle de droit européen* 1

Ladenburger, C. 'Police and Criminal Law in the Lisbon Treaty, A New Dimension for the Community Method' (2008) 4 *European Constitutional Law Review* 20

Leczykiewicz, D. 'Constitutional Conflicts and the Third Pillar' (2008) 33 *European Law Review* 230

Lenz, C.-O. *Frankfurter Allgemeine Zeitung*, 8 August 2009

Leparmentier, A. 'L'Allemagne apaisée enterre le rêve européen', *Le Monde*, 17 July 2009

Louis, J.-V. 'Le droit de retrait de l'Union européenne' (2006) *Cahiers de droit européen* 293

'National Parliaments and the Principle of Subsidiarity: Legal Options and Practical Limits' (2008) 4 *European Constitutional Law Review* 429

Magnette, P. and K. Nicolaïdis. 'The European Convention: Bargaining in the Shadow of Rhetoric' (2004) 27 *West European Politics* 381

Majone, G. *Dilemmas of European Integration. The Ambiguities and Pitfalls of Integration by Stealth* (Oxford University Press, 2005)

'Europe's Democratic Deficit' (1998) 4 *European Law Journal* 5

Marquardt, S. 'La capacité de l'Union européenne de conclure des accords internationaux dans le domaine de la coopération policière et judiciaire en matière pénale', in G. de Kerchove and A. Weyembergh (eds), *Sécurité et justice: enjeu de la politique extérieure de l'Union européenne* (Brussels: Institut d'Etudes Européennes, Université de Bruxelles, 2003), 179–94

'The Conclusion of International Agreements under Article 24 of the Treaty on European Union', in Vincent Kronenberger (ed.), *The European Union and the International Legal Order: Discord or Harmony?* (The Hague: T.M.C. Asser Instituut, 2001), 16333–49

Mény, Y. 'Europe, la grande hésitation', *Le Monde*, 12 June 2004

Milton, G. and J. Keller-Noëllet, with A. Bartol-Saurel. *The European Constitution: Its Origins, Negotiation and Meaning* (London: John Harper Publishing, 2005)

Moravcsik, A. 'Europe's Slow Triumph', *Newsweek*, 21 June 2004, 41

'Ignore the Skeptics; EU Democracy Is Doing Just Fine', *Newsweek*, 29 June 2009, 20

'In Defence of the "Democratic Deficit": Reassessing Legitimacy in the European Union' (2002) 40 *Journal of Common Market Studies* 603

The Choice for Europe: Social Purpose and State Power from Messina to Maastricht (Ithaca: Cornell University Press, 1998)

'The European Constitutional Settlement' (2008) 31 *World Economy* 158

'What We Can Learn from the Collapse of the European Constitutional Project' (2006) 47 *Politische Vierteljahresschrift* 219

Nicoll, W. and M. Bryan-Kinns. 'The Budget Procedure', in M. Westlake and D. Galloway (eds.), *The Council of the European Union*, 3rd edn (London: John Harper Publishing, 2004)

Norman, P. *The Accidental Constitution: The Making of Europe's Constitutional Treaty* (Brussels: EuroComment, 2005)

O'Brennan, J. and T. Raunio. *National Parliaments within the enlarged European Union: From 'Victims' of Integration to Competitive Actors* (New York: Routledge, 2007)

Patten, C. *European Voice*, 4 June 2009

Pech, L. 'Le référendum en Irlande pour ratifier les traités européens: obligatoire ou coutumier?', Questions d'Europe 115, Fondation Robert Schuman, 28 October 2008

Peers, S. 'EU Criminal Law and the Lisbon Treaty', (2008) 33 *European Law Review* 507

'The Beneš Decrees and the EU Charter of Fundamental Rights', University of Essex, 12 October 2009, available at www.statewatch.org/news/2009/oct/lisbon-benes-decree.pdf

Pilecka, M. 'Homework for the Irish, Reasons for the Rejection of the Lisbon Treaty as Seen through Opinion Polls', in *Lisbon Treaty – Provisions, Evaluation, Implications*, UKIE Analytical Paper Series 20, 2008, Office of the Committee for European Integration, Department of Analyses and Strategies, available at www.ukie.gov.pl

Piris, J.-C. 'Does the European Union Have a Constitution? Does It Need One?', (1999) 6 *European Law Review* 557

    Le Traité constitutionnel pour l'Europe: une analyse juridique (Brussels: Bruylant, 2006)

    'The 1996 Intergovernmental Conference' (1995) 20 *European Law Review* 235

    The Constitution for Europe: A Legal Analysis (Cambridge University Press, 2006)

    'The European Union: Towards a New Form of Federalism?', in J. Fedtke and B. Markesinis (eds.), *Patterns of Regionalism and Federalism, The Clifford Chance Lectures*, Vol. 8 (Oxford: Hart Publishing, 2006)

Potteau, A. 'Les finances publiques de l'Union européenne en 2007' (2009) 45(10) *Revue trimestrielle de droit européen* 105

Priollaud, F.-X. and D. Siritzky. *Le Traité de Lisbonne – Texte et commentaire article par article des nouveaux traités européens (TUE–TFUE)* (Paris: La Documentation française, 2008)

Reid, T. R. *The United States of Europe* (London: Penguin Press, 2005)

Rifkin, J. *The European Dream* (New York: Jeremy P. Tarcher/Penguin, 2004)

Roland, G. and E. Buyssens, 'La transformation d'Europol en agence de l'Union – Regards sur un nouveau cadre juridique', *Revue du Marché commun et de l'Union européenne*, February 2009

Rossi, L. S. 'Constitutionnalisation de l'UE et des droits fondamentaux' (2002) 38(1) *Revue trimestrielle de droit européen* 27

Roux, J. 'Le Conseil constitutionnel et le contrôle de constitutionnalité du Traité de Lisbonne: bis repetita' (2008) 44(1) *Revue trimestrielle de droit européen* 5

Rumford, C. *The European Union: A Political Sociology* (Oxford: Blackwell, 2002)

Rutten M. (compiler), *From St-Malo to Nice: European Defence: Core Documents*, Chaillot Paper 47 (Paris: EU Institute for Security Studies, 2001)

Schmidt, V. A. *Democracy in Europe: The EU and National Polities* (Oxford University Press, 2006)

Schoettl, J.-E. 'La ratification du "Traité établissant une Constitution pour l'Europe" appelle-t-elle une révision de la Constitution française?', (2004) 393(238) *Les Petites Affiches* 3

'Scientists for a democratic Europe', paper, available at www.ruhr-uni-bochum.de/mathphys/politik/eu/open-letter.htm.

Senate (France). *Les services d'intérêt général après le Traité de Lisbonne*, no. 376 (Paris: Délégation pour l'UE, Sénat, 2008)

Sieberson, S. C. 'The Treaty of Lisbon and its Impact on the EU's Democratic Deficit' (2008) 14 *Columbia Journal of European Law* 445

Siedentop, L. *Financial Times*, 30 September 2009

Straw, J. *The Economist*, 10 July 2004, 30

Toje, A. *The EU, NATO and European Defence – A Slow Train Coming*, Occasional Paper 74 (Paris: European Union Institute for Security Studies (2008)

Torrent, R. 'Whom is the European Central Bank the Central Bank of? Reaction to Zilioli and Selmayr' (1999) 36 *Common Market Law Review* 1229

Tridimas, T. and S. Poli. 'Locus Standi of Individuals under Article 230(4): The Return of Euridice?', in P. Moser and K. Sawyer (eds.), *Making Community Law: The Legacy of Advocate General Jacobs at the European Court of Justice* (Cheltenham: Edward Elgar Publishing, 2008), 70–89

Vigant Ryborg, O. *Det utoenkelige: NEJ . . . !* (Denmark: Informations Forlag, 1998)

Weiler, J. H. H. 'Does Europe Need a Constitution? Demos, Telos on the German Maastricht Decision' (1995) 1 *European Law Journal* 219

  The Constitution of Europe (Cambridge, MA: Harvard University Press, 1999)

Weiler, J. H. H., U. R. Haltern and F. C. Mayer. 'European Democracy and its Critique' (1995) 18(3) *West European Policies* 4

Werts, J. *The European Council* (London: John Harper, 2008)

Wessel, R. A. 'The State of Affairs in EU Security and Defence Policy: The Breakthrough in the Treaty of Nice' (2003) 8 *Journal of Conflict and Security Law* 265

Zilioli, C. and M. Selmayr. 'The European Central Bank: An Independent Specialized Organization of Community Law' (2000) 37 *Common Market Law Review* 591

  'The External Relations of the Euro Area: Legal Aspects' (1999) 36 *Common Market Law Review* 273

Zyczkowski, K. and W. Slomczynski. 'Voting in the European Union: The Square Root System of Penrose and a Critical Point', available at http://arxiv.org/ftp/cond-mat/papers/0405/0405396.pdf

Useful internet sites

EU and EC (europa), general Internet site: http://europa.eu

Archive of European Integration, University of Pittsburg: http://aei.pitt.edu

Convention for the Future of Europe: http://european-convention.europa.eu

Convention on the EU Charter of Fundamental Rights: www.europarl.europa.eu/charter

Council of the European Union: http://consilium.europa.eu

Council of the European Union, Registry of documents: http://register.consilium.europa.eu

European Court of Human Rights: http://cmiskp.echr.coe.int

European Parliament: www.europarl.europa.eu

INDEX

bold locators indicate box features and tables